THE

POLYGRAPH

AND LIE DETECTION

Committee to Review the Scientific Evidence on the Polygraph

Board on Behavioral, Cognitive, and Sensory Sciences

and

Committee on National Statistics

Division of Behavioral and Social Sciences and Education

NATIONAL RESEARCH COUNCIL
OF THE NATIONAL ACADEMIES

THE NATIONAL ACADEMIES PRESS
Washington, D.C.
www.nap.edu

THE NATIONAL ACADEMIES PRESS   500 Fifth Street, N.W.   Washington, DC 20001

NOTICE: The project that is the subject of this report was approved by the Governing Board of the National Research Council, whose members are drawn from the councils of the National Academy of Sciences, the National Academy of Engineering, and the Institute of Medicine. The members of the committee responsible for the report were chosen for their special competences and with regard for appropriate balance.

This study was supported by Contract No. DE-AT01-01DP00344 between the National Academy of Sciences and the U.S. Department of Energy. Any opinions, findings, conclusions, or recommendations expressed in this publication are those of the author(s) and do not necessarily reflect the views of the organizations or agencies that provided support for the project.

Library of Congress Cataloging-in-Publication Data

The polygraph and lie detection.
    p. cm.
Includes bibliographical references and index.
  ISBN 0-309-08436-9 (hardcover)
  1. Lie detectors and detection—Evaluation. I. Committee to Review the Scientific Evidence on the Polygraph (National Research Council (U.S.))
  HV8078 .P64 2003
  363.25'4—dc21
                              2002151541

Additional copies of this report are available from the National Academies Press, 500 Fifth Street, N.W., Lockbox 285, Washington, DC 20055; (800) 624-6242 or (202) 334-3313 (in the Washington metropolitan area); Internet, http://www.nap.edu

Printed in the United States of America.

Suggested citation: National Research Council (2003). *The Polygraph and Lie Detection.* Committee to Review the Scientific Evidence on the Polygraph. Division of Behavioral and Social Sciences and Education. Washington, DC: The National Academies Press.

THE NATIONAL ACADEMIES
Advisers to the Nation on Science, Engineering, and Medicine

The **National Academy of Sciences** is a private, nonprofit, self-perpetuating society of distinguished scholars engaged in scientific and engineering research, dedicated to the furtherance of science and technology and to their use for the general welfare. Upon the authority of the charter granted to it by the Congress in 1863, the Academy has a mandate that requires it to advise the federal government on scientific and technical matters. Dr. Bruce M. Alberts is president of the National Academy of Sciences.

The **National Academy of Engineering** was established in 1964, under the charter of the National Academy of Sciences, as a parallel organization of outstanding engineers. It is autonomous in its administration and in the selection of its members, sharing with the National Academy of Sciences the responsibility for advising the federal government. The National Academy of Engineering also sponsors engineering programs aimed at meeting national needs, encourages education and research, and recognizes the superior achievements of engineers. Dr. Wm. A. Wulf is president of the National Academy of Engineering.

The **Institute of Medicine** was established in 1970 by the National Academy of Sciences to secure the services of eminent members of appropriate professions in the examination of policy matters pertaining to the health of the public. The Institute acts under the responsibility given to the National Academy of Sciences by its congressional charter to be an adviser to the federal government and, upon its own initiative, to identify issues of medical care, research, and education. Dr. Harvey V. Fineberg is president of the Institute of Medicine.

The **National Research Council** was organized by the National Academy of Sciences in 1916 to associate the broad community of science and technology with the Academy's purposes of furthering knowledge and advising the federal government. Functioning in accordance with general policies determined by the Academy, the Council has become the principal operating agency of both the National Academy of Sciences and the National Academy of Engineering in providing services to the government, the public, and the scientific and engineering communities. The Council is administered jointly by both Academies and the Institute of Medicine. Dr. Bruce M. Alberts and Dr. Wm. A. Wulf are chair and vice chair, respectively, of the National Research Council.

www.national-academies.org

Contents

Preface

The polygraph, known more commonly as the "lie detector," has a long and controversial history as a forensic tool, but it has also been used in a variety of other contexts, including employment screening. The U.S. federal government, through a variety of agencies, carries out thousands of polygraph tests each year on job applicants and current employees, and there are inevitable disputes that are sometimes highly publicized when someone "fails" a polygraph test. The American Polygraph Association, the largest polygraph association consisting of examiners in the private, law enforcement, and government fields, claims that the polygraph has a high degree of accuracy in detecting truthfulness or deception, with research studies published since 1980 reporting average accuracy rates ranging from 80 to 98 percent. Yet others claim that the studies underlying the polygraph represent "junk science" that has no scientific basis. Can experienced polygraph examiners detect deception? Again there is a diversity of claims. The World Wide Web contains a myriad of web pages advertising methods to beat the polygraph, while some people say that if the examinee knowingly lies, the polygraph will detect the lie.

The Committee to Review the Scientific Evidence on the Polygraph was asked by the U.S. Department of Energy to conduct a scientific review of the research on polygraph examinations that pertain to their validity and reliability, particularly for personnel security screening, and to provide suggestions for further research. Over 19 months, the committee held a series of meetings, visited polygraph facilities at several government agencies, and examined large numbers of reports and published papers. We explored some historical dimensions of the research literature on the polygraph, including a link to work at the National Research Council (NRC) more than 80 years ago—and we learned how this led to the creation of the comic book character, Wonder Woman. We attempted to listen carefully to people representing both sides in the debate on polygraph accuracy, and we then stepped back and reviewed the evidence ourselves. The members of the committee brought to our deliberations diverse backgrounds and research perspectives, most of which had special relevance to one or more aspects of the research literature and practice of the polygraph. But we shared one thing in common: none of us had previously been engaged in polygraph research, per se, and each was intrigued by the claims in support of and against the polygraph.

Examining alternatives to the polygraph was also a key component of the committee's charge. We did this in a variety of ways, through input from agency representatives, visits to research laboratories, participation of committee members in outside workshops, presentations by researchers before the committee, and by reviewing relevant research literature shared with the committee by others or gathered by individual members and staff. We looked for polished alternatives and promising approaches and attempted to assess their scientific bases.

The committee tried to understand how the polygraph was used in different government agencies, for example, which format of polygraph test, what questions, with what instructions, etc. Andrew Ryan of the U.S. Department of Defense Polygraph Institute (DoDPI) served as a liaison to the committee from the government polygraph agencies, and was especially helpful in providing us with documentation and copies of research papers and manuscripts. David Renzelman and Anne Reed, Allen Brisentine, Paul Cully, and Alvina Jones arranged for visits with those in the polygraph programs at the Department of Energy, the National Security Agency, the Federal Bureau of Investigation, and the Central Intelligence Agency, respectively.

We also appreciate the information we received from many people who made presentations before the committee: Gary Berntson (Ohio State University), Senator Jeff Bingaman (D-New Mexico), Emanuel Donchin (University of Illinois), Lawrence Farwell (Brain Fingerprinting Laboratories, Inc.), General John A. Gordon (National Nuclear Security Administration), John Harris (Johns Hopkins University Applied Physics Laboratory), Charles Honts (Boise State University), William Iacono (University of Minnesota), Stephen Kosslyn (Harvard University), Peter Lyons (Office of Senator Peter Domenici), Joseph Mahaley (Department of Energy), George Maschke (antipolygraph.org), Anne Reed (Department of Energy), Sheila Reed (North Texas State Hospital), David Renzelman (Department of Energy), Drew Richardson (Federal Bureau of Investigation, retired),

Andrew Ryan (Department of Defense Polygraph Insitute), and Alan P. Zelicoff (Sandia National Laboratory).

The events of September 11, 2001, and their aftermath briefly interrupted the committee's activities, but more importantly, they reinforced for the committee the important roles that many of the agencies and organizations we had been visiting play in attempting to assure national security.

Late in the committee's deliberative process, one of the committee members, John Cacioppo, resigned from the committee to pursue research he had initiated as a consequence of his work on the committee. John was a major contributor to the committee's work, especially as it related to psychophysiology, and we owe him a great debt even though he was unable to assist us in the final revisions.

This report would not have been completed had it not been for the tremendous efforts of a number of key staff. Paul Stern served as study director and guided us from the outset, helping us to organize our work and to write the report. His insightful observations often forced us to rethink draft conclusions and summaries, and his good humor and gentle prodding made our writing tasks easier to accept. In summary, Paul was a partner in almost all of our tasks. Christine Hartel, director of the Board on Behavioral, Cognitive, and Sensory Sciences (BBCSS) stepped in at a crucial stage of the committee's work and played a lead staff role when Paul was temporarily absent and has provided input and wise counsel throughout. Andrew White, director of the Committee on National Statistics, also participated in our meetings and offered assistance and support. Susan McCutchen worked on the full spectrum of the committee's activities, secured documents for us, organized our research database, and interacted with representatives of the government polygraph agencies. Anne Mavor and James McGee, study directors, and Jerry Kidd, senior program officer on the BBCSS staff, assisted in the initial screening of articles for the committee's literature review. Deborah Johnson provided valuable project assistance, particularly in making arrangements for the committee's meetings and visits to agencies. Barbara Torrey, then executive director of the NRC's Division of Behavioral and Social Sciences and Education (DBASSE), and associate director Miron Straf, who developed the project initially, took a continuing interest in the work of the committee. We have also been fortunate to have the continuing wise counsel of Eugenia Grohman, director, DBASSE Reports Office, throughout the work of the committee. We are also grateful for help received from Nancy A. Obuchowski, at the Cleveland Clinic Foundation, and Kevin S. Berbaum, at the University of Iowa, in acquainting us with existing software for receiver operating characteristic (ROC) analysis. Finally, we thank Aleksandra Slavkovic who provided technical statistical assistance and support to the committee, especially in connection with the empirical analyses reported in Chapter 5 and Appendix F.

This report has been reviewed in draft form by individuals chosen for their diverse perspectives and technical expertise, in accordance with procedures approved by the NRC's Report Review Committee. The purpose of this independent review is to provide candid and critical comments that will assist the institution in making the published report as sound as possible and to ensure that the report meets institutional standards for objectivity, evidence, and responsiveness to the study charge. The review comments and draft manuscript remain confidential to protect the integrity of the deliberative process.

We thank the following individuals for their participation in the review of this report: John F. Ahearne, Sigma Xi and Duke University; Gershon Ben-Shakhar, Department of Psychology, Hebrew University, Jerusalem; Roy D'Andrade, Department of Anthropology, University of California, San Diego; Paul Gianelli, School of Law, Case Western Reserve University; Bert F. Green, Jr., Professor of Psychology, Emeritus, Johns Hopkins University; James A. Hanley, Department of Epidemiology and Biostatistics, McGill University, Canada; Barbara C. Hansen, School of Medicine, University of Maryland, Baltimore; Ray Hyman, Department of Psychology, University of Oregon; Sallie Keller-McNulty, Statistical Sciences, Los Alamos National Laboratory; John Kircher, Department of Educational Psychology, University of Utah; James L. McGaugh, Center for the Neurobiology of Learning and Memory, University of California, Irvine; Gregory A. Miller, University of Illinois; William Revelle, Northwestern University; Anthony E. Siegman, McMurtry Professor of Engineering, Emeritus, Stanford University; Robert M. Stern, Pennsylvania State University; Stephen Stigler, Department of Statistics, University of Chicago; and James Woolsey, Shea & Gardner, Washington, DC.

Although the reviewers listed above have provided many constructive comments and suggestions, they were not asked to endorse the conclusions or recommendations nor did they see the final draft of the report before its release. The review of this report was overseen by John Bailar, University of Chicago (emeritus), and Michael Posner, Department of Psychology, University of Oregon. Appointed by the National Research Council, they were responsible for making certain that an independent examination of this report was carried out in accordance with institutional procedures and that all review comments were carefully considered. Responsibility for the final content of this report rests entirely with the authoring committee and the institution.

> Stephen E. Fienberg, *Chair*
> Committee to Review the Scientific
> Evidence on the Polygraph

THE
POLYGRAPH
AND LIE DETECTION

Executive Summary

For as long as human beings have deceived one another, people have tried to develop techniques for detecting deception and finding truth. Lie detection took on aspects of modern science with the development in the 20th century of techniques intended for the psychophysiological detection of deception, most prominently, polygraph testing. The polygraph instrument measures several physiological processes (e.g., heart rate) and changes in those processes. From the charts of those measures in response to questions on a polygraph test, sometimes aided by observations during the polygraph examination, examiners infer a psychological state, namely, whether a person is telling the truth or lying.

Polygraph testing is used for three main purposes: event-specific investigations (e.g., after a crime); employee screening, and preemployment screening. The different uses involve the search for different kinds of information and have different implications. A question asked about a specific incident (e.g., "Did you see the victim on Monday" or "Did you take the file home yesterday?") often has little ambiguity, so it is clear what facts provide the criterion for a truthful answer.

For employee screening, there is no specific event being investigated, and the questions must be generic (e.g., "Did you ever reveal classified information to an unauthorized person?"). Both examinee and examiner may have difficulty knowing whether an answer to such a question is truthful unless there are clear and consistent criteria that specify what activities justify a "yes" answer. Examinees may believe they are lying when providing factually truthful responses, or vice versa. Polygraph tests might elicit admissions to acts not central to the intent of the question and these answers might be judged either as successes or failures of the test. In this regard, we have seen no indication of a clear and stable agreement on criteria for judging answers to security screening polygraph questions in any agency using them.

The use of polygraph testing for preemployment screening is even more complicated because it involves inferences about future behavior on the basis of information about past behaviors that may be quite different (e.g., does past use of illegal drugs, or lying about such use on a polygraph test, predict future spying?).

The committee's charge was specifically "to conduct a scientific review of the research on polygraph examinations that pertains to their validity and reliability, in particular for personnel security screening," that is, for the second and third purposes. We have focused mainly on validity because a test that is reliable (i.e., produces consistent outcomes) has little use unless it is also valid (i.e., measures what it is supposed to measure). Virtually all the available scientific evidence on polygraph test validity comes from studies of specific-event investigations, so the committee had to rely heavily on that evidence, in addition to the few available studies that are relevant for screening. The general quality of the evidence for judging polygraph validity is relatively low: the substantial majority of the studies most relevant for this purpose were below the quality level typically needed for funding by the National Science Foundation or the National Institutes of Health.

SCIENTIFIC EVIDENCE

Basic Science

Almost a century of research in scientific psychology and physiology provides little basis for the expectation that a polygraph test could have extremely high accuracy. Although psychological states often associated with deception (e.g., fear of being judged deceptive) do tend to affect the physiological responses that the polygraph measures, these same states can arise in the absence of deception. Moreover, many other psychological and physiological factors (e.g., anxiety about being tested) also affect those responses. Such phenomena make polygraph testing intrinsically susceptible to producing erroneous results. This inherent ambiguity of the physiological measures used in the polygraph suggests that further investments in improving polygraph technique and interpretation will bring only modest improvements in accuracy.

Polygraph research has not developed and tested theories of the underlying factors that produce the observed responses. Factors other than truthfulness that affect the physiological responses being measured can vary substantially across settings in which polygraph tests are used. There is little knowledge about how much these factors influence the outcomes of polygraph tests in field settings. For example, there is evidence suggesting that truthful members of socially stigmatized groups and truthful examinees who are believed to be guilty or believed to have a high likelihood of being guilty may show emotional and physiological responses in polygraph test situations that mimic the responses that are expected of deceptive individuals. The lack of understanding of the processes that underlie polygraph responses makes it very difficult to generalize from the results obtained in specific research settings or with particular subject populations to other settings or populations, or from laboratory research studies to real-world applications.

Evidence on Polygraph Accuracy

Scientific evidence relevant to the accuracy of polygraph tests for employee or preemployment screening is extremely limited. Only one field study, which is flawed, provides evidence directly relevant to accuracy for preemployment screening. A few additional laboratory studies are relevant to preemployment or employee screening, but they are more analogous to specific-incident investigations than to screening because the deceptive examinee is given a precise recent incident about which to lie.

Of the 57 studies the committee used to quantify the accuracy of polygraph testing, all involved specific incidents, typically mock crimes (four studies simulated screening in the sense that the incidents were followed by generic screening-type questions). The quality of the studies varies considerably, but falls far short of what is desirable. Laboratory studies suffer from lack of realism, and in the randomized controlled studies focused on specific incidents using mock crimes, the consequences associated with lying or being judged deceptive almost never mirror the seriousness of these actions in real-world settings in which the polygraph is used. Field studies have major problems with identifying the truth against which test results should be judged. In addition, they suffer from problems associated with heterogeneity and lack of control of extraneous factors and more generally, they have lower quality than could be achieved with careful study design. Moreover, most of the research, in both the laboratory and in the field, does not fully address key potential threats to validity. For these reasons, study results cannot be expected to generalize to practical contexts.

Estimates of accuracy from these 57 studies are almost certainly higher than actual polygraph accuracy of specific-incident testing in the field. Laboratory studies tend to overestimate accuracy because laboratory conditions involve much less variation in test implementation, in the characteristics of examinees, and in the nature and context of investigations than arises in typical field applications. Observational studies of polygraph testing in the field are plagued by selection and measurement biases, such as the inclusion of tests carried out by examiners with knowledge of the evidence and of cases whose outcomes are affected by the examination. In addition, they frequently lack a clear and independent determination of truth. Due to these inherent biases, observational field studies are also highly likely to overestimate real-world polygraph accuracy.

> **CONCLUSION: Notwithstanding the limitations of the quality of the empirical research and the limited ability to generalize to real-world settings, we conclude that in populations of examinees such as those represented in the polygraph research literature, untrained in countermeasures, specific-incident polygraph tests can discriminate lying from truth telling at rates well above chance, though well below perfection. Because the studies of acceptable quality all focus on specific incidents, generalization from them to uses for screening is not justified. Because actual screening applications involve considerably more ambiguity for the examinee and in determining truth than arises in specific-incident studies, polygraph accuracy for screening purposes is almost certainly lower than what can be achieved by specific-incident polygraph tests in the field.**

The accuracy levels in the four screening simulations in our sample, which include a validation study of the Test for Espionage and Sabotage (TES) used in the employee security screening program of the U.S. Department of Energy (DOE), are in the range reported for other specific-incident laboratory studies. The one field study of actual screening presents results consistent with the expectation that polygraph accuracy in true screening situations is lower.

Countermeasures

Countermeasures pose a potentially serious threat to the performance of polygraph testing because all the physiological indicators measured by the polygraph can be altered by conscious efforts through cognitive or physical means. Certain countermeasures apparently can, under some laboratory conditions, enable a deceptive individual to appear nondeceptive and avoid detection by an examiner. It is unknown whether a deceptive individual can produce responses that mimic the physiological responses of a nondeceptive individual well enough to fool an examiner trained to look for behavioral and physiological signatures of countermeasures. The available research provides no information on whether innocent examinees can increase their chances of achieving nondeceptive outcomes by using countermeasures. (It is possible that classified information exists on these topics; however, this committee was not provided access to such information and cannot verify its existence or relevance.)

CONCLUSION: Basic science and polygraph research give reason for concern that polygraph test accuracy may be degraded by countermeasures, particularly when used by major security threats who have a strong incentive and sufficient resources to use them effectively. If these measures are effective, they could seriously undermine any value of polygraph security screening.

POLYGRAPH USE FOR SECURITY SCREENING

The proportion of spies, terrorists, and other major national security threats among the employees subject to polygraph testing in the DOE laboratories and similar federal sites presumably is extremely low. Screening in populations with very low rates of the target transgressions (e.g., less than 1 in 1,000) requires diagnostics of extremely high accuracy, well beyond what can be expected from polygraph testing. Table S-1 illustrates the unpleasant tradeoffs facing policy makers who use a screen-

TABLE S-1 Expected Results of a Polygraph Test Procedure with an Accuracy Index of 0.90 in a Hypothetical Population of 10,000 Examinees That Includes 10 Spies

S-1A If detection threshold is set to detect the great majority (80 percent) of spies

| | Examinee's True Condition | | |
Test Result	Spy	Nonspy	Total
"Fail" test	8	1,598	1,606
"Pass" test	2	8,392	8,394
Total	10	9,990	10,000

S-1B If detection threshold is set to greatly reduce false positive results

| | Examinee's True Condition | | |
Test Result	Spy	Nonspy	Total
"Fail" test	2	39	41
"Pass" test	8	9,951	9,959
Total	10	9,990	10,000

ing technique in a hypothetical population of 10,000 government employees that includes 10 spies, even when an accuracy is assumed that is greater than can be expected of polygraph testing on the basis of available research. If the test were set sensitively enough to detect about 80 percent or more of deceivers, about 1,606 employees or more would be expected "fail" the test; further investigation would be needed to separate the 8 spies from the 1,598 loyal employees caught in the screen. If the test were set to reduce the numbers of false alarms (loyal employees who "fail" the test) to about 40 of 9,990, it would correctly classify over 99.5 percent of the examinees, but among the errors would be 8 of the 10 hypothetical spies, who could be expected to "pass" the test and so would be free to cause damage.

Available evidence indicates that polygraph testing as currently used has extremely serious limitations in such screening applications, if the intent is both to identify security risks and protect valued employees. Given its level of accuracy, achieving a high probability of identifying individuals who pose major security risks in a population with a very low proportion of such individuals would require setting the test to be so sensitive that hundreds, or even thousands, of innocent individuals would be implicated for every major security violator correctly identified. The only way to be certain to limit the frequency of "false positives" is to administer the test in a manner that would almost certainly severely limit the proportion of serious transgressors identified.

> **CONCLUSION: Polygraph testing yields an unacceptable choice for DOE employee security screening between too many loyal employees falsely judged deceptive and too many major security threats left undetected. Its accuracy in distinguishing actual or potential security violators from innocent test takers is insufficient to justify reliance on its use in employee security screening in federal agencies.**

Polygraph screening may be useful for achieving such objectives as deterring security violations, increasing the frequency of admissions of such violations, deterring employment applications from potentially poor security risks, and increasing public confidence in national security organizations. On the basis of field reports and indirect scientific evidence, we believe that polygraph testing is likely to have some utility for such purposes. Such utility derives from beliefs about the procedure's validity, which are distinct from actual validity or accuracy. Polygraph screening programs that yield only a small percentage of positive test results, such as those in use at DOE and some other federal agencies, might be useful for deterrence, eliciting admissions, and related purposes. However, in populations with very low base rates of the target transgressions they should not be counted on for detection: they will not detect more than a small proportion of major security violators who do not admit their actions.

We have thought hard about how to advise government agencies on whether or how to use information from a diagnostic screening test that has these serious limitations. We note that in medicine, such imperfect diagnostics are often used for screening, though only occasionally in populations with very low base rates of the target condition. When this is done, either the test is far more accurate than polygraph testing appears to be, or there is a more accurate (though generally more invasive or expensive) follow-up test that can be used when the screening test gives a positive result. Such a follow-up test does not exist for the polygraph. The medical analogy and this difference between medical and security screening underline the wisdom in contexts like that of employee security screening in the DOE laboratories of using positive polygraph screening results—if polygraph screening is to be used at all—only as triggers for detailed follow-up investigation, not as a basis for personnel action. It also underlines the need to pay close attention to the implications of false negative test results, especially if tests are used that yield a low proportion of positive results.

A belief that polygraph testing is highly accurate probably enhances its utility for such objectives as deterrence. However, overconfidence in the polygraph—a belief in its accuracy that goes beyond what is justified by the evidence—also presents a danger to national security objectives. Overconfidence in polygraph screening can create a false sense of security among policy makers, employees in sensitive positions, and the general public that may in turn lead to inappropriate relaxation of other methods of ensuring security, such as periodic security re-investigation and vigilance about potential security violations in facilities that use the polygraph for employee security screening. It can waste public resources by devoting to the polygraph funds and energy that would be better spent on alternative procedures. It can lead to unnecessary loss of competent or highly skilled individuals in security organizations because of suspicions cast on them by false positive polygraph exams or because of their fear of such prospects. And it can lead to credible claims that agencies that use polygraphs are infringing civil liberties for insufficient benefits to the national security. Thus, policy makers should consider each application of polygraph testing in the larger context of its various costs and benefits.

ALTERNATIVES AND ENHANCEMENTS TO THE POLYGRAPH

CONCLUSION: Some potential alternatives to the polygraph show promise, but none has yet been shown to outperform the poly-

graph. **None shows any promise of supplanting the polygraph for screening purposes in the near term.**

The polygraph is only one of many possible techniques for identifying national security risks among federal employees. Other techniques attempt to detect deception from facial expressions, voice quality, and other aspects of demeanor; from measurements of brain activity and other physiological indicators; and from background investigations or questionnaires. Computerized analysis of polygraph records has the potential to improve the accuracy of test results by using more information from polygraph records than is used in traditional scoring methods. This potential has yet to be realized, however, either in research or in practice.

We considered the potential to increase the capability to identify security risks by combining polygraph information with information from other screening techniques, for example, in serial screening protocols such as are used in medical diagnosis. There are good theoretical reasons to think appropriate procedures of this sort would improve detection of deception, but we found no serious investigations of such multicomponent screening approaches.

RESEARCH RECOMMENDATIONS

There has been no serious effort in the U.S. government to develop the scientific basis for the psychophysiological detection of deception by any technique, even though criticisms of the scientific grounding of polygraph testing have been raised prominently for decades. Given the heavy reliance of government on the polygraph, especially for screening for espionage and sabotage, the lack of a serious investment in such research is striking.

The limitations of the polygraph, especially for security screening, justify efforts to look more broadly for effective tools for deterring and detecting security violations. These might include modifications in the overall security strategies used in federal agencies, such as have been recommended by the Hamre Commission for DOE, as well as improved techniques for deterring and detecting security violations focused on individuals. Research offers one promising strategy for developing the needed tools.

We recommend an expanded research effort directed at methods for detecting and deterring major security threats, including efforts to improve techniques for security screening.

This effort should pursue two major objectives: (1) to provide federal agencies with methods of the highest possible scientific validity for protecting national security by deterring and detecting major security threats; and (2) to make these agencies fully aware of the strengths and limitations of the techniques they use. If the government continues to rely heavily on the polygraph in the national security arena, some of this research effort should be devoted to developing scientific knowledge that could put the polygraph on a firmer scientific foundation, develop alternative methods, or develop effective ways to combine techniques and methods. National security is best served by a broad research program on detecting and deterring security threats, not a narrow focus on polygraph research.

The research program should be open to supporting alternative ways of looking at the problems of deterrence and detection because there is no single research approach that clearly holds the most promise for meeting national security objectives. Thus, it might support research ranging from very basic work on fundamental psychological, physiological, social, and organizational processes related to deterring and detecting security threats to applied studies on implementing scientifically rooted methods in practical situations.

A substantial portion of our recommended expanded research program should be administered by an organization or organizations with no operational responsibility for detecting deception and no institutional commitment to using or training practitioners of a particular technique. The research program should follow accepted standards for scientific research, use rules and procedures designed to eliminate biases that might influence the findings, and operate under normal rules of scientific freedom and openness to the extent possible while protecting national security.

The mandate should be broad and should include both basic and applied research. The program should use standard scientific advisory and decision-making procedures, including external peer review of proposals, and should support research that is conducted and reviewed openly in the manner of other scientific research. Classified and restricted research should be limited only to matters of identifiable national security. Mission agencies might well continue to conduct implementation-focused research on detecting deception, but their work should be integrated with the broader research program proposed here.

1

Lie Detection and the Polygraph

For as long as human beings have deceived each other, people have tried to develop techniques for detecting deception and determining truth (see, e.g., Kleinmuntz and Szucko, 1984). These techniques have almost always included interviews and interrogations to try to see through deception and reveal what a deceiver will not freely admit. In the 20th century, lie detection took on scientific aspects with the development of techniques that use measures of physiological responses as indicators of deception. The best known of these is the polygraph. This technique, which relies on physiological measurements developed early in the century, has become for many in the U.S. law enforcement and intelligence communities (including counterintelligence officials in several agencies with whom we met) the most valued method for identifying criminals, spies, and saboteurs when direct evidence is lacking.

Polygraph examinations are widely used in the United States and in some other countries (notably, Israel, Japan, and Canada) for three main purposes:

(1) They are used for preemployment screening in law enforcement and preemployment or preclearance screening in agencies involved in national security. The great majority of U.S. police departments, for example, include polygraph examinations as part of their preemployment screening batteries. Preclearance screening may involve current employ-

ees who are being considered for new assignments, typically at a higher level of clearance.

(2) They are used for screening current employees, especially in security-sensitive occupations. For example, the U.S. Department of Energy polygraph program, established in 1999, mandated polygraph examinations for about 1,300 employees in sensitive positions; a year later, the program was expanded to cover several thousand additional employees (P.L. 106-65 and P.L. 106-398).

(3) They are used in investigations of specific events, for instance, in criminal cases. Although there are many restrictions on the use of polygraph results in courts, they are often used to help direct and focus criminal investigations.

These three uses of the polygraph raise very different scientific and practical questions, as discussed in this report.

The polygraph continues to be the subject of a great deal of scientific and public controversy in the United States. A 1983 report by the U.S. Office of Technology Assessment examining the validity of the polygraph raised many criticisms that are still being voiced. The 1988 Employee Polygraph Protection Act sharply limited the use of polygraphs in employment settings, largely because of doubts about its validity for screening. Different courts have different sets of rules about the admissibility of polygraph evidence and even about what test must be met for such evidence to be considered admissible. Many people find polygraph testing objectionable, and there are several websites and organizations devoted to discrediting the polygraph.

It is against this background of continuing controversy that the committee was given the charge to "conduct a scientific review of the research on polygraph examinations that pertain to their validity and reliability, in particular for personnel security screening." We were also asked to "review other techniques that may be adapted for similar purposes . . . in order to allow for a comparative evaluation of the polygraph and to suggest directions for future research that may include both polygraph and other tests." Based on our review, we were asked to present our "assessments of and recommendations for polygraph examinations for personnel security purposes" and to suggest further research.[1]

THE INSTRUMENT, THE TEST, AND THE EXAMINATION

Polygraph testing combines interrogation with physiological measurements obtained using the polygraph, or polygraph instrument, a piece of equipment that records physiological phenomena—typically, respiration, heart rate, blood pressure, and electrodermal response (electrical conductance at the skin surface).[2] A polygraph examination includes a series of yes/no questions to which the examinee responds while connected to sensors that transmit data on these physiological phenomena by wire to the instrument, which uses analog or digital technology to record the data. Because the original analog instruments recorded the data with several pens writing lines on a moving sheet of paper, the record of physiological responses during the polygraph test is known as the polygraph chart.

A variety of other technologies have been developed that purport to use physiological responses to make inferences about deceptiveness. These range from brain scans to analyses of voice tremors; some evidence relevant to these techniques is discussed in this report.

Physiological Phenomena

The physiological phenomena that the instrument measures and that the chart preserves are believed by polygraph practitioners to reveal deception. Practitioners do not claim that the instrument measures deception directly. Rather, it is said to measure physiological responses that are believed to be stronger during acts of deception than at other times. According to some polygraph theories, a deceptive response to a question causes a reaction—such as fear of detection or psychological arousal—that changes respiration rate, heart rate, blood pressure, or skin conductance relative to what they were before the question was asked and relative to what they are after comparison questions are asked. A pattern of physiological responses to questions relevant to the issue being investigated that are stronger than those responses to comparison questions indicates that the examinee may be deceptive.

The central issues in dispute about the validity of polygraph testing concern these physiological responses. For example, are they strongly and uniquely associated with deception, or are there conditions other than deception that could produce the same responses? Does this association depend on particular ways of selecting or asking questions, and if so, do examiners ask the right kinds of questions and make the right comparisons between the physiological responses to different questions? Is the same association of deception with physiological response observable across all kinds of examinees in all kinds of physical and emotional states? Does it depend on factors in the relationship between examiner and examinee? Is it influenced by an examiner's expectation about whether the examinee will be truthful? In Chapters 3, 4, and 5 we discuss in more detail the theory of the polygraph and two kinds of evidence on these questions. One comes from basic psychophysiological research on the phenomena the instrument measures. The other comes from research on polygraph testing itself.

Polygraph Test Techniques

Although the polygraph instrument is the centerpiece of the technique, the ability of the polygraph test to detect deception also depends critically on other elements of the process. One is the interpretation of the polygraph chart. Interpretation normally involves comparison of physiological responses to "relevant" questions (i.e., questions about the issue that is the focus of the examination) and responses to other questions that are asked for purposes of comparison.[3] Interpretation is often done by the examiner, who reviews the chart and may code it according to a standard protocol. People other than the examiner may also use such a protocol to code a chart. Chart interpretation can also be done by computer.

Different polygraph techniques are defined in part by the ways the relevant and comparison questions are selected and placed in a polygraph test. A considerable portion of the empirical research on polygraph testing focuses on validating particular techniques or comparing the performance of one technique with another. Three major classes of questioning techniques are in current use. In the oldest of these, the relevant-irrelevant technique, the relevant questions are typically very specific and concern an event under investigation: for example, "Did you rob the bank on Friday?" The irrelevant questions may be completely unrelated to the event and may offer little temptation to deceive: for example, "Is today Monday?" or "Are you in New Jersey?" Stronger physiological responses to relevant than to irrelevant questions are taken as indicative of deception. Although this technique has numerous limitations from a scientific standpoint (Raskin and Honts, 2002), it is used in criminal investigations and in some federal employee security screening programs, for instance, at the National Security Agency.

The second class of techniques, called control question or comparison question testing, compares responses to relevant questions with responses to other questions that are intended to generate physiological reactions even in nondeceptive examinees. In one version of this technique, the comparison questions are selected to create a temptation to deceive: for example, "Have you ever stolen a small object from your place of work?" or "Have you ever violated a minor traffic law?" Such so-called probable lie questions are presumed to be like the relevant questions in creating a level of concern related to truthfulness. For truthful examinees, this level of concern is presumed to be higher than for the relevant questions, about which the examinee can be truthful without much anxiety. For examinees who may be deceptive about the events under investigation, it is presumed that the relevant questions create the greater level of concern and therefore a stronger physiological response. Comparison question tests are used both for specific-event investigations and for screening. A version of the comparison question technique, the Test of Espionage and Sabotage (TES) is a staple of the U.S. Department of Energy's employee security screening polygraph program.

The third class of techniques, commonly called guilty knowledge polygraph testing, involves questions about details of an event under investigation that are known only to investigators and those with direct knowledge of the event. We refer to these tests as concealed information tests because they are applicable even when an examinee who possesses information is not guilty and even if the information is incorrect. The questions are presented in a multiple-choice format. For example, in a burglary investigation: "Where was the place of entry? Was it a: (1) front entrance? (2) kitchen door? (3) bathroom window? (4) balcony? (5) room on the second floor?" (Nakayama, 2002:50). If an examinee who denies knowledge of the event shows the strongest physiological response in several such sets of questions to the alternative that accurately describes the event, the examinee is concluded to have concealed information. Because this test format requires that the examiner have knowledge of the details of a specific event that is the topic of questioning, it cannot be used in typical security screening contexts.

Appendix A provides brief descriptions of these basic polygraph questioning techniques and some of their variants. More detail is available from several sources, including the recent *Handbook of Polygraph Testing* (Kleiner, 2002; especially chapters by Raskin and Honts, Nakayama, and Ben-Shakhar and Elaad). Appendix B provides more detail on how security screening polygraph examinations are conducted in the U.S. Department of Energy and other federal agencies.

As these brief descriptions make clear, polygraph testing techniques vary in the ways the relevant and comparison questions differ and in how these differences, combined with an examinee's physiological responses to them, are used to make inferences about whether the person may be lying in response to the relevant questions. We return to these differences in Chapter 3. In many applications, examiners take a stronger response than to comparison questions as an indication not necessarily of deception, but of the need for further interviewing or testing to determine whether deception is occurring. The lack of such a differential response or a stronger response to comparison questions generally leads to a conclusion that a respondent is being truthful.

Pretest Interview

A polygraph *test* is part of a polygraph *examination*, which includes other components. A critical one, particularly in comparison question tests, is the pretest interview. This interview typically has multiple purposes. It explains the test procedure to the examinee. It explains the questions to be asked so that examiners and examinees understand the questions in the same way. Shared understanding is especially important for screening polygraphs that ask about general categories of behavior, such as "Have you ever revealed classified information to an unauthorized individual?" The pretest interview shapes the expectations and emotional state of the examinee during the test. It may be used to convince the examinee that the polygraph instrument will detect any deception. This process often involves a demonstration in which the examinee is asked to lie about an unimportant matter, and the examiner shows the instrument's ability to detect the lie; these demonstrations sometimes involve deceiving the examinee.[4] In comparison question testing, the interview is also used to help the examiner decide which questions to ask for comparison purposes. It is important to note that each of these aspects of the pretest interview may influence an examinee's physiological responses to the relevant or comparison questions and, therefore, the result of the examination.

Finally, the polygraph examiner is likely to form impressions of the examinee's truthfulness, based on the examinee's demeanor and responses in the pretest interview and during the charting. These impressions, as well as any expectations the examiner may have formed in advance of the examination, are likely to affect the conduct and interpretation of the examination and might, therefore, influence the outcome and the validity of the polygraph examination.

Overall Examination

A polygraph test and its result are a joint product of an interview or interrogation technique and a psychophysiological measurement or testing technique. It is misleading to characterize the examination as purely a physiological measurement technique. Polygraph examiners' training implicitly recognizes this point in several ways. It provides instruction on the kind of atmosphere that is to be created in the pretest interview, advises on techniques for convincing examinees of the accuracy of the test, and offers guidance (in different ways for different test formats) for selecting comparison questions. Examiners are advised to control these details—sometimes following carefully specified procedures—because they can affect test results.

Polygraph examination procedures often explicitly combine and interweave testing and interviewing. When a polygraph chart indicates something other than an ordinary nondeceptive response to a relevant question, the examiner typically pursues this response with questioning during the course of the examination. For example, the examiner may say, "You seem to be having a problem in the area of X [the relevant item]" and ask the examinee if he or she can think of a reason for having a strong physiological reaction to that question. The interview may reveal a misunderstanding of the question, which is then explained and reasked in a subsequent charting. Or if the reaction remains unexplained to the examiner's satisfaction, the issue may be probed in more detail in the interview or with questions in a subsequent charting. Some examiners believe that an important use of polygraph testing is in helping narrow the range of issues that need to be investigated, using both polygraph and other investigative tools.

The important role of interview conditions is also recognized in much of the practice and lore of polygraph testing. For example, it is widely and plausibly believed that polygraph results are different for "friendly" and "unfriendly" examinations (e.g., examiners proffered by the defense or by the prosecution in criminal cases). Presumably, examinees are more relaxed with "friendly" examiners and less likely to have responses that indicate deception on the test. When interviewers are hostile or aggressive, examinees may be less relaxed and may produce different physiological responses than those they would produce in response to calm, friendly questioning.

Such effects of the interview situation are common in other settings, for example, the widely noted phenomenon of "white-coat hypertension," in which blood pressure is believed to increase because of the context of a medical examination. These situational effects represent a challenge to the validity of any physiological test that does not adequately reduce the influence of variations in the interview situation on the physiological responses being measured or separate the effects of the situation from the effects of the condition (such as deception) that the test is intended to measure. In polygraph testing, the use of initial buffer items is intended to reduce situational effects on the examinee's physiological responses. Comparison questions are also used to separate situational effects from the effects of deception by statistical means. Whether these procedures in fact have the desired effects is an empirical question, which is explored in this book.[5]

THE LIE DETECTION MYSTIQUE

In order to frame a scientific discussion about the polygraph, we consider the role of this method of detecting deception in American culture and compare it with methods of detecting deception that have been accepted in other cultures. The polygraph, perhaps more than any other apparently humane interrogation technique, arouses strong emotions. There is a mystique surrounding the polygraph that may account for much of its usefulness: that is, a culturally shared belief that the polygraph device is nearly infallible. Practitioners believe that criminals sometimes prefer to admit their crimes and that potential spies sometimes avoid certain job positions rather than face a polygraph examination, which they expect will reveal the truth about them. The mystique shows in other ways, too. People accused of crimes voluntarily submit to polygraph tests and publicize "passing" results because they believe a polygraph test can confer credibility that they cannot get otherwise. In popular culture and media, the polygraph device is often represented as a magic mind-reading machine. These facts reflect the widespread mystique or belief that the polygraph test is a highly valid technique for detecting deception—despite the continuing lack of consensus in the scientific community about the validity of polygraph testing.

Ritualized Lie Detection Across Cultures

Ritualized lie detection techniques in many groups, societies, and cultures through the ages share several characteristics that help create a mystique that enables the techniques to be effective. Lie detection rituals involve a socially certified administrator (an examiner or interrogator) and some device or procedure that purportedly can objectively and publicly identify lying on the part of the examinee. The administrator—in some cultures, a priest or shaman—has completed a secret or semi-secret training process. The keeping of the secrets of the ritual within a small, select group adds to the mystique (e.g., the belief that keepers of the secrets have good reason not to publicize them and should be trusted), and, consequently, adds to the power of the technique. The belief structure of the endorsing society includes beliefs about the special powers of the officials authorized to perform the ritual and about the ritual's ability to divine or elicit concealed truths. The examinee, as a member of the society or culture, generally accepts the importance of the lie detection ritual and believes that it is very accurate. Hence, if he or she is telling the truth, there is little or no reason to fear the examination, but if he or she is lying, there is reason to fear it. Many procedures and techniques have been used in lie detection rituals, including ones that in our society would be regarded as quite primitive and unscientific, such as immersion in water or placing a wafer on the tongue (see Kleinmuntz and Szucko, 1984). Despite the lack of scientific evidence supporting the validity of such techniques, they apparently are useful, as judged by their ability to elicit confessions of truths that are not forthcoming when other methods are used. Some or all of this usefulness is attributed to mystique—the systems of beliefs that surround and support the techniques.

The polygraph testing procedures currently used in the criminal justice system and in several government agencies in the United States and other countries fit this prototype ritual. A polygraph examiner subculture exists, complete with its own institutions (e.g., professional societies), norms, values, etc. Examiners are trained and certified expert by various training institutes, including some private ones and, importantly, by the U.S. Department of Defense Polygraph Institute. Members of the polygraph examiner culture have a particular jargon and shared lore that are generally unknown to others. They also maintain secrets because to reveal too much of their knowledge would enable targets of investigations to "beat" polygraph tests. The polygraph device or instrument is purported to have the power to discriminate lies from truths in the hands of a certified and experienced examiner.

The polygraph examination follows standardized, ritual-like procedures and usually occurs in a setting designed to evoke associations with science, medicine, or law enforcement, institutions whose certified practitioners are believed to have special powers to uncover truths. Claims that polygraph testing is a scientific method, together with the establishment of research programs to improve polygraph testing, are useful for building credibility in a society that confers credibility on scientific activities. Moreover, potential examinees are assumed to believe in the validity of polygraph testing, and its validity is supported by popular culture.

These similarities between current polygraph detection of deception procedures and the lie detection rituals of other and former cultures say nothing directly about the validity or invalidity of the polygraph testing for distinguishing truth from deception. They do, however, suggest that some of the value or utility of the polygraph for eliciting admissions and confessions undoubtedly comes from attributes other than the validity of the testing itself. Polygraph testing may work, in part, because it capitalizes on the mystique that is common to lie-detection rituals in many societies. Any investigation into the scientific validity of polygraph detection of deception must try to identify and distinguish between two kinds of scientific evidence: evidence bearing on the effects of the polygraph ritual and mystique and evidence bearing on the validity of polygraph testing and the polygraph device for detecting deception.

Any scientific investigation must also deal with some of the cognitive and organizational phenomena that go along with a ritual that has a mystique, a "priesthood," and a set of secrets. One of these is the difficulty of gaining access to information. Some information of interest to this study, such as the polygraph test records of known spies, is classified for national security reasons. Other information, such as the precise ways particular pieces of polygraph equipment measure physiological responses, is guarded by equipment manufacturers as trade secrets. Some manufacturers ignored our requests for such information, even though we offered to sign legally binding promises of nondisclosure. Information about computer scoring algorithms for polygraph tests was similarly withheld by some algorithm developers. All of this behavior makes scientific analysis difficult. Some of these "secrets" probably have good practical justification, but they are also very much like the activities of a priesthood keeping its secrets in order to keep its power.

Another aspect of the polygraph mystique that creates difficulties for scientific analysis is the strong, apparently unshakeable, beliefs of many practitioners in its efficacy on the basis of their experiences. We have heard numerous anecdotes about admissions of serious crimes and security violations that have been elicited in polygraph examinations even after background checks and ordinary interviews had yielded nothing. Many of these admissions have been later corroborated by other convincing evidence, indicating that the polygraph examination sometimes reveals truths that might otherwise have remained concealed indefinitely. We do not doubt the veracity of these anecdotes. However, they do not constitute evidence that the polygraph instrument conveys information that, in the context of the polygraph test, accurately identifies the locus of deception. Rather, they signify that something in the polygraph examination can have this result. It may be the test, the interviewer's skills, the examinee's expectation of detection, or some combination of these or other factors. From a scientific standpoint, these anecdotes are compelling indications that there is a phenomenon in need of explanation; they do not, however, demonstrate that the polygraph test is a valid indicator of deception.

Practical Implications

From a practical standpoint, it can make a considerable difference whether decisions that rely on polygraph evidence are resting on a scientifically proven device and procedures (that is, on the test), on the judgments of examiners, or on the expectation that guilty examinees will be sufficiently fearful of detection to confess. For example, if the apparent successes depend only on examinees' fear of detection and not on the test itself, the examination would fail with well-trained spies who know the test's limitations and do not respond to the mystique.

Polygraph examiners and the decision makers who use their reports do not always make such distinctions. The belief among many agency officials that the important questions about polygraph testing validity have already been favorably resolved makes it difficult to conduct scientific analysis of the components of polygraph testing, including the polygraph instrument itself, in those agencies. It also creates resistance to scientific evidence critical of the test's validity among practitioners whose personal experience has convinced them of the polygraph's utility. Finally, placing polygraphic detection of deception within the anthropological and historical context of lie detection rituals strongly suggests that the mystique will outlive current lie detection techniques, including the polygraph test. We surmise that if the mystique of lie detection no longer attaches to the polygraph, a new technique or instrument will take its place and assume its mystique. Indeed, some people argue that the mystique has already been dispelled, as exemplified by the controversy over polygraph security screening that led to the request for this study. It is therefore not surprising that in the current context of heightened concern about espionage and terrorism, there is a lot of publicity about new devices and techniques for the psychophysiological detection of deception. This interest reflects both the need for security and at least latent doubts about the validity of polygraph testing procedures. As discussed in this report, the scientific criteria that should be used to evaluate new devices and procedures are the same as those that apply to the polygraph.

SCIENTIFIC ISSUES

Detecting Deception and Eliciting Truth

For a criminal investigator or a counterintelligence officer, detecting deception and eliciting truth are opposite sides of the same coin. It does not matter whether deception is detected in an interviewee's physiological responses or whether truth is elicited in the form of an admission or revealed by a combination of physiological responses and further interrogation and investigation. Such distinctions are not made in official reports on polygraph screening programs. What matters most to investigators and is reported to Congress are the number of examinees who were ultimately "cleared," the number subjected to adverse personnel actions, and the security violations revealed.

From a scientific standpoint, however, detecting deception and revealing truth are two distinct purposes of polygraph examinations or any other technique for the psychophysiological detection of deception. The polygraph *test* is advocated as an accurate psychophysiological indicator of deception. The polygraph *examination*, which includes the test and the interrogation surrounding it, is a tool for revealing truth. To evaluate the accuracy of polygraph tests, it is imperative to distinguish several different roles of the polygraph test in polygraph examinations, some of which do not depend on whether the test provides a valid indicator of deception.

One role of the polygraph test is to help elicit admissions from people who believe, or are influenced to believe, that it will accurately detect any deception they may attempt. This role is demonstrated most clearly when a polygraph examination is terminated because of an admission before any charts are done. Such an examination can be thought of as an interrogation interview conducted in the presence of a polygraph. In this case, the polygraph test has a useful role independently of whether it can accurately detect deception: it is effective if the examinee believes it can detect deception. Admissions of this kind provide evidence of the value of the polygraph examination for investigative purposes, but they do not provide evidence that the polygraph test accurately detects deception.

Another role of the polygraph is to test cooperation with an investigative effort. Sometimes a polygraph examination is terminated or leads to an assessment that the examinee is deceptive because of detected or suspected countermeasures during the test.[6] If an examinee is judged to be using countermeasures, that is taken as evidence that the examinee is not cooperating with the investigation, particularly if the test protocol asks the examinee not to use countermeasures. Noncooperation is in turn taken as a reason to suspect deception. Holding aside the question of whether such inferences are valid, the use of the polygraph in this way does not depend on the scientific validity of the test.

A third role of the polygraph test is to influence the conduct of a polygraph interview. A polygraph examiner who detects what he or she believes to be deceptive responses during the polygraph test normally conducts the remainder of the interview differently than an examiner who sees no signs of deception. Such an examiner may ask more probing questions, do additional charting, shift to a different type of polygraph test protocol, or take a more confrontational attitude in the interview in an effort to elicit an admission or to "clear" the examinee of suspicion. In this situation, it is impossible without careful experimental analysis to disentangle the effect of polygraph validity from other elements of the interaction in the examination.

Finally, polygraph chart readings may be used directly to make inferences about truthfulness or deceptiveness. Assessments of the scientific validity of the polygraph test as a technique for the psychophysiological detection of deception should properly be made on test outcomes that depend only on chart scoring.[7] However, it can be difficult or impossible to consider chart results in isolation because of the likelihood that the examiner's behavior during the test is affected by prior expectations, the pretest interview, and his or her initial interpretations of a chart. Despite such difficulties, it is important to distinguish between the use of the polygraph as a diagnostic test of deception, in which the charts are scored and decisions are made on the basis of the score, and its use as part of an interrogation procedure.

Purposes of Polygraph Testing

As we note at the beginning of this chapter, polygraph testing and interviewing are used for three main purposes: event-specific investigation, employee screening, and preemployment (or preclearance) screening. These different purposes are reflected in different kinds of questions that are asked in polygraph tests.

For an event-specific investigation, the polygraph is used to investigate a specific incident, such as a crime or a specific act of sabotage or espionage. In this case, it is possible to ask relevant questions that are highly specific, such as "Did you plant the bomb that exploded at location X on June 12?" or "Was the murder committed with a knife?" Relevant questions like these are highly specific to a known event about which a guilty person may have a strong motive to lie or to conceal information.

For employee screening, the polygraph is used with current employees who may have committed acts prohibited by their employer or by law, but there is usually no specific known act that is the focus of the examination. Relevant questions in a security screening context might include "Have you released classified information to any unauthorized person?" or "Have you had any unreported contacts with a foreign government representative?" Some analysts believe that such questions, because they do not refer to specific past events, are more similar to comparison questions than are the relevant questions that can be asked in an event-specific investigation. For this reason, it has been argued that it is inherently more difficult to discriminate deception from truthfulness in a screening context (Murphy, 1993).

For preemployment screening or preclearance screening of employees being considered for new job assignments, the polygraph is used to try to determine the potential for future acts. For example, when someone is given a polygraph examination as part of an application to do intelligence work or for a new assignment that requires access to classified information, the employer's concern may be with the potential that the person may commit an act in the future that he or she is not at present in a position to commit. In this situation, "relevant" questions can only be about unspecific past acts that are different in kind from the ones of greatest concern. Deception can be inferred from the polygraph in the same way it is done in screening current employees. However, in making inferences from indications of deception, it is necessary to make one additional assumption: that a person who is deceptive about certain undesirable past acts is at risk for committing different kinds of undesirable acts in the future.[8]

Some polygraph test situations, which can be described as focused screening situations, do not fit neatly into the above three categories because they have attributes of both the screening and the specific-incident investigation purposes. An example might be the investigation of a fairly large group of individuals who are suspected of involvement with a known terrorist organization. Such investigations are like typical screening situations in that there is no known specific incident that can be the focus of questioning, but they are like specific-event investigations if it is possible to ask specific questions about the organization, its leaders, or the places in which it operates. Strong physiological responses to such specific questions might indicate that the examinee has information about the terrorist organization and should be investigated more fully regarding possible ties to it. If the answers to such questions are likely to be known only to the investigators and to the organization's members and close associates, the situation is amenable to the use of tests of the concealed information type, which are not otherwise considered to be applicable to screening situations.

The ability of polygraph testing to uncover the deceptions of interest and to serve broader law enforcement or national security goals may depend on the purpose of the test and the kinds of acts that are the subject of the relevant questions. It is plausible that the task of the polygraph is easiest in event-specific investigation and hardest in preemployment screening. The possibility that accuracy depends on the purpose of the test makes it unwise to assume that accuracy estimates calculated from data when the polygraph is used for one purpose are pertinent to its use for a different purpose.

Our study focused on the use of polygraph examinations for employee and preemployment screening. However, one of the critical limitations of the available research is the extreme paucity of studies that directly address the validity of the polygraph for current or preemployment screening. Most of the scientific research considered in this report deals with the use of the polygraph for event-specific investigations. Unfortunately, the relevance of such research for the screening context is not self-evident. As we note in Chapter 2, the sorts of decisions made in screening contexts (e.g., a forecast of whether a job applicant might pose a future risk) and event-specific investigations (e.g., an assessment of whether a suspect is truthful when denying a crime) are so fundamentally different that even the best event-specific research may not be relevant to the validity of the polygraph for employee or preemployment screening.

CONTEXT OF POLYGRAPH TESTS

Polygraph examinations are not the only source of information used to determine an examinee's truthfulness or deceptiveness. In event-specific investigations, a variety of techniques of criminal or security investigation are used, and it is often these that lead to the selection of the individuals (suspects) for polygraph testing. In pre-employment screening, employment questionnaires and interviews, as well as background checks, may supplement information from polygraph tests. In employee screening, periodic or occasional polygraph examinations may be supplemented by interviews and investigations, especially if the polygraph test result is inconclusive or shows a significant response that remains unexplained. In short, information from polygraph examinations may be combined in many ways with information from other sources in judging truthfulness or deception. Policy decisions on the use of the polygraph must therefore consider not only the information that can be gained from the polygraph alone, but also the value it may add to what can be learned from other available investigative techniques. Furthermore, besides the additive value of polygraph information, the polygraph test may influence or be affected by other forms of investigation in known and unknown ways. For example, evidence about a crime may identify certain suspects who are then given a polygraph test, or a polygraph test result may lead an ongoing investigation to focus on one person and turn away from others. Such interactions can make it difficult to separate the effects of the polygraph test from those of concurrent investigative methods.

The value, or utility, of polygraph testing does not lie only in its validity for detecting deception. It may have deterrent value, for instance, if people do not take certain actions because they fear that a polygraph examination will uncover them. It may help focus an investigation on particular aspects of a case highlighted by an examinee's physiological responses. And, as noted above, polygraph testing may elicit admissions or confessions of undesired activity from people who believe they are better off to admit certain activities voluntarily than to submit to a polygraph test and risk being accused of these or more serious activities, as well as being accused of deception. These admissions or confessions may occur during the polygraph examination, either before charts are collected or in response to an examiner's questions about the charts. These kinds of utility do not depend on validity in the sense that polygraph policies may yield deterrence, admissions, and confessions when a potential examinee believes that the polygraph will detect or has detected deception, even if scientific evidence does not support such a belief.[9] We discuss utility in more detail in Chapter 2, along with its relationship to the investigation of validity.

STRUCTURE OF THIS BOOK

This book reviews the scientific evidence on the validity of polygraph testing, giving special attention to the use of the polygraph for employee screening for national security purposes. To do this, we consider all the available scientific evidence on polygraph validity, as well as evidence on a number of alternative techniques and technologies for detecting deception.

Chapter 2 discusses the concept of validity as it applies to the psychophysiological detection of deception, distinguishes validity from utility, and explains the measure we have chosen as an index of the accuracy of the polygraph. It covers issues of definition and measurement that are important for understanding how we conducted this study but that may not be of interest to readers concerned mainly with its results. Chapter 3 discusses theories of the polygraph and summarizes the basic scientific knowledge, mainly in psychology and physiology, relevant to polygraph validity. A solid scientific base is necessary if one is to have confidence in the validity of psychophysiological detection of deception across a wide range of settings, and the chapter evaluates this scientific base. Chapters 4 and 5 summarize and evaluate the evidence on the accuracy with which polygraph tests detect deception in experimental simulations and field settings. Chapter 6 discusses a number of alternative techniques for detecting deception that have been suggested as supplements to or replacements for the polygraph and evaluates the research on them. Chapter 7 discusses the issues raised by using polygraph evidence for making practical decisions, particularly in security screening processes, including the issue of combining polygraph evidence with other sources of information. Chapter 8 presents the committee's conclusions about the validity of polygraph testing and its recommendations about the use of the polygraph in employee security screening. It also presents a set of guidelines that should be considered in evaluating emerging techniques for lie detection and offers recommendations for future research. The appendixes provide technical detail and documentation of certain points of the study and are designed for technically oriented readers.

NOTES

1. More specifically, the work plan for the study calls for the National Research Council "to conduct a scientific review of the research on polygraph examinations that pertain to their validity and reliability, in particular for personnel security screening. The review would include what is known about the effect of medications, sleep deprivation, and illnesses on the physiological responses measured. . . .

    "The panel would review other techniques that may be adapted to similar purposes, such as research on facial expressions and voice stress analysis, in order to allow for a comparative evaluation of the polygraph and to suggest directions for future research that may include both polygraph and other tests. The panel will not, however, independently review and assess these other techniques nor assess the use of the polygraph in conjunction with other techniques. . . .

    "The report would present the panel's assessments of and recommendations for polygraph examinations for personnel security purposes and the panel's suggestions for further research."

2. Some standard definitions of key terms can be found in the U.S. Department of Energy's Polygraph Examination Regulations (10 CFR, Part 709.3):

    > *Polygraph* means an instrument that (1) Records continuously, visually, permanently, and simultaneously changes in cardiovascular, respiratory, and electrodermal patterns as minimum instrumentation standards; and (2) Is used, or the results of which are used, for the purpose of rendering a diagnostic opinion regarding the honesty or dishonesty of an individual.

    > *Polygraph examination* means a process that encompasses all activities that take place between a polygraph examiner and individual during a specific series of interactions, including the pretest interview, the use of the polygraph instrument to collect physiological data from the individual while the polygraph examiner is presenting a series of tests, the test data analysis phase, and the post-test phase.

    > *Polygraph test* means that portion of the polygraph examination during which the polygraph instrument collects physiological data based upon the individual's responses to test questions from the examiner.

    Our usage is consistent with these definitions.

3. There is much debate in the polygraph research literature on the relative validity of control question or comparison question tests vis-à-vis other kinds of tests, particularly guilty knowledge or concealed information tests, which are not based on the same kinds of comparisons. Notwithstanding this scientific issue, all polygraph tests involve comparison of physiological responses to questions that bear directly on the issue being investigated with responses to other questions, however named, that are used for purposes of comparison.

4. These demonstrations are commonly referred to as stimulation tests or acquaintance tests. They are normally described to the examinee as procedures designed to acquaint the examinee with the equipment and to determine whether the examinee can make the physiological responses used in the test. The examinee is connected to the polygraph equipment and asked to pick a card or select a number within a specified range. He or she is then asked to respond "no" to each of a series of questions of the form, "Was the number 4?" After the series of questions, the examiner, who in some versions of the demonstration has knowledge of the examinee's choice by a subterfuge such as a stacked deck of cards, reviews the chart with the examinee and shows that the polygraph was able to detect deception when the examinee did lie.

5. Some researchers make the plausible claim that comparison questions are a more effective protection against situational effects in concealed information formats than in comparison question tests because an examinee who lacks the concealed information will be unable to discriminate between the relevant and comparison questions and will therefore not have a different physiological response to the relevant question.

6. Countermeasures are actions taken by an examinee to influence the physiological responses being measured and thereby produce a test result that indicates truthfulness.

7. When a polygraph test is scored from a chart alone, scorers are normally provided with the questions that were asked and the temporal point on the chart when each question was asked.

8. This assumption must be made in any preemployment screening test and is not unique to polygraph screening.

9. It is also possible for polygraph examinations to result in false confessions, just as with other interrogation techniques (Kassin, 1997, 1998). False confessions should probably be counted as evidence against the utility of polygraph examinations.

2

Validity and Its Measurement

I n this chapter we first define some terms needed to clarify what our study did and did not cover. We then discuss concepts of validity and the empirical measurement of the accuracy of polygraph testing. We discuss methods for measuring accuracy and present our rationale for our chosen method of measurement. We conclude by discussing two difficult issues in assessing polygraph validity: (1) distinguishing the validity of the polygraph as an indicator of deception from its utility for such purposes as deterring security threats and eliciting admissions, and (2) defining the appropriate baseline against which to draw inferences about accuracy.

RELIABILITY, ACCURACY, AND VALIDITY

Psychophysiological testing, like all diagnostic activities, involves using specific observations to ascertain underlying, less readily observable, characteristics. Polygraph testing, for example, is used as a direct measure of physiological responses and as an indirect indicator of whether an examinee is telling the truth. Claims about the quantity or attribute being measured are scientifically justified to the degree that the measures are *reliable* and *valid* with respect to the target quantities or attributes.

Reliability

The term *reliability* is generally used to indicate repeatability across different times, places, subjects, and experimental conditions. *Test-retest reliability* is the extent to which the same measurement procedure (with the polygraph, this includes the examiner, the test format, and the equipment) used to examine the same subject for the same purpose yields the same result on repetition.[1] *Inter-rater reliability* is the extent to which different examiners would draw the same conclusions about a given subject at a given time for a given examination. In practice and in the literature we have considered, discussions of inter-rater reliability have focused almost exclusively on the repeatability of chart scoring across human or computer raters. Inter-rater reliability has been a critical issue in some celebrated practical uses of the polygraph. (Appendix C describes the use of the polygraph in investigations of Wen Ho Lee for espionage or other security violations; part of the story concerns differing interpretations of the results of a 1998 polygraph ordered by the U.S. Department of Energy.)

There is also potentially large variability in ways an examination is conducted: which questions are asked, how they are asked, and the general atmosphere of the examination. This variability can in principle seriously threaten test-retest reliability to the extent that polygraph examiners have latitude in asking questions.[2] Reliability across examinees is another important component of overall test reliability. For example, two examinees may have engaged in the same behaviors and may give the same answers to the same test questions, but due to different interpretations of a question, may have differing beliefs about the truthfulness of their responses and so produce different polygraph readings.

Internal consistency is another aspect of reliability. For example, a polygraph test may be judged to indicate deception mainly because of a strong physiological response to a single relevant question. If the examinee shows similar responses to other relevant questions about the same event or piece of information, the test is internally consistent.

Reliability is usually defined as a property of a measure as used on a particular population of people or events being measured. If the polygraph is to be applied in standard ways across a range of people and situations, it is desirable that measures be reliable across the range of people and situations being measured—whether subjects and examiners are calm or nervous, alert or sleepy, relaxed or under time pressure, male or female, from the same or different cultural backgrounds, in the laboratory or in the field, etc.

Accuracy and Validity

Scientific inference requires measures that exhibit strong reliability. However, a highly reliable test has little use if it is measuring something different from its intended target. A measurement process is considered *valid* if it measures what it is supposed to measure. As with reliability, there are several aspects to validity. It is particularly important for the committee's work to distinguish between the empirical concept of *criterion validity*, or accuracy, and the theoretical concept of *construct validity*.

Criterion Validity (Accuracy)

Criterion validity refers to how well a measure, such as the classification of polygraph test results as indicating deception or nondeception, matches a phenomenon that the test is intended to capture, such as the actual deceptiveness or truthfulness of examinees on the relevant questions in the test. When the test precedes the criterion event, the term *predictive validity* is used; criterion validity is the more general term that applies even when the criterion event precedes the test, as it normally does with the polygraph. The term "accuracy" is often used as a nontechnical synonym for criterion validity, and it is used in that way in this report. Polygraph accuracy is the extent to which test results correspond to truth with actual examinees. The proportion of correct judgments made by a polygraph examiner is a commonly used measure of accuracy for the polygraph test. (We discuss the shortcomings of this measure of accuracy and propose a more appropriate one below.)

Individual polygraph validation studies typically include accuracy measures that apply to the specific population that was tested. Evidence of accuracy becomes more general to the extent that test results are strongly and distinctively associated with truthfulness or deception in a variety of populations. Populations of interest include those containing high proportions of individuals who can be presumed to be deceptive on the critical questions (e.g., criminal suspects); those with low proportions of such people (e.g., nuclear scientists, intelligence agents); special populations that may be likely to show false negative results (e.g., people who want to deceive the examiner and who use countermeasures to try to "beat" the test); and populations that may be likely to show false positive results (e.g., truthful people who are highly anxious about the test). The same is true for test situations. Evidence of accuracy becomes more general as test results correspond with actual truthfulness or deceptiveness across situations (e.g., in criminal investigations, in employee security screening, and so forth). It is possible for a test such as the polygraph to be more accurate in some situations (e.g., criminal investigations) than in others (e.g., employee screening).

Construct Validity

Accuracy, or criterion validity, is essential for the overall validity of a test: no test that lacks it can be accepted as valid. However, it is not sufficient: additional evidence of validity is needed to give confidence that the test will work well with kinds of examinees and in examination settings that have not yet been tested. Thus, another critical element of validity is the presence of a theory of how and why the test works and of evidence supporting that theory. *Construct validity* refers to how well explanatory theories and concepts account for performance of a test. Users can have greater confidence in a test when evidence of its accuracy is supported by evidence of construct validity, that is, when there is a chain of plausible mechanisms that explain the empirical findings and evidence that each mechanism operates as the theory prescribes.

In the case of lie detection by polygraph, one theory invokes the following presumed chain of mechanisms. Lying leads to psychological arousal, which in turn creates physiological arousal. The polygraph measures physiological responses that correspond to this arousal: galvanic skin response, respiration, heart rate, and relative blood pressure. The measurements taken by the polygraph machine are processed, combined, and then scored to compute an overall index, which is used to make a judgment about the examinee's truthfulness. The validity of psychophysiological detection of deception by the polygraph depends on validity all along this chain. Important threats to construct validity for this theory come from the fact that the physiological correlates of psychological arousal vary considerably across individuals, from the lack of scientific evidence to support the claim that deception has a consistent psychological significance for all individuals, and from the fact that psychological arousal is associated with states other than deception. We discuss these issues further in Chapter 3.

As just noted, evidence supporting the construct validity of the test is important to give confidence in its validity in settings where criterion validity has not yet been established. It is also important for refining theory and practice over time: according to the theory mentioned, better measures of psychological arousal should make a more valid test. And it is important for anticipating and defeating countermeasures: knowing the strengths and weaknesses of the theory tells practitioners which possible countermeasures to the test are likely to fail and which ones to worry about.

The strongest scientific basis for a test's validity comes from evidence of both criterion validity and construct validity. Nevertheless, it may be possible to demonstrate that an appropriately selected set of physiological measures has sufficient accuracy in certain settings to have practical value in those settings, despite lack of strong support for the underlying theory and even in spite of threats to construct validity.

A useful analogy for understanding the issues of reliability, accuracy, and validity is the use of X-ray equipment in airport security screening. The X-ray examination is reliable if the same items are detected on repeated passes of a piece of luggage through the detection machine (test-retest reliability), if the same items are detected by different operators looking at the same image (inter-rater reliability), and if the same items are detected when the test is conducted in different ways, for example, by turning the luggage on different sides (internal consistency). The examination is accurate at detection if, in a series of tests, the X-ray image allows the examiner to correctly identify both the dangerous objects that are the targets of screening and the innocuous objects. Confidence in the validity of the test is further increased by evidence supporting the theory of X-ray screening, which includes an understanding of how the properties of various materials are registered in X-ray images. Such an understanding would increase confidence that the X-ray machine could detect not only ordinary dangerous objects, but also objects that might be concealed or altered in particular ways to avoid detection—including ways that have not yet been used in any test runs with the equipment.

For X-ray detection, as for the polygraph, reliability and validity depend both on the measuring equipment and on the capabilities and training of the operators. Validity depends on the ability of the equipment and the operators to identify target objects or conditions even when they appear in unusual ways or when efforts have been made to make them less detectable. Successful countermeasures to X-ray detection would diminish the validity of the screening. It is important to note that successful countermeasures would only decrease the test's accuracy if they were used frequently in particular trial runs—accuracy might look quite impressive if such countermeasures had not yet been tested. This is one reason that evidence of accuracy, though necessary, is not sufficient to demonstrate test validity. X-ray screening is not presumed to have perfect validity: this is why objects deemed suspicious by X-rays are checked by direct inspection, thus reducing the number of false positive results on the X-ray examination. There is no corrective, however, for false-negative X-ray results that allow dangerous objects on an aircraft.

Measuring Accuracy

Because of the many elements that contribute to construct validity, it is difficult to represent the construct validity of a test by any single numerical indicator. This section therefore focuses on criterion validity, or accuracy, which can be measured on a single scale.

To measure criterion validity, it is necessary to have a clearly defined criterion. The appropriate criterion depends on whether the polygraph is being used for event-specific investigation, employee screening, or pre-employment screening. For *event-specific investigation,* the polygraph is intended to measure the examinee's truthfulness about a specific incident. The accuracy of the polygraph test is the correspondence of the test outcome with actual truthfulness, which in this context is easy to define (although not necessarily to ascertain). Thus, measurement of accuracy in the specific-event case is straightforward in principle. It can be difficult in practice, however, if there is no way of independently determining what actually occurred.

Measuring accuracy in the *employee screening polygraph* setting raises more difficult issues. The Test of Espionage and Sabotage (TES) polygraph examination commonly used for screening at the U.S. Department of Energy weapons laboratories is intended to test whether an individual has committed espionage, engaged in sabotage, provided classified information to an unauthorized person, or had unauthorized contact with a foreign national. The examination asks whether the examinee intends to answer the security questions truthfully and whether he or she has engaged in any of the target behaviors. Accuracy of this screening polygraph might be defined as the extent to which the polygraph scoring corresponds to actual truthfulness of responses to these target questions. It might also be defined for a multi-issue polygraph screening test as the extent to which the test results correctly identify which of the target behaviors an examinee may have engaged in.

These seem straightforward criteria at first glance. However, there often is a large class of events that may be relevant to the examination, and it may not be clear to the examinee which of these is intended to be covered. For example, if asked whether one has ever provided classified information to an unauthorized person, one employee might have an emotional reaction brought on by remembering an incident in which he or she failed to properly wrap a classified report for a one-minute trip outside a secured area. Another employee might not have such a reaction. Such an event is a security violation, but individuals may differ about how serious it is and how relevant it is to the test question.

The U.S. Department of Energy (DOE) has developed guidelines regarding the behaviors that are and are not covered by TES questions, which probably resolve many ambiguities for examinees (a detailed description of how the terms *espionage* and *sabotage* are explained to examinees in research uses of the TES appears in Dollins [1997]). However, there appear to be ambiguous, even inconsistent definitions for the target of the TES for examiners. Agency officials repeatedly told the committee that the counterintelligence program at DOE is intended to identify serious breaches of security, not minor security infractions (such as leaving a secure computer on when leaving one's office briefly or what examiners call "pillow talk"). Yet, we were also told that all examinees who showed "significant response" results, requiring additional charts or repeat tests, were "cleared" after admitting such minor infractions. We were told that there were 85 such cases among the first 2,000 tested in the DOE polygraph security screening program. Under the assumption that the TES is intended to find serious problems, these 85 are false positives—tests that give positive results even though the target violations did not occur— (assuming, of course, that there were no unadmitted major infractions). However, in discussions with the committee, DOE polygraph examiners seemed to indicate that an instance of "pillow talk" revealed in response to follow-up questions triggered by a polygraph chart indicating "significant response" was regarded as a true positive, suggesting that the target of the screening was any security infraction, regardless of severity. Under this broader target, the same minor infraction in an individual who showed "no significant response" should be regarded as a false negative, whereas the DOE polygraph examiners seemed to indicate that it would be counted as a true negative, suggesting a switch to the narrower definition of target.

Assessing the polygraph's accuracy for screening cannot be done without agreement on the criterion—what it is supposed to be accurate about. The committee has seen no indication of a clear and stable agreement on what the criterion is, either in general or within any particular organization that uses polygraph screening.

In addition to an agreed definition of the criterion, an appropriate point of comparison is necessary to assess accuracy. Some representatives of the DOE polygraph screening program believe that the program is highly accurate because all 85 employees whose polygraphs indicated deception eventually admitted to a minor security infraction. If detecting minor security violations is the target of a security polygraph screening test, then these 85 are all true positives and there are no false positives. However, the significance of these admissions for accuracy cannot be evaluated in the absence of data from an appropriate comparison group. Such a group might consist of examinees who were interrogated as if the polygraph test indicated deception, even though it did not. We have been told on numerous occasions that almost everyone who has held a security clearance has committed at least one minor security infraction. If this is true, the suggested interrogation of a comparison group whose polygraph tests did not indicate deception might have uncovered a large number of minor infractions that the polygraph did not detect. Such members of the comparison group would be false negatives. Thus, the high accuracy suggested by the lack of false positives would be undercut by the presence of perhaps many false negatives.

All these considerations make it obvious that evaluating the accuracy of the employee screening polygraph is a nontrivial task. It requires more care in defining the criterion than is evident in current practice; it also requires great care in analyzing the evidence.

When the polygraph is used for *preemployment screening*, defining and measuring accuracy poses additional challenges. In this setting, the polygraph test is being used, in effect, to predict particular aspects of future job performance, such as the likelihood that the examinee, if employed, will commit security violations in the future.[3] As is the case for employee screening, defining accuracy requires a clear statement of which specific aspects of future job performance constitute the appropriate criterion. Given such a statement, one way to measure the accuracy of a preemployment polygraph test would be to compare those aspects of job performance among people who are scored as deceptive with the same aspects of performance for people who are scored as nondeceptive. This is impractical if people who score as deceptive are not hired and therefore do not get the chance to demonstrate their job performance. It would be practical, however, to compare the job performance of employees whose scores on the preemployment polygraph varied across the range of scores observed among those hired. In particular, it would be useful to examine the extent to which a person's score on a preemployment screening polygraph correlated with later instances of target behaviors, such as security violations, that came to the attention of management. We know of no such studies.

Another difficulty in measuring the accuracy of preemployment polygraph tests is that adverse personnel decisions made on the basis of preemployment polygraph examinations are not necessarily due to readings on the polygraph chart.[4] For instance, we were told at the FBI that applicants might be rejected for employment for any of the following reasons:

(1) they make admissions during the polygraph examination that specifically exclude them from eligibility for employment (e.g., admitting a felony);

(2) they provide information during the polygraph interview that is not itself a bar to employment but that leads the applicant to be judged deceptive (e.g., admitting past activities that were not disclosed on the job application);

(3) their behavior during the polygraph interview leads to the conclusion that they are trying to evade detection (e.g., the examiner concludes that the applicant is using countermeasures); or

(4) the scoring of the polygraph chart supports an assessment that the applicant is deceptive.

Only the last of these reasons is unambiguously a function of the physiological responses measured by the polygraph.[5] For the other reasons, the chart itself is only one input to the decision-making process. The relative importance of physiological responses, interrogation technique, and astute observation by an examiner is difficult to determine and is rarely explored in research. These distinctions may not be considered important for judging the usefulness or utility of polygraph examinations as screening tools, but they are critical if the personnel decisions made on the basis of the polygraph examination are to be used for measuring accuracy.

There are difficulties with using polygraphs (or other tests) for preemployment screening that go beyond accuracy. Perhaps most critical, it is necessary to make inferences about future behavior on the basis of polygraph evidence about past behaviors that may be quite different in kind. The construct validity of such inferences depends on specifying and testing a plausible theory that links evidence of past behavior, such as illegal drug use, to future behavior of a different kind, such as revealing classified information. We have not found either any explicit statement of a plausible theory of this sort in the polygraph literature or any appropriate evidence of construct validity.

A CONSISTENT APPROACH TO MEASURING ACCURACY

For choosing appropriate measures of accuracy it is helpful to consider the polygraph as a diagnostic test of truthfulness or deception and the criterion as consisting of independent indicators of what actually occurred. In this respect, the polygraph is similar to other diagnostic tests; the scientific work that has gone into measuring the accuracy of such tests can be applied to measuring the accuracy of the polygraph. This section draws on this scientific work and explains the measure of accuracy we have chosen for this study. It introduces a number of technical terms that are needed for understanding our measure of accuracy.

Diagnostic tests generally result in a binary judgment—yes or no—concerning whether or not some condition is present. The tests themselves, however, usually give more than two values. For example, cholesterol tests give a range of values that are typically collapsed into two or three categories for purposes of medical decision: high risk, justifying medical intervention; low risk, leading to no intervention; and an intermediate category, justifying watchful waiting or low-risk changes in diet and life-style, but not medical intervention. Polygraph tests similarly give a range of values that are typically collapsed into a few categories for decision purposes, such as "significant response," "no significant response," and an intermediate category called "inconclusive."

There are two distinct aspects to accuracy. One is sensitivity. A perfectly sensitive indicator of deception is one that shows positive whenever deception is in fact present: it is a test that gives a positive result for all the positive (deceptive) cases; that is, it produces no false negative results. The greater the proportion of deceptive examinees that appear as deceptive in the test, the more sensitive the test. Thus, a test that shows negative when an examinee who is being deceptive uses certain countermeasures is not sensitive to deception. The other aspect of accuracy is specificity. An indicator that is perfectly specific to deception is one that always shows negative when deception is absent (is positive only when deception is present). It produces no false positive results. The greater the proportion of truthful examinees who appear truthful on the test, the more specific the test. Thus, a test that shows positive when a truthful examinee is highly anxious because of a fear of being falsely accused is not specific to deception because it also indicates fear. Box 2-1 gives precise definitions of sensitivity, specificity, and other key terms relevant to measuring the accuracy of polygraph testing. It also shows the quantitative relationships among the terms.

The *false positive index* (FPI) and the *positive predictive value* (PPV) are two closely related measures of test performance that are critical to polygraph screening decisions.[6] The FPI is the ratio of false positives to true positives and thus indicates how many innocent examinees will be falsely implicated for each spy, terrorist, or other major security threat correctly identified. The PPV gives the probability that an individual with a deceptive polygraph result is in fact being deceptive. The two are inversely related: $PPV = 1/(1 + FPI)$; the lower the PPV, the higher the FPI.

Much research on diagnostic accuracy draws on a general theory of signal detection that treats the discrimination between *signals* and *noise*. Signals are "positive" conditions—the polygraph test readings of respondents who are being deceptive, for example. Noise is any "negative" event that may mimic and be difficult to distinguish from a signal—such as the polygraph test readings of respondents who are not being deceptive (Peterson, Birdsall, and Fox, 1954; Green and Swets, 1966). Developed for radar and sonar devices during and following World War II, signal detection theory has since been applied extensively in clinical medicine (now upward of 1,000 articles per year) and also in nondestructive testing, information retrieval, aptitude testing, weather forecasting, cockpit warning systems, product inspection, survey research, clinical psychology, and other settings (see Swets, 1996).

In the model of diagnosis that is provided by the theory, a diagnosis

BOX 2-1
Terms Relevant to Measuring the Accuracy of Polygraph Testing

The table below shows the four possible combinations of actual truthfulness and polygraph test results. The text under the table defines terms that are used to describe the quantitative relationships among these outcomes.

Test Result	True Condition		
	Positive (truly deceptive)	Negative (truly truthful)	Total
Positive (testing deceptive)	a true positive	b false positive	$a + b$
Negative (testing truthful)	c false negative	d true negative	$c + d$
Total (n)	$a + c$	$b + d$	$a + b + c + d$

Sensitivity—The proportion of truly positive (deceptive) cases that give positive results on the test ($a/[a + c]$). This is also known as the conditional probability of a true-positive test or the true-positive proportion.

False negative probability—The proportion of truly positive cases that give negative results on the test ($c/[a + c]$). This quantity is the conditional probability of a false-negative test and is the complement of *sensitivity* (that is, the difference between sensitivity and 100 percent).

Specificity—The proportion of truly negative (truthful) cases that give negative results on the test ($d/[b + d]$). This quantity is also known as the conditional probability of a true-negative test.

False positive probability—The proportion of truly negative cases that give positive results on the test ($b/[b + d]$). This quantity is the conditional probability of a false-positive test and is the complement of *specificity*.

Three terms use test results as a reference point and reveal how well the test results indicate the true conditions (see text for further discussion).

Positive predictive value—The predictive value of a positive test, that is, the percentage of positive tests that are correct ($a/[a + b]$).

Negative predictive value—The predictive value of a negative test, that is, the percentage of negative tests that are correct ($d/[c + d]$).

False positive index—Number of false positives for each true positive (b/a). This is another way of conveying the information described by *positive predictive value,* in order to make clearer the tradeoffs between false positives and true positives.

depends on the degree of evidence favoring one or the other alternative. With a single diagnostic test, the raw score on the test is typically interpreted as indicating strength of evidence—for example, stronger differential responses to relevant questions on the polygraph are taken as stronger evidence of deception. A diagnostic decision is determined by how much positive evidence the diagnostician requires to make a positive diagnosis or how much negative evidence to make a negative diagnosis. This reasoning is the basis for the most common polygraph scoring systems, which base diagnostic decisions on numerical representations of the strength and consistency of physiological responses.

Degree of evidence can be represented along a decision axis as shown in the left panel of Figure 2-1. In general, greater amounts of positive evidence (higher eye pressure test scores, in this example) are associated with the presence of the underlying condition (the right-hand distribution, for glaucoma cases) than with its absence (the left-hand distribution, for healthy eyes). However, the two distributions overlap, and intermediate degrees of evidence are often interpreted as inconclusive. A diagnostician may use two cutoff points, as in the left panel of the figure (such as 10 and 40), and call the intermediate values inconclusive, or he or she may choose to make only a positive or negative decision, as based on a single cutoff point (e.g., 20, in the second panel of the figure). The choice of this particular cutoff point represents the judgment, common in medical diagnosis, that it is more important to avoid false negatives than to avoid false positives.

Accuracy and Decision Threshold

Signal detection theory distinguishes two independent features of a test that contribute to its diagnostic performance: (1) the *accuracy* of the test for the application being studied, which depends on the amount of overlap of the test score distributions when the target condition is present and absent (more accurate tests have less overlap), and (2) a measure of the *decision threshold(s)*—the cutoff point(s) along the decision or evidence axis—used by the diagnostician.

This distinction—and particularly the concept of decision threshold—deserves further explanation in relation to polygraph testing. The familiar scoring of each question comparison and each physiological response on a polygraph chart on a scale of +3 to –3 (Backster, 1963, 1973; Swinford, 1999) sets thresholds in the form of numerical scores (for example, sums of item scores) that must be attained for a chart to be considered conclusively indicating deception or nondeception. It is not always appreciated, however, that these thresholds are policy choices made by polygraph researchers or polygraph program managers. Thresholds could (and

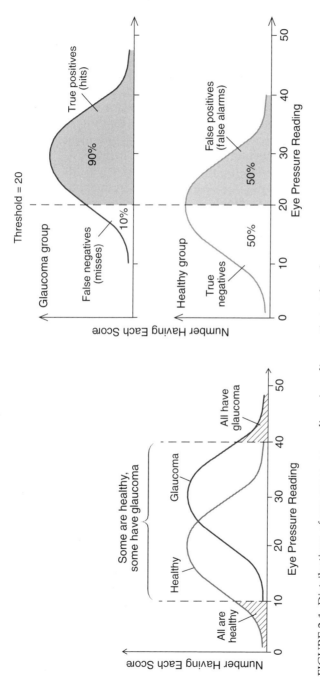

FIGURE 2-1 Distributions of eye pressure readings in a diagnostic test for glaucoma.

SOURCE: Swets, Dawes, and Monahan (2000). Copyright, John Swets; used by permission.

NOTE: The left panel shows the overlap between the distributions of eye pressures for people who are actually healthy and who actually have glaucoma. The right panel shows the same distributions (glaucoma above, healthy below) together with the consequences of using a pressure of 20 as a diagnostic threshold.

should) be set differently, depending on policy needs. (Considerations for setting thresholds are discussed below, "Selection of Decision Thresholds.")

The concept of a decision threshold (and other concepts from signal detection theory) have been little used in the U.S. government-supported polygraph research, though they have been used for decades in other studies (see, e.g., Ben-Shakhar, Lieblich, and Kugelmass, 1970; Ben-Shakar, Lieblich, and Bar-Hillel, 1982; Hammond, Harvey, Jr., and Hastie, 1992; Swets, 1992, 1996:Chapter 5; Szucko and Kleinmuntz, 1981). The committee's discussions with representatives of government agencies reveal little awareness of the concept in polygraph practice. There may indeed be some resistance to the idea that polygraph examiners can set various thresholds, perhaps because the idea makes the polygraph sound less scientific or objective. However, the need to set thresholds with diagnostic tests does not make them any less accurate or objective. Different thresholds simply reflect different tradeoffs between false positives and false negatives: for a test of any given level of accuracy, setting a threshold to decrease false negatives means accepting more false positives, and vice versa.

We have some concern that in practice, polygraph programs and examiners may ostensibly adhere to a given threshold—reflected by a mandated point on a scoring scale—while accomplishing the equivalent of varying the threshold in other ways, for instance, by altering the test conditions to affect the strength of the examinee's autonomic response. That examiners can do so is reflected in their own claims to the committee about their ability to influence examinees' physiological reactions and by the small worth typically assigned to a polygraph chart collected under circumstances friendly to an examinee. Test conditions may vary systematically according to such factors as expectancies of guilt about individuals and expected base rates of guilt in a population of examinees. If they do, and if different test conditions yield different physiological responses, the effect would be similar to varying the threshold—but less transparent and more difficult to control. The effect would be to undermine claims that the quality of polygraph examinations is sufficiently controlled that a polygraph test result has the same meaning across test formats, settings, and agencies.

As shown in the second panel of Figure 2-1, any given decision threshold will produce a certain proportion of true-positive decisions (equal to the shaded proportion of total area under the curve in the upper part of the panel, which represents examinees with the target condition present) and a certain proportion of false-positive decisions (similarly represented in the lower part of the panel). These two proportions vary together from 0 to 1 as the threshold is moved continuously from a value at the extreme right of the decision axis (no tests diagnosed as positive) to a value at the very left of that axis (all tests diagnosed as positive). If truth is known, these proportions can be used to estimate two probabilities: the conditional probability of a positive test result given the presence of the target condition (this probability—90 percent in the figure—is known as the sensitivity of the test) and the conditional probability of a positive result given the absence of the condition (which is the complement of the test's specificity—and is 50 percent in the figure). The second panel shows that the proportions of false negative and true negative results, respectively, are complements of the first two and add no additional information. They do not, therefore, require separate representation in a measure of accuracy.

Receiver Operating Characteristic (ROC)

Figure 2-2 presents a representative function that shows the true positive rate (percent of deceivers correctly identified) and the false positive rate (percent of nondeceivers falsely implicated) for a given separation of the distributions of scores for all possible choices of threshold. The curve would be higher for diagnostic techniques that provide greater separations of the distributions (i.e., have higher accuracy) and lower for techniques that provide lesser separations (i.e., have lower accuracy). Such a curve is called a receiver operating characteristic (ROC). The ROC of random guessing lies on the diagonal line. For example, imagine a system of guessing that randomly picks a particular proportion of cases (say, 80 percent) to be positive: this system would be correct in 80 percent of the cases in which the condition is present (80 percent sensitivity or true-positive probability), but it would be wrong in 80 percent of the actually negative cases (80 percent false-positive probability or 20 percent specificity). Any other guessing system would appear as a different point on the diagonal line. The ROC of a perfect diagnostic technique is a point (P) at the upper left corner of the graph, where the true positive proportion is 1.0 and the false positive proportion is 0.

Measure of Accuracy

The position of the ROC on the graph reflects the accuracy of the diagnostic test, independent of any decision threshold(s) that may be used. It covers all possible thresholds, with one point on the curve reflecting the performance of the diagnostic test for each possible threshold, expressed in terms of the proportions of true and false positive and negative results for each threshold. A convenient overall quantitative index of accuracy is the proportion of the unit area of the graph that lies under the

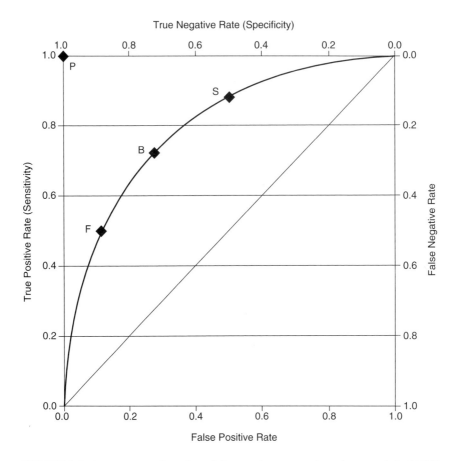

FIGURE 2-2 A representative plot of the receiver operating characteristic (ROC) curve for a diagnostic test with accuracy index (A) of 0.8, showing three threshold or cutoff values: F, a "friendly" threshold; B, a "balanced" threshold, with equal probabilities of false positive and false negative errors; and S, a "suspicious" threshold.

NOTE: The diagonal line represents an accuracy index of 0.50 (chance). The point P represents an accuracy index of 1.00.

ROC, as indicated in Figure 2-2. This area, denoted A, is the accuracy index used in this book.[7] Its possible range is from 0.5 at the "chance" diagonal to 1.0 for perfection. Figure 2-3 shows the ROCs for three values of A, 0.7, 0.8, and 0.9, and for the chance diagonal (0.50), under the assumption that the distributions of evidence follow a particular (Gaussian) symmetric form. Higher values of A indicate tests with greater accuracy. The curves for such tests are above and to the left of those for less accurate

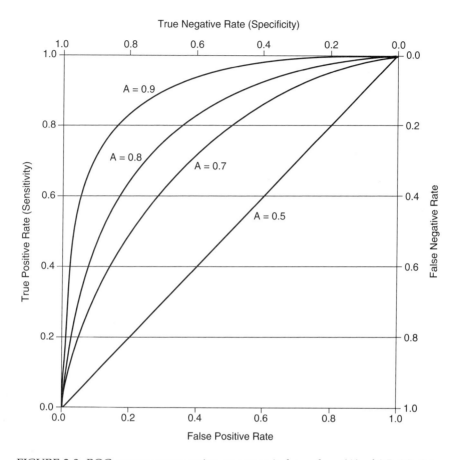

FIGURE 2-3 ROC curves representing accuracy index values (A) of 0.5, 0.7, 0.8, and 0.9.

tests. Reading across from the axis at the right of Figure 2-3 to the one at the left, one can see that for any fixed rate of correct identification of positive cases (sensitivity), the more accurate the test, the smaller the proportion of truly negative cases incorrectly judged positive, read from the axis at the bottom. Similarly, for any false positive rate, shown on the axis at the bottom of the figure, the more accurate the test, the greater the proportion of positive cases that are accurately identified.[8]

Decision Thresholds

Figure 2-2 shows three points corresponding to different thresholds on a curve with A = 0.8. The point B is the balanced threshold, meaning that at this threshold, the test is equally accurate with examinees who are deceptive and those who are nondeceptive. With a threshold set at that point, 72.5 percent of the deceptive examinees and 72.5 percent of the nondeceptive examinees would (on average) be correctly identified in a population with any proportion of examinees who are being deceptive. (For the curves shown in Figure 2-3 with A = 0.9 and A = 0.7, the corresponding balanced thresholds achieve 81.8 and 66.0 percent correct identifications, respectively.) Points F and S in Figure 2-2 represent two other possible thresholds. At point F (for friendly), few are called deceptive: only 12 percent of those who are nondeceptive and 50 percent of those truly deceptive. At point S (for suspicious), many more people are called deceptive: the test catches 88 percent of the examinees who are being deceptive, but at the cost of falsely implicating 50 percent of those who are not.[9]

Selection of Decision Thresholds

Decision theory specifies that a rational diagnostician faced with a set of judgment calls will adopt a threshold or cutoff point for making the diagnostic decisions that minimizes the net costs of false positive and false negative decisions. If all benefits and costs could be measured and expressed in the same units, then this optimal threshold could be calculated for any ROC curve and base rate of target subjects (e.g., cases of deception) in the population being tested (see Chapter 6 and Appendix J for details). A goal of being correct when the positive outcome occurs (e.g., catching spies) suggests a suspicious cutoff like S; a goal of being correct when a negative outcome occurs (avoiding false alarms) suggests a friendly cutoff point like F.

The optimum decision threshold also depends on the probability, or base rate, of the target condition in the population or in the sample at hand—for security screening, this might refer to the proportion of spies or terrorists or potential spies or terrorists among those being screened. Because the costs depend on the number of deceptive individuals missed and the number of nondeceptive individuals falsely implicated (not just on the proportions), wanting to reduce the costs of errors implies that one should set a suspicious cutoff like S when the base rate is high and a friendly cutoff like F when the base rate is low. With a low base rate, such as 1 in 1,000, almost all the errors will occur with truly negative cases (that is, they will be false positives). These errors are greatly reduced in number by using a friendly cutoff that calls fewer test results positive. With a high base rate, such as 8 in 10, most of the errors are likely to be false negatives, and these are reduced by setting a suspicious threshold. Thus, it makes sense to make a positive decision fairly frequently in a referral or adjudication setting, when other evidence indicates that the likelihood of a true positive outcome is high, because any set percentage of false positive errors will cost less when there are few negative cases to get wrong. In a screening setting, when the base rate of truly positive cases is low, a suspicious cutoff like S will lead to a very large number of false positives.

It is important to note here that accuracy and decision thresholds have very different practical implications depending on the base rate of the target population being tested. A test that may be acceptable for use on a population with a high base rate of deceivers (e.g., criminal suspects) may look much less attractive for use with a low base-rate population (e.g., employees in a nuclear weapons laboratory, because of the inherent properties of accuracy and thresholds.) This generalization, which holds true for all diagnostic techniques, is illustrated in Table 2-1 for a test with an accuracy of $A = 0.90$ and deceivers in two base rates of deception (see Chapter 6 for more detailed discussion). Table 2-1A shows the results of using this test with a threshold that correctly identifies 80 percent of deceivers on two hypothetical populations. In a population of 10,000 criminal suspects of whom 5,000 are expected to be guilty, the test will identify 4,800 examinees (on average) as deceptive, of whom 4,000 would actually be guilty. The same test, used to screen 10,000 government employees of whom 10 are expected to be spies, will identify an average of 1,606 as deceptive, of whom only 8 would actually be spies. Table 2-1B and Table 2-1C show that the high number of false positives in the screening situation can be reduced by changing the threshold, but the result is that more of the spies will get through the screen.

Empirical Variation in Decision Threshold

As already noted, polygraph examiners may vary considerably in the decision thresholds they apply. A study by Szucko and Kleinmuntz (1981) gives an idea of the variation in threshold that can occur across experienced polygraph interpreters under controlled conditions. In their mock crime study, six interpreters viewed the physiological data (the charts) of 30 individuals (15 guilty and 15 innocent) and made judgments on an eight-category scale of their confidence that a given subject was guilty or not. The eight-category scale allows for seven possible thresholds for dividing the charts into groups judged truthful or deceptive. An indication of the results of using different decision thresholds among polygraph interpreters is the false positive proportions that would result if each interpreter had set the threshold at the fifth of the seven possible thresholds and had made yes/no, binary judgments at that cutoff. Then the proportion of false positives would have varied across interpreters by almost 0.50—from 0.27 for the most conservative interpreter to 0.76 for

TABLE 2-1 Results of a Diagnostic Test of Deception of Accuracy (A) = 0.90, with Hypothetical Populations of 10,000 Examinees with Base Rates of Deception of 1 in 2 and 1 in 1,000

2-1A Sensitivity of 80 percent (i.e., threshold set to correctly identify 80 percent of deceivers)

Result	Criminal Suspects (Base Rate: 1 guilty of 2)			National Laboratory Employees (Base Rate: 1 spy of 1,000)		
	Guilty	Not Guilty	Total	Spy	Not Spy	Total
"Failed" test	4,000	800	4,800	8	1,598	1,606
"Passed" test	1,000	4,200	5,200	2	8,392	8,394
Total	5,000	5,000	10,000	10	9,990	10,000

2-1B Sensitivity of 50 percent (i.e., threshold set to correctly identify 50 percent of deceivers)

Result	Criminal Suspects (Base Rate: 1 guilty of 2)			National Laboratory Employees (Base Rate: 1 spy of 1,000)		
	Guilty	Not Guilty	Total	Spy	Not Spy	Total
"Failed" test	2,500	170	2,670	5	340	345
"Passed" test	2,500	4,830	7,330	5	9,650	9,655
Total	5,000	5,000	10,000	10	9,990	10,000

2-1C Sensitivity of 20 percent (i.e., threshold set to correctly identify 20 percent of deceivers)

Result	Criminal Suspects (Base Rate: 1 guilty of 2)			National Laboratory Employees (Base Rate: 1 spy of 1,000)		
	Guilty	Not Guilty	Total	Spy	Not Spy	Total
"Failed" test	1,000	19	1,019	2	39	41
"Passed" test	4,000	4,981	8,981	8	9,951	9,959
Total	5,000	5,000	10,000	10	9,990	10,000

the most liberal. Other possible thresholds would also have yielded substantial differences among interpreters in false-positive rates.

Producing an Empirical ROC Curve

It is possible to produce an empirical ROC curve on the basis of the performance of a diagnostic test in a field or laboratory setting. This can be accomplished in a few different ways. An efficient way is for the diagnostician to set several thresholds at once, in effect to use several categories of response, say, five or six categories ranging from "very definitely a signal" to "very definitely only noise." Points on the ROC curve are then calculated successively from each category boundary: first, considering only the top category positive and the rest negative; then considering the top two categories positive, and so on. This rating procedure can be expanded to have the diagnostician give probabilities from 0 to 1 (to two decimal places) that a signal is present. The 100 categories implied may then be used as is or condensed in analysis to perhaps 10, which would give nine ROC points to be fitted into a curve (the first point is always [0.0, 0.0], the point at which all tests are considered negative; the final point is always [1.0, 1.0], the point where all tests are considered positive). An example of this rating procedure is the use of three categories, corresponding to yes/no/inconclusive decisions in many polygraph diagnostic systems. Treating this three-alternative scoring system as a rating procedure gives a two-point ROC curve.[10] Because of the way polygraph data are most commonly reported, our analyses in Chapter 5 draw heavily on two-point ROC curves obtained when "no-opinion" or "inconclusive" judgments are reported.

Using the Percent Correct to Measure Accuracy

Treating no-opinion or inconclusive judgments as an intermediate category and estimating two ROC points handles neatly a problem that is not dealt with when percent correct is used to estimate accuracy. In that case, reported performance depends on how often given examiners use the inconclusive category, especially if examiners treat the "inconclusive" records, which are the ones they find most difficult to score, as if the subject had not been tested. Examiners vary considerably in how frequently their records are scored inconclusive. For example, nine datasets reported in four screening studies completed between 1989 and 1997 at the U.S. Department of Defense Polygraph Institute showed rates of no-opinion judgments ranging from 0 to 50 percent (materials presented to the committee, March 2001). By using the inconclusive category liberally and excluding inconclusive tests, an examiner can appear very accurate as measured by percent correct. For a measure of accuracy to be useful for comparing examiners, studies, or test techniques, it should not be affected by the number of inconclusive judgments an examiner chooses to give; however, percent correct is so affected. By contrast, the A measure is robust against varying uses of the inconclusive category of result.

Percent correct has three other difficulties that preclude our adoption of this widely used measure (see Swets, 1986a, 1996:Chapter 3). First, it depends heavily on the proportions of positive and negative cases (the base rates) in the population. This requirement poses acute difficulties in security screening applications, in which the base rates of activities such as espionage and sabotage are quite low: assuming that no one is being deceptive yields an almost perfect percent correct (the only errors are the spies). Second, the percent correct varies extensively with the diagnostician's decision threshold. The examples in Table 2-1 show these two difficulties concretely. When the base rate of guilt is 50 percent, the hypothetical polygraph test, which has an accuracy index of A = 0.90, makes 82, 73, and 60 percent correct classifications with the three thresholds given. When the base rate of guilt is 0.1 percent, it makes 84, 97, and 99.5 percent correct classifications with the same three thresholds. Finally, as a single-number index, the percent correct does not distinguish between the two types of error—false positives and false negatives—which are likely to have very different consequences. The problems with percent correct as an index of accuracy are best seen in the situation shown in the right half of Table 2-1c, in which the test is correct in 9,959 of 10,000 cases (99.5 percent correct), but eight out the ten hypothetical spies "pass" and are free to cause damage.

When percentages of correct diagnoses are calculated separately for positive and negative cases, there are two numbers to cope with, or four numbers when no-opinion judgments are included. Because these are not combined into a single-number index, it is difficult to offer a simple summary measure of accuracy for a single study or to order studies or testing techniques in terms of their relative accuracy. The difficulty of interpreting percent correct when inconclusive judgments vary haphazardly from one study to another is multiplied when two percentages are affected.

Accuracy Measures Used in This Study

For the reasons discussed in this section, we used the A index from signal detection theory to estimate the accuracy of polygraph testing. We calculated empirical ROC curves from data contained in those studies that met basic criteria of methodological adequacy and that also provided sufficient information about polygraph test results to make the calculation. Chapter 5 and Appendixes G and H report on the methods we used to select the studies and make the calculations and discusses the results.

VALIDITY AND UTILITY

The practical value of polygraph testing depends on at least five conceptually different factors that are often not distinguished:

- The ability to detect deception from polygraph charts—by analyzing the data collected by polygraph instruments (i.e., psychophysiological detection of deception).
- The ability of an examiner to detect deception by using other cues in the polygraph examination (what can be called detection of deception from demeanor).
- The deterrent effect of a screening procedure that potential examinees believe can detect their deception or falsely identify them as deceptive.
- The ability of the procedure to elicit admissions or confessions because of any of the above factors.
- The ability of the procedure to foster public confidence in law enforcement and national security.

The first of these corresponds to the validity of polygraph testing. The others, particularly the last three, relate to what can be termed the utility of polygraph testing.[11]

It is important to recognize that none of these five elements is unique to polygraph testing. Any interrogation technique that includes physiological measures may combine all of them; traditional investigative techniques that do not use physiological measures often combine all the others. It has been argued, however, that adding a credible physiological measure to an interrogation procedure increases utility not only because of the validity of the physiological test but also by enhancing the other elements. To evaluate polygraph testing for practical purposes, one must therefore consider not only its validity (normally defined in terms of the physiological test), but also its effects on other elements of the interrogation procedure.

What is unique to psychophysiological testing and not common to all interrogation techniques—and what is central to our investigation of its validity—is the capability for the detection of deception that comes from the physiological data collected and the way those data are analyzed. Although the polygraph may enhance the utility of interrogation in ways that are unrelated to its validity, such benefits would be shared equally by any other adjunct to interrogation that was applied similarly and that had other characteristics now associated with polygraph testing. For example, any other technique that potential examinees believed to be valid for detecting deception would be likely to elicit admissions and to have deterrent effects. Even a technique that examinees believed to be invalid but that they also believed would be treated as valid might bring some benefits of deterrence.

Psychophysiological Detection of Deception

The term *validity*, when applied to polygraph testing, normally refers only to the psychophysiological test. That is, the polygraph is said to be valid only if deception is strongly and uniquely associated with a discernable pattern in the record of physiological responses made on or from the polygraph. Chapter 3 discusses the scientific basis for believing that deception produces specific psychological and physiological processes that influence polygraph readings, which indicates the construct validity of the polygraph test. Chapters 4 and 5 discuss the evidence on the empirical association between deception and polygraph test results, which indicates the accuracy of the polygraph. As noted above, the utility of the polygraph depends on more than just its validity, but these utility aspects should be considered separately from the issue of validity of the instrument for measuring deception.

Detection of Deception from Demeanor

It is possible to assess the ability of interviewers to detect deception from visible and audible cues in the interview, generally referred to as demeanor (e.g., facial expression, posture, voice quality). Considerable scientific effort has been devoted to the development of techniques for detecting deception from such behavioral indicators. Although this is not a major focus of the present study, we discuss the research evidence on this detection briefly in Chapter 6. In the context of evaluating the validity of the polygraph instrument, it is necessary to exclude the possibility that the examiner's judgment was affected in part by the examinee's demeanor, since that is not what the polygraph instrument measures. This can be done in part by evaluating the performance of polygraph assessments made by computer programs or by trained examiners who have access only to the record of physiological responses. If examiners who actually interviewed the subject make the same judgments as result from these other methods, their assessments are unlikely to have been affected directly by the examinee's demeanor.[12]

Deterrent Effect

When polygraph testing is used for screening, one of its goals is deterrence: keeping people who have done or may do certain undesired things out of sensitive positions and keeping people already in sensitive positions from doing undesired things. Deterrence is distinct from the validity of polygraph testing because the polygraph can be an effective deterrent even if it does not provide valid information about deception. (An analogy would be the possible deterrent effect on burglars of a bogus window sticker saying that a house is protected by an alarm system.) In fact, it can be an effective deterrent even without being used. Individuals who are security risks may: (a) choose not to seek positions for which a polygraph examination is required; (b) decide not to engage in serious transgressions if they know they may undergo a polygraph examination; or (c) resign (and thus minimize the duration of acts of sabotage or espionage) if they are facing a polygraph examination. In addition, people in sensitive positions may take greater care to avoid even minor security infractions in order to avoid the possibility of a future deceptive reading on a polygraph test.

The committee heard numerous anecdotes of the deterrent value of policies of polygraph examination. For instance, we were told that John Anthony Walker, the retired Naval officer who pleaded guilty in 1985 to spying for the Soviet Union, was told by his handlers not to engage in espionage until he was promoted to the highest position in which a polygraph examination was not required, then to engage in espionage, to refuse promotion to a position in which a polygraph exam was required, and to retire when promotion to such a position was mandated. Notwithstanding such anecdotes, some observers have questioned the value of the polygraph as a deterrent (see, e.g., Aftergood, 2000).

Direct scientific research on the deterrent value of polygraph testing in any setting is lacking. However, research on social influence through surveillance or power (McGuire, 1969) is consistent with the underlying reasoning that the threat of polygraph testing might deter actions that threaten national interests if the perceived likelihood and consequences of detection by polygraph assessment are substantial. The logic is the same as that which applies to the use of radar speed traps as deterrents. Frequent and unpredictable use of radar increases the likelihood that a violator will be caught, and substantial consequences for detected speeders increase the expected cost for a potential violator. Following the same reasoning, predictable polygraph testing (e.g., fixed-interval testing of people in specific job classifications) probably has less deterrent value than random testing. Similar effects have been observed in research on the use of employee drug tests (National Research Council, 1994). In the

U.S. armed services, for example, the introduction of random and frequent drug testing has been associated with lower levels of drug use.

Deterrence effects depend on beliefs about the polygraph, which are logically distinct from the validity of the polygraph. The deterrent value of polygraph testing is likely to be greater for individuals who believe than who do not believe in its validity for detecting deception.

It is worth noting that deterrence has costs as well as benefits for an organization that uses polygraph testing. The threat of polygraph testing may lead desirable job candidates to forgo applying or good employees to resign for fear of suffering the consequences of a false positive polygraph result. The more accurate people believe the test to be—independent of its actual validity—the greater the benefits of deterrence relative to the costs. This is because a test that is believed to be highly accurate in discriminating deception from truthfulness will be more deterring to people whose actions might require deception and more reassuring to others who would be truthful than a test that is believed to be only moderately accurate.

It is also worth emphasizing that validity and utility for deterrence, while logically separable, are related in practice. The utility of the polygraph depends on the beliefs about validity and about how results will be used among those who may be subject to testing. Utility increases to the extent that people believe the polygraph is a valid measure of deception and that deceptive readings will have severe negative consequences. To the extent people hold these beliefs, they are deterred from engaging in behaviors they believe the polygraph might detect. If people came to have an equal or greater level of faith in some other technique for the physiological detection of deception, it would acquire a deterrent value equal to or greater than that now pertaining to polygraph testing.

Eliciting Admissions and Confessions

Polygraph testing is used to facilitate interrogation (Davis, 1961). Polygraph proponents believe that individuals are more likely to disclose information about behaviors that will lead to their punishment or loss of a valued outcome if they believe that any attempts to conceal the information will fail. As part of the polygraph pretest interview, examinees are encouraged to disclose any such information so that they will "pass" the examination. It can be important to security organizations to have their employees admit to past or current transgressions that might not disqualify them from employment but that might be used against them, for example, by an enemy who might use the threat of reporting the transgression to blackmail the employee into spying. Anecdotes suggest that the polygraph context is effective for securing such admissions. As reported by the U.S. Department of Defense (DoD) Polygraph Program (2000:4 of 14) on the cases in which significant information was uncovered during DoD counterintelligence-scope polygraph examinations covered in the report:

> It should be noted that all these individuals had been interviewed previously by security professionals and investigated by other means without any discovery of the information obtained by the polygraph examination procedure. *In most cases, the information was elicited from the subject in discussion with the examiner* [italics added].

There is no scientific evidence on the ability of the polygraph to elicit admissions and confessions in the field. However, anecdotal reports of the ability of the polygraph to elicit confessions are consistent with research on the "bogus pipeline" technique (Jones and Sigall, 1971; Quigley-Fernandez and Tedeschi, 1978; Tourangeau, Smith, and Rasinski, 1997). In bogus pipeline experiments, examinees are connected to a series of wires that are in turn connected to a machine that is described as a lie detector but that is in fact nonfunctional. The examinees are more likely to admit embarrassing beliefs and facts than similar examinees not connected to the bogus lie detector. For example, in one study in which student research subjects were given information in advance on how to respond to a classroom test, 13 of 20 (65 percent) admitted receiving this information when connected to the bogus pipeline, compared to only 1 of 20 (5 percent) who admitted it when questioned without being connected (Quigley-Fernandez and Tedeschi, 1978).

Admissions during polygraph testing of acts that had not previously been disclosed are often presented as evidence of the utility and validity of polygraph testing. However, the bogus pipeline research demonstrates that whatever they contribute to utility, they are not necessarily evidence of the validity of the polygraph. Many admissions do not depend on validity, but rather on examinees' beliefs that the polygraph will reveal any deceptions. All admissions that occur during the pretest interview probably fall into this category. The only admissions that can clearly be attributed to the validity of polygraph are those that occur in the posttest interview in response to the examiner's probing questions about segments of the polygraph record that correctly indicated deception. We know of no data that would allow us to estimate what proportion of admissions in field situations fall within this category.

Even admissions in response to questions about a polygraph chart may sometimes be attributable to factors other than accurate psychophysiological detection of deception. For example, an examiner may probe a significant response to a question about one act, such as revealing classified information to an unauthorized person, and secure an admission of a different act investigated by the polygraph test, such as having undis-closed contact with a foreign national. Although the polygraph test may have been instrumental in securing the admission, the admission's rel-evance to test validity is questionable. To count the admission as evidence of validity would require an empirically supported theory that could explain why the polygraph record indicated deception to the question on which the examinee was apparently nondeceptive, but not to the question on which there was deception.

There is also a possibility that some of the admissions and confessions elicited by interrogation concerning deceptive-looking polygraph re-sponses are false. False confessions are more common than sometimes believed, and standard interrogation techniques designed to elicit confes-sions—including the use of false claims that the investigators have defini-tive evidence of the examinee's guilt—do elicit false confessions (Kassin, 1997, 1998). There is some evidence that interrogation focused on a false-positive polygraph response can lead to false confessions. In one study, 17 percent of respondents who were shown their strong response on a bogus polygraph to a question about a minor theft they did not commit subsequently admitted the theft (Meyer and Youngjohn, 1991).

As with deterrence, the value of the polygraph in eliciting true admis-sions and confessions is largely a function of an examinee's belief that attempts to deceive will be detected and will have high costs. It likely also depends on an examinee's belief about what will be done with a "decep-tive" test result in the absence of an admission. Such beliefs are not necessarily dependent on the validity of the test.

Thus, admissions and confessions in the polygraph examination, as important as they can be to investigators, provide support for claims of validity only in very limited circumstances. Admissions can even ad-versely affect the assessment of validity in field settings because in field settings an admission is typically the end of assessment of the polygraph—even if interrogation and investigation continue. The polygraph exami-nation is concluded to have been productive. In our efforts to secure data from federal agencies about the specific circumstances of admissions se-cured during security screening polygraph examinations, we have learned that agencies do not classify admissions according to when in the exami-nation those admissions occurred. This practice makes it impossible to assess the validity of federal polygraph screening programs from the data those programs provide. Polygraph examinations that yield admissions may well have utility, but they cannot provide evidence of validity unless the circumstances of the admission are taken into account and unless the veracity of the admission itself is independently confirmed. Using the polygraph record to confirm an admission that was elicited because of the polygraph record does not count as independent confirmation.

Fostering Public Confidence

Another purpose of the polygraph is to foster public confidence in national security. Public trust is obviously challenged by the revelation that agents acting on behalf of foreign interests occupy sensitive positions in the U.S. government. Counterintelligence necessarily includes programs that are secret. Because these programs' responses to revelations of spying cannot be made public, they do little to reassure the public of the integrity of U.S. national security procedures. Calls for increased polygraph testing appear to us to be intended in part to reassure the public that all that can be done is being done to protect national security interests. To the extent that the public believes in the polygraph, attribution theory (Jones, 1991) suggests it may serve this function. We know of no scientific evidence to assess the net effect of polygraph screening policies on public confidence in national security or security organizations. We note that as with the value of the polygraph for deterrence and for eliciting admissions and confessions, its value for building confidence depends on people's beliefs about its validity and only indirectly on its proven validity.

Public confidence in the polygraph that goes beyond what is justified by evidence of its validity may be destructive to public purposes. An erroneously high degree of belief in validity can create a false sense of security among policy makers, among employees in sensitive positions, and in the general public. This false sense of security can in turn lead to inappropriate relaxation of other methods of ensuring security. In particular, the committee has heard suggestions that employees may be less vigilant about potential security violations by coworkers in facilities in which all employees must take polygraph tests. Some agencies permit new hires who have passed a polygraph but for which the background investigation is not yet complete to have the same access to classified material as other employees with no additional security precautions.

Implications for Assessing Validity of Polygraph Testing

The detection of deception from demeanor, deterrence, and effects on public confidence may all contribute to the utility of polygraph testing. These effects do not, however, provide evidence of the validity of the polygraph for the physiological detection of deception. Rather, those effects depend on people's *beliefs* about validity. Admissions and confessions, as noted above, provide evidence supportive of the validity of polygraph tests only under very restricted conditions, and the federal agencies that use the polygraph for screening do not collect data on admissions and confessions in a form that allows these field tests to be used to assess polygraph validity. Moreover, even with data on when in the examination admissions or confessions occurred and on whether the admitted acts corresponded to significant responses to relevant questions about those specific acts, information from current field screening examinations would have limited value for assessing validity because of the need for independent validation of the admissions and confessions.

There is in fact no direct scientific evidence assessing the value of the polygraph as a deterrent, as a way to elicit admissions and confessions, or as a means of supporting public confidence. What indirect scientific evidence exists does support the plausibility of these uses, however. This evidence implies that for the polygraph or any other physiological technique to achieve maximal utility, examinees and the public must perceive that there is a high likelihood of deception being detected and that the costs of being judged deceptive are substantial. If people do not have these beliefs, then the value of the technique as a deterrent, as an aid to interrogation, and for building public confidence, is greatly diminished. Indeed, if the public does not believe a technique such as the polygraph is valid, using it to help reinstate public trust after a highly visible security breach may be counterproductive.

Regardless of people's current beliefs about validity, if polygraph testing is not in fact highly accurate in distinguishing truthful from deceptive responses, the argument for utility diminishes in force. Convincing arguments could then be made that (a) polygraphs provide a false sense of security, (b) the time and resources spent on the polygraph would be better spent developing alternative procedures, (c) competent or highly skilled individuals would be or are being lost due to suspicions cast on them by erroneous decisions based on polygraph tests, (d) agencies that use polygraphs are infringing civil liberties for insufficient benefits to the national security, and (e) utility will decrease rapidly over time as people come to appreciate the low validity of polygraph testing. Polygraph opponents already make such arguments.

The utility benefits claimed for the polygraph, even though many of them are logically independent of its validity, depend indirectly on the polygraph being a highly valid indicator of deception. In the long run, evidence that supports validity can only increase the polygraph test's utility and evidence against validity can only decrease utility. The scientific evidence for the ability of the polygraph test to detect deception is therefore crucial to the test's usefulness. The evidence on validity is discussed in Chapters 3, 4, and 5.

CRITERION VALIDITY AS VALUE ADDED

For the polygraph test to be considered a valid indicator of deception, it must perform better against an appropriate criterion of truth than do indicators that have no validity. That is, it must add predictive value. It is therefore necessary to define the nonvalid indicators that serve as points of comparison.[13]

One possible reference point is the level of performance that would be achieved by random guessing about the examinee's truthfulness or deceptiveness on the relevant questions. In this comparison, the predictive validity of the polygraph test is the difference between its predictive value and that of random guessing. This reference point provides a minimal comparison that we consider too lenient for most practical uses, and particularly for employee screening applications. For the polygraph to have sufficient validity to be of more than academic interest, it must do considerably better than random guessing.

A second possible reference point is the extent to which deception is accurately detected by other techniques normally used in the same investigations as the polygraph (background checks, questionnaires, etc.). Comparisons of the *incremental validity* (Fiedler, Schmid, and Stahl, in press) of the polygraph consider the improvement provided by the polygraph over other methods of investigation (e.g., background checks). We consider this reference point to be important for making policy decisions about whether to use the polygraph (see Chapter 7), but not for judging validity. The scientific validity of the polygraph is unaffected by whether or not other techniques provide the same information.

A third possible reference point for the validity of polygraph testing is a comparison condition that differs from the polygraph examination only in the absence of the chart data, which is purportedly the source of the valid physiological detection of deception in the polygraph examination. This logic implies a comparison similar to the placebo control condition in medical research. The reference point is an experimental treatment condition that is exactly the same as the one being investigated, except for its active ingredient. For the polygraph, that would mean a test that both the examiner and examinee believed yielded valid detection of deception, but that in fact did not. Polygraph research does not normally use such comparisons, but it could. Doing so would help determine the extent to which the effectiveness of the polygraph is attributable to its validity, as distinct from other features of the polygraph examination, such as beliefs about its validity.

Bogus pipeline research illustrates what might be involved in assessing validity of the polygraph using an experimental condition analogous to a placebo. An actual polygraph test might be compared with a bogus pipeline test in which the examinee is connected to polygraph equipment that, unbeknownst both to examiners and examinees, produced charts that were not the examinee's (perhaps the chart of a second examinee whose actual polygraph is being read as the comparison to the bogus one). The polygraph's validity would be indicated by the degree to which it uncovered truth more accurately than the bogus pipeline comparison. Such a comparison might be particularly useful for examining issues of utility, such as the claimed ability of the polygraph to elicit admissions and confessions. These admissions and confessions might be appropriately attributed to the validity of the polygraph if it produced more true admissions and confessions than a bogus pipeline comparison condition. However, if similar proportions of deceptive individuals could be induced to admit transgressions when connected to an inert machine as when connected to a polygraph, their admissions could not be counted as evidence of the validity of the polygraph.

We believe that such a comparison condition is an appropriate reference point for judging the validity of polygraph testing, especially as that validity contributes to admissions and confessions during the polygraph interview. However, we have found no research attempting to assess polygraph validity by making this kind of comparison. This gap in knowledge may not present a serious threat to the quality of laboratory-based polygraph research, in which examinees normally do not admit their mock crimes, but it is important for making judgments about whether research on polygraph use under field conditions provides convincing evidence of criterion validity.

CONCLUSIONS

Validity and Utility

- The appropriate criteria for judging the validity of a polygraph test are different for event-specific and for employee or preemployment screening applications. The practical value of a polygraph testing and scoring system with any given level of accuracy also depends on the application because in these different applications, false positive and false negative errors differ both in frequency and in cost.

- No clear consensus exists on what polygraphs are intended to measure in the context of federal employee security screening.

- Evidence of the utility of polygraph testing, such as its possible effects of deterring potential spies from employment or increasing the frequency of admissions of target activities, is relevant to polygraph validity only under very restricted circumstances. This is true in part because any technique that examinees believe to be a valid test of deception is likely to produce deterrence and admissions, whether or not it is in fact valid.

• The federal agencies that use the polygraph for screening do not collect data on admissions and confessions in a form that allows these field tests to be used to assess polygraph validity.

• There is no direct scientific evidence assessing the value of the polygraph as a deterrent, as a way to elicit admissions and confessions, or as a means of supporting public confidence. The limited scientific evidence does support the idea that these effects will occur when examinees (and the public) perceive that there is a high likelihood of deception being detected and that the costs of being judged deceptive are substantial.

Measurement of Accuracy

• For the purposes of assessing accuracy, or criterion validity, it is appropriate to treat the polygraph as a diagnostic test and to apply scientific methods based on the theory of signal detection that have been developed for measuring the accuracy of such tests.

• Diagnostic test performance depends on both the accuracy of the test, which is an attribute of the test itself, and the threshold value selected for declaring a test result positive.

• There is little awareness in the polygraph literature and less in U.S. polygraph practice of the concept that false positives can be traded off against false negatives by adjusting the threshold for declaring that a chart indicates deception. We have seen indications that practitioners implicitly adjust thresholds to reflect perceived organizational priorities, but may not be fully aware of doing so. Explicit awareness of the concept of the threshold and appropriate policies for adjusting it to reflect the costs of different kinds of error would eliminate a major source of uncontrolled variation in polygraph test results.

• The accuracy of the polygraph is appropriately summarized by the accuracy index A, as defined in the theory of signal detection. To estimate the accuracy of the polygraph, it is appropriate to calculate values for this index for the validation studies that meet standards of scientific acceptability and to consider whether these values are systematically related to other factors, such as populations of examinees, characteristics of individual examinees or examiners, relationships established in the interview, testing methods, and the use of countermeasures.

NOTES

1. In practice, test-retest reliability can be affected by memory effects, the effects of the experience of testing on the examinee, the effects of the experience on the examiner, or all of these effects.

2. In most applications of the comparison question technique, for example, examiners select comparison questions on the basis of information gained in the pretest interview that they believe will produce a desired level of physiological responsiveness in examinees who are not being deceptive on the relevant questions. It is plausible that tests using different comparison questions—for example, tests by different examiners with the same examinee—might yield different test results (compromising test-retest reliability). Little research has been done on the test-retest reliability of comparison question polygraph tests. Some forms of the comparison question test, notably the Test of Espionage and Sabotage used in the U.S. Department of Energy's security screening program, offer examiners a very limited selection of possible relevant and comparison questions in an attempt to reduce variability in a way that can reasonably be expected to benefit test-retest reliability in comparison with test formats that allow an examiner more latitude.

3. The polygraph examination for preemployment or preclearance screening may have other purposes than the diagnostic purpose served by the test. For example, an employer may want to gain knowledge of information about the applicant's past or current situations that might be used to "blackmail" the individual into committing security violations such as espionage, but that could not be used in this way if the employer already had the information.

4. Policies for use of the polygraph in preemployment screening vary considerably among federal agencies.

5. We were told that the FBI administered approximately 27,000 preemployment polygraph examinations between 1994 and 2001. More than 5,800 of these tests (21 percent) led to the decision that the examinee was being deceptive. Of these, almost 4,000 tests (approximately 69 percent of "failures") involved obtaining direct admissions of information that disqualified applicants from employment (about 2,300 tests) or of information not previously disclosed in the application process that led to a judgment of deceptiveness (about 1,700 tests). More than 1,800 individuals who did not provide direct admissions also were judged deceptive; the proportion of these attributed to detected or suspected countermeasures is not known. Thus, only the remainder of those judged deceptive—less than 1,800—resulted from the direct and unambiguous result of readings of the polygraph chart.

6. The false positive index is not commonly used in research on medical diagnosis but seems useful for considering polygraph test accuracy.

7. Many statistics other than the ROC accuracy index (A) might have been used, but they have drawbacks relative to A as a measure of diagnostic accuracy. One class of measures of association assumes that the variances of the distributions of the two diagnostic alternatives are equal. These include the d' of signal detection theory (also known as Cohen's d). These measures are adequate when the empirical ROC is symmetrical about the negative diagonal of the ROC graph, but empirical curves often deviate from the symmetrical form. The measures A and d' are equivalent in the special case of symmetric ROCs, but even then A has the conceptual advantage of being bounded, by 0.5 and 1.0, while d' is unbounded. Some measures of association, such as the log-odds ratio and Yule's Q, depend only on the internal four cells of the 2-by-2 contingency table of test results and true conditions (e.g., their cross product) and are independent of the table's marginal totals. Although they make no assumptions about

equal variances per se, as measures of accuracy they share the same "symmetric" features of d'. A second class of standard measures of association, which do depend on marginal totals, are functions of the correlation coefficient; they include Cohen's kappa and measures derived from the Chi-square coefficient, such as the Phi, or four-fold point, coefficient. Like the "percentage correct" index, these measures vary with the base rate of positive cases in the study sample and with the diagnostician's decision threshold, in a way that is evident only when their ROCs are derived. Their ROCs are not widely known inasmuch as the measures were designed for single 2-by-2 or 2-by-3 tables, rather than for the 2-by-n table that represents the multiple possible thresholds used in estimating an ROC. However, these measures can be shown to predict an ROC of irregular form—one that is not concave downward or that intersects the ROC axes at places other than the (0.0, 0.0) and (1.0, 1.0) corners. Moreover, some of these latter measures were developed to determine statistical significance relative to hypotheses of no relationship, and they lack cogency for assessing degree of accuracy or effect size. Several of these alternative statistics have been analyzed and their theoretical ROCs compared with a broad sample of observed ROCs (Swets, 1986a, 1986b); the two classes of association statistics are discussed by Bishop, Fienberg, and Holland (1975).

8. The accuracy index (A) is equal to the proportion of correct signal identifications that would be made by a diagnostician confronted repeatedly by pairs of random test results, one of which was drawn from the signal category and one from the noise category. For example, a decision maker repeatedly faced with two examinees, one of whom is truthful, will make the correct choice 8 out of 10 times by using a test with A = 0.8. In other situations, A does not translate easily to percent correct. Under a great many assumptions about test situations that are realistic in certain applications, the percent correct is quite different from A, as is illustrated in Table 2-1. (The measure A is applied to diagnostic performance in several fields; see Swets, [1988, 1996:Chapter 4].)

9. A conventional way of representing decision thresholds quantitatively is as the slope of the tangent to the ROC curve drawn at the cutoff point that defines the threshold. It can be shown that this slope is equal to the ratio of the height of the signal distribution to the height of the noise distribution (the "likelihood ratio") at that threshold (see representations in Figure 2-1). At point F in Figure 2-2, this slope is 2, at point B it is 1, and at point S it is 1/2 (Swets, 1992, 1996:Ch. 5).

10. Computer software exists to give maximum-likelihood fits to empirical ROC points (e.g., Metz, 1986, 1989, 2002; Swets, 1996). There are two common approaches: to draw straight line segments interpolating between estimated ROC points and the lower left and upper right corners of the plotting square; or to assume a curved form that follows from underlying distributions of the measure of evidence that are normal (Gaussian), often with arbitrary variances but sometimes with these assumed equal, and to use maximum likelihood estimation. In either case, A is determined as the area under the estimated ROC; standard errors and confidence bounds for A may also be computed. These methods have technical limitations when used on relatively small samples, but they are adequate to the level of accuracy needed here.

11. A different distinction between validity and utility is made in some writings on diagnostic testing (Cronbach and Gleser, 1965; Schmidt et al., 1979). That distinction concerns the practical value of a test with a given degree of accuracy in particular decision-making contexts, such as screening populations with low base rates of the target condition. We address these issues in this report (particularly in Chapter 7), but do not apply the term "utility" in that context. Our usage of "utility" in discussing the polygraph follows the usage of the term by polygraph practitioners.

12. Using computers or "blind" scoring may not completely remove the effects of demeanor because cues in the examinee's demeanor can alter the way the examination is given, and this may in turn affect the examinee's physiological responses on the test.
13. We found many polygraph validation studies in which assessment was done only by tests of statistical significance without any attempt to estimate effect size or strength of association. We were unable to use these in our quantitative assessment of accuracy because they did not provide the raw data needed to calculate the accuracy index.

3

The Scientific Basis for
Polygraph Testing

Evidence relevant to the validity of polygraph testing can come from two main sources: basic scientific knowledge about the processes the polygraph measures and the factors influencing those processes, and applied research that assesses the criterion validity or accuracy of polygraph tests in particular settings. This chapter considers the first kind of evidence; the second is considered in Chapters 4 and 5.

We begin by discussing the importance of establishing a solid scientific basis, including empirically supported theory, for detection of deception by polygraph testing. We then present the main arguments that have been used to provide theoretical support for polygraph testing and evaluate them in relation to current understanding of human psychological and physiological responses. We also consider arguments based on current knowledge of psychology and physiology that raise questions about the validity of inferences of deception made from polygraph measures. We conclude with an assessment of the strength of the scientific base for polygraph testing.

THE SCIENTIFIC APPROACH

To an investigator interested in practical lie detection, basic science may seem irrelevant. The essential question is whether a technique works in practice: whether it provides information about guilty or deceptive individuals that cannot be obtained from other available techniques. As Chapter 2 makes clear, however, it can be very difficult in field situations to determine scientifically whether or how well the polygraph (or any other technique for the psychophysiological detection of deception) "works." The appropriate criterion of validity can be slippery; truth is often hard to determine; and it is difficult to disentangle the roles of physiological responses, interrogators' skill, and examinees' beliefs in order to make clear attributions of practical results to the validity of the test. Given all these confounding factors in the case evidence, even the most compelling anecdotes from practitioners do not constitute significant scientific evidence.

Evidence of scientific validity is essential to give confidence that a test measures what it is supposed to measure. Such evidence comes in part from scientifically collected data on the diagnostic accuracy of a test with certain examiners and examinees. Evidence of accuracy is critical to test validation because it can demonstrate that the test works well under specific conditions in which it is likely to be applied. Evidence of accuracy is not sufficient, however, to give confidence that a test will work well across all examiners, examinees, and situations, including those in which it has not been applied. This limitation is important whenever a test is used in a situation or on a population of examinees for which accuracy data are not available and especially when scientific knowledge suggests that the test may not perform in the same way in the new situation or with the new population. This limitation of accuracy data is particularly serious for polygraph security screening because the main target populations, such as spies and terrorists, have not been and cannot easily be subjected to systematic testing. Confidence in polygraph testing, especially for security screening, therefore also requires evidence of its construct validity, which depends, as we have noted, on an explicit and empirically supported theory of the mechanisms that connect test results to the phenomenon they purport to be diagnosing. A test with good construct validity is one that uses methods that are defensible in light of the best theoretical and empirical understanding of those mechanisms, the external factors that may alter the mechanisms and affect test results, and the measurement issues affecting the ability to detect the signal of the phenomenon being measured and exclude extraneous influences. Only to the extent that a diagnostic test meets these construct validity criteria can one have confidence that it will work well in new situations and with different kinds of examinees.

A well supported theory of the test is also essential to provide confidence that the test will work well in the face of efforts examinees may make to produce a false negative result. Spies and terrorists may be strongly motivated to learn countermeasures to polygraph tests and may develop potential countermeasures that have not been studied. To have confidence that such measures will fail or will be detected requires basic understanding of the physiological measures used in polygraph testing and of the ways they respond to various intentional activities of examinees. Issues of construct validity such as these are likely to arise in courts operating under *Daubert* and the Federal Rules of Evidence or under analogous state rules, which require that the admissibility of evidence be judged on the basis of the validity of the underlying scientific methods (see Saxe and Ben-Shakhar, 1999).

For polygraph lie detection, scientific validity rests on the strength of evidence supporting all the inferential links between deception and the test results. Inferences from polygraph tests presume that deception on relevant questions uniquely causes certain psychological states different from those caused by comparison questions, that those states are tied to certain physiological concomitants, that those physiological responses are the ones measured by the polygraph instrument, that polygraph scoring systems reflect the deception-relevant aspects of the physiological responses, and that the interpretation of the polygraph scores is appropriate for making the discrimination between deception and truthfulness.[1] Inferences also presume that factors unrelated to deception do not interfere with this chain of inference so as to create false test results that misdiagnose the deceptive as truthful or vice versa.

A knowledge base to support the scientific validity of polygraph testing is one that adequately addresses those inferences. It would include evidence that answers such questions as the following:

- Are the procedures used to measure the physiological changes said to be associated with deception standardized and scientifically valid?[2]
- Does the act of deception reliably cause identifiable changes in the physiological processes the polygraph measures (e.g., electrodermal, cardiovascular)?
- Is deception the only psychological state that would cause these physiological changes in the context of the polygraph test?
- Does the type of lie (rehearsed, spontaneous) affect the nature of the physiological changes?
- If the correlation between deception and the physiological response is not perfect, what are the mechanisms by which a truthful response can produce a false positive?
- Considering such mechanisms, how can the test procedure minimize the chances of false positive results?
- If the correlation between deception and the physiological response is not perfect, what are the mechanisms by which a deceptive response could produce a false negative result (i.e., mechanisms that would allow for effective countermeasures)?

• Considering such mechanisms, how can the test procedure minimize the chances of false negative results?

• Are the mechanisms relating deception to physiological responses universal for all people who might be examined, or do they operate differently in different kinds of people or in different situations? Is it possible that measured physiological responses do not always have the same meaning or that a test that works for some kinds of examinees or situations will fail with others?

• How might the test results be affected by the examinee's personality or frame of mind? For example, can recent stress change the likelihood that an examinee will be judged deceptive?

• How might expectancies and personal interactions between an examiner and an examinee affect the reliability and validity of the physiological measurements? For example, might a test result have been different if a different examiner had given the test?

• How might the wording or presentation of the relevant or comparison questions affect an examinee's differential physiological responses? For example, if a test procedure gives the examiner latitude in formulating relevant or comparison questions, might the test results be affected by the particular questions that are used?

• Which theory of psychophysiological detection of deception has the strongest scientific support? Which testing procedures are most consistent with this theory?

These questions are central to developing an approach to the psychophysiological detection of deception that is scientifically justified and that deserves the confidence of decision makers. Although many of the questions are in the realms of basic science in psychology, physiology, and measurement, answering them also has major practical importance. For example, a well-supported theory of the physiological detection of deception can clarify how much latitude, if any, examiners can be given in question construction without undermining the validity of the test. It may also specify countermeasures by which an examinee can act intentionally to create false readings that lead to misinterpretations of polygraph results and thus can help examiners anticipate their use and develop counterstrategies. Research focused only on establishing accuracy does not provide an adequate basis for confidence in a test because it inevitably leaves many critical questions unanswered. Consider, for example, some inherent limitations of a standard research approach in which some individuals are asked to lie about a mock crime they have committed and the polygraph is used to distinguish those examinees from others who have only witnessed the mock crime or who have no knowledge of it. If the polygraph performs well in this experiment, one can only conclude that it "works" for people like the examinees in situations like the mock crime. There would be many unanswered questions, including:

- Would the physiological responses be the same if the crime had been real?
- Would the test procedure perform as well if the deceptive examinees had been coached in ways to make it difficult for examiners to discriminate between their responses to relevant and comparison questions?
- Would the test procedure have performed as well if the examinees had been from different cultural backgrounds?
- Would the test procedure work as well for the people most likely to commit the target infractions as for other people (for example, are there systematic differences between these groups of people that could affect test results)?
- Would a polygraph test procedure that performs well in specific-event investigations perform as well in a screening setting, when the relevant questions must be asked in a generic form?
- Would different examiners who constructed the relevant and comparison questions in slightly different ways have produced equally good results?

Such questions can sometimes be answered by additional research, for instance, using different kinds of examinees or training some of them in countermeasures. But it is never possible to test all the possible kinds of examinees or countermeasures. A solid theoretical and scientific base is also valuable for improving a test because it can identify the most serious threats to the test's validity and the kinds of experiments that need to be conducted to assess such threats; it can also tell researchers when further experiments are unlikely to turn up any new knowledge. In such ways, a solid scientific base is important for developing confidence in any technique for the psychophysiological detection of deception and critical for any technique that may be used for security screening.

THEORIES OF POLYGRAPH TESTING

Polygraph specialists have engaged in extensive debate about theories of polygraph questioning and responding in the context of a controversy about the validity of comparison question versus concealed information test formats. We are more impressed with the similarities among polygraph testing techniques than with the differences, although some of the differences are important, as we note at appropriate places in this and the following chapters. The most important similarities concern the physiological responses measured by the polygraph instrument, which are essentially the same across test formats. Factors that affect these physiological responses, including many factors unrelated to deception or attempts to conceal knowledge, have similar implications for the validity of all tests that measure those responses.

Polygraph Questioning

Polygraph practice is built on comparing physiological responses to questions that are considered relevant to the investigation at hand, which evoke a lie from someone who is being deceptive, with responses to comparison questions to which the person responds in a presumably known way (e.g., tells the truth or a probable or directed lie). The responses are compared only for one individual because it is recognized that there are individual differences in basal physiological functioning, physiological reactivity, and physiological response hierarchies (for more information, see Davidson and Irwin, 1999; Cacioppo et al., 2000; Kosslyn et al., 2002). Because of individual differences, the absolute magnitude of an individual's physiological response to a relevant question cannot be a valid indicator of the truthfulness of a response.

According to contemporary theories of polygraph questioning, individuals who are being deceptive or truthful in responding to relevant questions show different patterns of physiological response when their reactions to relevant and comparison questions are compared. In the relevant-irrelevant test format, the theory is that a guilty person, who is deceptive only to the relevant questions, will react more to those questions; in contrast, an innocent person, who is truthful about all questions, will not respond differentially to the relevant questions. In the comparison question format, a guilty person lies both to the relevant and the comparison questions (which are constructed to generate probable or directed lies), while the innocent person lies to the comparison but not the relevant question. The theory is that the innocent person will show equal or less physiological responsiveness to relevant than comparison questions and that the guilty person will show greater responsiveness to relevant than comparison. In the concealed information format, the theory is that examinees will respond most strongly to questions related to their actual knowledge and experience, so that concealed information will be revealed by a stronger response to questions that touch on that information than to the comparison questions. Examinees without special information to conceal will not respond differentially across questions.

The specific nature of the relevant and comparison questions depends on the purpose and type of test. In specific-incident tests using the relevant-irrelevant format, the relevant question(s) focus on specifics of the target event about which a guilty individual would have to lie to conceal guilt. The typical comparison questions are very unlikely to yield deceptive responses (e.g., "Is today Friday?").

Specific-incident polygraph tests using comparison question test formats look like those in the relevant-irrelevant format. The comparison questions are specially formulated during a pretest interview with the intent to make an innocent examinee very concerned about them and either lie with high likelihood (a probable lie comparison question) or lie under instruction (a directed lie comparison question, such as, "During the first 18 years of your life did you ever steal something from someone who trusted you?"). Such comparison questions are often very similar to those used in lie scales or validity scales on personality questionnaires, except that the polygraph examiner is usually given latitude in choosing questions, so that different examinees may be asked different comparison questions at the same point in the test. The comparison questions tend to be more generic than the relevant questions in that they do not refer to a specific event known to the examiner.

Concealed knowledge specific-incident tests ask about specific details of the target event that the examinee would be unlikely to know unless present at the scene (e.g., "Was the victim wearing a red dress? A yellow dress? A blue dress?"). The relevant questions are those that note accurate details; the comparison questions present false details of the same aspect of the event. If the stimuli that produce the strongest responses consistently correspond to actual details of the incident, the respondent is judged to have concealed information about the incident.

In employee and preemployment screening tests, the relevant questions focus on generic acts, plans, associations, or behaviors (e.g., "Have you engaged in an act of sabotage?") because the examiner does not know of a specific event. Comparison questions are typically also generic, but unrelated to the target event, and may in fact be the same questions used in specific-incident testing using the comparison question format. The concealed information format cannot be used if the examiner lacks specific knowledge that can be used in formulating relevant questions.

Psychophysiological Responses

Polygraph testing is based on the presumptions that deception and truthfulness reliably elicit different psychological states across examinees and that physiological reactions differ reliably across examinees as a function of those psychological states. Comparison questions are designed to produce known truthful or deceptive responses and therefore to produce physiological responses that can be compared with responses to relevant questions to detect deception or truthfulness. To have a well-supported theory of psychophysiological detection of deception, it is therefore necessary to identify the relevant psychological states and to understand how those states are linked to characteristics of the test questions intended to create the states and to the physiological responses the states are said to produce.

Marston (1917), Larson (1922), and Landis and Gullette (1925) all found elevated autonomic (blood pressure) responses when individuals engaged in deception. Marston (1917) described the underlying psychological state as fear; other writers have conceived it as arousal or excitement. The idea that fear or arousal is closely associated with deception provides the broad underlying rationale for the relevant-irrelevant test format.[3] Subsequent research has confirmed that the polygraph instrument measures physiological reactions that may be associated with an examinee's stress, fear, guilt, anger, excitement, or anxiety about detection or with an examinee's orienting response to information (see below) that is especially relevant to some forbidden act.

The comparison question test and related formats are presumed to establish a context such that an examinee who is innocent of the acts identified in the relevant questions will be at least as concerned and reactive, if not more so, in relation to lying on the comparison questions as about giving truthful answers to the relevant questions. In contrast, the examinee guilty of some forbidden acts is assumed to be more fearful, anxious, or stressed about being detected for lying—and, therefore, more reactive—to the relevant questions than the comparison questions. Several theoretical accounts have been offered to lend support to these assumptions. Although there is evidence bearing on some of the propositions underlying some of these theories, none of them has been subjected to detailed investigation in the polygraph context.

Conflict Theory

According to the theory of conflict (Davis, 1961), two incompatible reaction tendencies aroused at the same time produce a large physiological reaction that is greater than the reaction to either alone. A life of answering questions straightforwardly would create one reaction tendency, and the circumstances that would motivate an examinee to deny the truth would create an incompatible reaction tendency. The assumption underlying variants of the comparison question technique is that a stronger reaction tendency (and, hence, greater reaction tendency incompatibility) will be aroused in response to relevant than control questions in guilty individuals than in others. Ben-Shakhar (1977) noted that the conflict hypothesis has trouble accounting for responses that are seen even when participants do not respond verbally to questions (e.g.,

Gustafson and Orne, 1965; Kugelmass, Lieblich, and Bergman, 1967). Moreover, a conflict between an examinee and examiner, for instance, about persistent questioning of a response to a relevant question or an expectation of being falsely accused, could in theory also create especially large and repeatable responses to relevant questions even in wrongly accused examinees.

Conditioned Response Theory

The conditioned response theory (Davis, 1961) holds that the relevant questions play the role of conditioned stimuli and evoke in deceptive individuals an emotional (and concomitant physiological) response with which lying has been associated during acculturation. A variation of this theory holds that the stimuli associated with a major transgression serve as conditioned stimuli while the act itself (e.g., a homicide), an uncondi-tioned stimulus, elicits a dramatic autonomic response (an unconditioned response) at the time of the transgression and produces single-trial emo-tional conditioning. Accordingly, the recollection of the act, elicited by the relevant question, acts as a conditioned stimulus for guilty individu-als and elicits a minor autonomic response (conditioned emotional re-sponse). Innocent individuals, according to this theory, never undergo this conditioning and therefore do not show a conditioned emotional response to stimuli about the target act. There is substantial evidence that autonomic responses can be classically conditioned (Diven, 1937; Tursky et al., 1976; LeDoux, 1995).

If this theory is correct, there are significant possibilities for the poly-graph to misinterpret an examinee's truthfulness because in conditioned response theory, lying is not the only possible elicitor of an autonomic response, and innocent individuals may show a conditioned emotional response triggered by some other feature of the relevant question or the manner in which it is asked. For example, questions related to traumatic experiences may produce large conditioned physiological responses even if the examinee responds truthfully—consider the psychological state of a victim or an innocent witness asked to recall specifics of a violent crime—while a lie about a trivial matter may elicit a much smaller response. Also according to this theory, relevant questions might also produce large responses in innocent examinees who have in the past experienced un-founded accusations that were associated with upsetting or punitive con-sequences that elevated autonomic activity. In such an examinee, a rel-evant question might serve as a conditioned stimulus for anger or fear similar to that associated with false accusations in the past.

Psychological Set and Related Theories

Psychological set theory (e.g., Barland, 1981) holds that when a person being examined fears punishment or anticipates serious consequences should he or she fail to deceive, such fear or anticipation produces a measurable physiological reaction (e.g., elevation of pulse, respiration, or blood pressure, or electrodermal activity) if the person answers deceptively. A variation on this theory, the threat-of-punishment theory (Davis, 1961), posits that lying is an avoidance reaction with considerably less than 100 percent chance of success, but the only one with any chance of success at all. If a person anticipates there is a good likelihood and serious consequences of being caught in the lie, then the threat of punishment when the person tries to deceive will be associated with a large physiological response. Because the consequences of lying to the comparison questions are thought to be less than lying to the relevant questions, the theory is that lying to relevant questions will be associated with larger physiological responses than lying to control questions. These theories suggest that the detection of deception will be more robust in real-life situations involving strong emotions and punishment than in innocuous interrogations or laboratory simulations. In another variation of this theory, Gustafson and Orne (1963) suggest that an individual's motivation to succeed in the detection task will be greater in real-life settings (because the consequences of failing to deceive are grave), and this elevated motivational state will also produce elevated autonomic activation.

This theoretical argument also leaves open significant possibilities for misinterpretation of the polygraph results of certain examinees. It is plausible, for instance, that a belief that one might be wrongly accused of deceptive answers to relevant questions—or the experience of actually being wrongly accused of a deceptive answer to a relevant question—might produce large and repeatable physiological responses to relevant questions in nondeceptive examinees that mimic the responses of deceptive ones.

The related arousal theory holds that detection occurs because of the differential arousal value of the various stimuli, regardless of whether or not there is associated fear, guilt, or emotion (Ben-Shakhar, Lieblich, and Kugelmass, 1970; Prokasy and Raskin, 1973). The card test illustrates this theory. The card test is an information test in which an examinee selects one item from a set of matched items (e.g., a card from a deck). This item produces a different response from the others, whether the examinee denies special knowledge about any of the items (i.e., lies about the selected item) or claims special knowledge about all of the items (i.e., lies about all but the selected item) (Kugelmass, Lieblich, and Bergman, 1967).

A related theory, Ben-Shakhar's (1977) dichotomization theory, is built on the concepts of orienting, habituation, and signal value (Sokolov, 1963). According to dichotomization theory, stimuli are represented in terms of one of two categories—relevant and neutral—which habituate independently. A response to a given stimulus is an inverse function of the number of previous presentations of stimuli in its category and is unrelated to the number of previous presentations of stimuli in the other category (Ben-Shakhar, 1977). Dichotomization theory is seen as additive with rather than in competition with other theories. Thus, dichotomization theory emphasizes a "relevance" factor, based on the signal value of the stimulus (Sokolov, 1963), in which stimuli that are personally relevant for historical reasons yield stronger responses than neutral material made relevant in the experimental context.

Orienting Theory

The above theoretical accounts, all of which have been used as justification for the comparison question test format, predict that deceptive individuals will show stronger physiological reactions on relevant than on comparison questions; however, they also predict that truthful examinees, under certain conditions, will show physiological response patterns similar to those expected from deceptive examinees. They thus suggest that comparison question polygraph testing has a significant potential to lead to inferences of deception when none has occurred: that is, they suggest that the polygraph test may not be specific to deception because other psychological states that can result from stimuli arising during the test mimic the physiological signs of deception. The possibility that truthful examinees will occasionally exhibit stronger physiological responses to relevant than control questions based on chance alone also increases the possibility of false alarms.

To address this issue, Lykken (1959, 1998) devised the guilty knowledge test (called here the concealed information test), based in part on orienting theory. The notion of an orienting or "what-is-it" response emerged from Pavlov's studies of classical conditioning in dogs. Pavlov (1927:12) observed that a dog's conditioned response to a stimulus would fail to appear if some unexpected event occurred:

> It is this reflex [the orienting response] which brings about the immediate response in men and animals to the slightest changes in the world around them, so that they immediately orientate their appropriate receptor organ in accordance with the perceptible quality in the agent bringing about the change, making a full investigation of it. The biological significance of this reflex is obvious.

An orienting response occurs in response to a novel or personally significant stimulus to facilitate a possible adaptive behavioral response to the stimulus (Sokolov, 1963; Kahneman, 1973). The phenomenon of orienting is illustrated in a cocktail party in which a person can converse with another, apparently oblivious to the din created by the conversations of others, yet the person stops and orients toward the source when his or her name is spoken in one of these other conversations. Lynn (1966) has summarized the physiological profile of an orienting response as decreased heart rate, increased sensitivity of the sense organs, increased skin conductance, general muscle tonus (but a decrease in irrelevant muscle activity), pupil dilation, vasoconstriction in the limbs and possibly vasodilation in the head, and more asynchronous, low-voltage electrical activity in the brain. There are individual differences in the presence and relative magnitude of these responses, however, and the orienting response is subject to habituation, which implies that false negatives may be particularly likely among the most sophisticated and well-prepared examinees.

The concealed information test format is designed to provide a quantitative specification of the relative probability of a given outcome based on the elicitation of an orienting response to a specific piece of information that differs from the other items only in the mind of an individual who is knowledgeable about details of a crime or other target incident. An innocent examinee would be expected to respond most strongly to the relevant item in a series of five similar items (e.g., "How much money was taken? $10, $20, $30, $40, $50"), by chance with a probability of 1 in 5 (0.20). Such a response on one question would not engender much confidence in the interpretation that the person had concealed knowledge of the true amount. However, if an examinee consistently responded most strongly to the one relevant item out of five, over five separate questions, then the probability of that combined outcome occurring by chance in the absence of concealed information is presumed to be 1 in 5^5 (0.00032).

It is important to keep in mind that there might be a distinction between physiological reactions to the stimuli (i.e., the questions) and reactions to the response (e.g., attempted deception). Arousal theory and orienting theory, both of which are commonly cited as justifications for the concealed information test format and related techniques, focus on reactions to the questions. From the perspective of these theories, it might not even be necessary for examinees to respond, and reactions might be the same regardless of whether the response is deceptive or honest. The theories that underlie the comparison question technique (e.g., set theory, theory of conflict, conditioned response theory) assume that it is the deceptive response that causes the reactions recorded by the polygraph.

Polygraph tests that use the comparison question technique are also sometimes justified in terms of orienting theory. Such a justification has been offered for the Test of Espionage and Sabotage (TES) used for security screening in the U.S. Department of Energy (DOE) and some other federal agencies (U.S. Department of Defense Polygraph Institute, 1995a). Strong responses to relevant questions are taken to indicate an orienting response, in turn indicating "the significance of the stimulus"—though not necessarily deception (U.S. Department of Defense Polygraph Institute, 1995a:4). Responses to the TES are scored as "significant responding," or "no significant responding" rather than the more traditional "deception indicated" or "no deception indicated." Orienting theory has recently been offered as theoretical justification for polygraph testing in general (e.g., Kleiner, 2002).

The claim that orienting theory provides justification for the comparison question technique of polygraph testing is radically at odds with the practices of polygraph examiners using that technique. If it is the orienting response to the stimulus rather than the physiological response to deceptiveness that drives the responses, many of the procedures that are common practice in comparison question polygraph testing should be revised. First, the practice of previewing questions with examinees is problematic under orienting theory. Exposure to the relevant questions prior to the examination would tend to decrease the differential orienting response to the relevant and comparison questions and weaken the test's ability to discriminate. Also, comparison questions would probably be constructed differently for a test based on orienting theory. Instead of designing them to induce reactions in nondeceptive subjects, they would probably be designed to be nonevocative, as they are in the relevant-irrelevant technique. Finally, a polygraph examination based on orienting theory would typically include multiple administrations of each class of questions (e.g., there would be several variations on an espionage question), to allow for a clear differentiation of orienting responses from others. Thus, we do not take very seriously the argument that the TES or other polygraph examination procedures based on the comparison question technique can be justified in terms of orienting theory.

It is possible that different theories are applicable in different situations. The dichotomization and orienting theories, for instance, may be more applicable to tests in which the signal value of the stimulus is more pertinent than the threat of severe consequences of detection: for example, when an investigation is aimed at identifying witnesses with knowledge about an incident even if they are innocent. The conflict, set, punishment, and arousal theories, in contrast, may be more applicable for identifying individuals guilty of serious crimes or those hiding dangerous plans or associations.

The early theoretical work assumed that polygraph responses associated with deception, or the fear of deception, were involuntary and quite large in comparison to other anxieties aroused by the test (Marston, 1917). Consistent with this line of thinking, theories of the psychophysiological detection of deception by polygraph assume that relevant, in contrast to comparison, questions are more stimulating to those giving deceptive than truthful answers. Interpretation of a polygraph test has typically been based on the relative size of the physiological responses elicited by relevant questions and the associated comparison questions (e.g., Podlesny and Raskin, 1977; Lykken, 1998). If the assumptions about large and involuntary responses to relevant questions are true, the polygraph test would be characterized by high sensitivity and specificity—it would discriminate very accurately between deception and truthfulness—and it would be immune to countermeasures.

Such assumptions are not tenable in light of contemporary research on individual and situational determinants of autonomic responses generally (Lacey, 1967; Coles, Donchin, and Porges, 1986; Cacioppo, Tassinary, and Berntson, 2000a) and on the physiological detection of deception in particular (e.g., Lykken, 2000; Iacono, 2000). There is no unique physiological response that indicates deception (Lykken, 1998). If deceivers in fact have stronger differential responses to relevant questions, it does not necessarily follow that an examinee who shows this response pattern was lying (see Strube, 1990; Cacioppo and Tassinary, 1990a) because differences in people's anticipation of and responses to the relevant and comparison questions other than differences in truthfulness can also produce differential physiological reactions. For example, relevant questions are sometimes inherently more threatening than comparison questions. Asking a weapons scientist "Have you committed espionage?" might generate a stronger response in some innocent examinees than "Have you ever taken something that did not belong to you?" Also, as noted above, individuals who have experienced punitive outcomes from being wrongly accused in the past or who believe the examiner suspects them of being the culprit may, in theory, be more reactive to relevant than control questions even when responding truthfully. No independent evidence has been reported in mock crime studies to verify that relevant questions are more stimulating than comparison questions to those giving deceptive answers or that comparison questions are equally or more stimulating than relevant questions to those giving truthful responses.

Most comparison question testing formats face the difficult challenge of calibrating the emotional content of relevant and comparison questions to elicit the levels of response that are needed in order to correctly interpret the test results. It has been argued that an unethical examiner could manipulate the questions and the way they are presented to produce

desired test results (Honts and Perry, 1992), and if this can be done intentionally, it might also be done unintentionally by an examiner who holds
a strong expectancy about the examinee's guilt or innocence (we discuss
the expectancy phenomenon later in this chapter). Even if this calibration
is not influenced by an examiner's intended or unintended bias, it may be
tipped one way or another by subtle variations in the ways an examiner
introduces or conducts the test (Abrams, 1999). This source of inconsistency and potential unreliability in test administration was a stimulus for
developing comparison question testing techniques that standardize the
relevant and comparison questions across examinations and examiners.
For example, directed-lie comparison question test formats have been
advocated as superior to probable-lie variants because in the latter format, "it is difficult to standardize the wording and discussion of the questions" (Raskin and Honts, 2002:22). Concealed information test formats
have also been advocated as superior to comparison question formats in
this respect.

While orienting theory appears somewhat more plausible than the
theories that underlie comparison question approaches, using the theory
in devising polygraph procedures is not without problems. In particular,
it is not clear how differences in stimulus familiarity affect orienting responses. Descriptions of this theory usually start with the assumption
that responses to familiar and important stimuli will be different from
those to novel, irrelevant stimuli, but in fact, the characteristics of stimuli
should be thought of as a continuum rather than a dichotomy. That is,
some stimuli are highly familiar and relevant and attract strong orienting
responses, while others are moderately familiar and might or might not
attract these responses. Orienting responses to familiar and important
stimuli might generalize to other similar stimuli in ways that would make
it difficult to distinguish true orienting responses from those bought on
by stimulus generalization. For example, suppose a murder is committed
using a nickel-plated revolver, and suppose an examinee owns an unreg-
istered pistol (a blue-steel semi-automatic). That examinee might show
enhanced responses to a variety of questions about handguns, even
though he has no concealed information about the actual murder weapon.

Theoretical Limitations

The possibility of systematic individual differences or variability in
physiological response has not been given much attention in polygraph
theories. For example, the unresolved theoretical questions about the
basis of inferences from the polygraph leave open the possibility, discussed below, that responses may be sensitive to effects of examiner expectations or witting or unwitting biases or to examinees' beliefs about

the polygraph's validity. Polygraph theories have been largely silent about these possibilities, and empirical polygraph research has made little effort to assess their influence on polygraph readings or interpretation.

Most alternative technologies for the psychophysiological detection of deception that are being pursued (see U.S. Department of Defense, 2000; U.S. General Accounting Office, 2001) rest on similar theoretical foundations and are subject to the same theoretical limitations. This statement holds both for measures of brain function and for peripheral measures of autonomic activity. The underlying assumption remains that someone who is trying to hide something will respond differently (i.e., show "leakage," physiological arousal, or orienting responses to specific questions) than someone who is not trying to hide something. The objective of the new approaches, therefore, continues to be to measure a naturally occurring physiological response or profile of responses that not only differentiates known deceptive from truthful answers but also allows accurate classification of answers as deceptive or truthful. Improvements have been and continue to be made in the design of transducers, amplifiers, data recording, and display techniques, and in the standardization of procedures and data reduction. Data interpretation, however, still depends on the validity of the assumption that relevant, in contrast to comparison, questions are more evocative to those giving deceptive answers and equally or less evocative to those giving true answers.

Screening uses of polygraph testing raise particular theoretical issues because when the examiner does not have a specific event to ask about, the relevant questions must be generic. If a comparison question testing format can meet the challenge of calibrating questions to elicit the desired level of response in a specific-incident test, it does not follow that the same format will meet the challenge in a screening application because the relevant questions do not refer to a specific event. It is reasonable to hypothesize that autonomic reactions are more intense, at least for guilty individuals, when a target event is described concretely than when it is merely implied by mention of a generic category of events. Nothing in current knowledge of psychophysiology gives confidence that a test format will work at the same level of accuracy in a screening setting that requires generic questioning as it does in a specific-incident application.

The theory of comparison question polygraph techniques as currently used for screening can be summarized as follows:

- An examinee will respond differently when trying to hide something (i.e., show leakage or greater physiological arousal or orienting responses to relevant questions) than when not trying to hide something.[4]
- Those who have nothing to hide will be less reactive to key (rel-

evant) questions than they are when lying on personally relevant (comparison) questions.[5]

• Examinees will not respond more strongly to the relevant than comparison questions based on chance alone.

• An examiner's pursuit of an explanation of an anomalous response and the consequent activation of social norms and fear of having been detected will lead to explanations, admissions, or confessions one otherwise might not obtain but will not produce false confessions or a specific fear or anxiety in response to relevant questions on a follow-up test.

To the extent that these principles do not hold universally, an examiner's rapport with the examinee, the desired understanding of the polygraph examination and questions, and the clinical skill in determining the person's veracity (i.e., detection of deception from demeanor) are all important in distinguishing among individuals who have physiological responses not indicative of deception (e.g., anxiety or anger regarding relevant questions, insufficient emotionality about the comparison questions), those who have physiological responses indicative of relatively innocuous transgressions, and those who have physiological responses indicative of significant transgressions. These distinctions are made on the basis of clinical judgment, which, though sometimes accurate, does not stand on a good foundation of theory or empirical evidence. There is little basis for relying on the accuracy of clinical judgments, especially in individual cases, without such a foundation.

Empirical Limitations

The scientific basis for polygraph testing rests in part on what is known about the physiological responses the polygraph measures—particularly, knowledge about how they relate to psychological states that may be associated with contemplating and responding to test questions and how they might be affected by other psychological phenomena, including conscious efforts at control. The polygraph machine usually measures three or four responses. Relative blood pressure is measured by a blood pressure cuff positioned over the biceps. Electrodermal activity (a measure of the activity of the eccrine sweat glands) is measured by electrodes placed on two fingers or the palm of the hand (Orne, Thackray, and Paskewitz, 1972). The rate and depth of respiration are measured by pneumographs positioned around the chest and abdomen. The contemporary scoring methods in most common use combine information from all these response systems under the assumption that each may provide a sensitive index of fear, arousal, or orienting response to a particular question in a given individual.[6]

The justification of these physiological measures was originally derived from arousal theory, which holds that the stronger the stimulus or event, the stronger the psychological reaction, and the more pronounced these particular physiological responses. In studies of the influence of emotional disturbances on what he termed the "emergency reaction," Cannon (1929) advanced the hypothesis that there is a diffuse, nonspecific sympathetic outflow through the interconnections in the sympathetic ganglia during emergency states and that this sympathetic discharge is integrated with behavioral states—the so-called "fight-or-flight" reaction. In Cannon's formulation, autonomic and neuroendocrine activation associated with emotional disturbances serves to mobilize metabolic resources to support the requirements of fight or flight, thereby promoting the protection and survival of the organism.[7]

Although the intensity of autonomic, electrocortical, and behavioral reactions does tend to covary with the intensity of the evocative stimulus, the prediction of a general and diffuse physiological activation has failed empirical tests. Correlations among autonomic measures both within and between individuals are commonly found to be weak. Moreover, negative correlations have been found to occur within individuals during some tasks (e.g., between heart rate and skin conductance responses; see Lacey et al., 1963). Negative correlations have also been reported between electrocortical and autonomic measures of activation and between facial expressiveness and autonomic responses. Contrary to the notion that sympathetic nervous activation is global and diffuse, highly specific regional sympathetic activation has been observed in response to stressors (Johnson and Anderson, 1990), even in extreme conditions such as panic attacks (Wilkinson et al., 1998). Research also shows that the same excitatory stimulus (e.g., stressor) can have profoundly different effects on physiological activation across individuals or circumstances (Cacioppo et al., 2000; Kosslyn et al., 2002).

Cardiovascular, electrodermal, and respiratory activity respond in different ways to various psychological states and behaviors. The cardiovascular system responds to stimuli that may be considered arousing, and even to the anticipation of such stimuli. The responses are multiply determined, however, and there are individual differences in the direction and extent of cardiovascular response. For example, active coping tasks (i.e., those that require cognitive responses, such as test taking or interrogation) tend to increase blood pressure, but through different mechanisms (i.e., cardiac activation or vasoconstriction) for different kinds of tasks; moreover, individuals differ in the reactivity of these mechanisms. The evidence does not support the assumption that cardiovascular signals of arousal are consistent across individuals.

Electrodermal activity can be measured by skin conductance between two electrodes on the fingers or palm (skin resistance measurements can give misleading indications of magnitudes of response). Skin conductance responses can be elicited by so many stimuli that it is difficult to isolate specific psychological antecedents. Respiration is easily brought under voluntary control, so it is unlikely by itself to be a robust indicator of any psychological state an examinee is trying to conceal. Variations in respiration can produce changes in heart rate and electrodermal activity. Therefore, respiration needs to be monitored to determine whether cardiovascular and electrodermal responses to relevant and comparison questions are artifacts of other changes. (Appendix D provides more detail about current knowledge of cardiovascular, electrodermal, and respiratory response systems.)

The physiological responses measured by the polygraph do not all reflect a single underlying process such as arousal. Similarly, arousing stimuli do not produce consistent responses across these physiological indicators or across individuals. This knowledge implies that there is considerable lack of correspondence between the physiological data the polygraph provides and the underlying constructs that polygraph examiners believe them to measure. On theoretical grounds, it is therefore probable that any standard transformation of polygraph outputs (that is, scoring method) will correspond imperfectly with an underlying psychological state such as arousal and that the degree of correspondence will vary considerably across individuals. Little is known from basic physiological research about whether there are certain types of individuals for whom detection of arousal from polygraph measures is likely to be especially accurate—or especially inaccurate.

Polygraph theories assume that differences in physiological responses are closely correlated with psychological differences between examinees' responses to relevant and comparison questions on the polygraph test. This assumption will be less plausible to the extent that a polygraph testing procedure gives an examiner discretion in selecting the relevant and comparison questions for each examinee. It is reasonable to expect that if a polygraph test procedure gives examiners more latitude in this respect, the results are likely to be less reliable across examiners, and more susceptible to examiner expectancies and influences in the examiner-examinee interaction.

INFERENCES FROM POLYGRAPH TESTS

Given the imperfect correspondence that can be expected between polygraph test results and the underlying state the test is intended to measure, inferences from polygraph tests confront both logical and empirical issues.

The Logic of Inference

When theory does not establish a tight link from the physiological responses to the psychological states presumably tied to deception, and particularly when theory raises the possibility that states other than deception may generate physiological responses from which deception is inferred, inference faces a major logical problem.[8] This problem is not obviated by advances in neural and physiological measurement, which is now often highly sophisticated and precise. The logical problem is generic to inferences about psychological states from physiological indicators.

Inference commonly follows the subtractive method, in which experimental and control or contrast conditions differ by one element, stage, or process (Strube, 1990; Cacioppo, Tassinary, and Berntson, 2000b). Outcome differences between the experimental and control conditions are then considered to reflect the effect of that single component. This method allows the construction of physiological indices of the psychological phenomena that have been varied in experiments, which are then used to develop concepts and test theories about those phenomena.

The subtractive method underlies the interpretation of the polygraph chart and of other indicators used for the psychophysiological detection of deception. If there are sufficiently more or stronger "arousal" responses to relevant than control questions, the polygraph chart is interpreted as "deception indicated" or as showing "significant response." This approach does not allow a strong inference (Cacioppo and Tassinary, 1990a).[9] The confidence in such an interpretation would be enhanced if the particular result (e.g., relatively large skin conductance responses) could be shown to arise consistently under a wide range of conditions of deception, and if the result could not be attributable to some other aspect of the stimulus or context (e.g., fear of being suspected or anxiety over trivial or irrelevant transgressions). Even then, however, the autonomic responses could not be used definitively to infer the presence of deception, as other antecedent conditions (e.g., emotional reactions) may yield the same result.[10]

In most polygraph research, a psychological factor (deception) serves as the independent variable and a physiological factor serves as the dependent variable. This format provides information about the likelihood of a physiological response given a person who is being deceptive. Such evidence is commonly offered to address the question of how good the polygraph test is as a diagnostic of lying. However, a polygraph test, like other diagnostic instruments, is actually used to make the reverse inference: about the likelihood of deception given the physiological response that is observed. The conditional probabilities on these two situations are not necessarily or typically equal; they are related as follows:

P(physiological activity given deception) × P(deception)
= P(deception given physiological activity) × P(physiological activity).[11]

A strong ability to distinguish deception from truthfulness on the basis of a positive polygraph result requires that the polygraph test have high specificity (a probability of physiological response given nondeception close to zero). For example, a positive result from a test with 50 percent sensitivity and 100 percent specificity implies the subject is deceptive, but 50 percent of deceptive subjects will not be caught. A strong inference of innocence from a negative polygraph result requires that the sensitivity of the test be very high. In that case, all the deceptive subjects are caught, but unless the specificity is also high, many nondeceptive subjects will also be "caught." Only with a test with an accuracy similar to that of DNA matching—which has both very high sensitivity and very high specificity—could one be confident that the test results correspond closely to truth.[12] However, as we have shown, the physiological measures used in polygraph testing do not have such close correspondence with deception or any other single psychological state (Davis, 1961; Orne, Thackray, and Paskewitz, 1972). Lacking a one-to-one correspondence between the psychological and physiological states, empirical evidence at the aggregate level showing that deception produces larger physiological responses than honest responding does not adequately address the validity of the reverse inference, that larger physiological responses can be caused only by deception. This misinterpretation of the import of the empirical evidence has been called the "fallacy of the transposed conditional" in the literature on legal decision making (the attribution is usually to the statistician Dennis Lindley; see, e.g., Balding and Donnelley, 1995; Fienberg and Finkelstein, 1996). It is also known as the prosecutor's fallacy because of the way it can arise in the courts. A prosecutor may offer forensic evidence that establishes the probability that a positive test result (a DNA match or a polygraph test indicating deception) would be observed if the defendant is innocent, but a jury's task is to determine the probability that the defendant is innocent, given a positive test result.[13] At least one jury decision has been overturned because of the confusion between these two probabilities (see Pringle, 1994).

Empirical Sources of Error

Compounding the logical problems, many factors associated with polygraph testing itself may introduce substantial error, both random and systematic, into the results of polygraph examinations. The implications of these errors for polygraph test interpretation depend on the nature of the error. If errors were known to be randomly distributed across individuals and physiological indicators, they would be reduced by multiple measurement across multiple channels—an approach commonly used in polygraph testing.

Of more serious concern are sources of error that may reflect consistent rather than random causes and that may lead guilty individuals to appear truthful on the test or innocent ones to appear deceptive, thus reducing the accuracy of the test. We have noted that one cannot rule out, on theoretical grounds, the possibility that polygraph responses vary systematically with characteristics of examiners, examinees, the test situation, the interview process, and so forth.[14] Such factors may cause systematic error in polygraph interpretation and need careful consideration, especially if basic scientific knowledge suggests that a particular factor might systematically affect polygraph test results. It is convenient to distinguish two classes of potential sources of systematic error: those that derive from stable or transient characteristics of examinees or examiners (endogenous factors) and those that derive from factors in the social context of the polygraph examination.

Endogenous Factors

Among the characteristics of examinees and examiners that could threaten the validity of the polygraph are personality differences affecting physiological responsiveness; temporary physiological conditions, such as sleeplessness or the effects of legal or illegal drug use; individual differences between examiners in the ways they conduct tests; and countermeasures. For such conditions to threaten the validity of the test, they would have to differentially affect responsiveness to relevant and comparison questions (e.g., by reducing a guilty examinee's responsiveness to relevant questions). Although there have been studies of the effects of some personality variables and some drugs on polygraph detection of deception (see Chapter 5), there have been few systematic efforts to ascertain whether and how any such relationships might vary across the particular indicators used in polygraph testing. We have not seen persuasive scientific arguments that any specific personality variable would influence polygraph accuracy. If such effects were found to exist, however, it would be possible in principle to use information on the personality variable to adjust polygraph test scores.

An example of an endogenous factor that could be imagined to decrease the specificity of the polygraph, mentioned at our visit to the U.S. Department of Energy (DOE), is what was termed the "guilty complex"—

an individual attribute that may lead innocent people to respond physiologically as do guilty people. Certain chronic medical conditions (e.g., tachycardia) could be imagined to have similar effects. We have not found scientific studies investigating the effects of these factors on polygraph test performance. In general, too little attention has been paid to the factors that may reduce the specificity of the polygraph (i.e., produce false positive results). Research has been done on one endogenous factor that may reduce the sensitivity of the polygraph—the use of countermeasures. The empirical evidence from studies of countermeasures is discussed in Chapter 5.

Contextual Factors

Factors in the social context of the polygraph examination may also threaten the validity of the test and lower its sensitivity and specificity. The possibility of systematic physiological effects from the examiner-examinee interaction is particularly troublesome for two reasons: the effects would be hard to control or correct, and there are plausible psychophysiological mechanisms by which this interaction could degrade polygraph test validity. Social interaction effects would be hard to correct because manipulation of the examiner-examinee social interaction is an integral part of the polygraph test, particularly in the relevant-irrelevant and some control question test formats, and is normally done in a clinical manner that relies heavily on examiner judgment. Examiners are instructed to create emotional conditions designed to lead to differential levels of arousal and physiological responsiveness in innocent and guilty examinees. How this is done is not standardized in polygraph practice nor measured in polygraph research. This uncontrolled variation is likely to reduce the test-retest reliability of polygraph tests when different examiners are used for different tests and to make the accuracy of test results more variable in test formats that depend on creating an emotional climate based on the examiner's judgment. It also creates extreme difficulty in correcting for the effects of social interaction factors on polygraph test results. Eliminating an examiner entirely from the polygraph test is likely to reduce some but not all of these effects.

Moreover, basic research in social psychophysiology gives reason for concern about important sources of systematic error that could arise in polygraph tests from social interactions in the examination situation. Over the past three decades or so, this research has demonstrated that individuals are quite autonomically sensitive to the characteristics of those with whom they interact (Cacioppo and Petty, 1983; Wagner, 1988; Gardner, Gabriel, and Diekman, 2000), especially in potentially threatening situations (e.g., Cacioppo and Petty, 1986; Hinton, 1988; Blascovich,

2000). This research suggests that at least two interpersonal phenomena might affect the sensitivity and specificity of polygraph tests: *stigma* and *expectancies*.

Stigma

Stigmas mark individuals who are members of socially devalued groups. Stigmas may be easily visible (e.g., gender, skin color, deformations of the body); not necessarily visible (e.g., socioeconomic status, religion); or usually invisible (e.g., sexual orientation, metaphysical beliefs, having been suspected of espionage). Many theorists have argued that stigmas cause perceivers to feel a sense of uncertainty, discomfort, anxiety, or even danger during social interactions (Crocker, Major, and Steele, 1998). Much recent physiological work also suggests that bearers of stigma are threatened during interactions with members of nonstigmatized groups. Recently, research has confirmed experimentally that both stigma bearers and perceivers exhibit cardiovascular patterns of response associated with threat during performance situations that are not metabolically demanding (e.g., Mendes, Seery, and Blascovich, 2000; Blascovich et al., 2001b). This research typically demonstrates these effects during task performance but not during baseline or resting periods, suggesting the possibility that physiological responses to relevant and comparison questions might be differentially affected on polygraph tests.

Research on members of racially stigmatized groups (particularly, African Americans) suggests that such individuals exhibit heightened cardiovascular threat responses in situations in which negative stereotypes about racially stigmatized groups are likely to exist (Blascovich et al., 2001a). For example, members of racially stigmatized groups exhibit increased blood pressure reactivity during testing that requires their cognitive responses to difficult test items.

The experimental situations in which these stigma studies have occurred bear a striking resemblance to polygraph testing situations, particularly employee screening tests. Participants are told the kind of tasks that they will undertake. Their written consent is obtained. Participants are given physiological tests in recording rooms. In most of these studies, participants are asked to cooperate with each other. Autonomic physiological sensors, including blood pressure cuffs, are attached to participants, and so forth.

One important difference between the testing situations in these studies and polygraph testing situations is that participants are not asked to lie. Neither are they told that the purpose of the physiological recording equipment is to detect lying (which it is not). Nonetheless, both perceivers and bearers of stigma, including visible and nonvisible stigmas, have been shown to exhibit cardiovascular patterns associated with threat, including increased myocardial contractility, decreased cardiac output, increased total peripheral resistance, and increases in blood pressure (Blascovich, 2000; Blascovich et al., 2001b).

These studies suggest that stigma may affect polygraph test accuracy. Specifically, they suggest that if either the examiner or the examinee bears a stigma, the examinee may exhibit heightened cardiovascular responses during the polygraph testing situation, particularly during difficult aspects of that situation such as answering relevant questions, independently of whether he or she is answering truthfully. Such responses would be likely to increase the rate of false positive results among examinees who are members of stigmatized groups, at least on relevant-irrelevant and comparison question tests.[15] (In Chapter 4, we discuss the very limited empirical research examining the effects of stigma-related characteristics of examiners and examinees, such as race and gender, on the accuracy of polygraph diagnoses of deception.)

Expectancies

Expectancies have been a subject of social-psychological research for the past 40 years. In the early 1960s, Robert Rosenthal began one major line of research, examining the social psychology of the research situation; he hypothesized and verified the so-called experimenter expectancy effects. He demonstrated that experimenter biases affected the results of experimental psychological studies in many situations, even when the experimenters had no intention to do so. Expectancy effects have been tested outside the research situation hundreds of times in a variety of settings (e.g., Rosenthal and Jacobson, 1968; Rosenthal and Rubin, 1978; Harris and Rosenthal, 1985; Rosenthal, 1994; McNatt, 2000; Kierein and Gold, 2000). The most familiar example of expectancy effects is the so-called "Pygmalion effect," in which teachers' initial expectancies about specific students' potential can affect the students' future performance in the classroom and on standardized tests.

Expectancies in the polygraph testing situation have the potential to affect the validity of such testing.[16] It is reasonable to assume, for instance, that an examiner's belief, or expectancy, about examinees' guilt or innocence in a criminal investigation setting may cause the examiner to behave differentially—for instance, in a more hostile manner—toward examinees believed to be guilty or deceptive. Such behavior would plausibly create differential emotional reactions in examinees that could affect physiological responses that are detected by the polygraph. These emotional reactions would plausibly be strongest in response to questions about which the examiner expects deceptive responses, thus possibly causing physiological responses to those questions, regardless of the examinee's truthfulness. It is also possible for an examiner's expectancy to influence the way questions are selected, explained, or asked, to the extent that the test format is not standardized (Honts and Perry, 1992; Abrams, 1999). Basic research shows that expectancies can affect responses even when the responder does not know which responses are expected (e.g., Rosenthal and Fode, 1963). Consequently, examiner expectancies might influence responses even among innocent examinees on concealed information tests.

In employee screening, examiners may have expectancies not only about the truthfulness of individual examinees, but also about the base rates of true positives and true negatives in the population tested. In the DOE security screening program, for example, examiners reasonably believe that the likelihood of any individual examinee being a spy is very low. Their interactions with examinees might therefore be relatively low-key and unlikely to generate differential responses to relevant questions.

In both event-specific and screening applications, it is also quite plausible that examinees may vary in their expectancies about how the test will be used or about the particular examiner's attitudes about them. Such responses, especially when specific to individuals, are very difficult to assess and take into account in interpreting polygraph charts.

It is easy to infer hypotheses from basic research in social psychology about the ways expectancies might affect polygraph test results. For example, examiners who have high expectancies of deceptive individuals among those they test may act in ways that elicit strong physiological responsiveness to relevant questions in their examinees, resulting in a high rate of false positives (lower specificity). Similarly, examiners with high expectancies of truthfulness might elicit weaker physiological responses, resulting in a high rate of false negatives (lower sensitivity). Or examiners who think an examinee is probably guilty can be hypothesized to elicit stronger emotional responses from the examinee than they would from the same examinee if they believed the person to be innocent. Expectancy research, as well as related research on behavioral confirmation (Snyder, Tanke, and Berscheid, 1977; Snyder, 1992; Snyder and Haugen, 1994), makes such hypotheses plausible, and polygraph theory provides no reasons to discount them as unreasonable. It therefore remains an empirical question whether polygraph test results and interpretations support such hypotheses and whether, in fact, test validity is diminished to any significant degree by examiner or examinee expectancies. (We discuss the limited empirical research on this question in Chapter 5.)

An important and somewhat special case of expectancies with great relevance to polygraph testing involves examinees' expectancies regarding the validity of the polygraph test itself. Indeed, much of the utility claimed for polygraph testing can be ascribed to the strength of the expectancy on the part of the examinee that any deception will be revealed by the polygraph. This expectancy can become so strong that it motivates the examinee to admit or confess to crimes or other transgressions. Such admissions are often counted as true positive results of polygraph examinations, even in the complete absence of physiological data or independent confirmation of the admissions. It seems plausible that a belief that is nearly strong enough to lead to a confession may lead to physiological response patterns indicative of deception if the examinee does not confess. If this hypothesis is correct, the polygraph would perform better with examinees who believe it is effective than with those who do not. This hypothesis is, in fact, the rationale for using stimulation tests during the pretest phase of the polygraph examination. Research on the effect of stimulation tests on polygraph accuracy gives mixed results, as is noted in Chapter 5.

Summary

Current knowledge about physiological responses to social interaction is consistent with the idea that certain aspects of the interaction in the polygraph testing context may constitute significant sources of systematic error in polygraph interpretation that can affect the specificity as well as the sensitivity of the test, reducing the test's validity. The usual strategy for addressing systematic error resulting from a testing interaction is to standardize the interaction, perhaps by automating it. However, this strategy might be very difficult to implement effectively, especially with comparison question polygraph testing, because elements of the interaction are integral to creating the expectations and emotional states in the examinee that are said to be necessary for accurate comparison of responses to relevant and comparison questions. Some standardization can be achieved within the comparison question test format—for example, by limiting the examiner's choice of questions, as is done in the Test of Espionage and Sabotage.

Although much of the knowledge relevant to expectancy effects is decades old, polygraph theory and practice have changed little in terms of their sensitivity to issues of social interaction in the examination setting. Polygraph theory does not give reason to discount the contextual hypotheses concerning possible systematic error.

THE STATE OF POLYGRAPH RESEARCH

Psychophysiological detection of deception is one of the oldest branches of applied psychology, with roots going back to the work of

Lombroso (1882, 1895) and with systematic applied research occurring at least since Marston's (1917) efforts in support of the U.S. war effort in World War I. (Appendix E summarizes the history of Marston's work, including his relationship to the National Research Council, as well as providing some historical context related to the use of polygraph tests in security screening.) Over more than a century of research, major advances have been made in fields of basic psychology, physiology, and measurement that are relevant to the psychophysiological detection of deception and have the potential to transform the field, possibly improving practice. Some of these advances have found their way into polygraph research. The applied field as a whole, however, has been affected relatively little by these advances.

Theoretical Development

A solid theoretical base is necessary to have confidence in tests for the psychophysiological detection of deception, particularly for security screening. This is the case, as we have noted, because theory suggests that polygraph tests may give systematically erroneous results in certain situations and with certain populations (e.g., expectancy and stigma effects); because purely empirical assessment of the accuracy of test procedures cannot be conducted in important target populations such as spies and terrorists; and because of the need to have tests that are robust against a variety of countermeasures, some of them unanticipated. A research effort appropriate to these challenges would have been characterized by a set of research programs, each of which would have attempted to build and test a theoretical base and to develop an associated set of empirically supported measures and procedures that could guide research and practice. It would have focused on the psychophysiology and neuroscience of deception and sought the best physiological indicators of deception and the best ways to measure each one.

There are a few research programs that exhibit some of these characteristics. However, for the most part, polygraph research has focused on a few physiological responses for which measures have been available since at least the 1920s and tried to make the best of them by testing variations of them in practice, without doing much to develop the underlying science. The research has tended to focus on the application without advancing the basic science. In recent years, the same sort of approach has been tried with newer measures (see Chapter 6). There has been no systematic effort to identify the best potential physiological indicators on theoretical grounds or to update theory on the basis of emerging knowledge in psychology or physiology.

There has not even been any systematic effort to develop theoretical clarity regarding the mechanisms purported to cause differential responses to relevant and comparison question in relevant-irrelevant or comparison question polygraph tests. Various theoretical accounts have been advanced to explain differential psychological responses to relevant and comparison questions (differential arousal, stress, anxiety, fear, attention, or orienting). Although these theories all concur that a guilty individual responding to relevant question should evince a different psychological state than when responding to a comparison question, these theories differ with respect to the variety of psychological states that an *innocent* individual might experience in responding to relevant question and comparison questions. Although these differences are important for understanding the possibilities for false positive test results, we have found no studies reporting tests among the theories. Relatedly, various theories have been proposed to map the diverse psychological states presumed to be associated with deception to peripheral physiological responses. We found no tests among these theories, either. Indeed, most research on the comparison question polygraph has been atheoretical about the underlying mechanisms.

The situation is somewhat different with research on concealed information polygraph testing, which has consistently drawn on the theory of the orienting response. This research has emphasized developing and testing procedures that are resistant to threats to validity that can arise from differential reactions to relevant and comparison questions among examinees who have no event-related information to conceal. It uses the same physiological measures as other polygraph research, however, and in this respect shares the limitations of other polygraph test formats.

Polygraph research has not made adequate use of well-developed theoretical models of the physiological processes underlying the peripheral measurements taken by the polygraph. Those models are not reflected in the instruments or measurement procedures used in polygraph testing. Theoretical developments about the separable neurophysiological control of peripheral responses that appear similar (e.g., Dienstbier, 1989; Berntson, Cacioppo, and Quigley, 1991, 1993; Cacioppo, 1994) have seldom been considered in polygraph research, nor do the physiological measurement procedures and devices used in polygraph tests conform to the standards established by the scientific research community (e.g., Dawson, Schell, and Filion, 1990; Dawson, 2000). There is now an extensive body of literature on the sympathetic and parasympathetic influences on many organs that are in turn reflected in psychophysiological measures. Many of the measures used in polygraph testing, such as heart rate, reflect both sympathetic and parasympathetic influences. Several very different physiological mechanisms can result in identical changes in heart rate. There are now measures available that allow for the disentangling of these separate contributions; however, few of these concepts and methods have been used in polygraph research. Moreover, applied polygraph research has not for the most part taken advantage of advances in the psychophysiology and neuroscience of emotion, motivation, attention, and other processes that can affect the measures taken in polygraph testing (see, e.g., Coles, Donchin, and Porges, 1986; Cacioppo and Tassinary, 1990b; Cacioppo et al., 2000).

Polygraph research has not paid sufficient attention to advances in inductive inference in psychophysiology that have underscored the need to examine the specificity as well as the sensitivity of the mapping between a psychological state and a physiological manifestation (Strube, 1990; Cacioppo and Tassinary, 1990a; Sarter, Berntson, and Cacioppo, 1996). Specificity of the polygraph is threatened by any physiological process unrelated to deception that can systematically affect polygraph test scores.[17] We have found very little research on ways that conditions other than deceptiveness might produce records that are judged deceptive and no evidence of any systematic attention to threats to specificity. As discussed in more detail in Chapter 5, empirical validation studies of the polygraph continue to emphasize the ability to make physiological differentiation between known lying and known truth-telling.

A particularly important gap is the absence of any theoretical consideration of the social (e.g., interpersonal) and physical context of the polygraph test. As already noted, an extensive basic scientific literature in social psychology and sociology details the myriad effects of perceptible personal features (e.g., status, race, gender), dispositions (e.g., traits), and histories (e.g., examinee expectancies, cultural norms, and values) on social perception (e.g., examiner expectancies) and on psychological and physiological processes within individuals (e.g., Shapiro and Crider, 1969; Waid, 1983; Cacioppo and Petty, 1983; Gardner, Gabriel, and Diekman, 2000; Hicks, Keller, and Miller, 2000; Blascovich et al., 2001b). We found no study of the mechanisms by which such variables might affect polygraph test outcomes: for instance, of the effects they might have on the selection of comparison questions, on the examinee's understanding of the questions and the examination, or on the examiner's behavior, subtle and otherwise, during the examination.

In short, the bulk of polygraph research, including almost all the research conducted by federal agencies that use the polygraph, can be accurately characterized as atheoretical. Studies report on efforts to improve accuracy by changing methods of test administration, physiological measurement, data transformation, and the like, but they rarely address the underlying psychological and physiological processes and mechanisms that determine how much accuracy might be achieved. Thus, for example, the field includes little or no research on the emotional corre-lates of deception; the psychological determinants of the physiological measures used in the polygraph; the robustness of these measures to demographic differences, individual differences, intra-individual variabil-ity, question selection, attempted countermeasures, or social interaction variables in the interview context; or the best ways of measuring and scoring each physiological response for tapping the underlying emotional states to be measured. Because empirical evidence of accuracy does not exist for polygraph testing on important target populations, particularly for security screening, the absence of answers to such theoretical ques-tions leaves important questions open about the likely accuracy of poly-graph testing with target populations of interest.

Relationships to Other Scientific Fields

Polygraph research has not been adequately connected to at least two major scientific literatures, other than basic psychophysiology, that are also of direct relevance to improving the psychophysiological detection of deception. One of these is the research on diagnostic testing. As noted in Chapter 2, polygraph researchers and practitioners do not generally con-ceive of the polygraph as a diagnostic test, nor does most of the field recognize the concept of decision thresholds that is central to the science of diagnostic testing. Researchers and practitioners rarely recognize that the tradeoff between false positives and false negatives can be made as a matter of policy by setting decision thresholds. As a result, practitioners seem to make this tradeoff implicitly, sometimes in the choice of which polygraph testing procedure to use and sometimes, perhaps, in judging the likelihood that a particular examinee will be deceptive. Polygraph research also does not consider systematically the possible use of the polygraph as part of a sequence of diagnostic tests, in the manner of medical testing, with tests given in a standard order according to their specificity, their invasiveness, or related characteristics. (This approach to interpreting information from polygraph tests is discussed further in Chapter 7.)

The other field that polygraph research has not for the most part benefited from is the science of psychological measurement. Psychologi-cal testing and measurement draws on nearly a century of well-devel-oped research and theory (Nunnally and Bernstein, 1994), which has led to the development of reliable and valid measures of a wide range of abilities, personality characteristics, and other human attributes. There is substantial research dealing with the evaluation of objective tests, person-ality inventories, interviews, and other assessment methods, and clear standards for assessing and interpreting the reliability, validity, and utility of tests and assessments have been articulated and adopted by test developers and users (see Society for Industrial and Organizational Psychology, 1987; American Psychological Association, 1999). The goal of virtually all evaluations of psychological tests and assessments is to provide evidence about their construct validity. A wide range of methods (e.g., factor analyses, correlations, laboratory experiments) and types of evidence are used in investigating construct validity.

Polygraph research and practice typically have not drawn on established psychometric theory or of current methods for developing and evaluating tests and measures. Some polygraph studies report inter-rater agreement in assessing charts and others report other types of reliability information, but there has been little serious effort to investigate the construct validity of the polygraph. Indeed, as already noted, it is rarely clear exactly what polygraph tests are designed to measure, or how the various pieces of data obtained from polygraph tests are thought to be linked to states or attributes of the examinee, making it difficult to even initiate the process of construct validation (Fiedler et al., in press). Despite several decades of polygraph research and practice, it is still difficult to determine the relationship, if any, between attributes of the examinee (e.g., deceptiveness, use of countermeasures) and the outcomes of a polygraph examination.

There has been substantial progress in the development of psychometric methods and theory in the last 30 years. Cronbach et al. (1972) developed generalizability theory, which provides a framework for assessing measurement methods that involve multiple components or facets (polygraph outcomes might be affected by the types of questions used, by the examiner, by the context in which the examination is carried out, and so forth). Item response theory (for an overview, see Hambleton, Swaminathan, and Rogers, 1991), the method of choice for modern psychometric theory and research, provides detailed information about the relationship between the attribute or construct a test is designed to measure and responses to items and tests. McDonald (1999) has proposed a unified test theory that links traditional psychometric approaches, item response theory, and factor analytic methods. Unfortunately, none of these developments has had a substantial effect on the administration, scoring, interpretation, or evaluation of the polygraph. Modern psychometric methods are rarely if ever cited or recognized in papers and reports dealing with the polygraph, and while some studies do attempt to estimate some aspects of the reliability of polygraph examinations, none focuses on the cornerstone of modern psychometric theory and practice— the assessment of construct validity.

Consequences for Practice

Partly as a consequence of the isolation of polygraph research from related fields, polygraph practice has been very slow to adopt new technologies and methods. For example, some polygraph equipment still displays electrodermal activity as skin resistance rather than conductance, despite the fact that it has been known for decades that the latter gives a more useful measure of electrodermal response (see Fowles, 1986; Dawson, Schell, and Filion, 1990).[18] There has been no systematic effort to address the basic question of how best to detect deception in criminal investigation or national security contexts. Such an effort would have led to earlier and more serious investigation of emerging physiological and neurological measurement techniques that might be expected on theoretical grounds to have potential for lie detection, particularly measurements of brain activity. Instead, there appears to be inertia among practitioners about using the familiar equipment and techniques that rely on 1920-era science and a lack of impetus from national security or criminal justice agencies, until quite recently, to develop methods and measures that might have a stronger base in modern psychophysiology and neuroscience.

The field has also failed so far to make the best of knowledge about new and promising methods of data analysis that might do a better job of linking theory to measurement, for example, research on computer-based models for scoring polygraph charts. Early efforts, such as those reported by Kircher and Raskin (1988), focused on statistical discriminant analysis and used general notions (such as latency, rise, and duration) and other measures for each channel, drawing on general constructs that underlie psychophysiological detection of deception in the psychophysiology literature. But there appears to be limited justification for most specific choices of key parameters used in the formal models, and the operational measures one finds in this work often closely resemble what polygraph examiners claim to do in practice. This work was followed in the 1980s and 1990s by government-funded studies aimed at developing computer-based polygraph scoring systems that take advantage of advances in statistical and machine-learning algorithms capable of making the most of polygraph data (e.g., see Raskin et al., 1988; Raskin, Horowitz, and Kircher, 1989; Olsen et al., 1997). Those studies have not led to significant changes in practice. To the extent that the polygraph instrument measures physiological responses relevant to deception, this approach holds promise, but much of that promise has yet to be realized (see Appendix F). Unfortunately, the most recent and complex studies of this type, conducted at the Applied Physics Laboratory at Johns Hopkins University, appear to have taken a largely atheoretical approach, aiming to build a logistic regression detection algorithm by purely empirical means from a subset of 10,000 features extracted from physiological signals. Those efforts have not apparently built on advances in psychophysiology that might have helped in selecting features with theoretical or empirical rationales for their relevance.

Social Context

The above discussion might easily be read as a broad indictment of polygraph researchers; we do not intend that interpretation. Polygraph research has attracted and continues to attract well-trained and qualified scientists. We believe that the lack of progress in polygraph research is attributable not so much to the researchers as to the social context and structure of the work.

Polygraph research has been guided, for the most part, by the perceived needs of law enforcement and national security agencies and the demands of the courts, rather than by basic scientific approaches to research. In this respect, polygraph research is like many other fields of forensic science. The 1923 decision in *Frye v. United States* (293 F.1013) did not support work on validity issues in forensic science because under *Frye*, courts accepted the judgment of communities of presumed experts. After *Frye*, the courts did not demand validation research or efforts to find the most scientifically defensible methods for the psychophysiological detection of deception. Not until the 1993 *Daubert* decision were courts asked to judge the admissibility of expert testimony on the basis of the scientific validity of the expert opinion. That decision brought validity issues to the fore and is likely to increase the demand for solid scientific validation. So far, however, the overall enterprise of forensic science and the subfield of polygraph research have not changed much.

Meanwhile, promising young scientists from a number of relevant fields have not flocked to forensic science to make their careers. The questions being pursued have seemed far from the cutting edge of the fields in which those scientists were trained and unrelated to the major theoretical issues in those fields. Consequently, advisers in those fields have not steered their best students into forensic science, and a career in the area does not confer academic prestige. Psychophysiology and its relation to polygraph research is a case in point. Polygraph research, which has focused mainly on making incremental improvements in the way 1920s technology is used, would seem particularly unattractive to any young scientist wanting to advance understanding of modern psychology or physiology. As a result, there have been few new ideas for the research on the psychophysiological detection of deception.

Polygraph and related research has been supported primarily by law enforcement and national security agencies whose concerns have been with practical detection of deception, not with advancing science. These concerns are perfectly valid, but they have impeded scientific progress. The fact that polygraph testing combines a diagnostic test and an interrogation practice in an almost inextricable way would be a major concern for any scientist seeking to validate the diagnostic test. The cultures of those parts of the agencies that deal with law enforcement and counterintelligence do not include traditions of scientific peer review, open exchange of information, and open critical debate that are common in scientific work. (The U.S. Department of Defense Polygraph Institute has, in the past few years, shown signs of becoming an exception to this generalization.) The culture of practice in security agencies, combined with the strong belief of practitioners in the utility of the polygraph, have made it easy for those agencies to continue their old practices. Thus, research has until quite recently focused almost exclusively on the polygraph and has been conducted within agencies that are committed to using the polygraph, believe strongly in its utility, and have seen little need to seek alternative techniques.

Our conversations with practitioners at several national security agencies indicate that there is now an openness to finding techniques for the psychophysiological detection of deception that might supplement or replace the polygraph. However, both these conversations and the recent research that these agencies have sponsored on alternatives to the polygraph show a continuing atheoretical approach that does not build on or connect with the relevant scientific research in other fields.

Assessment

Criticisms of the scientific basis of polygraph testing have been raised since the earliest days of the polygraph. An indication of the state of the field is the fact that the validity questions that scientists raise today include many of the same ones that were first articulated in criticisms of Marston's original work in 1917:[19]

> My greatest reason for persistent skepticism as to the real use of the test, however, arises from the history of the subject. . . . The net result has been, I think to show that organic changes are an index of activity, of "something doing," but not of any particular kind of activity . . . but the same results would be caused by so many different circumstances, anything demanding equal activity (intelligence or emotional) that it would be impossible to divide any individual case.

Another assessment remains as true today as when it was written a half century ago (Guertin and Wilhelm, 1954:153): "There has been relatively little theoretical evaluation of the processes underlying the responses to lie detector procedure since lie detection instruments and techniques have been developed empirically in the field."

That assessment was in the introduction to a study that used factor analysis to examine the relationships of ten indices of electrodermal response and reduced them to two factors believed to have different psychological significance—one related to deception and the other to "test fright" and adaptation. Their research goal, as appropriate now as then, was to reveal basic links between psychological and physiological processes and thereby build scientific support for the choice of particular indicators of deception. This style of research, aimed at building a theory of the psychophysiological detection of deception by careful evaluation of empirical associations, has been little pursued. The same can be said of other strategies of theory building that draw on direct measurement of physiological phenomena, the techniques for which have been revolutionized over the past several decades.

Essentially the same criticism was voiced two decades ago by the U.S. Office of Technology Assessment (1983:6):

> The basic theory of polygraph testing is only partially developed and researched. . . . A stronger theoretical base is needed for the entire range of polygraph applications. Basic polygraph research should consider the latest research from the fields of psychology, physiology, psychiatry, neuroscience, and medicine; comparison among question techniques; and measures of physiological research.

More intensive efforts to develop the basic science in the 1920s would have produced a more favorable assessment in the 1950s; more intensive efforts in the 1950s would have produced a more favorable assessment in the 1980s; more intensive efforts in the 1980s would have produced a more favorable assessment now. A research strategy with better grounding in basic science might have led to answers to some of the key validity questions raised by earlier generations of scientists. Polygraph techniques might have been modified to incorporate new knowledge, or the polygraph might have been abandoned in favor of more valid techniques for detecting deception. As we have suggested, the failure to make progress seems to be structural, rather than a failure of individuals. We continue this issue in Chapter 8, where we offer some recommendations for redesigning the research enterprise that might address the structural impediments to progress.

CONCLUSIONS

One cannot have strong confidence in polygraph testing or any other technique for the physiological detection of deception without an adequate theoretical and scientific base. A solid theoretical and scientific base can give confidence about the robustness of a test across examinees and settings and against the threat of countermeasures and can lead to its improvement over time. The evidence and analysis presented in this chapter lead to several conclusions:

- The scientific base for polygraph testing is far from what one would like for a test that carries considerable weight in national security decision making. Basic scientific knowledge of psychophysiology offers support for expecting polygraph testing to have some diagnostic value, at least among naive examinees. However, the science indicates that there is only limited correspondence between the physiological responses measured by the polygraph and the attendant psychological brain states believed to be associated with deception—in particular, that responses typically taken as indicating deception can have other causes.

- The accuracy of polygraph tests can be expected to vary across situations because physiological responses vary systematically across examinees and social contexts in ways that are not yet well understood and that can be very difficult to control. Basic research in social psychophysiology suggests, for example, that the accuracy of polygraph tests may be affected when examiners or examinees are members of socially stigmatized groups and may be diminished when an examiner has incorrect expectations about an examinee's likely innocence or guilt. In addition, accuracy can be expected to differ between event-specific and screening applications of the same test format because the relevant questions must be asked in generic form in the screening applications. Accuracy can also be expected to vary because different examiners have different ways to create the desired emotional climate for a polygraph examination, including using different questions, with the result that examinees' physiological responses may vary with the way the same test is administered. This variation may be random, or it may be a systematic function of the examiner's expectancies or aspects of the examiner-examinee interaction. In either case, it places limits on the accuracy that can be consistently expected from polygraph testing.

- Basic psychophysiology gives reason for concern that effective countermeasures to the polygraph may be possible. All of the physiological indicators measured by the polygraph can be altered by conscious efforts through cognitive or physical means, and all the physiological responses believed to be associated with deception can also have other causes. As a consequence, it is possible that examinees could take conscious actions that create false polygraph readings.

- Available knowledge about the physiological responses measured by the polygraph suggests that there are serious upper limits in principle to the diagnostic accuracy of polygraph testing, even with advances in measurement and scoring techniques. Polygraph accuracy may be reaching a point of diminishing returns. There is only limited room to improve the detection of deception from the physiological responses the polygraph measures.

• Although the basic science indicates that polygraph testing has inherent limits regarding its potential accuracy, it is possible for a test with such limits to attain sufficient accuracy to be useful in practical situations, and it is possible to improve accuracy within the test's inherent limits. These possibilities must be examined empirically with regard to particular applications. We examine the evidence on polygraph test performance in Chapters 4 and 5.

• The bulk of polygraph research can accurately be characterized as atheoretical. The field includes little or no research on a variety of variables and mechanisms that link deception or other phenomena to the physiological responses measured in polygraph tests.

• Research on the polygraph has not progressed over time in the manner of a typical scientific field. Polygraph research has failed to build and refine its theoretical base, has proceeded in relative isolation from related fields of basic science, and has not made use of many conceptual, theoretical, and technological advances in basic science that are relevant to the physiological detection of deception. As a consequence, the field has not accumulated knowledge over time or strengthened its scientific underpinnings in any significant manner.

• There has been no serious effort in the U.S. government to develop the scientific base for the psychophysiological detection of deception by the polygraph or any other technique, even though criticisms of the polygraph's scientific foundation have been raised prominently for decades. The reason for this failure is primarily structural. Because polygraph and other related research is managed and supported by national security and law enforcement agencies that do not operate in a culture of science to meet their needs for detecting deception and that also believe in and are committed to the polygraph, this research is not structured within these agencies to give basic science its appropriate place in the development of techniques for the physiological detection of deception.

NOTES

1. Proponents of concealed information tests argue that they rest on a different series of inferential links because the tests do not detect deception and that their admissibility in courts should therefore be judged against different criteria than comparison question tests under the *Daubert* rule (Ben-Shakhar, Bar-Hillel, and Kremnitzer, 2002). We discuss the different theoretical underpinnings of polygraph testing later in the chapter.

2. The questions in this section are phrased with the presumption that the polygraph is being used to detect deception. With slightly different phrasing, they can be used to assess the validity of a polygraph test procedure that is being used to detect the examinee's possession of concealed information.

3. The relevant-irrelevant test format has not been the subject of sophisticated theory development or of much testing to establish construct validity. Most polygraph researchers now consider the technique fundamentally flawed on a theoretical level (e.g., Raskin and Honts, 2002).

4. For this point to apply under orienting theory, it is necessary to assume that the orienting response is stronger for the specific issues covered by the relevant questions than for the issues evoked by the more generic comparison questions.

5. The theories of the relevant-irrelevant and concealed knowledge polygraph techniques are somewhat different on this point. In the relevant-irrelevant test, truthful people are expected to be equally reactive to relevant and irrelevant questions, while guilty people are expected to react more strongly to the relevant questions. In the concealed knowledge test format, people without concealed knowledge will have the same reaction to all the questions in a set, while people with concealed knowledge will show a stronger response to the relevant question—the one that touches on their concealed knowledge.

6. Some commonly used scoring systems give each physiological response equal weight. These include 7-point systems that compare each polygraph channel for each relevant question against the same channel for the appropriate comparison question and then sum these scores across channels. Other scoring methods, including the global, impressionistic scoring used for the relevant-irrelevant format and the various computerized scoring techniques for comparison question testing, do not treat the channels as having equal weight. Computer scoring systems give numerical weights to different channels (or measures using the channels) according to their value in discriminating truthful from deceptive responses in test samples.

7. More specifically, arousal theory reflects the following empirical observations (see Cacioppo et al., 1992): (a) the autonomic control of the heart, smooth muscles, and glands is divisible into the sympathetic and parasympathetic systems; (b) postganglionic sympathetic fibers innervate the effector, where their catabolic (energetic) actions are typically mediated directly by the postganglionic release of norepinephrine and indirectly through adrenal medullary catecholamines; and (c) postganglionic parasympathetic fibers innervate specific effectors, where their anabolic (energy-conserving) actions are mediated by the neurotransmitter acetylcholine through muscarinic receptors that are not activated by blood borne catecholamines.

8. We note that some psychological tests that have been constructed in a purely empirical manner can support fairly confident inferences about psychological processes. Confidence in such tests is based on a solid empirical record demonstrating that the particular test procedures used have consistently yielded accurate inferences with people like those being tested. This argument does not strongly justify polygraph testing for two reasons. One is that available theory raises specific doubts about the

validity of inferences of deception with certain populations and in certain situations that have not been resolved by empirical research. These issues are raised later in the chapter; the relevant empirical data are discussed in Chapter 5. The other is that in the case of polygraph security screening, the empirical record necessary for an atheoretical justification of the test does not exist, and is unlikely to be developed, because of the difficulty of building a large database of test results on active spies, saboteurs, or terrorists.

9.   This is the case even when the response reflects a change in the activation of a specific region of cortical tissue (see Sarter, Berntson, and Cacioppo, 1996).

10. Converging evidence is always important in making inferences using the subtractive method because this method assumes that components or processes can be inserted or deleted without altering other components or processes (e.g., relevant and control questions differ only because the relevant questions have special meaning to deceptive individuals). This may not be true in relevant-irrelevant and comparison question polygraph tests. In concealed information tests, when only those with the information can identify the relevant items, a differential physiological response provides the basis for a stronger inference.

11. Both terms are equal to P(deception AND physiological activity). Conditional probabilities show what proportion of a restricted sample have a certain property; thus they are ratios. The two conditional probabilities have the same numerator P(deception AND physiological activity), but different denominators p(deception) and p(physiological activity). With low base rates of deception and somewhat inaccurate tests, p(deception) can be orders of magnitude smaller than p(physiological activity), and so p(deception given physiological activity) can be orders of magnitude smaller than p(physiological activity given deception).

12. Tests that are less accurate than DNA matching can have diagnostic value for detecting deception even though they are imperfect. Chapter 7 discusses the policy issues raised by using such tests, either alone or in combination with other sources of information, in security screening and other applications.

13. If a test is 100 percent specific, the prosecutor's fallacy is not a fallacy. For example, given the current state of DNA matching, finding blood with DNA that matches the defendant's on the victim means it is virtually certain that the defendant was there and constitutes strong evidence against the defendant unless the defense has another reasonable explanation of how the blood got there.

14. Some of these threats to validity can be ruled out if the test design provides adequate standardization or other controls. Efforts to standardize the interview process and the specific relevant and comparison questions across examinations can be helpful in this regard, and there is some such standardization in some tests, such as the Test of Espionage and Sabotage, that are used in federal employee screening programs. In addition, the concealed knowledge test approach rules out the possibility that extraneous factors may elicit differential responses to relevant and comparison questions by innocent examinees because they have no way of knowing which are the relevant questions.

15. The effect might be different on concealed information tests. Examinees who do not have concealed information would not be able to respond differentially to relevant questions on these tests because they do not have the information needed to recognize those questions. Examinees who have concealed information, however, might respond differentially to relevant questions, with the possible result that the rate of false negative errors would be lower for stigmatized than unstigmatized groups.

16. According to signal detection theory, it would be appropriate for expectancies about the probability that an examinee is deceptive to be reflected in the decision about what

threshold to use for judging a test result to indicate deception (see Green and Swets, 1966). Such changes do not alter the accuracy of the test. We are referring here to a different phenomenon, in which expectancies alter the social interaction in the test and through this interaction, affect the examinee's physiological responses in ways unrelated to truth or deception. Such phenomena do alter the accuracy of the test.

17. This problem may be less serious for concealed knowledge tests than for other test formats because innocent examinees in that format cannot discriminate between relevant and comparison questions. The problem is not completely obviated, however, because extraneous psychological phenomena can differentially affect the responses of examinees who have concealed knowledge and of all examinees in the event that the examiner's knowledge of the identity of the relevant questions is subtly communicated to them.

18. In some cases, equipment manufacturers will not reveal exactly what is being measured.

19. Unpublished letter commenting on the work of Marston, dated December 14, 1917, from John F. Shepard to Major Robert M. Yerkes, attached to minutes of the 6th meeting of Committee on Psychology, National Research Council.

4

Evidence from Polygraph Research: Qualitative Assessment

The basic science relevant to the polygraph suggests that it can at best be an imperfect instrument, but it leaves unclear the degree of imperfection. In this and the next chapter we evaluate the empirical evidence on error rates from scientific studies of polygraph testing. Our dual purposes are to gauge the levels of accuracy (in technical terms, criterion validity) that have been observed in research contexts and to assess the extent to which results of past empirical polygraph research can be relied upon for estimates of the test's accuracy in real-world settings. We undertook this task through a systematic literature review (detailed in Appendix G). The literature review includes studies of specific-incident as well as screening polygraph testing, even though the main purpose of this study is to draw conclusions about screening. We examined the broader literature because the empirical research on polygraph screening is too limited to support any judgments and because it is possible to gain useful insights about the potential value of polygraph screening from examining the evidence on polygraph test accuracy in specific-incident applications.

This chapter provides a qualitative assessment of research on polygraph validity. The next chapter discusses the collective quantitative findings of the studies we reviewed and the empirical data pertaining to specific issues, including questioning technique, subpopulations of examinees, and countermeasures.

OVERVIEW

There have been a number of previous reviews of the validity of the polygraph and related techniques (e.g., Levey, 1988; U.S. Office of Technology Assessment, 1983; see also Lykken, 1981; Murphy, 1993), each of which has examined partially overlapping sets of studies, though it is unlikely that any review (including ours) covers every study done. What is remarkable, given the large body of relevant research, is that claims about the accuracy of the polygraph made today parallel those made throughout the history of the polygraph: practitioners have always claimed extremely high levels of accuracy, and these claims have rarely been reflected in empirical research. Levey's (1988) analysis suggests that conclusions about the accuracy of the polygraph have not changed substantially since the earliest empirical assessments of this technique and that the prospects for improving accuracy have not brightened over many decades.

We used several methods to gather as many polygraph validation studies for review as possible (see Appendix G). Our search resulted in 217 research reports of 194 separate studies (some studies appeared in more than one report). The committee next determined which studies were of sufficient quality to include in our review. We agreed on six minimal criteria for further consideration:

(1) documentation of examination procedures sufficient to allow a basic replication;

(2) independently determined truth;

(3) inclusion of both guilty and innocent individuals as determined by truth criteria;

(4) sufficient information for quantitative estimation of accuracy;

(5) polygraph scoring conducted blind to information about truth; and,

(6) in experimental studies, appropriate assignment to experimental groups germane to estimating accuracy (mainly, guilt and innocence).

Our detailed review by staff selected 102 studies that deserved further examination by the committee because they met all the criteria or were of sufficient interest on other grounds. Each of these studies was assigned to two committee members for coding on 16 study characteristics that the committee judged to be potentially relevant to an assessment of the polygraph's accuracy. (Appendix G provides details on the committee's process.)

We conducted a systematic review of research but not a meta-analysis for two basic reasons.[1] First, the studies of adequate quality are too heterogeneous and the numbers of each type too few to allow us to deal with the heterogeneity in an adequate statistical way. Second, because most of the available studies bear only indirectly on applications to security screening, using precise statistical models to summarize the findings would not contribute much to our purpose. Rather than developing and testing meta-analytic models, we have taken the simpler and less potentially misleading approach of presenting descriptive summaries and graphs. Because the studies vary greatly in quality and include several with extreme outcomes due to small size, sampling variability, bias, or nongeneralizable features of their study designs, we did not give much weight to the studies with outcomes at the extremes of the group. Instead, we focused on outcomes in the middle half of the range in terms of accuracy. For the purpose of this study, this focus reveals what the empirical research shows about the accuracy of polygraph testing.

The polygraph studies that met our criteria for consideration do not generally reach the high levels of research quality desired in science. Only 57 of the 194 studies (30 percent) that we examined both met minimal standards of scientific adequacy and presented useful data for quantifying criterion validity. Of these 57, only 18 percent and 9 percent, respectively, received average internal validity and salience ratings of 2 or better on a 5-point scale (on which 1 is the best possible score; see Appendix G for the rating system). These ratings mean that relatively few of the studies are of the quality level typically needed for funding by the U.S. National Science Foundation or the U.S. National Institutes of Health. This assessment of the general quality of this literature as relatively low coincides with the assessments in other reviews (e.g., U.S. Office of Technology Assessment, 1983; Levey, 1988; Fiedler, Schmid, and Stahl, 2002). It partly reflects the inherent difficulties of doing high-quality research in this area. The fact that a sizable number of polygraph studies have nevertheless appeared in good-quality, peer-reviewed journals probably reflects two facts: the practical importance of the topic and the willingness of journals to publish laboratory studies that are high in internal validity but relatively low in salience to real-world application.

The types of studies that are most scientifically compelling for evaluating a technology with widespread field application are only lightly represented in the polygraph literature. Laboratory or simulation studies are most compelling when they examine the theoretical bases for a technique or when they provide information on its performance that can be extrapolated to field settings on the basis of a relevant and empirically supported theoretical foundation. Field studies are most valuable when they involve controlled performance comparisons, where either the field system is experimentally manipulated according to the subtraction principle (see Chapter 3) or where observational data are collected systematically from the field system to develop models suggesting what actual manipulation might produce.

The relevance of the available research to security screening applications is far less than would be desirable. Only one flawed study investigates a real polygraph screening program, and the simulated screening studies are too closely tied to specific mock crimes to simulate adequately the generic nature of polygraph screening questions. Moreover, all of the studies available to us were conducted on samples with base rates of guilt far above the extremely low rates typical of employee security screening programs, so that generalization from those studies to screening applications is quite problematic. (We address the base rate problem in detail in Chapter 7.)

LABORATORY STUDIES

For a variety of understandable practical reasons, the great majority of polygraph validation studies have been laboratory based. This research has consisted predominantly of efforts to measure test accuracy in simulated settings or compare accuracy across methods of testing or test interpretation. There has been relatively little attention to issues of theory, as noted in Chapter 3. For instance, very few studies have investigated threats to validity that seem potentially important on theoretical grounds, such as effects of stigma and expectancy. As a result, serious open questions remain about the basis for generalizing beyond the laboratory situations. The laboratory studies are also inconsistent regarding their attention to methodological controls. We found numerous studies that provide tight control in one or more respects but omit control in others. In addition, most studies have presented the data in terms of one or two cutoff points for scoring, preventing exploration of how the tradeoff between false positives and false negatives might vary with slightly different applications of the same testing approach. Although valuable laboratory studies have been done, they are relatively few in number and leave us with limited enthusiasm for this body of research as a whole.

EXPERIMENTAL FIELD STUDIES

The most compelling type of field validation study is an experimental field study, one in which a variable of interest is manipulated among polygraph examinations given in a real-life polygraph testing context, for example, the context of an actual security screening program. The variable of greatest interest is usually guilt/innocence or deception/truthfulness on relevant questions, a variable that is difficult, though not impossible, to manipulate in a field setting. Other variables are also of considerable interest, including whether the polygraph leads are connected to a polygraph or a bogus source of chart output, how the physiological responses are translated into chart output (e.g., electrodermal response measured as resistance or conductance), how the questions are asked, and how often screening is done. We found no such field experiments in the entire literature on polygraph validity.

Significant obstacles to high-quality polygraph field research are readily apparent. Good field research may require substantial funding, interagency cooperation, and enough time to resolve major logistical, ethical, interprofessional, and political problems, especially when experimental manipulation is intended. Nevertheless, so long as these obstacles are allowed to impede research, the scarcity of good field studies will remain a substantial impediment to appraising the scientific validity of the polygraph.

Some of these obstacles could be overcome. For the sake of discussion, we suggest what field studies of polygraphy would be like if they adhered to the highest standards of scientific rigor. Experimental studies would randomly assign subjects to one of two or more methods for detection of deception. These might be selected using the subtraction principle: e.g., one method might be the Test of Espionage and Sabotage (TES), conducted according to current U.S. Department of Energy practice, while the other might be the same test using polygraph tracings fed into the instrument from another subject, perhaps in an adjacent room, a bogus pipeline. Or one method might be a specific-incident control question polygraph test that represented electrodermal response as either skin conductance or skin resistance, with all other factors totally comparable. In either case, research subjects and, to the extent feasible, polygraph examiners and quality control chart scorers would be blinded to which form of testing was used. Subsequently, information would be obtained about test accuracy for each individual by some method that assesses truth independently of the polygraph test result. (Perhaps the test results would be filed away and not acted on.) The data to support the truth categorization would be collected uniformly and in a standard fashion over time, without regard to which form of polygraph test the subject had taken or the test results. After testing a large number of examinees and observation over a sufficient period to determine truth, the best procedure would be determined according to some predetermined criterion, such as the method that identifies the most spies for each false positive result. If randomized experimentation could not be done, data would be collected in a uniform fashion on whatever testing was performed and compared against truth, determined in a uniform fashion independent of test results.

It is easy to see from an organizational point of view why such research has not been done. The logistics of blind administration of alternative polygraph tests would require a large staff, would be technically complex, and might even require the use of custom-designed physical facilities. A method for ultimately assessing truth independently of the polygraph test may not be readily available, or it may be unavailable at an acceptable cost (or even at any cost). Moreover, polygraph examiners and the law enforcement and intelligence agencies that employ them are confident from experience in the value of polygraph testing. They might therefore find any research that might degrade test performance or that requires withholding of the test results from use to be ethically unacceptable. Furthermore, in today's litigious environment, errors made under research conditions might expose individual researchers and government agencies to a liability risk. In combination, these are powerful impediments to high-quality experimental field research on polygraph testing.

However, polygraph testing leads to important, even life and death, decisions about the examinee, and it also affects families, associates, and national security; consequently, it is worth making an effort to use the best feasible research designs to evaluate it. All of the above obstacles have close counterparts in clinical medical research, and research methods have been developed over half a century to largely overcome them or limit their effects. Billions of dollars are now spent annually on medical clinical trials because the importance of high-quality research is clear, and researchers have developed effective ways of dealing with the obstacles. During this period the federal government, through the U.S. National Institutes of Health, promoted the development of an entire field of methodological research for medical science that now has its own professional societies and journals and provides the scientific basis for an evidence-based medicine movement that is growing rapidly worldwide. Important, related progress has been made in other fields of practice, such as education and public health. We do not mean to conclude that a methodologically clean, definitive "clinical trial" of polygraph testing is now or necessarily ever will be possible. The problems of designing experiments that randomly assign examinees to be truthful or deceptive in a situation with stakes high enough to approach those in a criminal investigation or employee security screening situation are extreme, and they may be insurmountable. For example, examinees assigned to be deceptive could be expected to differentially withdraw from the experiment. Nevertheless, the medical research experience shows that major scientific advances occur even in the face of methodological limitations similar to those affecting polygraph research and that such limitations can often be successfully addressed. Some polygraph researchers appreciate the potential gains from using stronger research designs, but the lesson has not been applied to field experimentation.

OBSERVATIONAL FIELD STUDIES

Observational field studies are useful when laboratory experimentation has limited external validity, and they are necessary when field experiments are impossible or impractical. Methodology for the design and interpretation of observational research has seen extensive development over many decades by researchers in the social sciences and public health. As with clinical experimentation, issues once addressed only with qualitative methods, such as causal inference from observational data, are now the focus of competing quantitative mathematical models.

In typologies of observational studies, the top rungs of a generally accepted quality hierarchy are occupied by studies that, despite the absence of experimental control, do incorporate controls for potential biases and for confounding by extraneous factors that most closely mimic those of designed experiments. The highest rated among these studies are prospective cohort studies, often termed quasi-experimental studies, in which a cohort (a sample that is scientifically chosen from a carefully defined population) is followed over time with data collected by a design specified in advance. Such studies differ from actual experiments in a single respect: the exposure of subjects to respective levels of the experimental variable of interest is not randomly assigned and is outside of the experimenter's control. In other respects, such studies incorporate uniform observational protocols designed to minimize measurement biases and to detect and allow statistical adjustment for inequities, due to selection biases or serendipity, that might distort (confound) statistical relationships of primary interest. Thus, measurement and collection of appropriate research data is under the control of the experimenter even though the experimental variable is not. For the polygraph, an example would be a screening program in which the decision about how often employees are retested is made by agency staff rather than assigned at random. It would be possible, at least in principle, to assess the deterrent value of polygraph rescreening by comparing the rates of independently verified security violations among subgroups that have been retested at different intervals.

Lower in the quality hierarchy are observational studies in which the selection, implementation, and recording of measurements, and hence data quality and potential for bias, are less subject to the experimenter's control. Since the timing of observation and data collection correspond less closely to those of an experiment, there is the possibility of inconsistency in the temporal sequencing of events and, thus, confusion between causes and effects. As a general rule, the best such studies are retrospective cohort studies, that is, cohort studies with data collection after the events of interest, and population-based case-control studies. An example is the comparison of past performances on screening polygraph examinations between a group of employees later found to have violated computer security protocols and another group of employees of the same agency, similarly observed, for whom no violations were found.

Below these in the hierarchy are case-control studies not linked to a defined population; cross-sectional surveys, in which correlations are observed among multiple variables ascertained at the same time (e.g., polygraph tests and intensive security investigations); case series without comparison groups for control; and finally, individual case studies. All these can provide useful information, especially for generating hypotheses, but they are vulnerable to error from too many sources to be considered scientifically reliable on their own except in very rare circumstances. We note that no matter how well they are conducted, none of these study designs is capable of estimating the probability of any future event, because they do not observe forward in time a representative group of individuals to determine the actual probability of the target events occurring in subgroups of interest (e.g., people given or not given polygraph examinations as part of a security investigation).

Two additional observations are necessary to place our views on polygraph field studies in perspective. First, the scientific value of any observational study assessing the connection between two variables, such as polygraph result and deception, or medical therapy and survival and therefore the study's position in the above hierarchy is critically dependent on the manner in which the study sample is assembled. In particular, if inclusion in the sample is related to both variables in the study design, there is a serious risk of major distortion of the statistical accounting process and of spurious scientific results. An example is the common procedure in polygraph field research of defining truth by confession of the polygraph examinee or someone else. Such research necessarily omits cases in which there was no confession. This procedure probably yields an upward bias in the estimates of polygraph accuracy because the relationship between polygraph results and guilt is likely to be stronger in cases that led to confessions than in the entire population of cases. This bias can occur because definitive polygraph results can influence the likelihood of confession and the direction taken by criminal investigations (see Iacono, 1991, for a discussion; we offer a quantitative example below).

Second, the effectiveness of opportunistic studies that do not control the data collection process is largely determined by the degree of completeness, objectivity, and accuracy with which relevant variables are recorded by individuals with no awareness of the research process. The reliability of clinical and administrative data tends to vary in proportion to the relevance and immediacy of their use to the staff recording the data (or their supervisors). In medical charts, for example, observations of the variables critical to immediate patient care are generally accurate while others perhaps needed later for retrospective research are often omitted or present only by implication. Polygraph research would present a similar situation.

We appreciate the inherent difficulty of determining the truth for observational polygraph field studies. Although we applaud the labor of those investigators who have undertaken such studies, we are unable to place a great deal of faith in this small body of work, especially regarding its implications for screening. We found only one field study of polygraph screening with verifiable outcome data relevant to assessing accuracy; its results and limitations are discussed in Chapter 5. The annual reports that polygraph programs provide to Congress do not provide a basis for assessing the accuracy of polygraph testing, as we have discussed.

We found no specific-incident field investigations at the higher levels of the research hierarchy outlined above. The literature revealed no experiments and no cohort or case-control studies that were prospectively designed and implemented. The best criminal field investigations we reviewed were observational case-control studies using data on truth obtained retrospectively from administrative databases. In these studies, the past polygraph judgments (or reevaluations of past polygraph records) with respect to individuals whose deceptiveness or nondeceptiveness had subsequently been established were reviewed, tabulated, and compared. This case-control approach is an observational research design of intermediate strength, weakened in most of these studies by heterogeneity of polygraph procedure; lack of prospective, research-oriented data collection; and the probable contamination of sample selection by the polygraph result. Data were generally not provided on whether confessions occurred during the polygraph examination or subsequently as a direct consequence of being judged deceptive on the polygraph examination. Neither were data provided on the extent to which a suspect's polygraph results led an investigation to be redirected, leading to the determination of the truth. Both these outcomes of the polygraph examination are good for law enforcement, but they lead to overestimates of polygraph accuracy.

Although we excluded studies that lack independent evidence of truth, field study procedures still tend to overestimate the accuracy of the polygraph. The problem, in technical terms, is that these studies use the probabilities of past truthful or deceptive polygraph outcomes among subsets of examinees later proven to be truthful or deceptive to estimate the probabilities of future polygraph outcomes among all examinees, including those for whom the truth cannot be independently established.

The failure to establish truth independently and the consequent reliance on the easy cases can lead to seriously distorted inferences.

We provide an example to show how this might occur. Suppose, for instance, that in a certain city (a) the polygraph correctly detects deception in two-thirds of guilty suspects; and (b) due to belief of both police and suspects in the polygraph's accuracy, police are three times as likely to elicit a confession from guilty suspects who appear deceptive on the polygraph as from those who appear truthful. For instance, suppose that of 300 guilty suspects, 200 fail the polygraph and 100 pass it, and that 30 percent of guilty suspects who fail the polygraph confess, compared with only 10 percent for guilty subjects who have passed. Then 10 percent of the 100 passing suspects, or 10 suspects, would be expected to confess, as would about 30 percent of the 200 failing suspects, or 60 suspects. If none of the remaining 230 guilty suspects is definitively proven innocent or guilty, only the 70 confessed suspects enter the population of a case-control study as guilty cases. Although only 67 percent of all guilty suspects appeared deceptive on the polygraph, the case-control study would show that 60 out of 70, or 86 percent of the guilty cases confirmed by confessions, had given deceptive polygraph results. A validity study that uses cases confirmed by confession would therefore estimate a sensitivity of 86 percent, while the sensitivity under actual field conditions is only 67 percent. If, instead of 67 percent, we suppose that the polygraph has a sensitivity of 80 percent, a similar calculation shows that the case-control study would include 78 guilty suspects and would overestimate the sensitivity as 92 percent. A similar bias could exaggerate the test's specificity and any other measures of polygraph accuracy estimated from the case-control sample.

In summary, we were unable to find any field experiments, field quasi-experiments, or prospective research-oriented data collection specifically designed to address polygraph validity and satisfying minimal standards of research quality. The field research that we reviewed used passive observational research designs of no more than moderate methodological strength, weakened by the admittedly difficult problem that truth could not be known in all cases and by the possible biases introduced by different approaches to dealing with this problem. In addition, because field examiners normally have background information about the examinees before the test begins, there is the possibility that their expectations have direct or indirect effects on the polygraph test data that cannot be removed even if the charts are independently scored. Thus, field studies contain a bias of potentially serious magnitude toward overestimating the accuracy that would be observed if the truth were known for everyone who took a polygraph test.

AN APPROACH FOR PLANNED FIELD RESEARCH

Polygraph field research poses difficult design issues, and we readily acknowledge the lack of a template for dealing simultaneously with all the problems and obtaining rapid, definitive results. Nevertheless, it is possible to do better field research than we have found in the literature and, over time, to use admittedly imperfect research designs, both experimental and observational, to advance knowledge and build methodological understanding, leading to better research design in the future. To accomplish these ends requires a key ingredient that has been missing from polygraph field research: active, prospective research planning. Prospectively planned field research generally produces better information than that obtained from opportunistic samples. As is true in most areas of human activity, higher quality comes at higher cost. Such research would require extensive participation by agencies that currently use polygraph testing and a dramatically higher level of research funding than is currently available for polygraph investigations.

We provide a few examples of the types of planned approaches that might be considered, but that we have not found in the publicly available polygraph research literature.

• Prospective, research-oriented polygraph logs might be recorded for an extended series of routine field examinations. These logs would include information on exactly which question or questions produced responses indicating deception, precisely when in the polygraph examination admissions were made (in particular, whether these were before, during, or after testing), and whether admissions were made in response to an examiner's claim of deception supported by a polygraph chart, or to other stimuli.

• Actors or other mock subjects could be trained to be deceptive or nondeceptive, much as in laboratory mock crime experiments but more elaborately, and inserted sporadically for polygraph testing in field settings: for example, they could be presented to polygraph examiners as applicants for sensitive security positions.

• Selected physiological responses of genuine polygraph subjects could be concealed from the examiner in favor of dummy tracings, for instance, of an alternate subject listening to the same questions in another room. The genuine responses of the examinee could be retained and still used to guide a follow-up interrogation or investigation if the charts indicate such a need.

• Polygraph machines that can record a physiological response in more than one way (e.g., electrodermal response presented as conductance or resistance or presented as a bogus signal) might be used in field or laboratory testing. The form of chart output provided to the examiner could be varied randomly, and the examiners' conclusions compared. In the example of electrodermal response, polygraph theory and basic physiology imply that conductance should give superior performance. This sort of test would bear on the construct validity of electrodermal response as an indicator of deception.

• "Blind" scorers might be used to score sets of polygraph charts, including charts of confessed foreign espionage agents whose activities were uncovered by methods independent of the polygraph and charts of other randomly selected individuals who underwent examinations in the same polygraph programs but who are not now known to be spies. While the bias issue raised above in connection with criminal incident field studies is also of concern here, its importance would be diminished by restricting the analysis to agents uncovered without the polygraph, by random selection of the comparison group, and by appropriately narrow interpretation of the results.

This list is not offered as a set of research recommendations, but as examples of the kinds of research activities that might be considered in a program of actively designed field research on methods for the psychophysiological detection of deception. Such a program would not be expected to yield dramatic short-term results, nor would its long-term evolution be predictable. Experience in many areas of science suggests, however, that a program of actively designed field research would lead to innovations and improvements in methodology and to observations that might justify the effort. (We discuss research priorities in Chapter 8.)

BIAS, CONFLICT OF INTEREST, AND
UNSCIENTIFIC DECISION MAKING

In the course of our study we have seen or heard numerous disturbing allegations about the way polygraph research decisions have been made, particularly in federal agencies that have supported this research. We have seen or heard reports of researchers being prohibited from presenting studies at professional society meetings (see, e.g., Honts, 1994: Note 5); a report of a researcher being required to remove his name from a refereed journal article, apparently because the content displeased his employer (Furedy, 1993); a report of potentially inflammatory findings being suppressed and recalled from distribution; and various reports of researchers having been removed summarily from their duties or their positions, with reasons to believe that this might have been done because of the directions or results of their research. These reports are not ancient history, though they are not current either: most appear to have dated from the early 1990s.[2] We have not investigated these reports to determine their veracity—this was not our charge—but they appear to us to be sufficient in number and credibility to deserve mention. It is important that polygraph research be organized so as to minimize the possibility of such situations in the future.

We have also experienced difficulty in gaining access to material necessary to evaluate reports of polygraph research. We wrote to all federal agencies that use the polygraph for employee screening to request studies and other information necessary to conduct a scientific evaluation of polygraph validity, including both unclassified and classified information. In some ways, the agencies were highly responsive. We received large amounts of useful information, and we learned that the kinds of data we wanted on some topics are not collected by any of the agencies in the desired form. In other instances, though, we were left unsatisfied. Two agencies did not provide us with specific unclassified research reports that we requested.[3] Also, we were advised by officials from DOE and DoDPI that there was information relevant to our work, classified at the secret level, particularly with regard to polygraph countermeasures. In order to review such information, several committee members and staff obtained national security clearances at the secret level. We were subsequently told by officials of the Central Intelligence Agency and DoDPI that there were no completed studies of polygraph countermeasures at the secret level; we do not know whether there are any such studies at a higher level of classification. Accordingly, our analyses of research on countermeasures are based only on unclassified studies.

These experiences leave us with unresolved concerns about whether federal agencies sponsoring polygraph research have acted in ways that suppress or conceal research results or that drive out researchers whose results might have questioned the validity of current polygraph practice. If the agencies have done or are doing these things, the result would be to introduce a pro-polygraph bias into polygraph research in general, as well as to raise doubts about whether it is advisable for reviewers to apply the usual practice of trusting in the accuracy and completeness of reports in the scientific literature. In addition, any review of the literature, including this one, would be subject to question on the grounds of bias in the entire body of polygraph research.

Such bias is possible because a large segment of polygraph research in the United States has been supported by a small number of agencies that depend on the polygraph in their counterintelligence work. The effect might be something like the "file-drawer effect" commonly noted in meta-analytic research (Rosenthal, 1979, 1980). The nature of the file-drawer problem is that studies that fail to find significant effects or associations are believed to be less likely to be published because journals are disinclined to publish studies that lack clear findings. Thus, they are not submitted for publication or are rejected, and the published literature is, in effect, incomplete. This effect biases the literature in the direction of appearing to show stronger relationships than would otherwise be evident. If research funding agencies are suppressing research, the effects would be similar, though for a different reason. Studies that call the validity of polygraph testing into question, whether by failing to find accurate detection or by finding that accuracy is not robust across the range of situations in which polygraph tests are used, would fail to appear in literature searches.

We have not investigated the various allegations, so we are not in a position to evaluate the extent to which the alleged activities may have biased the literature. In Chapter 5 we do compare the polygraph accuracy estimates that come from studies with different sources of funding as a way of shedding some light on the possible effect of bias on the research literature, and find little difference. However, the distinctions between funding sources of these studies were often blurred.

Issues of conflict of interest reflect a serious structural problem with polygraph research. For the most part, the scientists involved in this area and the agencies involved in sponsoring and funding this research have a vested interest in supporting particular sets of conclusions about the reliability and validity of the polygraph (Levey, 1988). For example, U.S. agencies charged with initiating and sponsoring polygraph research (e.g., the U.S. Department of Defense Polygraph Institute) are also charged with the mission of training polygraph examiners and developing new polygraph applications. The dual mission of acting as a sponsor for polygraph research and as a sponsor for polygraph practice creates an obvious conflict of interest. Any reasonable investigator would anticipate that certain research questions (e.g., those that question the theory or logic of the polygraph) or certain patterns of results (e.g., those that suggest limited validity or strong susceptibility to countermeasures) will be less welcome by such research sponsors than empirical demonstrations that the polygraph "works."

Because the great bulk of polygraph research has been funded by agencies that rely on the polygraph for law enforcement or counterintelligence purposes, there is a significant potential for bias and conflict of interest in polygraph research. Serious allegations suggest that this potential has at some times been realized. This possibility raises warnings that the entire body of research literature may have a bias toward claims of validity for the polygraph. Using a crude classification method (see Chapter 5), we did not see systematic differences in outcomes of polygraph validation studies between those conducted at or funded by polygraph-related agencies and those with a greater presumed degree of independence. However, this issue remains a concern because of the insularity and close connections among polygraph researchers in government and academia, the associations between some prominent researchers and manufacturers of polygraph equipment, and the limited accessibility of field polygraph data to researchers independent of the organizations that conduct polygraph tests. The credibility of future polygraph research would be enhanced by efforts to insulate it from such real or perceived conflicts of interest (see Chapter 8).

CONCLUSIONS

We find the general quality of research on the criterion validity of the polygraph to be relatively low. This assessment agrees with those of previous reviewers of this field. This situation partly reflects the inherent difficulties of doing high-quality research in this area, but higher quality research designs and methods of data analysis that might have been implemented have generally not been used. Laboratory studies, though important for demonstrating principles, have serious inherent limitations for generalizing to realistic situations, including the fact that the consequences associated with being judged deceptive are almost never as serious as they are in real-world settings. Field studies of polygraph validity have used research designs of no more than moderate methodological strength and are further weakened by the difficulties of independently determining truth and the possible biases introduced by the ways the research has addressed this issue.

NOTES

1. Our definition of meta-analysis is presented in Appendix G, along with a more detailed discussion of our rationale for not conducting one.
2. In recent years, the U.S. Department of Defense Polygraph Institute has been working to put polygraph research on more of a scientific footing by adopting a number of standard procedures for scientific quality control that can only serve to improve research management at the institute and that may already be having such an effect.
3. One of these agencies informed us that it could not provide the requested report in order to protect its sources and methods. The other agency informed us that it would handle our request under the Freedom of Information Act and advised us that its response would not be received until January 2003 at the earliest, well after the scheduled completion of our study. Both of these unclassified reports have been cited in the open literature.

5

Evidence from Polygraph Research: Quantitative Assessment

This chapter presents our detailed analysis of the empirical research evidence on polygraph test performance. We first summarize the quantitative evidence on the accuracy of polygraph tests conducted on populations of naïve examinees untrained in countermeasures. Although our main focus is polygraph screening, the vast majority of the evidence comes from specific-incident testing in the laboratory or in the field. We then address the limited evidence from studies of actual or simulated polygraph screening. Finally, we address several factors that might affect the accuracy of polygraph testing, at least with some examinees or under some conditions, including individual differences in physiology and personality, drug use, and countermeasures.

SPECIFIC-INCIDENT POLYGRAPH TESTING

Laboratory Studies

For our analysis, we extracted datasets from 52 sets of subjects in the 50 research reports of studies conducted in a controlled laboratory testing environment that met our criteria for inclusion in the quantitative analysis (see Appendix G). These studies include 3,099 polygraph examinations. For the most part, examinees in these studies were drawn by convenience from a limited number of sources that tend to be most readily available in polygraph research environments: university undergraduates (usually but not always psychology students); military trainees; other workplace volunteers; and research subjects recruited through employment agencies. Although samples drawn from these sources are not demographically representative of any population on which polygraph testing is routinely performed, neither is there a specific reason to believe such collections of examinees would be either especially susceptible or refractory to polygraph testing. Since the examinees thus selected usually lack experience with polygraph testing, we will loosely refer to the subjects from these studies as "naïve examinees, untrained in countermeasures." The degree of correspondence between polygraph responsiveness of these examinees and the special populations of national security employees for whom polygraph screening is targeted is unknown.

Many of the studies collected data and performed comparative statistical analyses on the chart scores or other quantitative measures taken from the polygraph tracings; however, they almost invariably reported individual test results in only two or three decision classes. Thus, 34 studies reported data in three categories (deception indicated, inconclusive, and no deception indicated, or comparable classifications), yielding two possible combinations of true positive (sensitivity) and false positive rates, depending on the treatment of the intermediate category. One study reported polygraph chart scores in 11 ranges, allowing extraction of 10 such combinations to be used to plot an empirical receiver operating characteristic (ROC) curve. The remaining 17 used a single cutoff point to categorize subjects relative to deception, with no inconclusive findings allowed. The median sample size of the 52 datasets from laboratory studies was 48, with only one study having fewer than 20 and only five studies having as many as 100 subjects.

Figure 5-1 plots the 95 combinations of observed sensitivity (percent of deceptive individuals judged deceptive) and false positive rate (percent of truthful people erroneously judged deceptive), with straight lines connecting points deriving from the same data set. The results are spread out across the approximately 30 percent of the area to the upper left. Figure 5-2 summarizes the distribution of accuracy indexes (A) that we calculated from the datasets represented in Figure 5-1. As Figure 5-2 shows, the interquartile range of values of A reported for these data sets is from 0.81 to 0.91. The median accuracy index in these data sets is 0.86. The two curves shown in the Figure 5-1 are ROC curves with values of the accuracy index (A) of 0.81 and 0.91.[1]

Three conclusions are clearly illustrated by the figures. First, the data (and their errors of estimate; see Appendix H, Figure H-3) clearly fall above the diagonal line, which represents chance accuracy. Thus, we conclude that features of polygraph charts and the judgments made from them are correlated with deception in a variety of controlled situations

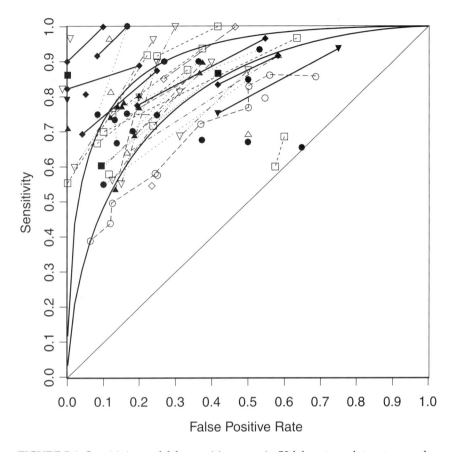

FIGURE 5-1 Sensitivity and false positive rates in 52 laboratory datasets on polygraph validity.
NOTES: Points connected by lines come from the same dataset. The two curves
are symmetrical receiver operating characteristic (ROC) curves with accuracy index (A) values of 0.81 and 0.91.

involving naïve examinees untrained in countermeasures: for such examinees and test contexts, the polygraph has an accuracy greater than chance.
Random variation and biases in study design are highly implausible explanations for these results, and no formal integrative hypothesis test
seems necessary to demonstrate this point.

Second, with few exceptions, the points fall well below the upper left-
hand corner of the figure indicative of perfect accuracy. No formal hypothesis test is needed or appropriate to demonstrate that errors are not
infrequent in polygraph testing.

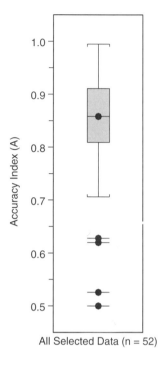

FIGURE 5-2 Accuracy index (A) values from 52 datasets from laboratory polygraph validation studies. The central box contains the middle half of the values of accuracy (A), with the median value marked by a dot and horizontal line. "Whiskers" extend to the largest and smallest values within 1.5 interquartile ranges on either side of the box. Values farther out are marked by detached dots and horizontal lines.

All Selected Data (n = 52)

Third, variability of accuracy across studies is high. This variation is likely due to a combination of several factors: "sampling variation," that is, random fluctuation due to small sample sizes; differences in polygraph performance across testing conditions and populations of subjects; and the varying methodological strengths and weaknesses of these diverse studies. The degree of variation in results is striking. For example, in different studies, when a cutoff is used that yields a false positive rate of roughly 10 percent, the sensitivity—the proportion of guilty examinees correctly identified—ranges from 43 to 100 percent. This range is only moderately narrower, roughly 64 to 100 percent, in studies reporting a cutoff that resulted in 30 percent of truthful examinees being judged deceptive. The errors of estimate for many of the studies fail to overlap with those of many other studies, suggesting that the differences between study results are due to more than sampling variation.

We looked for explanations of this variability as a function of a variety of factors, with little success. One factor on which there has been much contention in the research is test format, specifically, comparison question versus concealed information test formats. Proponents of concealed information tests claim that this format has a different, scientifically stronger rationale than comparison question tests in those limited situations for which both types of tests are applicable. Indeed, the concealed information tests we examined did exhibit higher median accuracy than the comparison question tests, though the observed difference did not attain conventional statistical significance. Specifically, the median accuracy index among 13 concealed information tests was 0.88, with an interquartile range from 0.85 to 0.96, while the corresponding median for 37 comparison question tests was 0.85, with an interquartile range from 0.83 to 0.90. (Two research reports did not fit either of these two test formats.) The arithmetic mean accuracies, and means weighted by sample size or inverse variance, were more similar than the reported medians. We regard the overall evidence regarding comparative accuracy of control question and concealed knowledge test formats as thus suggestive but far from conclusive.

Our data do not suggest that accuracy is associated with the size of the study samples, our ratings of the studies' internal validity and their salience to the field, or the source of funding.[2] We also examined the dates of the studies to see if research progress had tended to lead to improvements in accuracy. If anything, the trend ran against this hypothesis. (Appendix H presents figures summarizing the data on accuracy as a function of several of these other factors.)

It is important to emphasize that these data and their descriptive statistics represent the accuracy of polygraph tests under controlled laboratory conditions with naïve examinees untrained in countermeasures, when the consequences of being judged deceptive are not serious. We discuss below what accuracy might be under more realistic conditions.

Field Studies

Only seven polygraph field studies passed our minimal criteria for review. All involved examination of polygraph charts from law enforcement agencies' or polygraph examiners' case files in relation to the truth as determined by relatively reliable but nevertheless imperfect criteria, including confession by the subject or another party or apparently definitive evidence. The seven datasets include between 25 and 122 polygraph tests, with a median of 100 and a total of 582 tests. Figure 5-3 displays results in the same manner as in Figure 5-1. The accuracy index values (A) range from 0.711 to 0.999, with a median value of 0.89, which, given sampling and other variability, is statistically indistinguishable from the median of 0.86 for the 52 datasets from laboratory studies. There were no obvious relationships between values of A and characteristics of the studies. (Further discussion of these data appears in Appendix H.)

These results suggest that the average accuracy of polygraph tests examined in field research involving specific incident investigations is

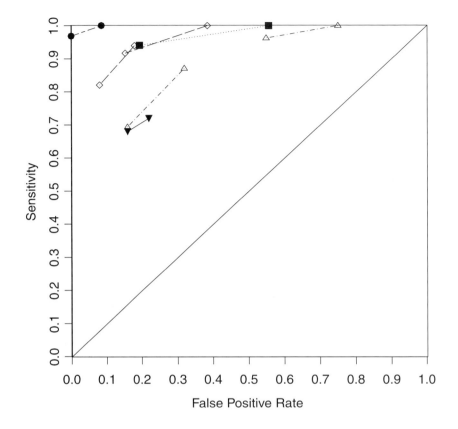

FIGURE 5-3 Sensitivity and false positive rate in seven field datasets on polygraph validity.
NOTE: Points connected by lines come from the same dataset.

similar to and may be slightly higher than that found from polygraph
validity studies using laboratory models. (The interquartile range of accuracy indexes for all 59 datasets, laboratory and field, was from 0.81 to
0.91, the same range as for the laboratory studies alone.) In the next
section, we discuss what these data suggest for the accuracy of the full
population of polygraph tests in the field.

From Research to Reality

Decision makers are concerned with whether the levels of accuracy
achieved in research studies correspond to what can be expected in field
polygraph use. In experimental research, extrapolation of laboratory re-

sults to the field context is an issue of "external validity" of the laboratory studies, that is, of the extent to which the study design, combined with any external knowledge that can be brought to bear, support the relevance of the findings to circumstances other than those of the laboratory study. For example, an externally valid polygraph study would suggest that the accuracy observed in it would also be expected for different types of examinees, e.g., criminals or spies instead of psychology students or respondents to newspaper advertising; interviews of different format or subject matter, e.g., comparison question tests for espionage screening instead of for investigations of a mock theft; examiners with differing backgrounds, e.g., police interrogators rather than full-time federally trained examiners; and in field situations as well as in the laboratory context.

If, as we believe, the polygraph is closely analogous to a clinical diagnostic test, then both psychophysiological theories of polygraph testing and experiences with other clinical diagnostic tests offer useful insights regarding the external validity of laboratory polygraph accuracy for field contexts. Each perspective raises serious concerns about the external validity of results from laboratory testing in the field context.

Higher Stakes. The theory of question construction in the comparison question polygraph technique relies at its core on the hypothesis that emotional or arousal responses under polygraph questioning increase the more concerned examinees are about being deceptive. Thus, innocent examinees are expected to show stronger responses to comparison than to relevant questions. This hypothesis suggests that factors that increase this concern, such as the costs of being judged deceptive, would increase emotional or arousal response and amplify the differences seen between physiological responses to relevant and comparison questions. On the basis of this hypothesis, one might expect polygraph accuracy in laboratory models to be on average somewhat below true accuracy in field practice, where the stakes are higher. There is a plausible contrary hypothesis, however, in which examinees who fear being falsely accused have strong emotional responses that mimic those of the truly deceptive. Under this hypothesis, field conditions might have more false-positive errors than are observed in the laboratory and less accuracy.

Under orienting theory, which provides the rationale for concealed information polygraph testing, it is the recognition of a novel or significant stimulus that is presumed to cause the autonomic response. Increasing the stakes might increase the significance of the relevant item and thus the strength of the orienting response for examinees who have concealed information, with the result that the test will do better at detecting such information as the stakes increase. However, as with arousal-based theories, various hypotheses can be offered about the effect of increased stakes on detection accuracy that are consistent with orienting theory (Ben-Shakhar and Elaad, 2002). Thus, theory and basic research give no clear guidance about whether laboratory conditions underestimate or overestimate the accuracy that can be expected in realistic settings.

Available data are inadequate to test these hypotheses. Two meta-analyses suggest that strength of motivation is positively associated with polygraph accuracy in comparison question (Kircher et al., 1988) and concealed information (Ben-Shakhar and Elaad, 2003) tests, but there are limitations to both analyses that preclude drawing any definite conclusions.[3] In the papers we reviewed, only one of the laboratory models under which specific-incident polygraph testing was evaluated included stakes that were significant to the subjects' future outside the polygraph room and so similar to those in field applications (Ginton et al., 1982). Unfortunately, that study was too small to be useful in evaluating polygraph accuracy.

Evidence from Medical Diagnostic Testing. Substantial experience with clinical diagnostic and screening tests suggests that laboratory models, as well as observational field studies of the type found in the polygraph literature, are likely to overstate true polygraph accuracy. Much information has been obtained by comparing observed accuracy when clinical medical tests are evaluated during development with subsequent accuracy when they become accepted and are widely applied in the field. An important lesson is that medical tests seldom perform as well in general field use as their performance in initial evaluations seems to promise (Ransohoff and Feinstein, 1978; Nierenberg and Feinstein, 1988; Reid, Lachs, and Feinstein, 1995; Fletcher, Fletcher, and Wagner, 1996; Lijmer et al., 1999).

The reasons for the falloff from laboratory and field research settings to performance in general field use are fairly well understood. Initial evaluations are typically conducted on examinees whose true disease status is definitive and uncomplicated by other conditions that might interfere with test accuracy. Samples are drawn, tests conducted, and results analyzed under optimal conditions, including adherence to optimal procedures of sample collection and preservation, use of fresh reagents, and evaluation by expert technicians in laboratories that participated in test development. In contrast, in general field use the test is used in a wide variety of patients, often with many concomitant disease conditions, possibly taking interfering medications, and often with earlier or milder cases of a disease than was the case for the patients during developmental testing. Sample handling, processing, and interpretation are also more variable.

Evaluation of a diagnostic test on general patient samples is often done within the context of ongoing clinical care. This may be problematic if the test is incorporated into the diagnostic process for these patients. Unless special care is taken, other diagnostic findings (e.g., an image) may then influence the interpretation of the test results, or the test result itself may stimulate further investigation that uncovers the final diagnosis against which the test is then evaluated. These types of "contamination" have been extensively studied in relation to what is termed "verification bias" (see Begg and Greenes, 1983). They artificially increase the correlation between a test result and its diagnostic reference, also exaggerating the accuracy of the test relative to what would be seen in field application.

Manifestations of these issues in evaluations of polygraph testing are apparent. Laboratory researchers have the capacity to exercise good control over contamination threats to internal validity. But such research typically uses subjects who are not representative of those examined in the field and are under artificial, uniform, and extremely clear-cut conditions. Polygraph instrumentation and maintenance and examiner training and proficiency are typically well above field situations. Testing is undertaken concurrent with or immediately after the event of interest, so that no period of potential memory loss or emotional distancing intervenes.

Thus, laboratory evaluations that correctly mirror laboratory performance are apt to overestimate field performance. But field evaluations are also apt to overestimate field performance for several reasons. The polygraph counterpart to contamination of the diagnostic process by the test result has been discussed in Chapter 4. So has the counterpart to evaluating only those cases for which the true condition is definitively known. In addition, expectancies, particularly those of examiners, are readily contaminated in both field applications and evaluations of field performance. Polygraph examiners typically enter the examination with information that shapes their expectations about the likelihood that the examinee is guilty. That information can plausibly influence the conduct of the examination in ways that make the test act somewhat as a self-fulfilling prophecy, thus increasing the apparent correspondence between the test result and indicators of truth and giving an overly optimistic assessment of the actual criterion validity of the test procedure.

In view of the above issues, we believe that the range of accuracy indexes (A) estimated from the scientifically acceptable laboratory and field studies, with a midrange between 0.81 and 0.91, most likely overstates true polygraph accuracy in field settings involving specific-incident investigations. We remind the reader that these values of the accuracy index do not translate to percent correct: for any level of accuracy, percent correct depends on the threshold used for making a judgment of deceptiveness and on the base rate of examinees who are being deceptive.

SCREENING STUDIES

The large majority of the studies we reviewed involve specific-issue examinations, in which relevant questions are tightly focused on specific acts. Such studies have little direct relevance for the usual employee screening situation, for three reasons. First, in screening, the test is not focused on a single specific act, so the examiner can only ask questions that are general in nature (e.g., have you had any unauthorized foreign contacts?). These relevant questions are arguably more similar to comparison questions, which also ask about generic past actions, than is the case in specific-incident testing. It is plausible that it will be harder to discriminate lying from truth-telling when the relevant and comparison questions are similar in this respect.

Second, because general questions can refer to a very wide range of behaviors, some of which are not the main targets of interest to the agencies involved (e.g., failure to use a secure screen saver on a classified computer while leaving your office to go to the bathroom), the examinee may be uncertain about his or her own "guilt." Examinees may need to make a series of complex decisions before arriving at a conclusion about what answer would be truthful before deciding whether to tell the truth (so defined) or fail to disclose this truthful answer. Instructions given by examiners may alleviate this problem somewhat, but they are not likely to do so completely unless the examinee reveals the relevant concerns.

Third, the base rate of guilt is usually very low in screening situations, in contrast with specific-incident studies, in which the percentage of examinees who are guilty is often around 50 percent and almost always above 20 percent. Examiners' expectations and the examiner-examinee interaction may both be quite different when the base rates are so different. In addition, the implications of judging an examinee deceptive or truthful are quite different depending on the base rate, as we discuss in detail in Chapter 7.

A small number of studies we reviewed did specifically attempt to estimate the accuracy of the polygraph for screening purposes. Given the centrality of screening to our charge, we offer detailed comments on the four studies that met our minimal quality standards as well as three others that did not. Four of these seven studies (Barland, Honts, and Barger, 1989; U.S. Department of Defense Polygraph Institute, 1995a, 1995b; Reed, no date) featured general questions used in examinations of subjects, some of whom had committed specific programmed transgressions. While this "mock screening situation," as it was termed by Reed (no date), is an incomplete model for actual polygraph screening, the resulting data seem reasonably relevant. An important screening-related question that can be addressed by such studies is whether polygraph-based judgments that an examinee was deceptive on the test are attributable to polygraph readings indicating deception on questions that the examinee actually answered deceptively or to false positive readings on other questions that were answered truthfully. While simply identifying that an examinee was deceptive may be sufficient for many practical purposes, scientific validity requires that polygraph charts show deception only when deception was actually attempted.

Barland, Honts, and Barger (1989) report the results of three experiments. In their first study, the questions and examination methods differed across examiners, and the false negative rate was extremely high (66 percent of the guilty examinees are not identified as deceptive). There was also wide variation in the formats and the standards used to review examinations. In their second study, the authors compared multiple-issue examinations with multiple single-issue examinations. While this study achieved higher overall sensitivity, there was little success in determining which guilty examinees committed which among a number of crimes or offenses. Their third study retested a number of subjects from the first study, and its results are hence confounded. Collectively, results of these three studies do not provide convincing evidence that the polygraph is highly accurate for screening.

Three U.S. Department of Defense Polygraph Institute (DoDPI) studies designed to validate and extend the Test of Espionage and Sabotage (TES) (U.S. Department of Defense Polygraph Institute, 1995a, 1995b; Reed, no date) showed overall results above chance levels of detection but far from perfect accuracy. One of these studies passed our screening (Reed, no date), and it reported data indicating an accuracy (A) of 0.90, corresponding to a sensitivity of approximately 85 percent and a specificity of approximately 78 percent. All three studies share biases that make their results less convincing than those statistics indicate. Deceptive examinees were instructed to confess immediately after being confronted, but nondeceptive examinees whose polygraph tests indicated deception were questioned further, in part to determine whether the examiner could find explanations other than deception for their elevated physiological responses. Such explanations led to removal of some subjects from the studies. Thus, an examiner classifying an examinee as deceptive received immediate feedback on the accuracy of his or her decision, and then had opportunity and incentive, if the result was a false positive error, to find an explanation that would justify removing the examinee from the study. No comparable search was conducted among true positives. This process biases downwards the false positive rate observed in association with any observed sensitivity of the test and therefore biases upwards estimates of accuracy.

The other two studies that passed our screening (Raskin and Kircher, 1990; Honts and Amato, 1999) dealt with deception on preemployment screening tests. They both were pilot studies, had small sample sizes, allocated subjects to other treatment categories than just deceptive/innocent, and had a variety of other methodological problems. The results we could extract that pertained to accuracy were unimpressive, in the bottom 25 percent of the studies from which we extracted data.

One study deserves special attention because, although it did not meet our minimal screening criteria, it is the only available study that reports results from a real screening situation. Brownlie, Johnson, and Knill (1998) reported a study of 769 relevant-irrelevant polygraph tests of applicants for security positions at Atlanta International Airport between 1995 and 1997. The tests included four relevant questions, on past convictions for traffic violations or felonies, past bankruptcies, and use of marijuana during the past 30 days. As is typical with relevant-irrelevant testing, scoring was done by examiners' impressions rather than any standardized method, a fact that makes generalization to other examiners very risky. The study reported results that correspond to an accuracy index of 0.81, a value well above chance, but still in the bottom 25 percent of the studies from which we extracted data.[4]

A desirable feature found in some screening studies is that examiners know neither which examinees are deceptive nor which of several questions a deceptive examinee will answer untruthfully (e.g., Barland, 1981; Correa and Adams, 1981; Honts and Amato, 1999; Raskin and Kircher, 1990; Timm, 1991). These studies mimic one aspect of true screening: the examiner is not certain which item is "relevant." But in other respects these studies they are still a far cry from normal screening, in which the examinee has not been instructed specifically to lie, the list of possible deceptive answers is effectively infinite, and examinees may be deceptive about multiple items. In mock screening experiments, the mock transgression is highly salient, at least to all "programmed guilty" examinees, and everyone involved in the situation knows that the critical event is a specific staged transgression (even if they do not know the precise one). In typical real-life screening applications, there are a wide range of behaviors that might lead examinees either to admit minor infractions or to deny them, based on their individual perceptions of what the examiner "really" wants to know. Thus, examinees in actual polygraph screening may not know or may not agree about precisely what constitutes an honest and complete answer to some questions. In contrast, mock screening studies include a narrow range of issues that might be the target for deception, and subjects are assigned to deceptive or nondeceptive roles, thus removing any internal sense of doubt about whether or not their responses are in fact deceptive. These differences between mock screening studies and real screening applications limit the external validity of the mock screening studies. The likely result is decreased random variation in physiological responses, and therefore higher accuracy, in mock screening studies than in actual screening settings.

Nevertheless, the results of these studies do shed some light on the possible accuracy of screening polygraphs. These studies do not provide strong evidence for the validity or utility of polygraph screening. First, the level of accuracy in distinguishing deceptive from nondeceptive examinees in these studies was generally lower than that achieved in comparison question test and concealed information test studies focused on specific-incident investigation. This finding, though not strongly supported because of the limitations of the evidence, is not surprising. It has been widely remarked that the psychological difference between relevant and comparison questions is probably smaller when both questions are generic than when the relevant questions address specific acts. This similarity would make it harder to distinguish the physiological concomitants of truthfulness from those of deception in screening tests than in specific-incident tests.

Second, these studies do not show consistent accuracy in identifying the specific questions that were answered deceptively (negative results are reported by Barland, Honts, and Barger [1989] and U.S. Department of Defense Polygraph Institute [1995a, 1995b]; positive results are reported by Brownlie et al. [1998] and Kircher et al. [1998]). The finding in several studies that examiners cannot reliably distinguish truthful from deceptive responses (even if they can distinguish truthful from deceptive examinees) directly contradicts the most basic assumptions that guide polygraph use. It also has practical implications. If examiners obtain evidence of a deceptive response and follow up by focusing on the question that triggered their judgment, they are no more likely to be focusing on the correct question than if their follow-up was guided by the flip of a coin. Thus, if an examinee is in fact guilty of deception with regard to a specific serious security violation, and the examiner concludes that deception is indicated, the follow-up interrogation may often be based on the wrong question. The examinee might well confess to some mild transgression in the area targeted by that question and subsequently satisfy the examiner that the problem is not serious, even though there may be a more serious problem in another area. We have been given conflicting reports from various agencies concerning the degree to which examiners focus on target questions in follow-up interrogation. The evidence from the existing screening studies makes it clear that it is wise to train examiners to treat a positive response as a possible indication of deception to *any* question, not necessarily the specific one for which deception was indicated.

We have also examined preliminary and as yet unfinished reports on two subsequent DoDPI "screening" studies, carried out in 1997 and in 2001. These studies share many characteristics of the earlier DoDPI research, and their results do little to assuage our concerns regarding the limited scientific support for the validity of the Test for Espionage and Sabotage (TES) as a screening instrument.

SPECIAL POPULATIONS AND CONDITIONS

This section summarizes the evidence on accuracy related to particular issues. Because the quantitative data are so sparse for many important issues, each section also includes qualitative judgments about the likely meaning of what we know for polygraph interpretation (e.g., judgments about the robustness of polygraph evidence across examinee populations).

Individual Differences in Physiology

Individual differences in psychophysiological measures are common. Such differences have been reported in measures of many response systems, including the electrodermal, cardiovascular, endocrine, and central nervous systems. A growing body of research indicates that such differences in adults are moderately stable over time and are associated with a wide range of theoretically meaningful behavioral measures (see Kosslyn et al., 2002, for a review).

One of the earliest reported individual differences in a psychophysiological measure that was meaningfully associated with behavior is in electrodermal lability (Crider and Lunn, 1971). This is defined as the frequency of "nonspecific" electrodermal responses—responses that are observed in the absence of any external eliciting stimulus. A few studies have investigated whether this individual difference variable affects the accuracy of the polygraph, with inconsistent results. In two studies, Waid and Orne (1980) found that electrodermally stabile subjects (those exhibiting relatively few spontaneous responses) were less frequently detected in a concealed information task in comparison with electrodermally labile subjects. The number of items detected on the concealed information test was positively correlated with the frequency of nonspecific electrodermal responses. In addition, among innocent subjects, those with higher levels of electrodermal lability were more frequently falsely identified as deceptive. These studies only analyzed electrodermal activity; consequently, is not clear how much the accuracy of a full polygraph would have been affected by individual differences in electrodermal lability in these examinees.

A subsequent DoDPI-sponsored study using a comparison question test (Ingram, 1994) found no relationship between electrodermal lability and the detection of deception by blind scorers. This study also found, however, that the proportion of the subject sample accurately detected as deceptive using skin conductance amplitudes was not significantly above chance. These are the only reports of such associations we were able to find, other than two doctoral dissertations that had other methodological problems and were never published.

We have found no studies of how any other individual differences in psychophysiological responsiveness may affect the accuracy of polygraph tests. In sum, investigation of whether individual differences in physiological responsiveness is associated with the accuracy of polygraph detection of deception has barely begun.[5]

Individual Differences in Personality

A small body of research addresses the question of whether the accuracy of polygraph testing is affected by the personality traits and characteristics of examinees. The research has addressed some personality traits characteristic of psychologically "normal" individuals and some characteristics of psychologically "abnormal" individuals. Various theoretical rationales have been offered for expecting that the investigated traits might affect physiological responses during polygraph testing.

Studies have been conducted comparing individuals in normal populations who are "high" and "low" on personality dimensions, such as trait anxiety (Giesen and Rollison, 1980), Machiavellianism (Bradley and Klohn, 1987), and self-monitoring (Bradley and Rettinger, 1992). Studies on abnormal individuals have been confined primarily to personality disorders (Gudjonsson, 1982) and psychopathy (e.g., Hammond, 1980; Patrick and Iacono, 1989; Raskin and Hare, 1978). These studies vary substantially in their internal and external validity. All of them were based on specific-incident scenarios, not screening scenarios.

Two studies found that "normal" personality traits moderated physiological indexes of deception. Giesen and Rollison (1980) found that the self-reported trait of anxiety affected skin conductance responsivity during a concealed information test such that subjects with high trait anxiety who were "guilty" of a mock crime responded more strongly than subjects low on trait anxiety. Subjects with low anxiety showed little skin conductance responsivity, regardless of whether they were innocent or guilty. Bradley and Klohn (1987:747) found that subjects high in Machiavellianism (i.e., those "able to focus more directly on the relevant aspects of the situation") were more physiologically responsive when "guilty" than when "innocent."

Other studies have failed to find effects of normal personality variation on polygraph accuracy. For example, Bradley and Rettinger (1992) found no differences with respect to polygraph detection of deception between subjects high and low in their propensity to monitor their own social demeanor. Gudjonsson (1982) found no consistent overall relationships between personality traits assessed by a battery of personality inventories (i.e., Eysenck Personality Inventory, Gough Socialization Scale, and the Arrow-Dot Test) and detection of deception using a concealed information test for normal or personality-disordered individuals.

Regarding psychopathy, Hammond (1980) found no differences in the detectability of deception using a mock crime scenario among normal individuals, alcoholics, and psychopaths. Similarly, neither Raskin and Hare (1978) nor Patrick and Iacono (1989) found any differences in the detectability of deception between psychopathic and nonpsychopathic prison inmates.

Although consistent personality effects on polygraph accuracy have not been found, it would be premature to conclude that personality traits in general have little effect: two studies did find such relationships, there is a paucity of relevant high-quality research, and the statistical power of the studies to find moderating effects if they exist is quite limited.

Sociocultural Group Identity

In Chapter 3 we discuss empirically supported theories relating physiological responses, including responses measured by the polygraph, to the interpersonal context. These theories have existed in the basic social psychological and sociological literature for some time (e.g., Goffman, 1963; Blascovich et al., 2000). The theories and associated research (Blascovich et al., 2001a) suggest that apparent stigmatizing qualities (e.g., race, age, gender, physical abnormalities, socioeconomic status) of the participants in situations like polygraph examinations might affect polygraph test results. However, relatively little work has been done to test these theories in the context of polygraph examiner-examinee interactions. There is some polygraph research bearing on the effects of sociocultural group identity, however. Some studies have reported polygraph accuracy as a function of the gender of examinees, fewer have reported on the race of examinees, and almost none on ethnicity. Only a few studies have data bearing on gender and race in combination, and only two have considered examiner and examinee characteristics in combination. As with the research on personality differences, the studies vary substantially in their internal and external validity.

Generally, the research on gender has failed to find effects, with most studies indicating no statistically reliable differences in detection of deception between males and females. Two studies (Bradley and Cullen, 1993; Matte and Reuss, 1992) found gender differences in specific physiological responses during polygraph tests, but the differences were not consistent across studies. The effect sizes in these gender studies are rarely calculable.

We found only two studies that compared polygraph accuracy by race of examinees (Reed, 1993; Buckley and Senese, 1991). Neither reported significant effects of examiner's race, examinee's race, or their interaction on polygraphic detection of deception. One of the studies, however (Buckley and Senese, 1991), reported only on blind rescoring of polygraph charts, so it is only partially relevant to the question of whether racial variables in the social interaction of the polygraph examination affect test results. The sample size is not large enough (40 polygraph records in all) to support any firm conclusions. Reed (1993) reported on a larger sample of 375 polygraph tests given by trainees at DoDPI and found no statistically reliable differences in accuracy between tests given to Caucasian and African American examinees. Reed also mentions an earlier dataset of 1,141 examinations, also given in DoDPI training classes, in which false positive results were significantly more common among the 81 nondeceptive African American examinees than among the 320 nondeceptive Caucasian examinees, as might be expected from the theoretical arguments presented in Chapter 3. However, there is no research report available on this dataset. We found only one study on ethnicity, conducted on different Bedouin groups in Israel; this study was so poorly reported that no objective interpretation can be made.

In our view, the effects of sociocultural group identity of examiners and examinees on the polygraphic detection of deception have been investigated only minimally, with little methodological sophistication, and with no attention to theoretically significant variables or mechanisms. In the reported research, effect sizes are rarely calculable. That some studies have found gender differences on intensity of physiological responses of one sort or another appears to have been ignored in the rest of the research literature (and the practice of polygraph testing). Finally, the preponderance of white male examiners has made it extremely difficult to develop and implement research studies that would examine interactions between examiner and examinee race with sufficient statistical power to draw conclusions. For the most part, the concerns about the possible decrement in accuracy in polygraph tests on stigmatized groups that were raised in Chapter 3 on the basis of basic research in social psychophysiology have not been addressed by polygraph research.

Expectancy Effects

Given the operation of expectancy effects in many social interactions (see discussion in Chapter 3), one might expect that examiner expectancies of examinee guilt might influence not only examiners' judgments of charts, but also examinees' physiological responses during polygraph tests. However, we could find very little research on these issues. In one study, expectancies affected examiners' scoring of charts that had previously been judged inconclusive, but not of charts with conclusive results (Elaad, Ginton, and Ben-Shakhar, 1994). We found only one small study (28 polygraph examinations) that considered the effects of examiners' expectancies that were induced in advance of the polygraph examination (Elaad, Ginton, and Ben-Shakhar, 1998): The expectancy manipulation produced no discernible effect on test results. This evidence is too limited to draw any strong conclusions about whether examiners' expectancies affect polygraph test accuracy.

There is a small body of research on the effects of examinees' expectancies, conducted in part to test the hypothesis that so-called stimulation tests, which are intended to convince examinees of the polygraph's ability to detect deception, improve detection accuracy. Although the results are mixed, the research provides some support for the hypothesis (e.g., Bradley and Janisse, 1981; Kircher et al., 2001).

Drug Effects

The potential effect of drugs on polygraph outcomes has received scant attention in the experimental literature. An early report examined the possible effect of the anxiolytic meprobamate (sometimes prescribed under brand names including Equanil and Miltown) on a concealed information task (Waid et al., 1981). This experiment was performed on a small sample of undergraduates and found that meprobamate in doses that were not detectable by the examiner significantly impaired the detection of deception in a concealed information analogue task. In a replication and extension of this study, Iacono and colleagues (Iacono et al., 1992) compared the effects of meprobamate, diazepam (a benzodiazepine) and propranolol (a beta-blocker) on detection of guilt with a concealed information task. Contrary to the findings of Waid et al. (1981), this study found that none of the drugs evaluated had a significant effect on the detection of deception, nor was there even a trend in the direction reported by Waid et al. The nature of the mock crimes was different in these studies, though drug dose was identical. Using diazepam and methylphenidate, a stimulant, in separate groups of subjects, Iacono, Boisvenu, and Fleming (1984) evaluated the effect of these drugs and a placebo on the electrodermal detection of deception, using a concealed information task with examiners blind to drug condition. The results indicated that the drugs had no effect. O'Toole et al. (1994) studied the effect of alcohol intoxication at the time of the mock crime on the detection of deception in a concealed information task. Intoxication at the time of the mock crime had no significant effect on the detection of deception though it did affect memory for crime details. Bradley and Ainsworth (1984), however, found that alcohol intoxication at the time of a mock crime reduced the accuracy of detection.

Overall, there has been little research on the effect of drugs on the detection of deception. The subjects tested have been exclusively undergraduates, dose-response effects have not been evaluated, and the mock crimes have been highly artificial with no consequence for detection. The weight of the published evidence suggests little or no drug effects on the detection of deception using the concealed information test, but given the few studies performed, the few drugs tested, and the analogue nature of the evidence, a conclusion that drugs do not affect polygraph validity would be premature.

COUNTERMEASURES

Perhaps the most serious potential problem with the practical use of the polygraph is the possibility that examinees—particularly deceptive ones—might be able to decrease the test's accuracy by engaging in certain behaviors, countermeasures, designed to produce nondeceptive test results. A wide range of potential countermeasures has been suggested (Krapohl, 1995, presents a taxonomy), and the effectiveness of some of these countermeasures has been examined in the empirical literature. Major classes of countermeasures include using drugs and alcohol to dampen polygraph responses (Cail-Sirota and Lieberman, 1995), mental countermeasures (e.g., relaxation, production of emotional imagery, mental disassociation, counting backwards, hypnotic suggestion, and attention-focusing techniques), and physical countermeasures (e.g., breath control, behaviors that produce pain before or during questioning, such as biting one's tongue, or behaviors that produce muscle tension before or during questioning, such as pressing one's toe to the floor or contracting a variety of muscles in the body). Advice about how to use countermeasures to "beat" the polygraph is readily available (e.g., Maschke and Scalabrini, no date; Williams, 1996) and there is anecdotal evidence of increasing levels of countermeasure use in federal security screening programs.

Countermeasures have long been recognized as a distinct threat to the validity and utility of the polygraph (U.S. Office of Technology Assessment, 1983). Guilty examinees have incentives to try to influence the examination in ways that reduce the likelihood that their deception will be detected. Some examinees who have not committed crimes, security breaches, or related offenses, or who have little to hide, might nevertheless engage in countermeasures with the intent to minimize their chances of false positive test results (Maschke and Scalabrini, no date). This strategy is not risk-free for innocent examinees. There is evidence that some countermeasures used by innocent examinees can in fact increase their chances of appearing deceptive (Dawson, 1980; Honts, Amato, and Gordon, 2001). Also, several agencies that use the polygraph in screening job applicants or current employees have indicated that examinees who are judged to be using countermeasures may, on these grounds alone, be subject to the same personnel actions that would result from a test that indicated deception. Because countermeasures might influence test outcomes and personnel actions, and because the effects of countermeasures on test validity and utility might depend on the examiner's ability to detect these behaviors, it is important to examine the empirical research on the effects and the detectability of physical and mental countermeasures.

Rationale

Most methods of polygraph examination rely on comparisons between physiological responses to relevant and comparison questions. Examinees who consistently show more pronounced reactions to relevant questions than to comparison or irrelevant questions are most likely to be judged deceptive. Maschke and Scalabrini (no date:68), referring to the comparison (control) question test format suggest that ". . . the key to passing a polygraph test . . . is to produce stronger physiological responses when answering control questions than when answering the relevant questions." They advise examinees that they can beat the comparison question test by identifying comparison questions and producing stronger-than-normal reactions to these questions.[6]

Most of the physical countermeasures described in the literature appear to be designed to strengthen responses to comparison questions. For example, there are a number of ways of inducing mild pain when responding to comparison questions (e.g., biting one's tongue, stepping on a hidden tack in one's shoe), and it is possible that the heightened physiological responses that accompany pain can mimic the responses polygraph examiners take as indicators of deception when they appear after relevant questions. Muscle contraction might produce similar reactions and might be difficult to detect, depending on the amount of training and the muscle groups involved (Honts, 1986). Mental countermeasures have also been suggested as a method for enhancing responses to comparison questions. For example, Honts (1986) and Maschke and Scalabrini (no date) suggest that the use of exciting or arousing mental imagery during comparison questions might lead to stronger physiological responses. A second strategy for reducing differences between responses to relevant and to comparison questions is to dampen responses to relevant questions. The mental countermeasures described in the literature (e.g., mental imagery, attention focusing) might be used for this purpose. It is widely believed that physical and mental countermeasures are ineffective for reducing physiological responses to relevant questions in polygraph examinations, but investigations of this strategy have not been reported.

Our review of basic theory and research in physiological psychology (see Chapter 3) makes it clear that a wide range of physiological responses can be brought under some level of conscious control. Countermeasure research has examined a limited set of strategies for influencing the readings obtained by the polygraph (e.g., muscle tensing, self-inflicted pain), but many other possibilities remain, including the use of biofeedback and conditioning paradigms. It is entirely plausible, from a scientific viewpoint, to develop a range of countermeasures that might effectively mimic specific physiological response patterns that are usually the focus of a polygraph test. It is not clear whether there would be individual differences in physiological response patterns with particular countermeasures or in the ease with which specific countermeasures are mastered. Nor is it clear whether examinees can learn to replicate faithfully their responses to comparison questions when answering relevant questions: systematic differences between comparison and relevant responses, even those that are not part of the standard scoring criteria for evaluating polygraph charts, might make it possible to detect countermeasures.

Most studies of countermeasures have focused on the effects of these measures on test outcomes and on the accuracy of polygraph tests, without directly examining whether these measures in fact produced their desired physiological effects. For example, Honts, Hodes, and Raskin (1985) and Honts, Raskin, and Kircher (1987) focus on the overall effects of countermeasures use without determining whether specific countermeasures (e.g., self-induced pain) lead to increased reactions to comparison questions. Some studies, however (e.g., Honts, 1986), have looked at the physiological responses to specific questions when countermeasures have or have not been attempted and provide some evidence that it is possible to produce more pronounced reactions to comparison questions with countermeasures. Some studies (e.g., Kubis, 1962) have examined the effects of particular countermeasures on accuracy of detection through specific physiological channels, as well as when all channels are examined.

The empirical research on countermeasures has not provided enough information to determine whether specific countermeasures have the specific physiological effects that would lead a polygraph examiner to judge an examinee as nondeceptive. Consequently, it is difficult to determine why specific countermeasure strategies might or might not work. We would not expect specific countermeasures (e.g., biting one's tongue) to have uniform effects on all of the chart readings obtained during a polygraph test, and studies that focus exclusively on the effects of countermeasures on accuracy do not allow one to determine why specific approaches might work or fail to work in different contexts.

Effects

Drugs

Studies of the effects of countermeasures on the outcomes of polygraph examinations have yielded mixed outcomes. Studies on the effects of drugs, already discussed, are a good example. An early study by Waid et al. (1981) suggested that the use of the drug meprobamate reduced the accuracy of polygraph examinations, but subsequent studies (Iacono, Boisvenu, and Fleming, 1984; Iacono et al., 1992) suggest that similar drugs, such as diazepam (Valium) and methlyphenidate (Ritalin), have little effect on the outcomes of polygraph examinations.

It is difficult to draw firm conclusions from research on the effects of drugs and alcohol on polygraph examinations for two reasons: there are relatively few studies that provide data, and these studies share a central weakness that is endemic in most of the polygraph research we have reviewed—a failure to articulate and test specific theories or hypotheses about how and why drugs might influence polygraph outcomes. These studies have rarely stated or tested predictions about the effects of specific classes of drugs on specific physiological readings obtained using the polygraph, on the examiner's interpretations of those readings, or of other behaviors observed during a polygraph examination. Different classes of drugs are likely to affect different physiological responses, and the effects of one class of drugs (e.g., benzodiazepines used to treat anxiety) might be qualitatively different from the effects of alcohol or some other drug. Research on drug and alcohol effects has not yet examined the processes by which these substances might influence polygraph outcomes, making it difficult to interpret any studies showing that particular drug-based countermeasures either work or fail to work.

Mental and Physical Strategies

Studies of mental countermeasures have also produced inconsistent findings. Kubis (1962) and Wakamatsu (1987) presented data suggesting that some mental countermeasures reduce the accuracy of polygraph tests. Elaad and Ben-Shakhar (1991) present evidence that certain mental countermeasures have relatively weak effects, findings that are confirmed by Ben-Shakhar and Dolev (1996). Timm (1991) found that the use of post-hypnotic suggestion as a countermeasure was ineffective. As with the research reviewed above, studies of the effects of mental countermeasures have failed to develop or test specific hypotheses about why specific countermeasures might work or under which conditions they are most likely to work. There is evidence, however, that their effects operate particularly through the electrodermal channel (Ben-Shakhar and Dolev, 1996; Elaad and Ben-Shakhar, 1991; Kubis, 1962).

A series of studies by Honts and his colleagues suggests that training subjects in physical countermeasures or in a combination of physical and mental countermeasures can substantially decrease the likelihood that deceptive subjects will be detected by the polygraph (Honts, 1986; Honts et al., 1996; Honts, Hodes and Raskin, 1985; Honts, Raskin, and Kircher, 1987, 1994; Raskin and Kircher, 1990). In general, these studies suggest that physical countermeasures are more effective than mental ones and that a combination of physical and mental countermeasures is probably most effective. These studies have involved very short periods of training and suggest that countermeasures are effective in both comparison question and concealed information test formats.

Limitations of the Research

Several important limitations to the research on countermeasures are worth noting. First, all of the studies have involved mock crimes and most use experimenters or research assistants as polygraph examiners. The generalizability of these results to real polygraph examinations—where both the examiner and the examinee are highly motivated to achieve their goals (i.e., to escape detection and to detect deception, respectively), where the examiners are skilled and experienced interrogators, where admissions and confessions are a strong factor in the outcome of the examination, and where there are important consequences attached to the polygraph examination—is doubtful. It is possible that the effects of countermeasures are even larger in real-life polygraph examinations than in laboratory experiments, but it is also possible that those experiments overestimate the effectiveness of the measures. There are so many important differences between mock-crime laboratory studies and field applications of the polygraph that the external validity of this body of research is as much in doubt as the external validity of other laboratory studies of polygraph test accuracy.

Second, the bulk of the published research lending empirical support to the claim that countermeasures substantially affect the validity and utility of the polygraph is the product of the work of Honts and his colleagues. It is therefore important to obtain further, independent confirmation of these findings from multiple laboratories, using a range of research methods to determine the extent to which the results are generalizable or limited to the particular methods and measures commonly used in one laboratory.

There are also important omissions in the research on countermeasures. One, as noted above, is that none of the studies we reviewed adequately investigated the processes by which countermeasures might affect the deception of deception. Countermeasures are invariably based on assumptions about the physiological effects of particular mental or physical activities and their implications for the outcomes of polygraph tests. The first step in evaluating countermeasures should be a determination of whether they have their intended effects on the responses measured by the polygraph, followed by a determination of whether these specific changes in physiological responses affect the outcomes of a polygraph test. Countermeasure studies usually omit the step of determining whether countermeasures have their intended physiological effects, making any relationships between countermeasures and polygraph test outcomes difficult to evaluate.

Another omission is the apparent absence of attempts to identify the physiological signatures associated with different countermeasures. It is very likely that specific countermeasures (e.g., inducing pain, thinking exciting thoughts) produce specific patterns of physiological responses (not necessarily limited to those measured by the polygraph) that could be reliably distinguished from each other and from patterns indicating deceptive responses. Polygraph practitioners claim that they can detect countermeasures; this claim would be much more credible if there were known physiological indicators of countermeasure use.

A third omission, and perhaps the most important, is the apparent absence of research on the use of countermeasures by individuals who are highly motivated and extensively trained in using countermeasures. It is possible that classified research on this topic exists, but the research we reviewed does not provide an answer to the question that might be of most concern to the agencies that rely on the polygraph—i.e., whether agents or others who are motivated and trained can "beat" the polygraph.

Detection

Polygraph examiners commonly claim to be able to detect the use of countermeasures, both through their observations of the examinee's behavior and through an assessment of the recorded polygraph chart. Some countermeasures, such as the use of psychoactive drugs (e.g., diazepam, commonly known as Valium), have broad behavioral consequences and should be relatively easy to detect (Iacono, Boisvenu, and Fleming, 1984). Whether polygraph examiners can detect more subtle countermeasures or, more importantly, can be trained to detect them, remains an open question.

Early empirical work in this area by Honts, Raskin, and Kircher (1987) suggested that countermeasures could be detected, but later work by Honts and his colleagues suggests that polygraph examiners do a poor job in detecting countermeasures (Honts, 1986; Honts, Amato, and Gordon, 2001; Honts and Hodes, 1983; Honts, Hodes, and Raskin, 1985; Honts, Raskin, and Kircher, 1994). Unfortunately, this work shares the same limitations as the work suggesting that countermeasures have a substantial effect and is based on many of the same studies. There have been reports of the use of mechanisms to detect countermeasure in polygraph tests, notably, reports of use of motion sensors in some polygraph equipment to detect muscle tensing (Maschke and Scalabrini, no date). Raskin and Kircher (1990) present some evidence that these sorts of detectors can be effective in detecting specific types of countermeasures, but their general validity and utility remain a matter for conjecture. There is no evidence that mental countermeasures are detectable by examiners. The available research does not address the issue of training examiners to detect countermeasures.

Incentives for Use

Honts and Amato (2002) suggest that the proportion of subjects who attempt to use countermeasures could be substantial (see also Honts, Amato, and Gordon, 2001). In particular, they report that many "innocent" examinees in their studies claim to use countermeasures in an effort to produce a favorable outcome in their examinations (the studies are based on self-reports). Even if these self-reports accurately represent the frequency of countermeasure use in the laboratory, it is unwise to conclude that countermeasures are equally prevalent in high-stakes field situations.

Because it is possible that countermeasures can increase "failure" rates among nondeceptive examinees and because a judgment that an examinee is using countermeasures can have the same practical effect as the judgment that the test indicates deception, their use by innocent individuals may be misguided. Yet, it is certainly not irrational. Examinees who are highly motivated to "pass" their polygraph tests might engage in a variety of behaviors they believe will improve their chances, including the use of countermeasures. It is therefore reasonable to expect that the people who engage in countermeasures include, in addition to the critical few who want to avoid being caught in major security violations, people who are concerned that their emotions or anxieties (perhaps about real peccadilloes) might lead to a false positive polygraph result, and people who simply do not want to stake their careers on the results of an imperfect test. Unfortunately, there is no evidence to suggest how many of the people who use countermeasures fall in the latter categories. The proportion may well have increased, though, in the face of widespread claims that countermeasures are effective and undetectable.

Of course, the most serious concern about countermeasures is that guilty individuals may use them effectively to cover their guilt. The studies we reviewed provide little useful evidence on this critical question because the incentives to "beat the polygraph" in the experiments are relatively small ones and the "guilt" is nominal at best. The most troubling possibility is that with a serious investment of time and effort, it might be possible to train a deceptive individual to appear truthful on a polygraph examination by using countermeasures that are very difficult to detect. Given the widespread use of the polygraph in screening for security-sensitive jobs, it is reasonable to expect that foreign intelligence services will attempt to devise and implement methods of assuring that their agents will "pass" the polygraph. It is impossible to tell from the little research that has been done whether training in countermeasures has a good possibility of success or how long such training would take. The available research does not engender confidence that polygraph test results will be unaffected by the use of countermeasures by people who pose major security threats.

In screening employees and applicants for positions in security-related agencies, because the prevalence of spies and saboteurs is so low, almost all the people using countermeasures will not be spies, particularly if, as we have heard from some agency officials, the incidence of the use of countermeasures is increasing. To the extent that examiners can accurately identify the use of countermeasures, people using them will be detected and will have to be dealt with. Policies for doing so will be complicated by the likelihood that most of those judged to be using countermeasures will in fact be innocent of major security infractions. They will include both individuals who are using countermeasures to avoid being falsely suspected of such infractions and individuals falsely suspected of using countermeasures.

Research Questions

If the U.S. government established a major research program that addressed techniques for detection of deception, such a program would have to include applied research on countermeasures, addressed to at least three questions: (1) Are there particular countermeasures that are effective against all or some polygraph testing formats and scoring systems? (2) If so, how and why do they work? (3) Can they be detected and, if so, how?

The research would aim to come as close as possible to the intended settings and contexts in which the polygraph might be used. Countermeasures that work in low-stakes laboratory studies might not work, or might work better, in more realistic polygraph settings. Also, different countermeasure strategies might be effective, for example, in defeating screening polygraphs (where the distinction between relevant and comparison questions might not always be obvious) and in defeating the polygraph when used in specific-incident investigations. Studies might also investigate how specific countermeasures relate to question types and to particular physiological indicators, and whether specific countermeasures have reliable effects.

Countermeasures training would also be a worthy subject for study. Authors such as Maschke and Williams suggest that effective countermeasure strategies can be easily learned and that a small amount of practice is enough to give examinees an excellent chance of "beating" the polygraph. Because the effective application of mental or physical countermeasures on the part of examinees would require skill in distinguishing between relevant and comparison questions, skill in regulating physiological response, and skill in concealing countermeasures from trained examiners, claims that it is easy to train examinees to "beat" both the polygraph and trained examiners require scientific supporting evidence to be credible. However, we are not aware of any such research. Additional questions for research include whether there are individual differences in learning and retaining countermeasure skills, whether different strategies for countermeasure training have different effects, and whether some strategies work better for some examinees than for others.

Research could also address methods of detecting countermeasures. The available research suggests that detection is difficult, especially for mental countermeasures, but the studies are weak in external validity (e.g., low stakes for examiners and examinees), and they have rarely systematically examined specific strategies for detecting physical or mental countermeasures.

Research on countermeasures and their detection has potentially serious implications for security, especially for agencies that rely on the polygraph, and it is likely that some of this research would be classified. Elsewhere, we advocate open public research on the polygraph. In areas for which classified research is necessary, it is reasonable to expect that the quality and reliability of this research, even if conducted by the best available research teams, will necessarily be lower than that of unclassified research, because classified research projects do not have access to the self-correcting mechanisms (e.g., peer review, free collaboration, data sharing, publication, and rebuttal) that are such an integral part of open scientific research.

CONCLUSIONS

Overall Accuracy

Theoretical considerations and data suggest that any single-value estimate of polygraph accuracy in general use would likely be misleading. A major reason is that accuracy varies markedly across studies. This variability is due in part to sampling factors (small sample sizes and different methods of sampling); however, undetermined systematic differences between the studies undoubtedly also contribute to variability.

The accuracy index of the laboratory studies of specific-incident polygraph testing that we found that had at least minimal scientific quality and that presented data in a form amenable to quantitative estimation of criterion validity was between 0.81 and 0.91 for the middle 26 of the values from 52 datasets. Field studies suggest a similar, or perhaps slightly higher, level of accuracy. These numerical estimates should be interpreted with great care and *should not* be used as general measures of polygraph accuracy, particularly for screening applications. First, none of the studies we used to produce these numbers is a true study of polygraph screening. For the reasons discussed in this chapter, we expect that the accuracy index values that would be estimated from such studies would be lower than those in the studies we have reviewed.[7]

Second, these index values do not represent the percentage of correct polygraph judgments except under particular, very unusual circumstances. Their meaning in terms of percent correct depends on other factors, particularly the threshold that is set for declaring a test result positive and the base rate of deceptive individuals tested. In screening populations with very low base rates of deceptive individuals, even an extremely high percentage of correct classifications can give very unsatisfactory results. This point is illustrated in Table 2-1 (in Chapter 2), which presents an example of a test with an accuracy index of 0.90 that makes 99.5 percent correct classifications in a hypothetical security screening situation, yet lets 8 of 10 spies pass the screen.

Third, these estimates are based only on examinations of certain populations of polygraph-naïve examinees untrained in countermeasures and so may not apply to other populations of examinees, across testing situations, or to serious security violators who are highly motivated to "beat" the test. Fourth, even for naïve populations, the accuracy index most likely overestimates performance in realistic field situations due to technical biases in field research designs, the increased variability created by the lack of control of test administration and interpretation in the field, the artificiality of laboratory settings, and possible publication bias.

Thus, the range of accuracy indexes, from 0.81 to 0.91, that covers the bulk of polygraph research studies, is in our judgment an overestimate of likely accuracy in field application, even when highly trained examiners and reasonably well standardized testing procedures are used. It is impossible, however, to quantify how much of an overestimate these numbers represent because of limitations in the data. In our judgment, however, reliance on polygraph testing to perform in practical applications at a level at or above A = 0.90 is not warranted on the basis of either scientific theory or empirical data. Many committee members would place this upper bound considerably lower.

Despite these caveats, the empirical data clearly indicate that for several populations of naïve examinees not trained in countermeasures, polygraph tests for event-specific investigation detect deception at rates well above those expected from random guessing. Test performance is far below perfection and highly variable across situations. The studies report accuracy levels comparable to various diagnostic tests used in medicine. We note, however, that the performance of medical diagnostic tests in widespread field applications generally degrades relative to their performance in validation studies, and this result can also be expected for polygraph testing. Existing polygraph field studies have used research designs highly vulnerable to biases, most of which exaggerate polygraph accuracy. We also note that the advisability of using medical diagnostic tests in specific applications depends on issues beyond accuracy, particularly including the base rate of the condition being diagnosed in the population being tested and the availability of follow-up diagnostic tests; these issues also pertain to the use of the polygraph.

Screening

The great bulk of validation research on the polygraph has investigated deception associated with crimes or other specific events. We have found only one true screening study; the few other studies that are described as screening studies are in fact studies focused on specific incidents that use relatively broad "relevant" questions. No study to date addresses the implications of observed accuracy for large security screening programs with very low base rates of the target transgressions, such as those now being conducted by major government agencies.

The so-called screening studies in the literature report accuracy levels that are better than chance for detecting deceptive examinees, but they show inconsistent results with regard to the ability of the test to detect the specific issue on which the examinee is attempting to deceive. These results indicate the need for caution in adopting screening protocols that encourage investigators to follow up on some issues and ignore others on the basis of physiological responses to specific questions on polygraph charts.

There are no studies that provide even indirect evidence of the validity of the polygraph for making judgments of future undesirable behavior from preemployment screening tests. The theory and logic of the polygraph, which emphasizes the detection of deception about past acts, is not consistent with the typical process by which forecasts of future security-related performance are made.

Variability in Accuracy Estimates

The variability in empirical estimates of polygraph accuracy is greater than can be explained by random processes. However, we have mainly been unable to determine the sources of systematic variability from examination of the data. Polygraph test performance in the data we reviewed did not vary markedly with several objective and subjective features coded by the reviewers: setting (field, laboratory); type of test (comparison question, concealed information); funding source; date of publication of the research; or our ratings of the quality of the data analysis, the internal validity of the research, or the overall salience of the study to the field. Other reviews suggest that, in laboratory settings, accuracy may be higher in situations involving incentives than in ones without incentives, but the evidence is not definitive and its relevance to field practice is uncertain.

The available research provides little information on the possibility that accuracy is dependent on individual differences among examinees in physiology or personality, examinees' sociocultural group identity, social interaction variables in the polygraph examination, or drug use by the examinee. There is evidence in basic psychophysiology to support an expectation that some of these factors, including social stigmas attached to examiners or examinees and expectancies, may affect polygraph accuracy. Although the available research does not convincingly demonstrate any such effects, replications are very few and the studies lack sufficient statistical power to support negative conclusions.

Countermeasures

Any effectiveness of countermeasures would reduce the accuracy of polygraph tests. There are studies that provide empirical support for the hypothesis that some countermeasures that can be learned fairly easily can enable a deceptive individual to appear nondeceptive and avoid detection by the examiners. However, we do not know of scientific studies examining the effectiveness of countermeasures in contexts where systematic efforts are made to detect and deter them.

There is also evidence that innocent examinees using some countermeasures in an effort to increase the probability that they will "pass" the exam produce physiological reactions that have the opposite effect, either because their countermeasures are detected or because their responses appear more rather than less deceptive. The available evidence does not allow us to determine whether innocent examinees can increase their chances of achieving nondeceptive outcomes by using countermeasures.

The most serious threat of countermeasures, of course, concerns individuals who are major security threats and want to conceal their activities. Such individuals and the organizations they represent have a strong incentive to perfect and use countermeasures. If these measures are effective, they could seriously undermine any value of polygraph security screening. Basic physiological theory suggests that training methods might allow individuals to succeed in employing effective countermeasures. Moreover, the empirical research literature suggests that polygraph test results can be affected by the use of countermeasures. Given the potential importance of countermeasures to intelligence agencies, it is likely that classified information on these topics exists. In open communications and in a classified briefing for some of the committee, we have not been told of any such research, so we cannot verify its existence or relevance.

NOTES

1. Appendix H explains how we estimated the ROC curves and values of A. It also presents additional descriptive statistics on these A values.

2. Two published meta-analyses claim to find associations between accuracy and characteristics of the studies, and therefore deserve discussion. In one, Kircher and colleagues (1988) reported that polygraph accuracy (measured as Pearson's r between test results and actual truthfulness or deception) was correlated with three study characteristics across 14 polygraph studies of comparison question tests. The characteristics were examinee population (college students or others), incentive strength (the presence or absence of a tangible consequence of being judged deceptive, for both innocent and guilty examinees), and whether or not the study used field testing techniques that allowed examiners to conduct three or more charts in order to get a conclusive result. Because these characteristics were highly correlated with each other in the 14 studies, and with whether or not the studies were conducted in the authors' laboratory, it is difficult to attribute the observed associations to any specific characteristic. We do not place much confidence in the reliability of the correlations because of the instability of the estimates for such a small number of studies and because of the inherent limits of Pearson's r as an index of polygraph accuracy. Moreover, our examination of one of these variables (strength of incentive) failed to reveal an association with test accuracy in our sample of studies, which is larger and covers a broader range of incentives. Kircher and colleagues coded incentive strength as high for studies that offered as little as a $5 bonus to examinees for producing a nondeceptive result; only one study in the Kircher meta-analysis involved an incentive stronger than a $20 bonus. In the other meta-analysis, Ben-Shakhar and Elaad (2002b) examined 169 experimental conditions from 80 laboratory studies of concealed information tests. The study included a large number of studies that did not meet our quality criteria or that we did not use to estimate accuracy because they did not include a comparison group that lacked any concealed information. Its overall results were generally consistent with ours, but it did find positive associations of accuracy with three moderator variables: number of sets of relevant and comparison questions, the presence of motivational instructions or monetary incentives, and the presence of the requirement that deceptive examinees make a deceptive answer (rather than a nonresponse). We cannot compare their results directly with ours because of the large number of studies that support their analysis of moderator variables that are not in our dataset. For example, all but one of the studies covered in this meta-analysis that are also in our dataset were coded by Ben-Shakhar and Elaad as positive for the motivation variable. These meta-analyses cover only laboratory studies, so their relevance to field practice is uncertain.

3. As stated in Note 2, Kircher et al. (1988) evaluated only 14 studies and considered bonuses of $5 to $20 as strong motivations. Ben-Shakhar and Elaad (2002) included a considerable number of studies in their analysis that did not meet our basic quality criteria or that we excluded from our analysis because they lacked a comparison group of examinees who had no concealed information. We consider their evidence suggestive of a motivation effect but not definitive.

4. This study shares important features with true screening studies and with specific-incident studies. The questions are broader in scope than in a traditional specific-incident study, but still deal with specific, discrete, and potentially verifiable events. For example, one relevant question in this study was "Have you been convicted of a felony in the state of Georgia?" There is little room for ambiguity in interpreting the question or the answer, in contrast with typical screening questions, which are more

ambiguous (e.g., "Have you ever committed a security violation?"). Also, the base rate for deception in this study was quite high (over three-quarters of examinees were confirmed as deceptive on one or more questions); in security and espionage screening, the base rate is likely to be extremely low. For these reasons, generalizing from this study to other screening applications is risky. In addition, determination of truth is problematic for this study because truth was defined by a mixture of criteria, including the search of public records for convictions and bankruptcies, a urine test for marijuana, and, in an unreported number of instances, confession. Truth established by confession may not be independent of the polygraph test. A reasonable guess is that polygraph testing in other kinds of security screening situations will be less accurate than in this one.

5. We note that although the use of comparison questions is undoubtedly helpful in controlling for such differences, it is a misconception to assume this strategy to be fully effective, for a variety of reasons. For instance, differential electrodermal responses to different stimuli may be especially hard to detect in individuals who are highly reactive or highly nonreactive to all stimuli. We also note that polygraph tests achieve accuracy greater than chance despite the failure of most scoring systems to control for these differences.

6. This strategy can also be applied to the relevant-irrelevant test. With concealed information tests, however, it can only be used by examinees who have concealed information because only they can distinguish relevant from comparison questions.

7. The only true screening study we found, which did not meet our standards for inclusion in the quantitative analysis because it did not use a replicable scoring system, yielded an accuracy index of 0.81.

6

Alternative Techniques
and Technologies

Public officials responsible for maintaining national security should consider polygraph policies in relation to other policy options that rely on alternative means of detecting deception and deterring violations to security. Their decisions must consider the net benefits and costs of a range of options for achieving these objectives by using the polygraph and other techniques for detecting deception that may supplement or substitute for the polygraph.

This chapter considers some of those alternative techniques. It focuses in particular on the potential of recently emerging technologies, including those that measure brain activity, some of which have recently received considerable attention, and those that rely on measures of externally observable behaviors. In Chapter 7 we take up issues involved in making policy decisions about the use of these techniques, including ways of assessing the costs and benefits of using particular techniques and ways of combining techniques.

Techniques for detecting real and potential violations of security can be roughly divided into four classes. The first class includes, but is not restricted to, the polygraph itself. This class considers physiological indicators of autonomic and somatic activity that are not detectable without special sensing equipment. In this chapter we discuss some of the members of this class other than the polygraph. The second class includes techniques involving observations of brain function. This class is attractive on grounds of basic psychophysiology because of the possibility that appropriately selected brain measures might get closer than any autonomic measures to psychological processes that are closely tied to deception. Brain activity can be measured with modern functional imaging techniques such as positron emission tomography (PET) and magnetic resonance imaging (MRI, often referred to as functional MRI or fMRI when used to relate brain function to behavior), as well as by recording event-related potentials, characteristics of brain electrical activity following specific discrete stimuli or "events." The third class of techniques attempts to achieve detection of deception from demeanor: these techniques usually involve careful observation of specific behaviors of examinees (e.g., voice, facial expression, body movements, choice of words) that can be observed with human sense organs but may also be measured with scientific equipment. The fourth class is based on overt, direct investigations and includes employment questionnaires; background checks; and employee surveys, questionnaires, and paper-and-pencil tests. We consider each of these in turn.

AUTONOMIC INDICATORS

The polygraph is the best-known technique for psychophysiological detection of deception. The goal of all of these techniques is to detect deception by analyzing signals of changes in the body that cannot normally be detected by human observation. The physiological phenomena recorded by the polygraph are only a few of the many physiological phenomena that have been characterized since the polygraph was first introduced and that might, in principle, yield signals of deception.

The polygraph relies on measurements of autonomic and somatic activity. That is, it analyzes signals of peripheral physiological activities associated with arousal and emotion. The traditional measures used in polygraph testing are cardiovascular (i.e., changes in heart rate and blood pressure), electrodermal (i.e., changes in the electrical properties of the skin that vary with the activity of the eccrine sweat gland), and respiratory (see Chapter 3). These are among the oldest measures used by psychophysiologists.

A wider variety of visceral events can now be recorded noninvasively, including myocardial contractility, cardiac output, total peripheral resistance, skin temperature (thermography), and vascular perfusion in various cutaneous tissue beds (Blascovich, 2000; Cacioppo, Tassinary, and Berntson, 2000a). Several of these measures provide clearer information than traditional polygraph measurements about the underlying neurophysiological events that produce visceral adjustments. Given appropriate measurement contexts and controls, for instance, respiratory sinus arrhythmia can be used to reflect cardiac vagal activation, and myocardial contractility (e.g., as assessed by pre-ejection period) can be used to measure cardiac sympathetic activation (e.g., Berntson et al., 1994; Cacioppo et al., 1994).

Because some of these measures are closer than polygraph-based measures to the specific physiological processes associated with arousal, there are theoretical reasons to expect that they might offer better indicators of arousal than those used in polygraph testing. However, although some of these measures have advantages over polygraph measures on grounds of theoretical psychophysiology, they may not actually map more closely to psychological variables. Like the polygraph indicators, measures such as myocardial contractility and respiratory sinus arrhythmia are influenced by sundry social and psychological factors (e.g., Berntson et al., 1997; Gardner, Gabriel, and Diekman, 2000). These factors might result in false positive test results if an examinee is aroused by something other than deception (e.g., a concern about false accusations) or might provide a basis for countermeasures.

Despite these caveats, various researchers have proposed the use of some of these autonomic measurements as alternatives or adjuncts to the four basic channels that are part of the standard polygraph measurement instrument. The limited research on these measures does not offer any basis for determining where they may fit in the array of possible physiological measurements. The studies generally report on the accuracy of tests using a particular measure in small samples or in uncontrolled settings.

A recent report on thermal imaging illustrates the difficulties we have had in assessing whether these peripheral measures are promising and precisely how research on them should be pursued. In 2001, investigators at the U.S. Department of Defense Polygraph Institute (DoDPI), collaborating with outside researchers, carried out a pilot study (Pollina and Ryan, 2002) using a comparison question format polygraph for a mock crime scenario with 30 examinees who were trainees at an army base. Their goal was to investigate the possible utility of a new device for thermography that measures the radiant energy emitted from examinees' faces, as an adjunct or alternative to the traditional polygraph measurements. Thermography has an important potential advantage over the polygraph in that it does not require an examinee to be hooked up to a machine.

Five of the original examinees in the study were dropped because they were uncooperative or had other problematic behavior. Of the remaining 25, 12 were programmed to be deceptive and 13 were programmed to be nondeceptive. The outside researchers published a report (Pavlidis, Eberhardt, and Levine, 2002) claiming that the thermal imaging results alone achieved higher accuracy than the polygraph on nondeceptive examinees (11 of 12 subjects correct for thermal imaging compared with 8 of 12 for the polygraph) and equivalent accuracy on deceptive ones (6 of 8 correct). Unfortunately, the published report uses only a subset of the examinees and offers no information on the selection process. It also gives no information on the decision criteria used for judging deceptiveness from the thermographic data.

The DoDPI researchers were interested in the possibility of combining the new information with that from the traditional polygraph channels. This required a new effort at computer scoring, as well as an explicit effort at extracting statistical information from the thermal recordings. The DoDPI report indicates moderately high correspondence with experimental conditions for polygraph testing (an accuracy index [A] of 0.88), relatively low correspondence with thermal signals alone (A of 0.70), and some incremental information when the two sets of information are combined (A of 0.92). Despite the public attention focused on the published version of this study in *Nature* (Pavlidis, Eberhardt, and Levine, 2002), it remains a flawed and incomplete evaluation based on a small sample, with no cross-validation of measurements and no blind evaluation. It does not provide acceptable scientific evidence to support the use of facial thermography in the detection of deception.

MEASUREMENTS OF BRAIN FUNCTION

The polygraph and other measures of autonomic and somatic activity reflect the peripheral manifestations of very complex cognitive and affective operations that occur when people give deceptive or nondeceptive answers to questions. By their very nature, polygraph measurements provide an extremely limited and indirect view of the complex underlying brain processes. A reasonable hypothesis is that by looking at brain function more directly, it might be possible to understand and ultimately detect deception. This section discusses some brain measurement technologies that are beginning to be explored for their ability to yield techniques for the psychophysiological detection of deception.

Functional Brain Imaging

Over the past 15 years, the field of cognitive neuroscience has grown significantly. Cognitive neuroscience combines the experimental strategies of cognitive psychology with various techniques to actually examine how brain function supports mental activities. Leading this research are two new techniques of functional brain imaging: positron emission tomography (PET) and magnetic resonance imaging (MRI) (see Buxton [2002] and Carson, Daube-Witherspoon, and Herscovitch [1997] for comprehensive general reviews). Over the past 5 years, these techniques have been used to study affective processes (see Davidson and Irwin, 1999), and there is a burgeoning literature on the neural correlates of cognitive and affective processes that is potentially relevant to psychophysiological detection of deception. Their use to study brain activity associated with deception is only beginning.

PET uses a measure of local blood flow, which invariably accompanies changes in the cellular activity of the brain of normal, awake humans and unanesthetized laboratory animals (for a review, see Raichle, 1987). More recently it has been appreciated that these changes in blood flow are accompanied by much smaller changes in oxygen consumption (Fox and Raichle, 1986; Fox et al., 1988). These changes lead to changes in the actual amount of oxygen remaining in blood vessels at the site of brain activation (i.e., the supply of oxygen is not matched precisely with the demand). Because MRI signal intensity is sensitive to the amount of oxygen carried by hemoglobin (Ogawa et al., 1990), this change in blood oxygen content at the site of changes in brain activity can be detected with MRI (Bandettini et al., 1992; Frahm et al., 1992; Kwong et al., 1992; Ogawa et al., 1992). The detection of these blood-oxygen-level-dependent (BOLD) signals with MRI has become known as functional magnetic resonance imaging or fMRI. Research with fMRI is now providing increasingly detailed maps of human brain function.

Several recent studies provide the beginnings of a scientific underpinning for using fMRI measures for detecting deception. These studies include research on knowledge and emotion. For example, some recent work (e.g., Shah et al., 2001; Tsivilis, Otten, and Rugg, 2001) suggests that seeing familiar names or faces produces distinctively different areas of brain activation than unfamiliar names or faces. In addition, to the extent that deception is associated with increased activation of circuitry associated with anxiety, activation of the amygdala and regions of the prefrontal cortex both reliably accompany certain forms of anxiety (Davidson, 2002). Such studies can help build a theory linking deception to psychological states and specific physiological correlates that might be applied in the future to develop neuroimaging methods for the detection of deception.

Other research is examining the connections between brain activity and phenomena that the polygraph measures. For example, at least five studies combining functional imaging (both PET and fMRI) with simultaneous measurements of the skin conductance response have investigated the brain basis of the conductance response (Critchley et al., 2000; Fredrikson et al., 1998; Raine, Reynolds, and Sheard, 1991; Williams et al., 2000, 2001). These studies show that it reflects a complex interplay in areas of the brain implicated in both emotion regulation and attention. These studies are complemented by parallel studies in patients with well-characterized lesions (Tranel and Damasio, 1994; Zahn, Grafman, and Tranel, 1999). The results of these studies underscore the complexity of the circuitry involved and also illustrate how the relationship between brain function and behavior can be understood in more detail when information on the former is directly available.

More immediately relevant to the use of fMRI for the detection of deception are the very few recent studies that use fMRI to identify associations between deception and specific brain activity. One recent study adapted the guilty knowledge test format for use with fMRI (Langleben et al., 2001). In 23 normal subjects, it was possible to detect localized activity changes in the brain that were uniquely associated with deception. Remarkably, these changes occurred in areas of the brain known to participate in situations involving response conflict (Miller and Cohen, 2001). In the study, the conflict involved overriding one (correct) response and providing a second (false or deceptive) response to a question.

Another study (Spence et al., 2001) used fMRI to study deception in an autobiographical memory task in which examinees were instructed to be truthful or to lie. The findings from this experiment indicated that during lying, compared with truthful responding, examinees exhibited significantly greater activation in the ventrolateral prefrontal cortex and the medial prefrontal cortex. Activation in several additional regions differentiated less strongly between the experimental conditions. In yet another recent study, Lee and colleagues (2002) instructed some subjects to feign a memory problem and deliberately do poorly on two memory tasks. One involved memorizing a three-digit number and reporting its correspondence with another number presented 2.25 seconds later; the other involved memory for the answers to such autobiographical questions such as "Where were you born?" The researchers reported differential patterns of activation that held across the two tasks when feigned memory impairment was compared with control conditions. The findings from this study revealed a distributed set of activations that included several regions of the prefrontal, parietal, and temporal cortices, the caudate nucleus, and the posterior cingulate gyrus.

The above studies suggest what might in principle be achieved by using a technique such as fMRI for the detection of deception. They also suggest the kinds of information needed in brain-based studies of detecting deception. These investigations seek to identify signatures of particular kinds of cognitive activity in brain processes. Yet even if fMRI studies could eventually identify signatures of acts of deception, it would be premature to conclude that fMRI techniques would be useful in practice for lie detection. Applied fMRI studies of the kinds done so far have similar limitations to those of typical laboratory polygraph research. They have limited external validity: the experimental lies were not high-stakes ones, and no penalty was presented for a failure to successfully deceive. They also have some similar limitations at the level of the basic science. For example, the brain regions activated by deception in the research on feigned memory impairment are activated not only during deception. Their activation probably reflects the very complicated constellation of cognitive and affective processes that are involved in particular kind of task. Identifying areas of brain activation that are specific to deception is not on the horizon, and it is by no means clear that such areas will ever be identified.

There are also several major methodological obstacles to be overcome in the use of fMRI for the detection of deception. First, studies with fMRI, including those mentioned here, involve the averaging of information over examinees. While such a strategy is enormously powerful for understanding general processes within the human brain, it ignores the need to obtain information on particular individuals that is central to the use of fMRI in the detection of deception. Only recently has work begun on the study of individual differences with fMRI, and much more will need to be done to optimize signal and reduce noise in such images so as to take individual differences into account. While this is very likely to be achieved in time, fMRI analysis is expensive and time-consuming (sometimes as long as 2 to 3 hours per examinee), and the analysis of these data is likely to remain complex for the foreseeable future. For these reasons, fMRI is not presently useful for the psychophysiological detection of deception in many applied settings, and the complexity of analysis may be a prohibitive factor for all applications, for quite some time. Nonetheless, much valuable new information can be learned from research using this powerful technique to advance theoretical understanding of the kinds of cognitive processes involved in deception and perhaps to identify the brain mechanisms underlying countermeasures designed to prevent its detection. Acquisition of such information will be important if new and more effective techniques for detecting deception are to be developed.

EEG and Event-Related Potentials

Caton (1875) was the first to show that electrical activity of the human brain can be detected from electrodes placed on the scalp. It was Berger's invention of the electroencephalogram (EEG) some years later (Berger, 1929) that made recording of these signals a practical reality. Since then they have been successfully exploited for diagnostic as well as research purposes. Davis (1939) was the first to notice event-related changes in the EEG that have subsequently become known as event-related potentials.

He observed a large negative response in the EEG about 100 to 200 milliseconds after each presentation of an auditory stimulus.

Brain electrical activity is typically measured in terms of either frequency or time. In frequency analyses, the complex waveforms recorded from the scalp are decomposed into underlying frequencies (using a mathematical transformation, such as the Fourier transformation). Time analyses are often referred to as event-related potentials, which represent averages of the brain electrical signals in relation to an external stimulus or subject response after a certain time interval. There are many advantages and a number of distinct disadvantages of this method for measuring human brain function. One of the key advantages is that brain electrical activity measures have excellent time resolution, allowing researchers to resolve changes that occur in milliseconds. Another distinct advantage is that measurement is completely noninvasive and so can be used repeatedly in an individual and can be made relatively portable. The major disadvantage is that event-related potentials provide only coarse information about the neural sources of the activity that is measured at the scalp.

There is an established tradition of using measures of brain electrical activity to make inferences about neural correlates of cognitive and affective processes (see Hugdahl, 1995, for review). The fact that brain electrical activity can be clearly connected in time to the occurrence of discrete external events provides a potentially powerful tool for investigating the neural correlates of deception.

A number of studies have attempted to use event-related potentials to examine different aspects of deception. In one of the earliest applications of this methodology, Rosenfeld and his colleagues (1987) allowed examinees to choose an item to keep from a box that contained nine items and used a form of the guilty knowledge test to tell which one was selected. Examinees were instructed not to react as the items were named, to try to defeat this test of deception. A large positive component was present in the event-related potentials between 400 and 700 milliseconds after the presentation of the chosen item but not after the other items. In another study, Rosenfeld and colleagues (Rosenfeld et al., 1991) investigated the modulation the P300 component of the event-related potential during deception (P300 is a positive wave of the event-related potential that occurs approximately 300 milliseconds following a stimulus). There is a very large literature on the psychological significance of the P300, and it appears to reflect task relevance, stimulus probability, or information processing resources being used (see Donchin and Coles, 1988, for a review). Rosenfeld et al. (1991) used a hybrid test format that they characterized as a control question test to ask about a series of antisocial acts, one of which the guilty examinees had conducted in a simulation. When the acts were reviewed and rehearsed on the day of the study, 12 of 13 guilty subjects and 13 of 15 innocent subjects were correctly classified on the basis of the P300 amplitude. However, when evaluation of the event-related potentials was conducted on a separate day from the review and rehearsal of the target acts, only 3 of 8 subjects were correctly classified.

Variants of these studies using concealed information formats have since appeared. They typically indicate that the P300 component of the event-related potential, when examined under specific restricted laboratory conditions, can accurately classify approximately 85 percent of examinees in simulation experiments (e.g., Farwell and Donchin, 1991; Johnson and Rosenfeld, 1992; Allen and Iacono, 1997). This level of accuracy is roughly the same as that reported for simple electrodermal measures (see MacLaren, 2001, for review).

In a recent study, Farwell and Smith (2001) used a composite measure of brain electrical activity, including the P300 and other metrics, to examine reactivity to autobiographical information. They report extremely high accuracies of classifying examinees according to the knowledge they possess. However, the range of stimuli to which examinees were exposed was small, and the sample size was very small (only three examinees per condition). Whether these findings generalize to other, more complex contexts in larger groups is not known.

Three recent unpublished studies (Johnson et al., 2002a, b, c) further explore the role of event-related potentials (the P300, the N100, and related measures) and behavioral measurements in understanding the underlying mechanisms involved in making deceptive responses. This work deals with issues such as response conflict and the conscious regulation of actions; it is similar to work in cognitive neuroscience using fMRI techniques. Both approaches emphasize the importance of specific control processes in the mental activities that must underlie deception. They also have similar shortcomings in terms of their applicability to the psychophysiological detection of deception. As with the fMRI studies, this research has not yet included controlled trials that allow assessment of regularities within individual examinees.

These studies have not systematically investigated the incremental validity of event-related potential measures in comparison with what might be achieved with the indicators traditionally used in the polygraph or the possibility that combining the polygraph with P300 might yield better classification than either approach alone. In addition, it is not known whether simple countermeasures could potentially defeat this approach by generating brain electrical responses to comparison questions that mimic those that occur with relevant questions.

DETECTION OF DECEPTION FROM DEMEANOR

Some techniques for detecting deception are based on the interpretation of subtle signals in behavior or demeanor, defined here as activities of an individual that can be observed with the usual human senses, without physical contact with the individual and therefore, potentially, without the individual's knowledge. Demeanor includes, among other things, gaze, posture, facial expressions, body movements, sound of the voice, and the patterns and content of speech when one person talks to another during an interview, interrogation, or any other conversation. We use the term detection of deception from demeanor to refer to efforts to discriminate lying from truth-telling on the basis of such cues. There can be a fine line between such detection and peripheral measurement of autonomic responses, as suggested, for example, by thermal imaging techniques. These techniques can detect both phenomena that a trained observer can learn to discriminate (such as blushing) and others that are beyond the capabilities of human senses because they involve infrared emissions. Because thermal imaging primarily measures infrared emissions, we classify it with techniques for the psychophysiological detection of deception.

Several authors have reviewed the large body of research connecting lying or truth-telling to cues from demeanor (Zuckerman, DePaulo, and Rosenthal, 1981, 1986; Zuckerman and Driver, 1985; DePaulo, Stone, and Lassiter, 1985; DePaulo et al., 2001; Ekman, 2001). Because this research is rooted in social psychology more than in law enforcement or counterintelligence practice, it has a somewhat different flavor and focus than the polygraph research (reviewed in Chapters 4 and 5). Many of the studies, for example, concern everyday "white lies" and other deliberate untruths that may be quite different psychologically from serious lies or truth telling, such as occur about suspected criminal activity or espionage. Their findings may not transfer to such practical settings. Some of the reviews do not analyze results in a way that shows how many subjects were correctly or incorrectly classified as liars or truth-tellers and how many could not be classified. Also, many of the studies focus on specific demeanor cues or classes of cues, rather than on building a full capability for detecting deception from demeanor by combining information on any aspects of demeanor that might provide useful information. For such reasons, large segments of the research have very limited practical relevance for criminal or security investigation contexts. In addition, most of the research has limitations in terms of external validity, as does most polygraph research: for example, the stakes are almost always low, and there are no negative consequences for being judged to be lying. In this context, it is worth noting the results from one meta-analytic study (DePaulo et al., 2001) indicating that the associations of demeanor indicators with deception tended to increase when people were more highly motivated to succeed and when lies were about transgressions rather than about less personally significant matters. If these findings are robust, the accuracy of detection of deception from demeanor may be expected to increase with the stakes, so that it would perform better in real criminal or security investigation settings than in much of the research literature.

This section is organized by classes of demeanor cues for which there has been significant research attention to the detection of deception. We conclude with an assessment of the potential of cues from demeanor as tools in criminal and security screening.

Facial and Body Movement

Some studies of demeanor and deception show internally reliable associations of facial or movement cues with deception. Few of these associations, however, have appeared consistently across large numbers of studies, and some cues associated with deception in conventional wisdom, such as avoidance of eye contact, have not shown reliable associations with deception in research studies (DePaulo et al., 2001). The meta-analytic literature fails to identify any pattern of facial or body movement that generally signals deception. However, some studies designed to develop indicators based on these movements show some ability to discriminate lying from truth-telling. For example, Ekman and his colleagues studied lying or truth-telling under fairly strong motivational conditions about three different matters: emotions felt at the moment (Ekman et al., 1991), a strongly held belief, and whether money was taken (Frank and Ekman, 1997). The motivation for the liar was either career success (for lies about emotions) or $100 (for the belief and money scenarios). Punishment involving loss or money and isolation in a dark room was also threatened for anyone, truthful or not, who was judged to be lying. An index based on precise measurement of all facial movement, voice pitch, and one body movement yielded a hit rate of 58 percent of all examinees lying about their emotions—86 percent of those who could be classified by the index. The study of lies about actions and beliefs with only measures of facial behavior yielded a hit rate of 75 percent for the lie about beliefs and 70 percent for the lie about actions. These studies suggest that the right measures of facial and motion features can offer accuracy better than chance for the detection of deception from demeanor in somewhat realistic situations. At present, the measurement of facial behavior and body movement is very labor intensive; recent work suggests, however, that it will be possible to automate the measurement of facial movements (Bartlett et al., 1999; Cohn et al., 1999).

Linguistic Analysis

Several different aspects of language use seem to be consistently associated with deception. For some of the strongest associations, such as with immediacy of expression (e.g., using active or passive voice, affirmations or negations), observers' subjective impressions have been more strongly correlated with deception than the objective measures that have been tested (DePaulo et al., in press). This finding suggests that efforts to design measures for the detection of deception based on language use may have untapped potential.

There have been a few efforts to develop such techniques. For example, one field study (Smith, 2001) evaluated scientific content analysis, developed by Sapir (1987), using statements made by criminal suspects who were later confirmed to be either lying or truthful. This approach can only be applied to written statements made by the suspect without assistance. Trained policemen correctly detected 80 percent of truthful statements and 75 percent of deceptive statements, but experienced policemen not trained in the technique were just as accurate. The study design did not make it possible to tell whether the examiners might have been making judgments based on their own experience rather than by using the principles for the technique. In either case, the study strongly suggests that close examination of how a suspect describes an incident of interest is likely to be fruitful. Pennebaker, Francis, and Booth (2001) and Newman and colleagues (2002) applied a computer program for analyzing five different aspects of language usage (e.g., first person or third person pronouns) to interviews about laboratory lies when the stakes were minimal. The program accurately classified 68 percent of those who lied and 66 percent of those who were truthful.

Another technique for analyzing cues in language is statement validity analysis (Horowitz, 1991; Lamb et al., 1997; Porter and Yuille, 1996; Steller and Koehnken, 1989). This technique, which involves content analysis of in-depth accounts of alleged events, has been used primarily to assess statements of victims or witnesses. There is evidence that credible accounts are more likely to contain an appropriate amount of detail about the alleged event (e,g., Steller and Koehnken, 1989; Porter and Yuille, 1996). Very little research has been done, however, on the technique's applicability to statements by criminal suspects, some of whom may be unwilling or unable to provide detailed accounts (Porter and Yuille, 1995).

In sum, the available evidence suggests that analysis of language usage and of facial and body movement might be useful in distinguishing lies from truth. It is reasonable to expect that accuracy can be improved by using measures that combine information from several channels (e.g., facial expression, various body movements, posture, and various mea-sures of speech). The evidence suggests that such measures are likely to have the greatest success when lies have high personal relevance, when the stakes are high, when the liar knows he or she is telling a lie when it is being told, and before there has been opportunity to practice and rehearse the lie (Ekman, 2001; DePaulo et al., 2001). So far, however, no research has been done combining all of the behavior measures and testing their accuracy under the appropriate circumstances.

Training Observers

Given the apparent potential for the detection of deception from de-meanor and the difficulty and limited effectiveness of objective measure-ment so far, the question arises whether it might be possible to train observers to make accurate judgments from demeanor without formal measurements. Without training, most observers, even experienced law enforcement personnel or security officers, cannot do much better than chance, and their confidence in their judgment is unrelated to accuracy (Ekman and O'Sullivan, 1991; Ekman, O'Sullivan, and Frank, 1999). Some groups, however, do perform better than chance in detecting lies from demeanor just by viewing videotapes. A group of U.S. Secret Service agents averaged 64 percent correct judgments when chance performance was 50 percent, with about half of them achieving an accuracy level of 70 percent or more (Ekman and O'Sullivan, 1991). No studies have yet been done to determine if those who do poorly in detecting deception from demeanor can be trained to become very accurate. However, a review of the research on training effects in deception studies showed a moderate improvement (Frank and Feeley, 2002).

Voice Stress Analysis

The research on the detection of deception from demeanor includes the presumption that liars experience more stress than truth-tellers, espe-cially in high-stakes circumstances, and that this stress shows in various channels, including in the voice. Recent meta-analytic evidence shows consistent associations of lying with vocal tension and high pitch (DePaulo et al., in press). Applied efforts to develop measures of voice stress for the detection of deception have not been very successful, however.

As early as 1941, Faye and Middleton attempted to use human judg-ment of voice responses to determine deceptions of subjects told to an-swer a series of questions either truthfully or untruthfully. Their method-ology yielded correct judgments for truthful responses at essentially chance levels and slightly higher rates of correct judgments for untruthful responses. Other studies, for example by Motley (1974), Horvath (1978, 1979), Lynch and Henry (1979) and Brenner, Branscomb, and Schwartz (1979), have attempted, with limited success at best, to extract information from recorded voice signals to measure stress in analogue studies and then to use the resulting determination as an indirect indicator of deception in much the same way as is done in polygraph research.

Various instruments have been developed over the past 20 years or more that purport to detect deception by means of signals of "voice stress" as reflected in intensity, frequency, pitch, harmonics, and even microtremors. One of the more widely used devices is the computer voice stress analyzer, manufactured by the National Institute for Truth Verification (NITV), which is now used by a number of law enforcement agencies. The underlying theory for the analyzer and some of its predecessor instruments is that the instrument detects physiological microtremors in muscles in the voice mechanism that are associated with deception.

In addition to manufacturing the computer voice stress analyzer, NITV publishes its own journal reporting on the ease of use of the analyzer and its utility in obtaining confessions. NITV also trains and certifies voice stress analysts using protocols for question format and sequences of relevant and irrelevant questions that are remarkably like those used for polygraph testing. The polygraph seems to be the reference point and the target of marketing for NITV and the analyzer. For example, Tippett (1995), writing in the NITV journal, argues that earlier failures to obtain high accuracy rates with the analyzer and similar devices were largely due to the low levels of jeopardy involved in the analog studies. He reports on a study of 54 subjects undergoing mandatory therapy as a condition of probation for past sex offenses and claims to have found "100 percent agreement between the [computer voice stress analyzer] and the polygraph" in the judgments of examiners for the respective techniques. The article does not report on the methods used for scoring or for determining truth, so is not usable for judging the accuracy of the analyzer.

Although proponents of voice stress analysis claim high levels of accuracy, empirical research on the validity of the technique has been far from encouraging. First, the reliability of this method is highly suspect (Horvath, 1978; Waln and Downey, 1987). The agreement between readings of the same voice stress charts by independent analysts is generally low, and correlations of test results between interviews in their original form and recordings of the same interviews transmitted over the telephone are also low (Waln and Downey, 1987). Second, the validity of judgments made on the basis of voice stress analysis appears to be questionable (Lykken, 1981). For example, Horvath (1979) showed approximately chance level of success in identifying deception in mock crime situations, and O'Hair and Cody (1987) found voice stress analyses to be unsuccessful in detecting spontaneous lies in a simulated job interview. Voice stress analysis may be more successful in detecting real crimes or other nontrivial deceptions, when the level of stress is presumably higher, but even in these cases the evidence of accuracy is rather slim.

During the 1990s, the U.S. Department of Defense Polygraph Institute (DoDPI) carried out a series of laboratory tests comparing the use of the computer voice stress analyzer and the polygraph using peak of tension and control question test formats. Cestaro and Dollins (1994) used a peak of tension test to compare with the analyzer in a standard laboratory comparison, and Cestaro (1996) and Janniro and Cestaro (1996) carried out comparisons with control question test formats for mock crime scenarios. These studies, which suffer from the same methodological deficiencies as most polygraph research, found that the computer voice stress analyzer was never significantly superior in its detection accuracy to the polygraph and that neither had exceptionally high correct detection rates. Palmatier (1996) conducted the only field test comparison, in collaboration with the Michigan Department of Police, using confirmed guilty and a group of presumably truthful examinees. Again, the analyzer results were close to chance levels (polygraph results were not reported). The detailed administration of the analyzer tests was severely criticized by the NITV, and the details of these criticisms are appended to the report. The most recently completed DoDPI study (Meyerhoff et al., 2000) compared the computer voice stress analyzer with biochemical and direct physiological measures of stress and concluded that the analyzer scores did not reflect the acute stress observed by more traditional stress measurements.

Overall, this research and the few controlled tests conducted over the past decade offer little or no scientific basis for the use of the computer voice stress analyzer or similar voice measurement instruments as an alternative to the polygraph for the detection of deception. The practical performance of voice stress analysis for detecting deception has not been impressive. It is possible that research conducted in high-stakes situations would give better results, but we have not found reports of the accuracy of voice stress analysis in such situations.

Graphology

Handwriting analysis, or graphology, is sometimes used to make inferences about honesty, integrity, or dependability. The underlying theory is that various characteristics of a person's handwriting provide information about his or her personality, including such traits as honesty or loyalty. Although there are serious questions regarding the validity of assessments provided by this technique (Bar-Hillel and Ben-Shakhar, 1986; Ben-Shakhar, 1989), it is widely used, especially in Israel (Ben-Shakhar et al., 1986) and Europe (Ben-Shakhar and Furedy, 1990). In the United States, more than 2,000 employers were thought to be using graphology in preemployment screening in the 1980s (Sinai, 1988).

Graphologists examine a number of specific structural characteristics of a handwriting sample (e.g., letter shapes and sizes) to make inferences about the writer. Graphologists typically insist that the sample must be spontaneous and that handwriting samples that involve copying text from a book or writing a passage from memory will not yield a valid reading. Graphologists often request a brief autobiographical sketch or some other sort of self-description (Ben-Shakhar, 1989; Ben-Shakhar et al., 1986).

Although there is some evidence of temporal stability and interrater agreement in graphological analyses (Tziner, Chantale, and Cusson, 1993), evidence regarding validity is limited, at best. Graphologists claim that their assessments and evaluations are the result only of close examination of the features of letters, words, and lines in the sample and are not influenced by the content or the quality of the writing sample (e.g., fluency, clarity of expression). This claim is called into question by two lines of evidence. First, when the same biographical passages are examined by graphologists and other analysts, their assessments of individual examinees tend to agree, and graphologists are no more accurate in their assessments than the other analysts (Ben-Shakhar et al., 1986; Ben-Shakhar, 1989). Indeed, predictions based solely on the content of writing samples, using a simple unweighted linear model based on information from the passages, were more accurate than those obtained from professional graphologists (Ben-Shakhar et al., 1986). Second, when the content of passages is not biographical in nature (e.g., meaningless text or text copied from some standard source), graphologists seldom make valid predictions. These findings strongly suggest that the graphological features of the writing do not increase the ability to make assessments of the writer.

The available evidence also casts doubt on graphologists' ability to make even the most general assessments of individuals more accurately than others given the same materials (Ben-Shakhar, 1989; Jansen, 1973; Murphy, 1993; Neter and Ben-Shakhar, 1989; Rafaeli and Klimoski, 1983). This research suggests that assessments of specific characteristics, such as honesty and integrity, by graphology will not be successful. There is little, if any, empirical research that adequately assesses the accuracy of specific assessments made by graphologists (e.g., assessments of a candidate's honesty), but given the generally dismal track record of graphologists in making global predictions, there is very little reason to believe that their more specific predictions will be any better.

Overall Assessment

Theoretically, it should be possible to detect deception from demeanor with some skill. And evidence from experimental and field studies has identified some cues emitted by people who are deceptive, particularly in high-stakes situations, that can be observed with human sense organs. Moreover, a small proportion of experienced interviewers exhibit skill in detecting deception from such cues. However, attempts to systematize such skill have so far been disappointing. Voice stress analysis and graphology, two commonly used techniques, have not convincingly demonstrated accuracy for detecting deception.

The gap between the promise and the practice of the detection of deception from demeanor has several possible explanations. It may be that different liars emit different cues, so that any standard protocol would have only limited accuracy. It may also be that research has not yet identified the most valid behavioral indicators of deception. The research has seemed to focus mostly on particular channels (e.g., facial expression, voice quality) rather than on developing an underlying theory of behavioral indicators or searching for several indicators, possibly including disparate channels, that have high accuracy in situations of interest. It seems possible that such approaches could lead to methods of detecting deception from demeanor with practical value. It is also possible that such methods might add information to what can be achieved by physiological indicators—though that possibility has not to our knowledge been investigated. In our judgment, the search for useful methods of detecting deception should not exclude efforts to find valid indicators in the subtleties of behavior.

DIRECT INVESTIGATION

Methods of direct investigation, such as background checks, interviews, and the like are already used for making personnel decisions, both with and without the polygraph as accompaniment. This section reviews what is known about the ability of these techniques to detect individuals who pose risks to their employers' objectives.

Background Checks

Little scientific evidence is available about the validity of the background checks and other investigative methods that have been used to identify individuals who create threats to national security. There is some anecdotal evidence, however, on the value of these methods. Publicly available reports indicate that the spies who have been detected within the U.S. government have been detected by normal investigative techniques. This track record supports the validity of investigations; it does not provide scientific evidence on their incremental value over polygraph testing or the incremental value of polygraph testing over background checks.

Some scientific evidence exists on reference checks and background investigations as used in the private sector for preemployment screening. Schmidt and Hunter's (1999) meta-analysis on preemployment reference checks suggests that the information gained has at best only a modest correlation with performance on the job and in training.[1] Background investigations are used by almost all police departments as part of their personnel selection processes (Decicco, 2000; Nelson, 1999). Researchers have advocated the development of structured protocols for investigating previous behaviors of job applicants (e.g., Dwyer, Prien, and Bernard, 1990), but there is little evidence of scientifically based approaches to background checks. On the contrary, background investigators are often untrained (Fuss, McSheey, and Snowden, 1998), and their investigations are rarely standardized. Background investigations might include obtaining photographs and fingerprints, conducting in-depth personal interviews, drug screens, the compilation and assessment of criminal history, employment history, military service, and driving records, as well as interviews with family members and persons familiar with the candidate (Harvey and Ward, 1996; Kirksey and Smith, 1998; Wright, 1991). These investigations often take 40 or more hours to complete (Harvey and Ward, 1996).

Empirical assessments of the validity of background investigations are rare. As with polygraph tests, the fact that background checks often yield derogatory or disqualifying information about those being evaluated is taken as *prima facie* evidence of their value. However, there have been instances where so much derogatory information is obtained that it becomes impossible to fill positions. Dickson (1986) described a program combining polygraphs with background investigations used in screening police applicants. Of the 2,711 applicants screened with this program, 1,626 (60 percent) were rejected, many of whom had committed serious felony crimes. Because a majority of applicants had used illegal drugs at some time, rejection standards had to be amended.

There are two factors that limit the utility of background checks as a general screening tool. First, they are time-consuming and expensive, and in most police departments and many other security-sensitive employers, staffing and budgetary constraints make it impossible to carry out background checks for most or all candidates. Second, these investigations can be intrusive, and applicants and the general public may regard the invasions of privacy that accompany background examinations as unwarranted unless the candidate is under serious consideration for hiring. Most agencies that use background checks do so late in the selection process, after most applicants have been screened out and the applicant pool has been narrowed down to qualified candidates who have a reasonable chance of being considered for the job.

Standardized Tests

Standardized tests, though not commonly used to assess deceptiveness, are widely used by employers to assess conscientiousness, dependability, and integrity. These techniques have improved over time as a result of refinements and learning from research.[2]

An example is integrity testing. Such tests were used by 10 to 15 percent of all U.S. employers in the 1980s, concentrated in the retail sales, banking, and food service industries, and over 2.5 million tests were given by over 5,000 employers each year (O'Bannon, Goldinger, and Appleby, 1989). Current figures for integrity test use are probably even higher because of increasing awareness of the cost and extent of employee theft and increasing evidence of the validity of several widely distributed tests.

Virtually all integrity tests include items that refer to one or more of the following areas: (a) direct admissions of illegal or questionable activities, (b) opinions regarding illegal or questionable behavior, (c) general personality traits and thought patterns thought to be related to dishonesty (e.g. the tendency to constantly think about illegal activities), and (d) reactions to hypothetical situations that may or may not feature dishonest behavior.

Several reviews of research are available on the reliability, validity, and usefulness of integrity tests (Sackett, Burris, and Callahan, 1989; Goldberg et al., 1991; U.S. Office of Technology Assessment, 1983). The early reviews of research on integrity tests were sharply critical, but both the research and the tests themselves appear to have improved, partly as a result of the earlier criticism. There is now a substantial body of evidence showing that integrity tests have some validity for predicting a variety of criteria that are relevant to organizations. This research does not say that tests of this sort will eliminate theft or dishonesty at work, but it does suggest that individuals who receive poor scores on these tests tend to be less desirable employees.

Although the reviews all raise concerns and several lament the shortcomings of research on the validity of integrity tests, the general conclusion of the more recent reviews is positive. A large-scale meta-analysis that quantitatively summarized the outcomes of multiple validity studies (Ones, Viswesvaran, and Schmidt, 1993), found that scores on integrity tests were related to measures of job performance and counterproductivity.[3] Different specific criteria have been used to assess validity in different studies: some studies have validated integrity tests against measures of counterproductive behavior; others have validated the tests against measures of general job performance. These two criteria are clearly not independent: employees who engage in a wide variety of counterproductive behavior are unlikely to be good performers. Nevertheless, there are important differences between the two criteria, and more important, differences in the validity of integrity tests for predicting the two. There is no literature correlating the results of these tests with indicators of the more specific kinds of counterproductive behavior of interest in national security settings.

Interviews

Early research on the validity of employment interviews portrayed a consistently negative picture, with correlations to job performance often embarrassingly close to zero (Arvey and Campion, 1982; Hunter and Hunter, 1984; Reilly and Chao, 1982). More recent research suggests that structured interviews—for example, those that include questions about past and potential job situations—can be a useful and valid method of selecting employees (Campion, Pursell, and Brown, 1988; Wiesner and Cronshaw, 1988; Campion, Palmer, and Campion, 1997).

The applicability of these employee screening techniques to the national security context is unclear. The correlations alone do not suggest that they are likely to provide reasonable and valid alternatives to the polygraph. The evidence does suggest, however, that more focused questioning in an interview or testing format is likely to have greater predictive value than unfocused questioning and that standardized measures with acceptable reliability do better than unstandardized methods.

CONCLUSIONS

Various techniques for detecting deception have been suggested or might be used as substitutes for or supplements to the polygraph. None of them has received as much research attention as the polygraph in the context of detecting deception, so evidence on accuracy is only minimal for most of the techniques. Some of the potential alternatives show promise, but none has yet been shown to outperform the polygraph. None shows any promise of supplanting the polygraph for screening purposes in the near term. Our conclusions are based on basic scientific knowledge and available information about accuracy.

Autonomic Measures

Some new or additional autonomic measures for detecting deception seem, on theoretical grounds, to be closer than polygraph measures to the psychological phenomena believed to be signals of deception. Some of them, such as facial thermography, may have practical advantages over the polygraph because they may be quicker, easier, or less invasive. Members of this class of measures that have any of these advantages may be promising alternatives to the polygraph that may be worthy of further investigation. They may have only limited value as supplements, however, if in fact they are measuring the same underlying phenomena. If so, their only potential value as supplements would be to help correct for error in polygraph-based estimates of those phenomena.

Measurements of Brain Function

Functional brain imaging techniques have important advantages over the polygraph, in theory, because they examine directly what the brain is doing. However, they are far from providing a practical alternative or supplement to the polygraph. Part of the limitation is theoretical. Not enough is yet known about the specific cognitive or emotional processes that accompany deception, about their localization in the brain, or about whether imaging signals can differentiate the brain activity associated with these processes from brain activity associated with other processes to make an assessment of the potential validity of these techniques on the grounds of the basic science. Further research with fMRI, coupled with a scientifically based cognitive psychological approach to deception, will be needed to determine if these issues can be addressed. Such research is likely to identify some signals of deception and localize some relevant processes, but not enough is known yet to guess whether the signals will be specific to deception. Functional imaging might also be used in efforts to identify brain signatures of mental activities that might be used as countermeasures to the psychophysiological detection of deception. If a research effort is undertaken to find improved scientific techniques for the detection of deception, basic research on brain imaging would be a top candidate for the research agenda.

There are also major practical problems at present with using brain imaging techniques for the psychophysiological detection of deception. The most likely technique to be used, fMRI, is both time consuming and expensive to perform. A typical research study with fMRI presently takes 2 to 3 hours to perform and many hours thereafter to analyze. Furthermore, almost all research to date has focused on results averaged over groups of individuals. While such an averaging approach is important for understanding basic brain processes, it is antithetical to the use of imaging for detecting deception in individuals. Some recent fMRI studies on individual differences do suggest the possibility of a future role for brain imaging in detecting deception, but much additional research must be done to move that prospect beyond mere possibility.

Measurement of event-related potentials has shown some promise as a way to assess orienting responses that are believed to signal the presentation of material that is familiar to the examinee. If this theory is accurate, they would be appropriate for lie detection in settings when questions can be asked about concealed information. The mechanisms linking deception to event-related potentials have not been clearly elucidated. In fact, it will be difficult to establish the mechanisms because measurement of the potentials is too diffuse to localize the underlying brain activity. Nevertheless, the basis for the orienting response is plausible and the very limited data on accuracy suggest a level similar to that of the polygraph. It seems plausible that event-related potentials tap different underlying phenomena than the polygraph measures, so that combining the two techniques might provide some added validity. This possibility is worth investigating. Some believe that event-related potentials are less vulnerable to countermeasures than the polygraph, which, if true, would make them useful as a substitute for the polygraph when questions about concealed information can be asked. The basic science, however, is unclear on whether or not people can learn to manipulate event-related potentials. There are as yet no empirical data on countermeasures and event-related potentials. In sum, the limited available knowledge justifies further research investigation of measurement of event-related potentials as an alternative or supplement to the polygraph.

Detection of Deception from Demeanor

Although there is considerable research on cues to deception in demeanor, there is relatively little on any one cue and much less on finding combinations of cues that might accurately discriminate lying from truthtelling. Most of the research on deception and demeanor has not been seriously applied to criminal or security investigation contexts. The evidence indicates that the right measure or measures might achieve a useful level of accuracy in those contexts, even though some techniques on the market, such as voice stress analysis, have not demonstrated such accuracy. It is unclear whether accurate demeanor measures would provide information different from the polygraph in terms of the underlying processes assessed: the theory of demeanor indicators is not well enough developed to judge.

Valid demeanor measures would have a significant practical advantage over the polygraph because tests could be conducted noninvasively and even without the examinee's knowledge. We note but do not judge the significant ethical and legal issues raised by this practical advantage. There is also the potential that interrogators might be taught to improve their skills by becoming more sensitive to demeanor indicators. In our judgment, any systematic effort to improve techniques for detecting deception should include attention to measures of demeanor.

Direct Investigation

Available evidence does not suggest that any direct investigation method is likely to provide a reasonable and valid alternative to the polygraph. The evidence does suggest ways to improve these techniques. Studies assessing whether they provide incremental accuracy over the polygraph, or whether the polygraph provides incremental accuracy over direct investigation, have not been done.

Need for Evaluation

Our conclusions about specific potential alternatives or supplements to the polygraph are all tentative and made with limited confidence because of the limited base these techniques now have in either basic science or empirical criterion validation. We have much greater confidence in concluding that security and law enforcement agencies need to improve their capability to independently evaluate claims proffered by advocates of new techniques for detecting deception. The history of the polygraph makes clear that such agencies typically let clinical judgment outweigh scientific evidence in their assessment of the validity of techniques for the psychophysiological detection of deception or the detection of deception from demeanor. Although it is probable that belief in a technique can go a long way in making it useful for deterrence and for eliciting admissions, overconfidence does not in the long run contribute positively to national security or law enforcement goals. Agencies that use such techniques should support independent scientific evaluation so that they can be fully informed when making decisions on whether and how to use the techniques and on how to use the test results they produce. We return to this issue in Chapter 8.

NOTES

1. Reported correlations (Pearson r) are typically between 0.13 and 0.17.
2. Integrity tests, conscientiousness measures, and structured interviews typically show correlations in the range of 0.30 to 0.40 with indicators of job performance (Schmidt and Hunter, 1999).
3. Test scores showed average correlations of 0.21 and 0.33 with job performance and counterproductivity, respectively; correcting for unreliability and a variety of statistical artifacts, the estimated population correlations were 0.34 and 0.47.

7

Uses of Polygraph Tests

Then available evidence indicates that in the context of specific-incident investigation and with inexperienced examinees untrained in countermeasures, polygraph tests as currently used have value in distinguishing truthful from deceptive individuals. However, they are far from perfect in that context, and important unanswered questions remain about polygraph accuracy in other important contexts. No alternative techniques are available that perform better, though some show promise for the long term. The limited evidence on screening polygraphs suggests that their accuracy in field use is likely to be somewhat lower than that of specific-incident polygraphs.

This chapter discusses the policy issues involved in using an imperfect diagnostic test such as the polygraph in real-life decision making, particularly in national security screening, which presents very difficult tradeoffs between falsely judging innocent employees deceptive and leaving major security threats undetected. We synthesize what science can offer to inform the policy decisions, but emphasize that the choices ultimately must depend on a series of value judgments incorporating a weighting of potential benefits (chiefly, deterring and detecting potential spies, saboteurs, terrorists, or other major security threats) against potential costs (such as of falsely accusing innocent individuals and losing potentially valuable individuals from the security related workforce). Cost-benefit tradeoffs like this vary with the situation. For example, the benefits are greater when the security threat being investigated is more serious; the costs are greater when the innocent individuals who might be accused are themselves vital to national security. For this reason, tradeoff decisions are best made by elected officials or their designees, aided by the principles and practices of behavioral decision making.

We first summarize what scientific analysis can contribute to understanding the tradeoffs involved in using polygraph tests in security screening. (These tests almost always use the comparison question or relevant-irrelevant formats because concealed information tests can only be used when there are specific pieces of information that can form the basis for relevant questions.) We then discuss possible strategies for making the tradeoffs more attractive by improving the accuracy of lie detection—either by making polygraph tests more accurate or by combining them with other sources of information. We also briefly consider the legal context of policy choices about the use of polygraph tests in security screening.

TRADEOFFS IN INTERPRETATION

The primary purpose of the polygraph test in security screening is to identify individuals who present serious threats to national security. To put this in the language of diagnostic testing, the goal is to reduce to a minimum the number of false negative cases (serious security risks who pass the diagnostic screen). False positive results are also a major concern: to innocent individuals who may lose the opportunity for gainful employment in their chosen professions and the chance to help their country and to the nation, in the loss of valuable employees who have much to contribute to improved national security, or in lowered productivity of national security organizations. The prospect of false positive results can also have this effect if employees resign or prospective employees do not seek employment because of polygraph screening.

As Chapter 2 shows, polygraph tests, like any imperfect diagnostic tests, yield both false positive and false negative results. The individuals judged positive (deceptive) always include both true positives and false positives, who are not distinguishable from each other by the test alone. Any test protocol that produces a large number of false positives for each true positive, an outcome that is highly likely for polygraph testing in employee security screening contexts, creates problems that must be addressed. Decision makers who use such a test protocol might have to decide to stall or sacrifice the careers of a large number of loyal and valuable employees (and their contributions to national security) in an effort to increase the chance of catching a potential security threat, or to apply expensive and time-consuming investigative resources to the task of identifying the few true threats from among a large pool of individuals who had positive results on the screening test.

Quantifying Tradeoffs

Scientific analysis can help policy makers in such choices by making the tradeoffs clearer. Three factors affect the frequency of false negatives and false positives with any diagnostic test procedure: its accuracy (criterion validity), the threshold used for declaring a test result positive, and the base rate of the condition being diagnosed (here, deception about serious security matters). If a diagnostic procedure can be made more accurate, the result is to reduce both false negatives and false positives. With a procedure of any given level of accuracy, however, the only way to reduce the frequency of one kind of error is by adjusting the decision threshold—but doing this always increases the frequency of the other kind of error. Thus, it is possible to increase the proportion of guilty individuals caught by a polygraph test (i.e., to reduce the frequency of false negatives), but only by increasing the proportion of innocent individuals whom the test cannot distinguish from guilty ones (i.e., frequency of false positives). Decisions about how, when, and whether to use the polygraph for screening should consider what is known about these tradeoffs so that the tradeoffs actually made reflect deliberate policy choices.

Tradeoffs between false positives and false negatives can be calculated mathematically, using Bayes' theorem (Weinstein and Fineberg, 1980; Lindley, 1998). One useful way to characterize the tradeoff in security screening is with a single number that we call the false positive index: the number of false positive cases to be expected for each deceptive individual correctly identified by a test. The index depends on the accuracy of the test; the threshold set for declaring a test positive; and the proportion, or base rate, of individuals in the population with the condition being tested (deception, in this case). The specific mathematical relationship of the index to these factors, and hence the exact value for any combination of accuracy (A), threshold, and base rate, depends on the shape of the receiver operating characteristic (ROC) curve at a given level of accuracy, although the character of the relationship is similar across all plausible shapes (Swets, 1986a, 1996:Chapter 3). Hence, for illustrative purposes we assume that the ROC shapes are determined by the simplest common model, the equivariance binormal model.[1] Because this model, while not implausible, was chosen for simplicity and convenience, the numerical results below should not be taken literally. However, their orders of magnitude are unlikely to change for any alternative class of ROC curves that would be credible for real-world polygraph test performance, and the basic trends conveyed are inherent to the mathematics of diagnosis and screening.

Although accuracy, detection threshold, and base rate all affect the false positive index, these determinants are by no means equally important. Calculation of the index for diagnostic tests at various levels of accuracy, using various thresholds, and with a variety of base rates shows clearly that base rate is by far the most important of these factors. Figure 7-1 shows the index as a function of the base rate of positive (e.g., deceptive) cases for three thresholds for a diagnostic test with A = 0.80. It illustrates clearly that the base rate makes more difference than the threshold across the range of thresholds presented. Figure 7-2 shows the index as a function of accuracy with the threshold held constant so that the diagnostic test's sensitivity (percent of deceptive individuals correctly identified) is 50 percent. It illustrates clearly that base rate makes more difference than the level of accuracy across the range of A values represented.

Figures 7-1 and 7-2 show that the tradeoffs involved in relying on a diagnostic test such as the polygraph, represented by the false positive index values on the vertical axis, are sharply different in situations with high base rates typical of event-specific investigations, when all examinees are identified as likely suspects, and the base rate is usually above 10 percent, than in security screening contexts, when the base rate is normally very low for the most serious infractions. The false positive index is

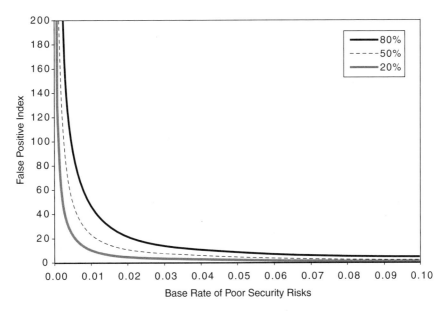

FIGURE 7-1 Comparison of the false positive index and base rate for three sensitivity values of a polygraph test protocol with an accuracy index (A) of 0.80.

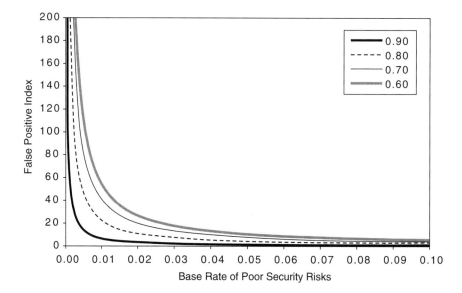

FIGURE 7-2 Comparison of the false positive index and base rate for four values of the accuracy index (A) for a polygraph test protocol with threshold set to correctly identify 50 percent of deceptive examinees.

about 1,000 times higher when the base rate is 1 serious security risk in 1,000 than it is when the base rate is 1 in 2, or 50 percent.

The index is also affected, though less dramatically, by the accuracy of the test procedure: see Figure 7-2. (Appendix I presents the results of calculations of false positive indexes for various levels of accuracy, base rates, and thresholds for making a judgment of a positive test result.) With very low base rates, such as 1 in 1,000, the false positive index is quite large even for tests with fairly high accuracy indexes. For example, a test with an accuracy index of 0.90, if used to detect 80 percent of major security risks, would be expected to falsely judge about 200 innocent people as deceptive for each security risk correctly identified. Unfortunately, polygraph performance in field screening situations is highly unlikely to achieve an accuracy index of 0.90; consequently, the ratio of false positives to true positives is likely to be even higher than 200 when this level of sensitivity is used. Even if the test is set to a somewhat lower level of sensitivity, it is reasonable to expect that each spy or terrorist that might be correctly identified as deceptive by a polygraph test of the accuracy actually achieved in the field would be accompanied by at least hundreds of nondeceptive examinees mislabeled as deceptive. The spy or terrorist would be indistinguishable from these false positives by poly-

graph test results. The possibility that deceptive examinees may use countermeasures makes this tradeoff even less attractive.

It is useful to consider again the tradeoff of false positives versus false
negatives in a manner that sets an upper bound on the attractiveness of
the tradeoff (see Table 2-1, p. 48). The table shows the expected outcomes
of polygraph testing in two hypothetical populations of examinees, assuming that the tests achieve an accuracy index of 0.90, which represents
a higher level of accuracy than can be expected of field polygraph testing.
One hypothetical population consists of 10,000 criminal suspects, of whom
5,000 are expected to be guilty; the other consists of 10,000 employees in
national security organizations, of whom 10 are expected to be spies.

The table illustrates the tremendous difference between these two
populations in the tradeoff. In the hypothetical criminal population, the
vast majority of those who "fail" the test (between 83 and 98 percent in
these examples) are in fact guilty. In the hypothetical security screening
population, however, because of the extremely low base rate of spies, the
vast majority of those who "fail" the test (between 95 and 99.5 percent in
these examples) are in fact innocent of spying. Because polygraph testing
is unlikely to achieve the hypothetical accuracy represented here, even
these tradeoffs are overly optimistic. Thus, in the screening examples, an
even higher proportion than those shown in Table 2-1 would likely be
false positives in actual practice. We reiterate that these conclusions apply to any diagnostic procedure that achieves a similar level of accuracy.
None of the alternatives to the polygraph has yet been shown to have
greater accuracy, so these upper bounds apply to those techniques as
well.

Tradeoffs with "Suspicious" Thresholds

If the main objective is to screen out major security threats, it might
make sense to set a "suspicious" threshold, that is, one that would detect
a very large proportion of truly deceptive individuals. Suppose, for instance, the threshold were set to correctly identify 80 percent of truly
deceptive individuals. In this example, the false positive index is higher
than 100 for any base rate below about 1 in 500, even with A = 0.90. That
is, if 20 of 10,000 employees were serious security violators, and polygraph tests of that accuracy were given to all 10,000 with a threshold set to
correctly identify 16 of the 20 deceptive employees, the tests would also
be expected to identify about 1,600 of the 9,980 good security risks as
deceptive.[2]

Another way to think about the effects of setting a threshold that
correctly detects a very large proportion of deceptive examinees is in
terms of the likelihood that an examinee who is judged deceptive on the

test is actually deceptive. This probability is the positive predictive value of the test. If the base rate of deceptive individuals in a population of examinees is 1 in 1,000, an individual who is judged deceptive on the test will in fact be nondeceptive more than 199 times out of 200, even if the test has A = 0.90, which is highly unlikely for the polygraph (the actual numbers of true and false positives in our hypothetical population are shown in the right half of part a of Table 2-1). Thus, a result that is taken as indicating deception on such a test does so only with a very small probability.

These numbers contrast sharply with their analogs in a criminal investigation setting, in which people are normally given a polygraph test only if they are suspects. Suppose that in a criminal investigation the polygraph is used on suspects who, on other grounds, are estimated to have a 50 percent chance of being guilty. For a test with A = 0.80 and a sensitivity of 50 percent, the false positive index is 0.23 and the positive predictive value is 81 percent. That means that someone identified by this polygraph protocol as deceptive has an 81 percent chance of being so, instead of the 0.4 percent (1 in 250) chance of being so if the same test is used for screening a population with a base rate of 1 in 1,000.[3]

Thus, a test that may look attractive for identifying deceptive individuals in a population with a base rate above 10 percent looks very much less attractive for screening a population with a very low base rate of deception. It will create a very large pool of suspect individuals, within which the probability of any specific individual being deceptive is less than 1 percent—and even so, it may not catch all the target individuals in the net. To put this another way, if the polygraph identifies 100 people as indicating deception, but only 1 of them is actually deceptive, the odds that any of these identified examinees is attempting to deceive are quite low, and it would take strong and compelling evidence for a decision maker to conclude on the basis of the test that this particular examinee is that 1 in 100 (Murphy, 1987).

Although actual base rates are never known for any type of screening situation, base rates can be given rough bounds. In employee screening settings, the base rate depends on the security violation. It is probably far higher for disclosure of classified information to unauthorized individuals (including "pillow talk") than it is for espionage, sabotage, or terrorism. For the most serious security threats, the base rate is undoubtedly quite low, even if the number of major threats is 10 times as large as the number of cases reported in the popular press, reflecting both individuals caught but not publicly identified and others not caught. The one major spy caught in the FBI is one among perhaps 100,000 agents who have been employed in the bureau's history. The base rate of major security threats in the nation's security agencies is almost certainly far less than 1 percent.

Appendix I presents a set of curves that allow readers to estimate the false positive index and consider the implied tradeoff for a very wide range of hypothesized base rates of deceptive examinees and various possible values of accuracy index for the polygraph testing, using a variety of decision thresholds. It is intended to help readers consider the tradeoffs using the assumptions they judge appropriate for any particular application.

Thus, using the polygraph with a "suspicious" threshold so as to catch most of the major security threats creates a serious false-positive problem in employee security screening applications, mainly because of the very low base rate of guilt among those likely to be screened. When the base rate is one in 1,000 or less, one can expect a polygraph test with a threshold that correctly identifies 80 percent of deceptive examinees to incorrectly classify at least 100 nondeceptive individuals as deceptive for each security threat correctly identified. Any diagnostic procedure that implicates large numbers of innocent employees for each major security violator correctly identified comes with a variety of costs. There is the need to investigate those implicated, the great majority of whom are innocent, as well as the issue of the civil liberties of innocent employees caught by the screen. There is the potential that the screening policy will create anxiety that decreases morale and productivity among the employees who face screening. Employees who are innocent of major security violations may be less productive when they know that they are being tested routinely with an instrument that produces a false positive reading with non-negligible probability and when such a reading can put them under suspicion of disloyalty. Such effects are most serious when the deception detection threshold is set to detect threats with a reasonably high probability (above 0.5), because such a threshold will also identify considerable numbers of false positive outcomes among innocent employees. And there is the possibility that people who might have become valued employees will be deterred from taking positions in security agencies by fear of false positive polygraph results.

To summarize, the performance of the polygraph is sharply different in screening and in event-specific investigation contexts. Anyone who believes the polygraph "works" adequately in a criminal investigation context should not presume without further careful analysis that this justifies its use for security screening. Each application requires separate evaluation on its own terms. To put this another way, if the polygraph or any other technique for detecting deception is more accurate than guesswork, it does not necessarily follow that using it for screening is better than not using it because a decision to use the polygraph or any other imperfect diagnostic technique must consider its costs as well as its benefits. In the case of polygraph screening, these costs include not only the civil liberties issues that are often debated in the context of false positive test results, but also two types of potential threats to national security. One is the false sense of security that may arise from overreliance on an imperfect screen: this could lead to undue relaxation of other security efforts and thus increase the likelihood that serious security risks who pass the screen can damage national security. The other cost is associated with damage to the national security that may result from the loss of essential personnel falsely judged to be security risks or deterred from employment in U.S. government security agencies by the prospect of false-positive polygraph results.

Tradeoffs with "Friendly" Thresholds

The discussion to this point assumes that policy makers will use a threshold such that the probability of detecting a spy is fairly high. There is, however, another possibility: they may decide to set a "friendly" threshold, that is, one that makes the probability of detecting a spy quite low. To the extent that testing deters security violations, such a test might still have utility for national security purposes. This deterrent effect is likely to be stronger when there is at least a certain amount of ambiguity concerning the setting of threshold. (If it were widely known that no one "failed" the test, its deterrent effect would be considerably lessened.) It is possible, however, to set a threshold such that almost no one is eventually judged deceptive, even though a fair number undergo additional investigation or testing. There is a clear difference between employment in the absence of security screening tests, a situation lacking in deterrent value against spies, and employment policies that include screening tests, even if screening identifies few if any spies.

Our meetings with various federal agencies that use polygraph screening suggest that different agencies set thresholds differently, although the evidence we have is anecdotal. Several agencies' polygraph screening programs, including that of the U.S. Department of Energy, appear to adopt fairly "friendly" effective thresholds, judged by the low proportion of polygraph tests that show significant response. The net result is that these screening programs identify a relatively modest number of cases to be investigated further, with few decisions eventually being made that the employee has been deceptive about a major security infraction.

There are reasons of utility, such as possible deterrent effects, that might be put forward to justify an agency's use of a polygraph screening policy with a friendly threshold, but such a polygraph screening policy will not identify most of the major security violators. For example, the U.S. Department of Defense (2001:4) reported that of 8,784 counterintelligence scope polygraph examinations given, 290 (3 percent) individuals gave "significant responses and/or provided substantive information." The low rate of positive test results suggests that a friendly threshold is being used, such that the majority of the major security threats who took the test would "pass" the screen.[4]

On April 4, 2002, the director of the Federal Bureau of Investigation (FBI) was quoted in the *New York Times* as saying that "less than 1 percent of the 700" FBI personnel who were given polygraph tests in the wake of the Hanssen spy case had test results that could not be resolved and that remain under investigation (Johnston, 2002). Whatever value such a polygraph testing protocol may have for deterrence or eliciting admissions of wrongdoing, it is quite unlikely to uncover an espionage agent who is not deterred and does not confess. A substantial majority of the major security threats who take such a test would "pass" the screen.[5] For example, if Robert Hanssen had taken such tests three times during 15 years of spying, the chances are that, even without attempting countermeasures, he would not have been detected before considerable damage had been done. (He most likely would never have been detected unless the polygraph protocol achieved a criterion validity that we regard as unduly optimistic, such as A = 0.90.) Furthermore, if Hanssen had been detected as polygraph positive (along with a large number of non-spies, that is, false positives), he would not necessarily have been identified as a spy.

There may be justifications for polygraph screening with a "friendly" threshold on the grounds that the technique may have a deterrent effect or may yield admissions of wrongdoing. However, such a screen will not identify most of the major security threats. In our judgment, the accuracy of polygraph testing in distinguishing actual or potential security violators from innocent test takers is insufficient to justify reliance on its use in employee screening in federal agencies.

Although we believe it likely that polygraph testing has utility in screening contexts because it might have a deterrent effect, we were struck by the lack of scientific evidence concerning the factors that might produce or inhibit deterrence. In order to properly evaluate the costs and benefits associated with polygraph screening, research is needed on deterrence in general and, in particular, on the effects of polygraph screening on deterrence.

Recent Policy Recommendations on Polygraph Screening

We have great concern about the dangers that may arise for national security if federal agencies use the polygraph for security screening with an unclear or incorrect understanding of the implications of threshold-setting choices for the meaning of test results. Consider, for instance, decisions that might be made on the basis of the discussion of polygraph screening in the recent report of a select commission headed by former FBI director William H. Webster (the "Webster Commission") (Commission for the Review of FBI Security Programs, 2002). This report advocates expanded use of polygraph screening in the FBI, but does not take any explicit position on whether polygraph testing has any scientific validity for detecting deception. This stance is consistent with a view that much of the value of the polygraph comes from its utility for deterrence and for eliciting admissions. The report's reasoning, although not inconsistent with the scientific evidence, has some implications that are reasonable and others that are quite disturbing from the perspective of the scientific evidence on the polygraph.

The Webster Commission recognizes that the polygraph is an imperfect instrument. Its recommendations for dealing with the imperfections, however, address only some of the serious problems associated with these imperfections. First, it recommends increased efforts at quality control and assurance and increased use of "improved technology and computer driven systems." These recommendations are sensible, but they do not address the inherent limitations of the polygraph, even when the best quality control and measurement and recording techniques are used. Second, it takes seriously the problem of false positive errors, noting that at one point, the U.S. Central Intelligence Agency (CIA) had "several hundred unresolved polygraph cases" that led to the "practical suspension" of the affected officers, sometimes for years, and "a devastating effect on morale" in the CIA. The Webster Commission clearly wants to avoid a repetition of this situation at the FBI. It recommends that "adverse personnel actions should not be taken solely on the basis of polygraph results," a position that is absolutely consistent with the scientific evidence that false positives cannot be avoided and that in security screening applications, the great majority of positives will turn out to be false. It also recommends a polygraph test only for "personnel who may pose the greatest risk to national security." This position is also strongly consistent with the science, though the commission's claim that such a policy "minimizes the risk of false positives" is not strictly true. Reducing the number of employees who are tested will reduce the total number of false positives, and therefore the cost of investigating false positives, but will not reduce the risk that any individual truthful examinee will be a false positive or that any individual positive result will be false. That risk can only be reduced by finding a more accurate test protocol or by setting a more "friendly" threshold.

Because the Webster Commission report does not address the problem of false-negative errors in any explicit way, it leaves open the possibility that federal agency officials may draw the wrong conclusions from negative polygraph test results. On the basis of discussions with polygraph program and counterintelligence officials in several federal agencies (including the FBI), we believe there is a widespread belief in this community that someone who "passes" the polygraph is "cleared" of suspicion. Acting on such a belief with security screening polygraph results could pose a danger to the national security because a negative polygraph result provides little additional information on deceptiveness, beyond the knowledge that very few examinees are major violators, especially when the test protocol produces a very small percentage of positive test results. As already noted, a spy like Robert Hanssen might easily have produced consistently negative results on a series of polygraph tests under a protocol like the one currently being used with FBI employees. Negative polygraph results on individuals or on populations of federal employees should not be taken as justification for relaxing other security precautions.

Another recent policy report raises some similar issues in the context of security in the U.S. Department of Energy (DOE) laboratories. The Commission on Science and Security (2002:62), headed by John H. Hamre (the "Hamre Commission") issued a recommendation to reduce the use of polygraph testing in the laboratories and to use it "chiefly as an investigative tool" and "sparingly as a screening tool." It recommended polygraph screening "for individuals with access only to the most highly sensitive classified information"—a much more restricted group than those subjected to polygraph screening under the applicable federal law.

Several justifications are given for reducing the use of polygraph screening, including the "severe morale problems" that polygraph screening has caused, the lack of acceptance of polygraph screening among the DOE laboratory employees, and the lack of "conclusive evidence for the effectiveness of polygraphs as a screening technique" (Commission on Science and Security, 2002:54). The report goes so far as to say that use of polygraphs "as a simplistic screening device . . . will undermine morale and eventually undermine the very goal of good security" (p. 55). Much of this rationale thus concerns the need to reduce the costs of false positives, although the report makes no reference to the extent to which false positives may occur.

The Hamre Commission did not address the false negative problem directly, but its recommendations for reducing security threats can be seen as addressing the problem indirectly. The commission recommended various management and technological changes at the DOE laboratories that would, if effective, make espionage more difficult to conduct and easier to detect in ways that do not rely on the polygraph or other methods of employee screening. Such changes, if effective, would reduce the costs inflicted by undetected spies, and therefore the costs of false negatives from screening, regardless of the techniques used. Given the limitations of the polygraph and other available employee screening techniques, any policies that decrease reliance on employee screening for achieving security objectives should be welcomed.

Although the commission recommended continued polygraph security screening for some DOE employees, it did not offer any explicit rationale for continuing the program, particularly considering the likelihood that the great majority of positive test results will be false. It did not claim that screening polygraphs accurately identify major security threats, and it left open the question of how DOE should use the results of screening polygraphs. We remain concerned about the false negative problem that can be predicted to occur if people who "pass" a screening polygraph test that gives a very low rate of positive results are presumed therefore to be "cleared" of security concerns. Given this concern, the Hamre Commission's emphasis on improving security by means other than screening makes very good sense.

Both the Webster and Hamre Commission reports make recommendations to reduce the costs associated with false positive test results, although neither takes explicit cognizance of the extent to which such results are likely to occur in security screening. More importantly, neither report explicitly addresses the problem that can arise if negative polygraph screening results are taken too seriously. Overconfidence in the polygraph—belief in its validity that goes beyond what is justified by the evidence—presents a danger to national security objectives because it may lead to overreliance on negative polygraph test results. The limited accuracy of all available techniques of employee security screening underlines the importance of pursuing security objectives in ways that reduce reliance on employee screening to detect security threats.

Making Tradeoffs

Because of the limitations of polygraph accuracy for field screening applications, policy makers face very unpleasant tradeoffs when screening for target transgressions with very low base rates. We have summarized what is known about the likely frequencies of false positive and false negative results under a range of conditions. In making choices about employee security policies, policy makers must combine this admittedly uncertain information about the performance of the polygraph in detecting deception with consideration of a variety of other uncertain factors, including: the magnitude of the security threats being faced, the potential effect of polygraph policies on staff performance, morale, recruitment, and retention; the costs of back-up policies to address the limitations of screening procedures; and effects of different policies on public confidence in security organizations.

In many fields of public policy, such tradeoffs are informed by systematic methods of decision analysis. Appendix J describes what would be involved in applying such techniques to policy decisions about polygraph screening. We were not asked to do a formal policy analysis, and we have not done so. Considering the advantages and disadvantages of quantitative benefit-cost analysis, we do not advocate its use for making policy decisions about polygraph security screening. The scientific basis for estimating many of the important parameters required for such an analysis is quite weak for supporting quantitative estimation. Moreover, there is no scientific basis for comparing on a single numerical scale some of the kinds of costs and of benefits that must be considered. Reasonable and well-informed people may disagree greatly about many important matters critical for a quantitative benefit-cost analysis (e.g., the relative importance of maintaining morale at the national laboratories compared with a small increased probability of catching a spy or saboteur or the value to be placed on the still-uncertain possibility that polygraph tests may treat different ethnic groups differently). When social consensus appears to be lacking on important value issues, as is the case with polygraph screening, science can help by making explicit the possible outcomes that people may consider important and by estimating the likelihood that these outcomes will be realized under specified conditions. With that information, participants in the decision process can discuss the relevant values and the scientific evidence and debate the tradeoffs. Given the state of knowledge about the polygraph and the value issues at stake, it seems unwise to put much trust in attempts to quantify the relevant values for society and calculate the tradeoffs among them quantitatively (see National Research Council, 1996b). However, scientific research can play an important role in evaluating the likely effects of different policy options on dimensions of value that are important to policy makers and to the country.

Other Potential Uses of Polygraph Tests

The above discussion considered the tradeoffs associated with polygraph testing in employee security screening situations in which the base rate of the target transgressions is extremely low and there is no specific transgression that can be the focus of relevant questions on a polygraph test. The tradeoffs are different in other applications, and the value of polygraph testing should be judged on the basis of an assessment of the aspects of the particular situation that are relevant to polygraph testing

choices. Because of the specific considerations involved in making decisions for each application, we have not attempted to draw conclusions
about other applications. Here, we note some of the important ways in
which polygraph testing situations differ and some implications for deciding whether and how to use polygraph testing.

A critically important variable is the base rate of the target transgressions or, put another way, the expected likelihood that any individual
potential examinee is guilty or has the target information. We have already discussed the effects of base rate on the tradeoffs involved in making decisions from polygraph tests and the way the use of polygraph
testing as an aid to decision making becomes drastically less attractive as
the base rate drops below a few percent.

The costs of false positive and false negative errors are also important
to consider in making policy choices. Consider, for example, the difference between screening scientists employed in the DOE laboratories and
preemployment screening of similar scientists. False positives are likely
to cost both government and examinee less in preemployment screening
because the people who test positive have not yet been trained in the
laboratories and do not yet possess critical, specialized skills and national
security information. The costs of false positives also vary across different preemployment screening applications. For example, these costs are
likely to be greater, for both the government and the potential employee,
if the job requires extensive education, training, or past experience, because it is harder for the employer to find another suitable candidate and
for the applicant to find another job. Thus, denying employment to a
nuclear physicist is probably more costly both to the government and the
individual than denying employment to a prospective baggage screener.
When false positive errors have relatively low cost, it makes sense to use
a screening test with a fairly suspicious threshold.

The costs of false negative errors rise directly with the amount of
damage a spy, saboteur, or terrorist could do. Thus, they are likely to be
greater in preclearance screening in relation to the sensitivity of the information to which the examinee might gain access. This observation suggests that if polygraph testing is used for such screening, more suspicious
thresholds make the most sense when a false negative result is a major
concern. The incentive to use countermeasures is also greater when the
cost of a false negative result is greater. Thus, the possibility of effective
and undetectable polygraph countermeasures is a more important consideration in very high-stakes screening situations than in other applications.

Another important factor is whether or not the situation allows for
asking questions about specific events, activities, places, and so forth.
Theory and limited evidence suggest that polygraph testing can be more

accurate if such questions can be asked than if they cannot. In addition, if the target answers to these questions are known only to examiners and to the individuals who are the targets of the investigation or screening, it is possible to use concealed information polygraph test formats or to use other tests that rely on orienting responses, such as those based on brain electrical activity. Thus, polygraph testing in general and concealed information tests (either with the polygraph or other technologies) are more attractive under these conditions than otherwise.

Employee security screening in the DOE laboratory is a situation that is quite unfavorable for polygraph testing in terms of all of the factors just discussed. Other potential applications should be evaluated after taking these factors into account. Polygraph testing is likely to look more attractive for some of these applications, even though in all applications it can be expected to yield a sizable proportion of errors along with the correct classifications.

In this connection, it is worth revisiting the class of situations we describe as focused screening situations. Events occurring since the terrorist attacks of September 11, 2001, suggest that such situations may get increased attention in the future. Focused screening situations differ both from event-specific investigations and from the kinds of screening used with employees in national security organizations. An illustrative example is posed by the need to screen of hundreds of detainees captured in Afghanistan in late 2001 to identify those, perhaps a sizable proportion, who were in fact part of the Al Qaeda terrorist network. Such a focused screening situation is like typical security screening in that there is no specific event being investigated, but it is different in that it may be possible to ask specific relevant questions, including questions of the concealed information variety.[6] It is thus possible to use concealed information polygraph tests or other tests that require the same format and that are not appropriate for screening situations in which specific questions cannot be constructed. For example, members of Al Qaeda might be identifiable by the fact that they have information about the locations and physical features of Al Qaeda training camps that is known to interrogators but not to very many other people. Another example might be the screening of individuals who had access to anthrax in U.S. biological weapons facilities to identify those who may be concealing the fact that they have the specific knowledge needed to produce the grade of anthrax that killed several U.S. citizens in the fall of 2001. Again, even though the examiners do not know the specific target action, they can ask some focused relevant questions.

The tradeoffs in focused screening are often very different from those in other screening situations because the base rate of the target activities may lie below the 10 percent or higher typical of criminal investigations and above the small fractions of 1 percent typical with employee security screening in national security organizations. Tradeoffs may also be different in terms of the relative costs of false positive and false negative test results and in terms of incentives to use countermeasures. A polygraph or other screening procedure that is inappropriate or inadvisable for employee security screening may be more attractive in some focused screening situations. As with other applications, the tradeoffs should be assessed and the judgment made on how and whether to use polygraph screening on the basis of the specifics of the particular situation. We believe that it will be helpful in most situations to think about the tradeoffs in terms of which sensitivities might be used for the screening test, which false positive index values can be expected with those sensitivities, and whether these possibilities include acceptable outcomes for the purpose at hand.

USING THE POLYGRAPH MORE EFFECTIVELY

One way to make the tradeoffs associated with polygraph screening more attractive would be to develop more accurate screening protocols for the use of the polygraph. This section discusses the two basic strategies for doing this: improving polygraph scoring and interpretation and combining polygraph results with other information.

Improving Scoring and Interpretation

The 11 federal agencies that use polygraph testing for employee screening purposes differ in the test formats they use, the transgressions they ask about in the polygraph examination, the ways they combine information from the polygraph examination with other security-relevant information on an examinee, and the decision rules they use to take personnel actions on the basis of the screening information available. Despite these differences, many of the agencies have put in place quality control programs, following guidance from the U.S. Department of Defense Polygraph Institute (DoDPI), that are designed to ensure that all polygraph exams given in a particular agency follow approved testing procedures and practices, as do the reading and interpretation of polygraph charts.

Quality Control

Federal agencies have established procedures aimed at standardizing polygraph test administration and achieving a high level of reliability in the scoring of charts. The quality control procedures that we have observed are impressive in their detail and in the extent to which they can remove various sources of variability from polygraph testing when they are fully implemented. We have heard allegations from polygraph opponents, from scientists at the DOE laboratories, and even from polygraph experts in other agencies that official procedures are not always followed—for example, that the atmosphere of the examination is not always as prescribed in examiners' manuals and that charts are not always interpreted as required by procedure. A review of testing practice in agency polygraph programs is beyond this committee's scope. We emphasize two things about reliable test administration and interpretation. First, reliable test administration and interpretation are both desirable in a testing program and essential if the program is to have scientific standing. Second, however, it is critical to remember that reliability, no matter how well ensured, does not confer validity on a polygraph screening program.

Attempts to increase reliability can in some cases reduce validity. For example, having N examiners judge a chart independently, and averaging their judgments, can produce a net validity that increases when N increases, because the idiosyncratic judgments of different examiners tend to disappear in the process of averaging. Having independent judgments produces what appear to be unreliable results, i.e., the examiners disagree. If examiners see the results of previous examiners before rendering a judgment, apparent reliability would increase because the judgments would probably not differ much among examiners, but such a procedure would likely reduce the accuracy of the eventual decision. Even worse, suppose instructions given to the examiners regarding scoring are made increasingly precise, in an effort to increase reliability, but the best way to score is not known, so that these instructions cause a systematic mis-scoring. The result would increase reliability, but would also produce a systematic error that would decrease accuracy. A group of examiners not so instructed might use a variety of idiosyncratic scoring methods: each would be in error, but the errors might be in random directions, so that averaging the results across the examiners would approach the true reading. Here again there is a tradeoff between reliability and validity. These are just illustrations. We can envision examples in which increases in reliability would also increase accuracy. The important point is that one should not conclude that a test is more valid simply because it incorporates quality control procedures that increase reliability.

Computerized Scoring

In addition to establishing examiner training and quality control practices at DoDPI and other agencies, the federal government has sponsored a number of efforts to use computing technology and statistical techniques to improve both the reliability of polygraph test interpretation and its ability to discriminate between truthful and deceptive test records. This approach holds promise for making the most of the data collected by the polygraph. Human decision makers do not always focus on the most relevant evidence and do not always combine different sources of information in the most effective fashion. In other domains, such as medical decision making (Weinstein and Fineberg, 1980) computerized decision aids have been shown to produce considerable increases in accuracy. To the extent that polygraph charts contain information correlated with deception or truth-telling, computerized analysis has the potential for increasing accuracy beyond the level available with hand scoring.

The most recent computerized scoring systems, and perhaps the ones that use the most complex statistical analyses, are being developed at the Applied Physics Laboratory at Johns Hopkins University (JHU-APL). The investigators from JHU-APL, in their publications and in oral presentations to the committee, have made claims about their methodology and its successful testing on criminal case data through cross-validation. We made extensive efforts to be briefed on the technical details of the JHU-APL methodology, but although we were supplied with the executable program for the algorithms, the documentation provided to us offered insufficient details to allow for replication and verification of the claims made about their construction and performance. JHU-APL was unresponsive to repeated requests for detail on these matters, as well as on its process for building and validating its models. On multiple occasions we were told either that the material was proprietary or that reports and testing were not complete and thus could not be shared. Appendix F documents what we have learned about (a) the existing computerized algorithms for polygraph scoring, both at JHU-APL and elsewhere, (b) the one problematic effort at external independent validation carried out by DoDPI (Dollins, Kraphol, and Dutton, 2000), and (c) our reservations and concerns about the technical aspects of the JHU-APL work and our inability to get information from APL.

From the information available, we find that efforts to use technological advances in computerized recording to develop computer-based algorithms that can improve the interpretations of trained numerical evaluators have failed to build a strong theoretical rationale for their choice of measures. They have also failed to date to provide solid evidence of the performance of their algorithms on independent data with properly determined truth for a relevant population of interest. As a result, we believe that their claimed performance is highly likely to degrade markedly when applied to a new research population and is even vulnerable to the prospect of substantial disconfirmation. In conclusion, computerized scoring theoretically has the potential to improve on the validity of hand scoring systems; we do not know how large an improvement might be made in practice; and available evidence is unconvincing that computer algorithms have yet achieved that potential.

We end with a cautionary note. A polygraph examination is a process involving the examiner in a complex interaction with the instrument and the examinee. Computerized scoring algorithms to date have not addressed this aspect of polygraph testing. For example, they have treated variations in comparison questions across tests as unimportant and have not coded for the content of these questions or analyzed their possible effect on the physiological responses being measured. Also, examiners may well be picking up a variety of cues during the testing situation other than those contained in the tracings (even without awareness) and letting those cues affect the judgments about the tracings. It is, therefore, possible that the examiner's judgments are based on information unavailable for a computerized scoring algorithm and that examiners may be more accurate for this reason. Little evidence is available from the research literature on polygraph testing concerning this possibility, but until definitive evidence is available, it might be wise to include both computerized scoring and independent hand scoring as inputs to a decision process.

Combining Polygraph Results with Other Information

In most screening applications, information from polygraph examinations (chart and interview information) is not by itself determinative of personnel actions. For example, the DOE's polygraph examination regulation reads in part, "DOE or its contractors may not take an adverse personnel action against an individual solely on the basis of a polygraph examination result of 'deception indicated' or 'no opinion'; or use a polygraph examination that reflects 'deception indicated' or 'no opinion' as a substitute for any other required investigation" (10 CFR 709.25 [a]; see Appendix B). Thus, polygraph information is often combined in some way with other information.

We have been unable to determine whether DOE or any other federal agency has a standard protocol for combining such information or even any encoded standard practice, analogous to the ways the results of different diagnostic tests are combined in medicine to arrive at a diagnosis. We made repeated requests for the DOE adjudication manual, which is supposed to encode the procedures for considering polygraph results and other information in making personnel decisions. We were initially told that the manual existed as a privileged document for official use only; after further requests, we were told that the manual is still in preparation and is not available even for restricted access. Thus it appears that various information sources are combined an in informal way on the basis of the judgment of adjudicators and other personnel. Quality control for this phase of decision making appears to take the form of review by supervisors and of policies allowing employees to contest unfavorable personnel decisions. There are no written standards for how polygraph information should be used in personnel decisions at DOE, or, as far as we were able to determine, at any other agency. We believe that any agency that uses polygraphs as part of a screening process should, in light of the inherent fallibility of the polygraph instrument, use the polygraph results only in conjunction with other information, and only as a trigger for further testing and investigation. Our understanding of the process at DOE is that the result of additional investigations following an initial positive reading from the polygraph test almost always "clears" the examinee, except in those cases where admissions or confessions have been obtained during the course of the examination.

Incremental Validity

Policy decisions about using the polygraph must consider not only its accuracy and the tradeoffs it presents involving true positives and false positives and negatives, but also whether including the polygraph with the sources of information otherwise available improves the accuracy of detection and makes the tradeoffs more attractive. This is the issue of incremental validity discussed in Chapter 2. It makes sense to use the polygraph in security screening if it adds information relevant to detecting security risks that is not otherwise available and with acceptable tradeoffs.

Federal agencies use or could use a variety of information sources in conjunction with polygraph tests for making personnel security decisions: background investigations, ongoing security checks by various investigative techniques, interviews, psychological tests, and so forth (see Chapter 6). We have not located any scientific studies that attempt directly to measure the incremental validity of the polygraph when added to any of these information sources. That is, the existing scientific research does not compare the accuracy of prediction of criminal behavior or any other behavioral criterion of interest from other indicators with accuracy when the polygraph is added to those indicators.

Security officials in several federal agencies have told us that the polygraph is far more useful to them than background checks or other investigative techniques in revealing activities that lead to the disqualification of applicants from employment or employees from access to classified information. It is impossible to determine whether the incremental utility of the polygraph in these cases reflects validity or only the effect of the polygraph mystique on the elicitation of admissions. If the value of the polygraph stems from the examinees' belief in it rather than actual validity, any true admissions it elicits are obviously valuable, but that is evidence only on the utility of having a test that examinees believe in and not on the incremental validity of the polygraph.

Ways of Combining Information Sources

There are several scientifically defensible approaches to combining different sources of information that could be used as part of polygraph policies. The problem has been given attention in the extensive literature on decision making for medical diagnosis, classification, and treatment, a field that faces the problem of combining information from clinical observations, interviews, and a variety of medical tests (see the more detailed discussion in Appendix K).

Statistical methods for combining data of different types (e.g., different tests) follow one of two basic approaches. In one, called independent parallel testing, a set of tests is used and a target result on any one is used to make a determination. For example, a positive result on any test may be taken to indicate the presence of a condition of interest. In the other approach, called independent serial testing, if a particular test in the sequence is negative, the individual is concluded to be free of the condition of interest, but if the test is positive, another test is ordered. Validating a combined test of either type requires independent tests or sources of information *and* a test evaluation sample that is representative of the target population.[7]

Polygraph security screening more closely approximates the second, serial, approach to combining information: people who "pass" a screening polygraph are not normally investigated further. Serial screening and its logic are familiar from many medical settings. A low-cost test of moderate accuracy is usually used as an initial screen, with the threshold usually set to include a high proportion of the true positive cases (people with the condition) among those who test positive. Most of those who test positive will be false positives, especially if the condition has a low base rate. In this approach, people who test positive are then subject to a more accurate but more expensive or invasive second-stage test, and so on through as many stages as warranted. For example, mammograms and prostate-specific antigen (PSA) tests are among the many first screens used for detecting cancers, with biopsies as possible second-stage tests.

The low cost of polygraph testing relative to detailed security investigation makes the polygraph attractive for use early in the screening series. Detailed investigation could act as the second-stage test. According to the security screening policies of many federal agencies, including DOE, this is how the polygraph is supposed to be used: personnel decisions are not to be made on the basis of polygraph results that indicate possible security violations without definitive confirming information.

Such a policy presents a bit of a dilemma. If the purpose of using the polygraph is like that of cancer screening—to avoid false negatives—the threshold should be set so as to catch a high proportion of spies or terrorists. The result of this approach, in a population with a low base rate of spies or terrorists, is to greatly increase the number of false positives and the accompanying expense of investigating all the positives with traditional methods. The costs of detailed investigations can be reduced by setting the threshold so that few examinees are judged to show significant response. This approach appears to be the one followed at DOD, DOE, and the FBI, judging from the low rate of total positive polygraph results reported. However, setting such a friendly threshold runs the risk of an unacceptably high number of false negative results.

A way might be found to minimize this dilemma if there were other independent tests that could be added in the sequence, either before the polygraph or between the polygraph and detailed investigation. Such tests would decrease the number of people who would have to pass the subsequent screens. If such a screen could be applied before the polygraph, its effect would be to increase the base rate of target people (spies, terrorists, or whatever) among those given the polygraph by culling out large numbers of the others. The result would be that the problem of high false positive rates in a population with a low base rate would be significantly diminished (see Figures 7-1 and 7-2, above). If such an independent screen could be applied after the polygraph, the result would be to reduce the numbers and costs of detailed investigations by eliminating more of the people who would eventually be cleared. However, there is no test available that is known to be more accurate than the polygraph and that could fill the typical role of a second-stage test in serial screening.

We have not found any scientific treatments of the relative benefits of using the polygraph either earlier or later in a series of screening tests, nor even any explicit discussion of this issue. We have also not found any consideration or investigation of the idea of using other tests in sequence with the polygraph in the manner described above. The costs and benefits of using the polygraph at different positions in a sequence of screening tests needs careful attention in devising any policy that uses the polygraph systematically as a source of information in a serial testing model for security screening.

Some people have suggested that polygraph data could be analyzed and combined with other data by nonstatistical methods that rely on expert systems. There is disagreement on how successful such systems have been in practice in other areas, but the most "successful" expert systems for medical diagnosis require a substantial body of theory or empirical knowledge that link clearly identified measurable features with the condition being diagnosed (see Appendix F). For screening uses of the polygraph, it seems clear that no such body of knowledge exists. Lacking such knowledge, the serious problems that exist in deriving and adequately validating procedures for computer scoring of polygraph tests (discussed above) also exist for the derivation and validation of expert systems for combining polygraph results with other diagnostic information.

Insufficient scientific information exists to support recommendations on whether or how to combine polygraph and other information in a sequential screening model. A number of psychophysiological techniques appear promising in the long run but have not yet demonstrated their validity. Some indicators based on demeanor and direct investigation appear to have a degree of accuracy, but whether they add information to what the polygraph can provide is unknown (see Chapter 6).

LEGAL CONTEXT

The practical use of polygraph testing is shaped in part by its legal status. Polygraph testing has long been the subject of judicial attention, much more so than most forensic technologies. In contrast, courts have only recently begun to look at the data, or lack thereof, for other forensic technologies, such as fingerprinting, handwriting identification and bite marks, which have long been admitted in court. The attention paid to polygraphs has generally led to a skeptical view of them by the judiciary, a view not generally shared by most executive branch agencies. Judicial skepticism results both from questions about the validity of the technology and doubt about its need in a constitutional process that makes juries or judges the finders of fact. Doubts about polygraph tests also arise from the fact that the test itself contains a substantial interrogation component. Courts recognize the usefulness of interrogation strategies, but hesitate when the results of an interrogation are presented as evidentiary proof. Although polygraphs clearly have utility in some settings, courts have been unwilling to conclude that utility denotes validity. The value of the test for law enforcement and employee screening is an amalgam of utility and validity, and the two are not easily separated.

An early form of the polygraph served as the subject of the well-known standard used for evaluating scientific evidence—general acceptance—announced in *Frye v. United States* (1923) and still used in some courts (see below). It has been the subject of a U.S. Supreme Court decision, *United States v. Scheffer* (1998), and countless state and federal decisions (see Appendix E for details on the *Frye* case). In *Scheffer*, the Court held that the military's per se rule excluding polygraphs was not unreasonable—and thus not unconstitutional—because there was substantial dispute among scientists concerning the test's validity.

Polygraphs fit the pattern of many forensic scientific fields, being of concern to the courts, government agencies and law enforcement, but largely ignored by the scientific community. A recent decision found the same to be true for fingerprinting (*United States v. Plaza*, 2002). In *Plaza*, the district court initially excluded expert opinion regarding whether a latent fingerprint matched the defendant's print because the applied technology of the science had yet to be adequately tested and was almost exclusively reviewed and accepted by a narrow group of technicians who practiced the art professionally. Although the district court subsequently vacated this decision and admitted the evidence, the judge repeated his initial finding that fingerprinting had not been tested and was only generally accepted within a discrete and insular group of professionals. The court, in fact, likened fingerprint identification to accounting and believed it succeeded as a "specialty" even though it failed as a "science."[8] Courts have increasingly noticed that many forensic technologies have little or no substantial research behind them (see e.g., *United States v. Hines* [1999] on handwriting analysis and the more general discussion in Faigman et al. [2002]). The lack of data on regularly used scientific evidence appears to be a systemic problem and, at least partly, a product of the historical divide between law and science.

Federal courts only recently began inquiring directly into the validity or reliability of proffered scientific evidence. Until 1993, the prevailing standard of admissibility was the general acceptance test first articulated in *Frye v. United States* in 1923. Using that test, courts queried whether the basis for proffered expert opinion is generally accepted in the particular field from which it comes. In *Daubert v. Merrell Dow Pharmaceuticals, Inc.* (1993), however, the U.S. Supreme Court held that *Frye* does not apply in federal courts. Under the *Daubert* test, judges must determine whether the basis for proffered expertise is, more likely than not, valid. The basic difference between *Frye* and *Daubert* is one of perspective: courts using *Frye* are deferential to the particular fields generating the expertise, whereas *Daubert* places the burden on the courts to evaluate the scientific validity of the expert opinion. This difference of perspective has begun to significantly change the reception of the scientific approach in the courtroom.[9]

Much of the expert opinion that has been presented as "scientific" in courts is not based on what scientists recognize as solid scientific evidence, or even, in some cases, rudimentary scientific methods and principles. The polygraph is not unusual in this regard. In fact, topics such as bite mark and hair identification, fingerprinting, arson investigation, and tool mark analysis have a less extensive record of research on accuracy than does polygraph testing. Historically, the courts relied on experts in sundry fields in which the basis for the expert opinion is primarily assertion rather than scientific testing and in which the value of the expertise is measured by effectiveness in court rather than scientific demonstration of accuracy or validity.

These observations raise several issues worthy of consideration. First, if the polygraph compares well with other forensic sciences, should it not receive due recognition for its relative success? Second, most forensic sciences are used solely in judicial contexts, while the polygraph is also used in employment screening: Do the different contexts in which the technique is used affect the determination of its usefulness? And third, since mainstream scientists have largely ignored forensic science, how could this situation be changed? We consider these matters in turn.

Polygraph Testing as a Forensic Science

Without question, DNA profiling provides the model of cooperation between science and the law. The technology was founded on basic science, and much of the early debate engaged a number of leading figures in the scientific community. Rapidly improving technology and expanded laboratory attention led to improvements in the quality of the data and the strengths of the inferences that could be drawn. Even then, however, there were controversies regarding the statistical inferences (National Research Council, 1992, 1996a). Nonetheless, from the start, judges understood the need to learn the basic science behind the technology and, albeit with certain exceptions, largely mastered both the biology and the statistics underlying the evidence.

At the same time, DNA profiling might be somewhat misleading as a model for the admissibility of scientific evidence. Although some of the forensic sciences, such as fingerprinting (see Cole, 2001), started as science, most have existed for many decades outside mainstream science. In fact, many forensic sciences had their start well outside the scientific mainstream. Moreover, although essentially probabilistic, DNA profiling today produces almost certain conclusions—if a sufficient set of DNA characteristics is measured, the resulting DNA profiles can be expected to be unique, with a probability of error of one in billions or less (except for identical twins) (National Research Council, 1996a). This near certainty of DNA evidence may encourage some lawmakers' naive view that science, if only it is good enough, will produce certain answers. (In fact, the one area in which DNA profiling is least certain, laboratory error, is the area in which courts have had the most difficulty in deciding how to handle the uncertainty.)

The accuracy of polygraph testing does not come anywhere near what DNA analysis can achieve. Nevertheless, polygraph researchers have produced considerable data concerning polygraph validity (see Chapters 4 and 5). However, most of this research is laboratory research, so that the generalizability of the research to field settings remains uncertain. The field studies that have been carried out also have serious limitations (see Chapter 4). Moreover, there is virtually no standardization of protocols; the polygraph tests conducted in the field depend greatly on the presumed skill of individual examiners. Thus, even if laboratory-based estimates of criterion validity are accurate, the implications for any particular field polygraph test are uncertain. Without the further development of standardized polygraph testing techniques, the gulf between laboratory validity studies and inferences about field polygraph tests will remain wide.

The ambiguity surrounding the validity of field polygraphs is complicated still further by the structure of polygraph testing. Because in practice the polygraph is used as a combination of lie detector and interrogation prop, the examiner typically is privy to information regarding the examinee. While this knowledge is invaluable for questioning, it also might lead to examiner expectancies that could affect the dynamic of the polygraph testing situation or the interpretation of the test's outcome. Thus, high validity for laboratory testing might again not be indicative of the validity of polygraphs given in the field.

Context of Polygraph Testing

The usefulness of polygraph test results depends on the context of the test and the consequences that follow its use. Validity is not something that courts can assess in a vacuum. The wisdom of applying any science depends on both the test itself and the application contemplated. A forensic tool's usefulness depends on the specific nature of the test (i.e., in what situation might it apply?), the import or relevance of the test (i.e., what inferences follow from "failing" or "passing" the test?), the consequences that follow the test's administration (e.g., denial of employment, discharge, criminal prosecution), and the objective of the test (lie detection or interrogation).

A principal consideration in the applied sciences concerns the content of a test: what it does, or can be designed to, test. Concealed information polygraph tests, for example, have limited usefulness as a screening device simply because examiners usually cannot create specific questions about unknown transgressions. (There may be exceptions, as in some focused screening applications, as discussed above.) The application of any forensic test, therefore, is limited by the test's design and function. Similarly, the import of the test itself must be considered. For instance, in the judicial context, the concealed information test format might present less concern than the comparison question format, even if they have comparable accuracy. The concealed information test inquires about knowledge that is presumed to be possessed by the perpetrator; however, a "failed" test might only indicate that the subject lied about having been at the scene of the crime, not necessarily that he or she committed the crime. Like a fingerprint found on the murder weapon, knowledge of the scene and, possibly, the circumstances of the crime, is at least one inferential step away from the conclusion that the subject committed the crime. There may be an innocent explanation for the subject's knowledge, just as there might be for the unfortunately deposited fingerprint.

In contrast, the comparison question test requires no intervening inferences if the examiner's opinion is accepted about whether the examinee was deceptive when asked about the pivotal issue. With this test, such an expert opinion would go directly to the credibility of the examinee and thus his or her culpability for the event in question. This possibility raises still another concern for courts, the possibility that the expert will invade the province of the fact finder. As a general rule, courts do not permit witnesses, expert or otherwise, to comment on the credibility of another person's testimony (Mueller and Kirkpatrick, 1995). This is the jury's (and sometimes the judge's) job. As a practical matter, however, witnesses, and especially experts, regularly comment on the probable veracity of other witnesses, though almost never directly. The line between saying that a witness cannot be believed and that what the witness has said is not believable, is not a bright line. Courts, in practice, regularly permit experts to tread on credibility matters, especially psychological experts in such areas as repressed memories, post-traumatic stress disorder, and syndromes ranging from the battered woman syndrome to rape trauma syndrome.

The legal meaning of a comparison question test polygraph report might be different if the expert opinion is presented in terms of whether the examinee showed "significant response" to relevant questions, rather than in terms of whether the responses "indicated deception." Significant response is an inferential step away from any conclusion about credibility, in the sense that it is possible to offer innocent explanations of "significant response," based on various psychological and physiological phenomena that might lead to a false positive test result.

When courts assess the value of forensic tools, the consequences that follow a "positive" or "negative" outcome on the test are important. Although scientific research can offer information regarding the error rates associated with the application of a test, it does not provide information on what amount of error is too much. This issue is a policy consideration that must be made on the basis of understanding the science well enough to appreciate the quantity of error, and judgment about the qualitative consequences of errors (the above discussion of errors and tradeoffs is thus relevant to considerations likely to face a court operating under the *Daubert* rule).

Finally, evaluating the usefulness of a forensic tool requires a clear statement of the purpose behind the test's use. With most forensic science procedures, the criterion is clear. The value of fingerprinting, handwriting identification, firearms identification, and bite marks is closely associated with their ability to accomplish the task of identification. This is a relatively straightforward assessment. Polygraph tests, however, have been advocated variously as lie detectors and as aids for interrogation. They might indeed be effective for one or the other, or even both. However, these hypotheses have to be separated for purposes of study. For purposes of science policy, policy makers should be clear about for which use they are approving—or disapproving—polygraphs.

Courts have been decidedly more ambivalent toward polygraphs than the other branches of government. Courts do not need lie detectors, since juries already serve this function, a role that is constitutionally mandated. Policymakers in the executive and legislative branches, in contrast, do perceive a need for lie detection and may not care about whether the polygraph's contribution is due to its scientific validity or to its value for interrogation.

Mainstream Science and Forensic Science

Many policy makers, lawyers, and judges have little training in science. Moreover, science is not a significant part of the law school curriculum and is not included on state bar exams. Criminal law classes, for the most part, do not cover forensic science or psychological syndromes, and torts classes do not discuss toxicology or epidemiology in analyzing toxic tort cases or product liability. Most law schools do not offer, much less require, basic classes on statistics or research methodology. In this respect, the law school curriculum has changed little in a century or more.

The general acceptance test of admissibility enunciated in the *Frye* decision expects little scientific sophistication of lawyers or judges. Courts, and presumably juries as well, have thus evaluated expertise based on consensus. The problem with this test has come in fields that purport to be rigorous but may not be. For instance, if the question is the validity of bite mark identification analysis, researchers who study the various factors that challenge this expertise (e.g., uniqueness of the mark, the identification of the mark in different substances, proficiency testing, etc.) would probably give the courts a solid scientific evaluation of the value of this kind of evidence. However, if the courts only consider the expert opinions of forensic odontologists who do bite mark identifications for police laboratories, they are unlikely to get a full view of the value of this kind of evidence. Unfortunately, in many fields of forensic science there are no communities of scientists conducting basic research and the only people who are asked as expert witnesses are interested practitioners with little proficiency in scientific methods.

Good forensic science can have salutary results and, in some cases, profound consequences. DNA profiling is a particularly salient example of how good science can be used for both good law enforcement and in the interests of the falsely accused. Lawyers, under the influence of *Daubert*, are beginning to open their eyes and ears to empirical criticisms of fields long thought settled. In the area of lie detection, good forensic research could directly contribute to national security.

Forensic science has not kept up with the state of science more generally for two basic reasons: the legal community's basic ignorance of science and statistics, and the lack of interest among research scientists in the practical (and especially forensic) applications of science. In lie detection, for instance, policy makers have not demanded better work, and few scientists have been interested in pursuing the subject. This powerful combination of ignorance and apathy has, in general, deprived policy makers of good scientific data. More particularly, it has led to convictions of the innocent (see Scheck, Neufeld, and Dwyer, 2000), acquittals for the guilty, and numerous costs to individuals, ranging from job loss to social ostracism.

Another institutional reality bears mentioning. The law very often asks empirical questions to which there are no scientific answers. Moreover, while science can take any amount of time to pursue a question and develop an answer, the law has to render a decision in a short time frame. A particularly good example of this is clinical prediction of violence. A large number of legal contexts call for predictions of future violence. These include capital sentencing, parole and pardon hearings, ordinary civil commitment, sexual predator commitments, and community notification laws. Courts and legislatures have been undeterred by the fact that psychologists and psychiatrists readily admit that science cannot provide such predictions—though the state of the art is improving. For policy makers, the inability to accomplish some task scientifically does not always mean that it cannot be done legally. In *Schall v. Martin* (1984), for instance, the Supreme Court upheld the pretrial detention of juveniles on a finding that there is a "serious risk" that if released the juvenile would commit a crime before his next court appearance. Responding to the argument that such predictions could not be made reliably, the Court said that "our cases indicate, however, that from a legal point of view there is nothing inherently unattainable about a prediction of future criminal conduct" (at 278).

CONCLUSIONS

Decisions about whether or how to use polygraph tests in particular applications must consider these tests' capabilities and limitations, as well as the tradeoffs posed by any imperfect diagnostic procedure.

Tradeoffs in Interpretation

The tradeoffs of false positives and false negatives are strikingly different in event-specific and screening applications, primarily because of the great difference in the base rate of guilt in the two settings. Even those who believe the polygraph "works" adequately in a criminal investigation should not presume without further careful analysis that this justifies its use for security screening.

Given the very low base rates of major security violations, such as espionage, that almost certainly exist in settings such as the national weapons laboratories, as well as the scientifically plausible accuracy level of polygraph testing, polygraph screening is likely to identify at least hundreds of innocent employees as guilty for each spy or other major security threat correctly identified. The innocent will be indistinguishable from the guilty by polygraph alone. Consequently, policy makers face this choice: either the decision threshold must be set at such a level that there will be a low probability of catching a spy (thereby reducing the number of innocent examinees falsely identified), or investigative resources will have to be expended to investigate hundreds of cases in order to find whether there is indeed one guilty individual (or more) in a pool of many individuals who have positive polygraph results. Although there are reasons of utility that might be put forward to justify an agency's use of a polygraph screening policy that produces a very low rate of positive results, such a policy will not identify most of the major security violators. In our judgment, the accuracy of polygraph testing for distinguishing actual or potential security violators from innocent test takers is insufficient to justify reliance on its use in employee security screening in federal agencies.

Although formal benefit-cost analysis might in principle be used to help decision makers evaluate the difficult tradeoffs posed by the use of the polygraph for security screening, in actuality the scientific basis for estimating many of the important parameters required for a benefit-cost analysis is too weak to support quantitative estimates. Moreover, no scientific basis exists for comparing on a single numerical scale many of the qualitatively different kinds of costs and of benefits that must be considered.

The tradeoffs presented by polygraph testing vary with the application. For example, some focused screening applications may present more favorable tradeoffs for polygraph use than those involved in employee security screening in the DOE laboratories.

Increasing Polygraph Effectiveness

The quality control program organized by DoDPI and implemented by DOE in its screening activities is impressive in its rigor and the extent to which it has removed various sources of examiner and other variability. Highly reliable polygraph scoring and interpretation, such as these programs aim to provide, are essential if polygraph screening is to have scientific standing. Reliability, however, is insufficient to establish the validity of the polygraph for screening purposes. The effects of DoDPI efforts to increase reliability on the validity of polygraph screening are untested and unknown.

The primary advances in polygraph technology since the 1983 Office of Technology Assessment report have come in the computerization of physiological responses and their display. Computerized polygraph scoring procedures have the potential in theory to increase the accuracy of polygraph testing because they improve the ability to extract and appropriately combine information from features of psychophysiological responses, both obvious and subtle, that may have differing diagnostic values. However, existing computerized polygraph scoring methods have a purely empirical base and are not backed by validated theory that would justify use of particular measures or features of the polygraph data. Such theory simply does not yet exist. Moreover, existing computerized polygraph scoring methods have not been tested on a sufficient number and variety of examinees after development to generate confidence that their validity is any greater than that of traditional scoring methods.

Although in theory, combining the results of polygraph tests with information from other sources is possible—for example, in serial screening protocols—such approaches have not been seriously investigated. Similarly, evidence on the incremental validity of the polygraph, that is, its ability to add predictive value to what can be achieved by other methods, has not been gathered. Moreover, the difficulties that exist with computerized scoring of polygraph tests also exist, and may be multiplied, with possible expert systems for combining polygraph results with other data.

Polygraphs in Legal Contexts

Courts following the *Daubert* rule on admissibility of scientific evidence are likely to look increasingly to scientific validation studies in judging the uses of polygraph data in court. The existing validation studies have serious limitations. Laboratory test findings on polygraph validity are not a good guide to accuracy in field settings. They are likely to overestimate accuracy in field practice, but by an unknown amount. The available field studies are also likely to overestimate the accuracy achieved in actual practice. Assessments of the polygraph for the purposes of forensic science should take into account the test's design, function, and purpose because both the accuracy of the test and the practical meaning of particular accuracy levels are likely to depend on these factors.

NOTES

1. This is the model we used to extrapolate A from reports that provided single sensitivity-specificity combinations (see Appendix H).

2. If A = 0.80, the false positive index is greater than 100 for any base rate below 1 in 250, and if A = 0.70, it is greater than 100 for any base rate below about 1 in 160. If the actual base rate is equal to or less than 1 in 1,000, the false positive index is at least 208 if the test has A = 0.90; at least 452 if A = 0.80; at least 634 if A = 0.70, and at least 741 if A = 0.60. Thus, if there are 10 serious security violators among 10,000 employees who are polygraphed and the criterion is set to correctly identify 8 of the 10, the test could be expected to erroneously classify as deceptive at least 1,664, 3,616, 5,072, or 5,928 of the 9,990 nonviolators, depending on which of the accuracy indexes applied to the test.

3. Other assumptions about the accuracy and sensitivity of polygraph testing procedures yield similarly dramatic differences between the predictive values of positive test results in screening versus event-specific investigation contexts.

4. A polygraph screening policy that produces 3 percent positive results, of which virtually all are false positives, will have a sensitivity of 48 percent (that is, it will correctly identify 48 percent of major violators) if the test procedure's actual accuracy index (A) is 0.90; 25 percent if its accuracy index is 0.80; or 14 percent if its accuracy index is 0.70.

5. A polygraph screening policy that produces 1 percent positive results, of which virtually all are false positives, will have a sensitivity of 30 percent (identify 30 percent of the major violators) if the test procedure's actual accuracy index (A) is 0.90; 13 percent if its accuracy index is 0.80; and 7 percent if its accuracy index is 0.70.

6. Polygraph testing of suspected Al Qaeda members is different from security screening of federal employees in other ways that should be recognized explicitly. Problems of language translation and of possible cultural differences in the meanings of deception and truthfulness are likely to create uncertainty in the meaning of polygraph charts and raise questions about whether these tests can be as accurate as similar tests conducted on English-speaking Americans.

7. We note that this criterion was rarely met in the simulation studies that have been used to assess polygraph validity for screening to date.

8. See *United States v. Plaza*, 188 F. Supp.2d 549, 2000 WL 389163 [E.D.Pa. March 13, 2002] vacating *United States v. Plaza*, 179 F. Supp.2d 492, 2002 WL 27305 [E.D.Pa Jan. 7, 2002].

9. The implications of *Daubert* for polygraph evidence are not straightforward. Some courts have interpreted *Daubert* to undermine the *per se* rule excluding polygraph evidence (e.g., *United States v. Posado*, 57 F.3d 428, 429 [5th Cir. 1995]), and some federal district courts have admitted polygraph evidence. It is reasonable to expect continued argument in the courts over whether or not the scientific evidence on polygraph testing justifies the use of test results as evidence.

8

Conclusions and Recommendations

We have reviewed the scientific evidence on the polygraph with the goal of assessing its validity for security uses, especially those involving the screening of substantial numbers of government employees. Overall, the evidence is scanty and scientifically weak. Our conclusions are necessarily based on the far from satisfactory body of evidence on polygraph accuracy, as well as basic knowledge about the physiological responses the polygraph measures. We separately present our conclusions about scientific knowledge on the validity of polygraph and other techniques of detecting deception, about policy for employee security screening in the context of the U.S. Department of Energy (DOE) laboratories, and about the future of detection and deterrence of deception, including a recommendation for research.

SCIENTIFIC KNOWLEDGE

Basic Science

Polygraph Accuracy *Almost a century of research in scientific psychology and physiology provides little basis for the expectation that a polygraph test could have extremely high accuracy.* The physiological responses measured by the polygraph are not uniquely related to deception. That is, the responses measured by the polygraph do not all reflect a single underlying process: a variety of psychological and physiological processes, including some that can be consciously controlled, can affect polygraph measures and test results. Moreover, most polygraph testing procedures allow for uncontrolled variation in test administration (e.g., creation of the emotional climate, selecting questions) that can be expected to result in variations in accuracy and that limit the level of accuracy that can be consistently achieved.

Theoretical Basis *The theoretical rationale for the polygraph is quite weak, especially in terms of differential fear, arousal, or other emotional states that are triggered in response to relevant or comparison questions.* We have not found any serious effort at construct validation of polygraph testing.

Research Progress *Research on the polygraph has not progressed over time in the manner of a typical scientific field. It has not accumulated knowledge or strengthened its scientific underpinnings in any significant manner.* Polygraph research has proceeded in relative isolation from related fields of basic science and has benefited little from conceptual, theoretical, and technological advances in those fields that are relevant to the psychophysiological detection of deception.

Future Potential *The inherent ambiguity of the physiological measures used in the polygraph suggest that further investments in improving polygraph technique and interpretation will bring only modest improvements in accuracy.*

Evidence of Polygraph Accuracy

Source of Evidence *The evidence for polygraph validity lies primarily in atheoretical, empirical studies showing associations between summary scores derived from polygraph measures and independent indicators of truth or deception, in short, in studies that estimate the accuracy of polygraph tests.* Accuracy—the ability to distinguish deceptive from truthful individuals or responses—is an empirical property of a test procedure administered under specific conditions and with specific examinees. Consequently, it may vary with a number of factors, such as the population of examinees, characteristics of individual examinees or examiners, relationships established in the interview, testing methods, and the use of countermeasures. Despite efforts to create standardized polygraph testing procedures, each test with each individual has significant unique features.

Realism of Evidence *The research on polygraph accuracy fails in important ways to reflect critical aspects of field polygraph testing, even for specific-incident investigation.* In the laboratory studies focused on specific incidents using mock crimes, the consequences associated with lying or being judged deceptive almost never mirror the seriousness of those in real-world settings in which the polygraph is used. Polygraph practitioners claim that such studies underestimate the accuracy of the polygraph for motivated examinees, but we have found neither a compelling theoretical rationale nor a clear base of empirical evidence to support this claim; in our judgment, these studies overestimate accuracy. Virtually all the observational field studies of the polygraph have been focused on specific incidents and have been plagued by measurement biases that favor overestimation of accuracy, such as examiner contamination, as well as biases created by the lack of a clear and independent measure of truth.

Overestimation For the reasons cited, we believe that estimates of polygraph accuracy from existing research overestimate accuracy in actual practice, even for specific-incident investigations. The evidence is insufficient to allow a quantitative estimate of the size of the overestimate.

Estimate of Accuracy Notwithstanding the limitations of the quality of the empirical research and the limited ability to generalize to real-world settings, we conclude that in populations of examinees such as those represented in the polygraph research literature, untrained in countermeasures, specific-incident polygraph tests for event-specific investigations can discriminate lying from truth telling at rates well above chance, though well below perfection.

Accuracy may be highly variable across situations. The evidence does not allow any precise quantitative estimate of polygraph accuracy or provide confidence that accuracy is stable across personality types, sociodemographic groups, psychological and medical conditions, examiner and examinee expectancies, or ways of administering the test and selecting questions. In particular, the evidence does not provide confidence that polygraph accuracy is robust against potential countermeasures. There is essentially no evidence on the incremental validity of polygraph testing, that is, its ability to add predictive value to that which can be achieved by other methods.

Utility Polygraph examinations may have utility to the extent that they can elicit admissions and confessions, deter undesired activity, and instill public confidence. However, such utility is separate from polygraph validity. There is substantial anecdotal evidence that admissions and confessions occur in polygraph examinations, but no direct scientific evidence assessing the utility of the polygraph. Indirect evidence supports the idea that a technique will exhibit utility effects if examinees and the public believe that there is a high likelihood of a deceptive person being detected and that the costs of being judged deceptive are substantial. Any technique about which people hold such beliefs is likely to exhibit utility, whether or not it is valid. For example, there is no evidence to suggest that admissions and confessions occur more readily with the polygraph than with a bogus pipeline—an interrogation accompanying the use of an inert machine that the examinee believes to be a polygraph. In the long run, evidence that a technique lacks validity will surely undercut its utility.

Polygraph Screening

Criterion of Truthfulness *There are inherent difficulties in assessing the accuracy of polygraph testing in the screening situations of greatest concern to this study.* Although the criterion of truthfulness is easy to establish in laboratory simulations, we have seen no indication of a clear and stable agreement on what criteria are used in practice for assessing the accuracy of security screening polygraph tests in any federal agency that uses the tests. In particular, there is inconsistency about whether the polygraph test is being judged on its ability to detect major security violations or on its ability to elicit admissions of security violations of any magnitude. Moreover, the federal agencies that use the polygraph for screening do not collect data in a form that allows data from the ongoing administration of polygraph programs to be used to assess polygraph accuracy.

Generalizing from Research *Because the studies of acceptable quality all focus on specific incidents, generalization from them to uses for screening is not justified.* For this reason, uncertainty about the accuracy of screening polygraphs is greater than for specific-incident polygraph testing.

Estimate of Accuracy *Because actual screening applications involve considerably more ambiguity for the examinee and in determining truth than arises in specific-incident studies, polygraph accuracy for screening purposes is almost certainly lower than what can be achieved by specific-incident polygraph tests in the field.* Accuracy can be expected to be lower because of two major differences between screening and specific-incident polygraph testing. First, because a screening examiner does not know what specific transgressions an examinee may be concealing, it is necessary to ask generic questions rather than specific ones. Such questions create considerably more ambiguity for examinees than specific questions, such that two examinees who have committed the same minor infraction might have very different interpretations of its relevance to a test question, and very different emotional and physiological reactions. Instructions to examinees may reduce, but will not eliminate such variations, which can only degrade the accuracy of a test. Second, the appropriate criteria for judging accuracy are different in the two situations. In the typical screening situation, it is difficult in principle to assess whether a negative answer is truthful, and therefore it is much harder to establish truth and estimate accuracy than in event-specific testing. Moreover, the experimental studies that somewhat approximate screening situations all have serious methodological flaws. These studies typically involve mock-crime simulations very much like those used in other polygraph research; consequently, we believe these studies have more relevance for real-world specific-incident settings than for real-world screening settings.

Preemployment Screening   The relevance of available research to preemployment polygraph screening is highly questionable because such screening involves inferences about future behavior on the basis of polygraph evidence about past behaviors that are probably quite different in kind. The validity for such inferences depends on specifying and testing a plausible theory that links evidence of past behavior, such as illegal drug use, to future behavior of a different kind, such as revealing classified information. We have not found any explicit statement of a plausible theory, let alone evidence appropriate for judging either construct or criterion validity for this application. Conclusions about polygraph accuracy for these applications must be drawn by educated extrapolation from research that addresses situations that differ systematically from the intended applications.

Locus of Deception   Evidence from screening simulation studies is inconsistent concerning the ability of screening polygraph tests to identify which of several question areas is the correct locus of deception.

Countermeasures

Effectiveness   Basic science and polygraph research give reason for concern that polygraph test accuracy may be degraded by countermeasures, particularly when used by major security threats who have a strong incentive and sufficient resources to use them effectively. If these measures are effective, they could seriously undermine any value of polygraph security screening. All of the physiological indicators measured by the polygraph can be altered by conscious efforts through cognitive or physical means, and there is enough empirical research to justify concern that successful countermeasures may be learnable. Research does not clarify, however, whether users of countermeasures can be detected in contexts in which systematic efforts are made to detect and deter them. The available evidence does not allow us to determine whether innocent examinees can increase their chances of achieving nondeceptive outcomes by using countermeasures. It is possible that classified information on countermeasures and their detection exists; however, our specific requests to the relevant federal agencies for such information, including a classified briefing, did not reveal any such research. Thus, we cannot verify its existence or relevance.

Alternatives and Enhancements to the Polygraph

Alternative Techniques *Some potential alternatives to the polygraph show promise, but none has yet been shown to outperform the polygraph. None shows any promise of supplanting the polygraph for screening purposes in the near term.* Some potential alternatives may be useful as supplements, though the necessary research to explore that potential has not been done. Some, particularly techniques based on measurement of brain activity through electrical and imaging studies, have good potential on grounds of basic theory. However, research is at a very early stage with the most promising techniques, and many methodological, theoretical, and practical problems would have to be solved for these techniques to yield improvements on the polygraph. Not enough is known to tell whether it will ever be possible in practice to identify deception in real time through brain measurements.

Computerized Analysis *Computerized analysis of polygraph records may be able, in theory, to improve test accuracy. This potential has not yet been demonstrated, however, either in research or in practice, and it is likely to be only modest.* There have been major developments in computerized acquisition, summarization, display, and scoring of polygraph data, and further advances are likely. Computerized polygraph scoring procedures have the theoretical potential to increase the accuracy of polygraph interpretation because they allow analysis to use more information from the polygraph record and to weight different polygraph features more appropriately than do traditional scoring methods. Despite considerable government investment in computerized polygraph scoring methods, however, the existing approaches have at best an empirical base and are only loosely justified in terms of the features they extract from the polygraph record. These methods have a problematic statistical basis and have not been tested widely enough to generate confidence that their accuracy is any greater than that of traditional scoring methods. The difficulties that exist with computerized scoring of polygraph tests also exist, and may be multiplied, with possible expert systems for combining polygraph results with other forms of data.

Combining Information Sources *It may be possible to improve the ability to identify major security risks by combining polygraph information with information from other screening techniques, for example, in serial screening protocols such as those used in medical diagnosis.* We found no serious investigations of such multicomponent screening approaches.

DOE POLYGRAPH SCREENING POLICY

Every situation in which polygraph testing might be contemplated, including each security screening situation, has its own characteristics in terms of the types and magnitudes of the costs and benefits presented by polygraph testing. These costs and benefits are of many types, some of which are impossible to estimate quantitatively with available knowledge. The choices should therefore be evaluated for each application on the basis of the characteristics of that application, available scientific knowledge about the test's performance, and informed judgments about the values at stake. We have carefully examined the situation of employee security screening at the DOE laboratories, and the conclusions below apply to that situation. They are likely also to apply to other situations in which the base rates of the target transgressions are extremely low, the costs of false negative results can be very high, and the costs associated with using a screening procedure that produces a large number of false positive results would be very high.

Limitations for Detection The polygraph as currently used has extremely serious limitations for use in security screening to identify security risks and to clear valued employees. In populations with extremely low base rates of major security violations, such an application requires greater accuracy than polygraph testing achieves. In addition, there is a realistic possibility that the polygraph might be defeated with countermeasures, at least by the most serious security violators. The potential that a polygraph policy may deter security threats and elicit admissions and confessions may justify using the polygraph in security screening, but this rationale does not rest on the validity of the polygraph for psychophysiological detection of deception. Rather, it rests on the expectation that examinees' behavior will be shaped by their concerns that they may be judged (rightly or wrongly) to be deceptive on the polygraph. Because of these limitations, even if the polygraph has some accuracy in actual field use, it does not follow that it should be used for screening because of the potential costs of such use, including the possibilities that it will lower morale and productivity in national security organizations and deter people with scarce and highly valuable skills from working, or continuing to work, in these organizations.

False Positives with "Suspicious" Thresholds Polygraph screening protocols that can identify a large fraction of serious security violators can be expected to incorrectly implicate at least hundreds, and perhaps thousands, of innocent employees for each spy or other serious security violator correctly identified. Given the range of scientifically plausible accuracy levels for polygraph testing, this conclusion applies to any population of examinees that has the very low base rates of major security violations, such as espionage, that almost certainly exist among the employees subjected to polygraph screening in the DOE laboratories. Because the innocent will be indistinguishable from the guilty by polygraph alone, investigative resources would have to be expended to investigate hundreds of cases in order to find whether there is indeed one guilty individual (or more) in a pool of many individuals who "fail" a polygraph test. The alternative is to terminate or interrupt the careers of hundreds of innocent and productive individuals in an attempt to prevent the activity of one potential spy or saboteur.

Failure to Detect with "Friendly" Thresholds *Polygraph screening programs can reduce the costs associated with false positive findings by adopting techniques that reduce the likelihood that innocent examinees will "fail" a polygraph test. However, polygraph screening programs that produce very small proportions of positive results, such as those reported by DOE, the U.S. Department of Defense (DoD), and the Federal Bureau of Investigation (FBI), can do so only at the cost of failing to accurately identify the majority of deceptive examinees.* This conclusion applies to any population with extremely low base rates of the target transgressions, and it holds true even if none of the deceptive examinees uses countermeasures.

Use in DOE Employee Security Screening *Polygraph testing yields an unacceptable choice for DOE employee security screening between too many loyal employees falsely judged deceptive and too many major security threats left undetected. Its accuracy in distinguishing actual or potential security violators from innocent test takers is insufficient to justify reliance on its use in employee security screening in federal agencies.* If polygraph screening is considered because of its potential utility for such purposes as deterrence and elicitation of admissions, it should be remembered that a policy with a relatively friendly threshold that might enhance these forms of utility cannot be counted on to detect more than a small proportion of major security violators.

Danger of Overconfidence *Overconfidence in the polygraph—a belief in its accuracy not justified by the evidence—presents a danger to national security objectives.* A false faith in the accuracy of polygraph testing among potential examinees may enhance its utility for deterrence and eliciting admissions. However, we are more concerned with the danger that can arise from overconfidence in polygraph accuracy among officials in security and counterintelligence organizations, who are themselves potential examinees. Such overconfidence, when it affects counterintelligence and security policy choices, may create an unfounded, false sense that because employees have appeared nondeceptive on a polygraph, security precautions can be relaxed. Such overconfidence can create a false sense of security among policy makers, employees in sensitive positions, and the public that may in turn lead to inappropriate relaxation of other methods of ensuring security. It can waste public resources by devoting to the polygraph funds that would be better expended on developing or implementing alternative security procedures. It can lead to unnecessary loss of competent or highly skilled individuals because of suspicions cast on them as a result of false positive polygraph exams or because they avoid or leave employment in federal security organizations in the face of such prospects. And it can lead to credible claims that agencies that use polygraphs are infringing on individuals' civil liberties for insufficient benefits to national security.

Broader Approaches *The limited usefulness of the polygraph for security screening justifies efforts to look more broadly for ways to improve security.* Modifications in the overall security strategies used in federal agencies, such as have been recommended by the Hamre Commission for the U.S. Department of Energy (Commission on Science and Security, 2002), deserve consideration. Ways of improving the accuracy of screening, including alternatives and supplements to the polygraph and innovative ways to combine information sources, also deserve consideration.

Recent Policy Recommendations on Polygraph Screening *Two recent reports that advocate continued use of polygraph tests for security screening in federal agencies are partly, but not completely, consistent with the scientific evidence on polygraph accuracy.* The Hamre Commission report recommends more restricted use in DOE; the Webster Commission report (Commission for the Review of FBI Security Programs, 2002) recommends expanded polygraph testing in the FBI. Both reports recommend using the polygraph only on individuals who are in positions where they could gravely threaten national security, a stance consistent with the objective of reducing the total costs of false positive errors in testing.

Both reports presumably based their recommendations at least in part on a belief in the utility of the polygraph that goes beyond issues regarding the scientific validity and accuracy.

Neither report explicitly addresses two inherent problems of using a test with the approximate accuracy of the polygraph for screening in populations with very low base rates of spies and terrorists. One is the false positive problem created by the likelihood that the great majority of positive test results will come from innocent examinees. The other, potentially more serious problem, is the false negative problem created by the likelihood that with polygraph screening programs such as are being operated at both DOE and FBI, which yield a very low proportion of negative results, the majority of spies are likely to "pass" at least one polygraph test without being detected, even if they do not use counter-measures. Thus, as we note above, a policy of screening that may be justified on the basis of utility for deterrence and elicitation of admissions cannot be counted on to detect more than a small proportion of major security violators.

Federal officials need to be careful not to draw the wrong conclusions from negative polygraph test results. Our discussions with polygraph program and counterintelligence officials in several federal agencies suggest that there is a widespread belief in this community that someone who "passes" the polygraph is "cleared" of suspicion. Acting on such a belief with the results of security screening polygraph tests could pose a danger to national security because a negative polygraph test result in a population with a low base rate, especially when the test protocol produces a very small percentage of positive test results, provides little information on deceptiveness beyond what was already known prior to the test, that the probability of true transgression is very low.

FUTURE DIRECTIONS

Although the scientific base for detecting deception remains weak, scientific analysis remains the best way for government agencies to assess techniques that are presented as useful for detecting and deterring criminals and national security threats and to develop improved methods. This section suggests ways that federal agencies should evaluate purported techniques for detection of deception or of concealed information. The next section recommends a program of research aimed at improving the capability for detection and deterrence.

Evaluating Methods for Detecting Deception

Need for Scientific Evaluation *Techniques for detecting deception should be subjected to independent scientific evaluation before any agency relies on them.* Government agencies will continue to seek accurate ways to detect deception by criminals, spies, terrorists, and others who threaten public safety and security interests. These agencies need to be able to make objective evaluations of new techniques offered to them by entrepreneurs who claim that these techniques are based on science. Recent experience suggests that many such techniques are likely to be developed in the coming years and that many of them will be oversold. In particular, proponents are likely to present evidence that a technique discriminates accurately between truthfulness and deception in a particular sample of examinees as proof of the overall validity of the technique. As Chapters 2 and 3 make clear, such evidence is insufficient to demonstrate general validity.

Our efforts in conducting this study may be useful in suggesting what kinds of scientific evaluation are needed for future claims of scientific detection of deception. We offer a set of questions that indicate the kinds of studies that would provide credible evidence for supporting techniques for the detection of deception. We have also identified a set of characteristics of high-quality studies that address issues of accuracy. We present these questions and characteristics with the hope that they may help government agencies to use solid independent evidence as the basis for their judgments about proposed techniques for the scientifically based detection of deception, including some that may not yet have been developed.

Questions for Assessing Validity

• Does the technique have a plausible theoretical rationale, that is, a proposed psychological, physiological, or brain mechanism that is consistent with current physiological, neurobiological, and psychological knowledge?

• Does the psychological state being tested for (deception or recognition) reliably cause identifiable behavioral, physiological, or brain changes in individuals, and are these changes measured by the proposed technique?

• By what mechanisms are the states associated with deception linked to the phenomena the technique measures?

• Are optimal procedures being used to measure the particular states claimed to be associated with deception?

• By what mechanisms might a truthful response produce a false positive result with this technique? What do practitioners of the technique do to counteract or correct for such mechanisms? Is this response to the possibility of false positives reasonable considering the mechanisms involved?

• By what means could a deceptive response produce a false negative result? That is, what is the potential for effective countermeasures? What do practitioners of the technique do to counteract or correct for such phenomena? Is this response to the possibility of false negatives and effective countermeasures reasonable considering the mechanisms involved?

• Are the mechanisms purported to link deception to behavioral, physiological, or brain states and those states to the test results universal for all people who might be examined, or do they operate differently in different kinds of people or in different situations? Is it possible that measured responses do not always have the same meaning or that a test that works for some kinds of examinees or situations will fail with others?

• How do the social context and the social interactions that constitute the examination procedure affect the reliability and validity of the recordings that are obtained?

• Are there plausible alternative theoretical rationales regarding the underlying mechanisms that make competing empirical predictions about how the technique performs? What is the weight of evidence for competing theoretical rationales?

Research Methods for Demonstrating Accuracy

Claims that a technique is valid for the detection of deception should be accompanied by evidence of accuracy. The broader the range of examinees, examiners, situations, and social contexts in which accuracy is demonstrated, the greater the confidence that a technique will perform well across various applications. Agencies assessing claims of accuracy should consider the degree to which the studies offered to support the claims embody a number of features shared by good validation research in this area.

• **Randomized Experimentation** In analog studies, this means that examinees are randomly assigned to be truthful or deceptive. It is also useful to have studies in which examinees are allowed to decide whether to engage in the target behavior. Such studies gain a degree of realism for what they lose in experimental control.

• **Manipulation Checks** If a technique is claimed to measure arousal, for example, there should be independent evidence that experimental manipulations actually create different levels of arousal in the different groups.

• **Blind Administration and Blind Evaluation of the Technique** Whoever administers and scores tests based on the technique must do so in the absence of any information on whether the examinee is truthful or deceptive.

• **Adequate Sample Sizes** Most of the studies we examined were based on relatively small sample sizes that were sometimes adequate to allow for the detection of statistically significant differences but were insufficient for accurate assessment of accuracy. Changing the results of only a few cases might dramatically affect the implications of these studies.

• **Appropriate Comparison Conditions and Experimental Controls** These conditions and controls will vary with the technique. A suggestion of what may be involved is the idea in polygraph research of comparing a polygraph examination with a bogus polygraph examination, with neither the examiner nor the examinee knowing that the test output might be bogus.

• **Cross-Validation of Any Exploratory Data Analytic Solution on Independent Data** Any standardized or computerized scoring system for measurements from a technique cannot be seriously considered as providing accurate detection unless it has been shown to perform well on samples of examinees different from those on whom it was developed.

• **Examinees Masked to Experimental Hypotheses if Not to Experimental Condition** It is important to sort out precisely what effect is being measured. For example, the results of a countermeasures study would be more convincing if examinees were instructed to expect that the examiner is looking for the use of countermeasures, among other things, rather than being instructed explicitly that this is a study of whether countermeasures work and can be detected.

• **Standardization** An experiment should have sufficient standardization to allow reliable replication by others and should analyze the results from all examinees. It is important to use a technique in the same way on all the examinees, which means: clear reporting of how the technique was administered; sharply limiting the examiner's discretion in administering the technique and interpreting its results; and using the technique on all examinees, not only the ones whose responses are easy to classify. If some examinees are dropped from the analysis, the reasons should be stated explicitly. This is a difficult test for a procedure to pass, but it is appropriate for policy purposes.

• **Analysis of Sensitivity and Specificity or Their Equivalents** Data should be reported in a way that makes it possible to calculate both the sensitivity and specificity of the technique, preferably at multiple thresholds for diagnostic decision making or in a way that allows comparisons of the test results with the criterion on other than binary scales.

A PROGRAM OF RESEARCH

Our conclusions make clear that polygraph testing, though exhibiting accuracy considerably better than chance under a variety of conditions, has characteristics that leave it far short of what would be desirable for screening programs to distinguish individuals who pose threats to national security from innocent examinees. The research base for precisely quantifying the accuracy of polygraph testing is also far from what would be desirable. During our deliberations we repeatedly discussed how polygraph research might have been done better, what alternatives to the current instruments and tests would most sensibly take modern psycho-physiological understanding into account, and what evidence we ourselves would find compelling as support for a technique for the physiological detection of deception. We also asked ourselves whether there would be much practical or scientific gain from incremental research on polygraph testing and scoring techniques and on the other detection techniques discussed throughout this report.

Expanded Research Effort *We recommend an expanded research effort directed at methods for deterring and detecting major security threats, including efforts to improve techniques for security screening.* Research offers one promising strategy for meeting the national need to deter and detect security threats. It is not, of course, the only appropriate strategy. Traditional methods of maintaining the security of classified material, controlling and monitoring access, investigating security threats, and so forth, continue to be extremely important. In fact, to the extent that techniques of detecting deception are likely to remain imperfect, such other security strategies gain in importance because they decrease the burden that detection techniques must carry in meeting security objectives.

We cannot guarantee that research related to techniques for detecting deception will yield valuable practical payoff for national security, even in the long term. However, given the seriousness of the national need, an expanded research effort appears worthwhile.

Objectives *The research program we envision would seek any edge that science can provide for deterring and detecting security threats. It would have two major objectives: (1) to provide federal agencies with methods of the highest possible scientific validity for protecting national security by deterring and detecting espionage, sabotage, terrorism, and other major security threats; and (2) to make these agencies fully aware of the strengths and limitations of the techniques they use.*

Deterring and Detecting Security Threats

If the government continues to rely heavily on the polygraph in the national security arena, some of this research effort should be devoted to developing scientific knowledge that could either put the polygraph on a firmer scientific foundation or lead to its supplementation or replacement. We have identified a considerable number of open scientific questions about the polygraph throughout this report that could be addressed as part of the research program. We do not think, however, that national security is best served by a narrow focus on polygraph research.

Scope The research program should have a far broader scope than polygraph testing, broader even than psychophysiological detection of deception and specific alternative approaches to detecting deception (discussed in Chapter 6). It should include, but not necessarily be limited to, approaches involving testing, interrogating, and investigating individuals. For instance, the recommendations of the Hamre Commission (Commission on Science and Security, 2002) suggest the need for research on approaches to deterrence and detection that can be implemented at the organizational level as well as through the testing of individuals. Research on such approaches would be appropriate for consideration and support under the program. It is important that the research program be broadly conceived and open to supporting alternative ways of looking at these problems because there is no single research approach that clearly holds the most promise for meeting national security objectives. Thus, the research program might support research ranging from very basic work on fundamental psychological, physiological, social, and organizational processes related to deterring and detecting security threats, on one hand, to applied studies implementing scientifically sound methods in practical situations, on the other.

We have investigated only a part of this large domain. We present below some ideas about potentially promising lines of research in the areas we have investigated, and our expectations about what concerted research efforts along each line of research might yield.

Polygraph Research

- Scientifically based efforts could be made to develop, define, and validate improved indicators derived from polygraph measurements for use in computerized scoring. These efforts would have to improve on the approaches currently being used. They might lead to marginal improvements in the overall performance of polygraph testing over several years, but major increases in accuracy are unlikely to be achieved.
- Serious investigations could be focused on explaining the variation in accuracy estimates from polygraph research. This might yield more confident estimates of accuracy, which would help inform decisions about the conditions under which polygraph testing is useful and about how much reliance to place on the results when it is used.
- The previous line of investigation would have to be supplemented by research into the major threats to polygraph validity. Two that deserve special attention are polygraph performance with stigmatized populations and as a function of examiners' expectancies. Such studies would resolve concerns that polygraph accuracy may be seriously reduced with certain examinees or under certain conditions. It is possible that such research would result in reduced confidence in the scientific value of the

polygraph. In our judgment, even such a result would be positive because it would help agencies make more accurate interpretations of the information they have.

• Research could be conducted on the effectiveness of polygraph countermeasures and on their detectability. Great progress can be made in learning how polygraph measures respond to different kinds of countermeasures, how much effort is needed to learn effective countermeasures, and how otherwise effective countermeasures can be detected. The value of this research depends on the usefulness of the polygraph for detection in particular contexts, which could be made clearer with the other suggested research.

• Careful documentation of polygraph examinations as they are being administered, combined with individual background information and reports on subsequent outcomes, would generate a valuable body of epidemiological data that could provide better estimates of the accuracy of field polygraph testing, both generally and with specific populations.

• Planned experiments, embedded in the operation of an ongoing polygraph program, in which examiners might potentially be experimental subjects uninformed about certain aspects of the research design, might be used to separate the effects of different components of the polygraph examination, elucidate the impact of expectancies, and more generally improve understanding of the polygraph examination process in real-world populations of examinees on whom the outcome has potentially serious impact.

Other Approaches to Detection of Deception in Individuals

• Research on indicators of deception from demeanor have not been given much systematic attention, even though some of them might yield measures of comparable or perhaps greater accuracy than the polygraph. This line of research might yield practical supplements or complements to the polygraph in the relatively near term because demeanor indicators may yield indicators of deception that are somewhat different from those measured by the polygraph.

• Investigations of brain activity through electrical and imaging studies may yield basic understanding of neural processes in deception. Such investigations, especially if theoretically grounded in central nervous system psychophysiology, have the potential in principle to yield techniques of deception more accurate than the polygraph, as well as to supplement information from polygraph and other sources and to identify signatures in the brain of particular polygraph countermeasures. Not enough is known, however, to tell whether it will ever be possible in practice to identify deception in real time through brain measurement. We are confident that it will not happen within the next decade. Moreover, brain-based indicators will not necessarily be resistant to countermeasures.

• Research could be conducted to seek physiological measures other than brain measures, developed since the advent of the polygraph, that might have greater validity than the polygraph or yield improvements in accuracy when combined with polygraph or other measures. Such research will be most promising if it is guided by empirically supported theory about the underlying psychological and physiological mechanisms. We anticipate that research on such measures will, at best, yield incremental improvement over the performance of the polygraph.

• Investigation of statistical and computer-based ways to combine diverse indicators of truthfulness or deception might yield composite indicators or serial testing protocols that would noticeably improve accuracy of detection beyond what the polygraph achieves with general populations. This strategy may be the most promising way to achieve noticeable improvements in the accuracy of detection of deception in the fairly short run. We caution, however, that this research is likely to be atheoretical, so that it will be very important to investigate carefully threats to validity, including the threat of countermeasures, for both composite indicators and serial testing protocols.

Broader Approaches

• Explicit research on policies for detection of deception would help agencies make better informed decisions on how to use uncertain information. This research might address questions of the incremental validity of new information, the policy implications of setting thresholds for tests of deception, and the estimation of tradeoffs involved in alternative detection policies.

• Systematic research on the bogus pipeline phenomenon can help with deterring and detecting security threats in more than one way. It can clarify the extent to which the practical value of the polygraph (or analogous techniques) for eliciting admissions results from test validity or merely from examinees' beliefs and concerns. This will help agencies better interpret the information they get from using the polygraph and analogous techniques. It may also help improve interrogation techniques. We note that ethical issues will arise with some uses of interrogation techniques that rely on elements known to be bogus.

• The problem of deterrence of security threats might be addressed explicitly with research. It is, after all, an empirical question how polygraph policies or other security policies affect the behavior of federal employees and potential employees—both those who may act against the national security and those who will not, but whose productivity or employment futures may be affected by security policies aimed at deterring breaches of security. Better understanding of such effects could give valuable insight to decision makers in the near term.

• Various lines of organizational research may also be useful in developing effective policies for deterring and detecting security threats. We have not considered the possibilities, but are convinced that useful research can be done on deterrence and detection from the perspective of policy design and implementation.

Potential Payoff We cannot predict with confidence that an investment by the federal government in the kind of research program envisioned here will yield substantial improvement in the ability to deter and detect threats to the national security. We would expect at least marginal improvement in this ability and more significant improvement in the government's ability to evaluate the information available from techniques for detecting deception. The basic research may have large practical value in the long run, as well as spillover effects through contributions to basic science, but these cannot be foreseen with any confidence.

The approaches that have the greatest overall promise for detecting deception, such as direct measurement of brain activity, will take a long time to produce any practical payoff. Even then, we have much more confidence that they will advance cognitive and social psychophysiology than that they will advance practical detection of deception. They constitute a long-term speculative investment. At the other extreme, research on the polygraph may have quick benefits, but they are likely to be small. Such research may also undermine confidence in the technique, leaving the government with the task of finding new instruments and new approaches to deterrence and detection. It is because of this real possibility that we advocate a program that has a broad vision: some of the best practical ideas may be ones that have not yet been researched. Some of them may not even directly involve efforts to detect deception.

Organization of a Research Program

Organizational Emphasis A substantial portion of our recommended expanded research program should be administered by an organization or organizations with no operational responsibility for detecting deception and no institutional commitment to using or training practitioners of a particular technique. The research program should follow accepted standards for scientific research, use rules and procedures designed to eliminate biases that might influence the findings, and operate under normal rules of scientific freedom and openness to the extent possible while protecting national security.

We recommend this organizational emphasis because many past research efforts on detection of deception in the U.S. government, though well intentioned, have suffered from a separation from mainstream scientific thinking and from their organizational location within agencies strongly committed to one technique. This has hampered progress in polygraph research and largely prevented the government from giving adequate attention to alternative and supplementary approaches.

We wish to note explicitly that in recent years, the DoD Polygraph Institute (DoDPI) has been working to put polygraph research on a more scientific footing. For example, technical reports are being submitted to peer-reviewed journals, and outside academic reviewers are providing advice on improving the scientific quality of DoDPI-funded research. These are salutary developments for polygraph science and should be commended, but they have not gone far enough. The effectiveness of DoDPI as a source of solid scientific knowledge on detecting deception is significantly undermined by two structural/institutional factors: (1) that its mission is narrowly defined in terms of the polygraph rather than the larger purpose of detecting deception; and (2) that the research activities are housed in an organization whose mission involves promoting and training personnel in a specific technique of detecting deception. These factors create real and perceived conflicts of interest with respect to research that might question polygraph validity or support an alternative method as superior.

The organizations that carry out the expanded research program should support both basic and applied research. They should follow standard scientific advisory and decision-making procedures, including external peer review of proposals, and they should support research that is conducted and reviewed openly in the manner of other scientific research. Classified and restricted research should be limited only to matters of identifiable national security.

The fundamental research sponsored in the research program should not be totally separate from other related scientific efforts (for example, research on brain imaging supported by basic science and health research agencies), but some separation is essential to ensure that mechanisms are in place for periodically assessing progress toward national security goals and for assuring that promising approaches move from the laboratory to testing in applied settings.

Expanding basic research on deception and deterrence as outlined above does not lessen the need the for government to review and assess the implications and uses of the research for defense and homeland security, and specifically to develop and test operational versions of procedures that can enhance such security and to train those who will be charged with implementing these procedures. Thus, at least some of the applied research in the expanded program should be sponsored by or linked to organizations with operational responsibilities for national security to ensure its relevance to these missions. Mission-oriented agencies should continue to conduct implementation-focused research, such as studies of quality control, examiner training effectiveness, and so forth. In addition, mission-oriented agencies should be encouraged and even mandated to cooperate with the broader research effort, for example, by providing archival data and cooperating in field research.

Countermeasures and Classified Research The problem of countermeasures highlights some important questions about how future research on detecting deception should be structured. Concerns about countermeasures arise in all lie detection contexts, not only polygraph testing. Research on countermeasures poses the prospect of discovering techniques that might be exploited by the very people lie detectors seek to catch. Thus, many people have argued that research on countermeasures should be classified or otherwise conducted outside the public domain. It is true that removing countermeasures research from public view may lessen the danger that these techniques will fall into the wrong hands, but such removal would also carry with it certain possible negative consequences. Classification would limit the number and, in all likelihood, the quality of the scientists available to study countermeasures. The more robust the scientific exploration of the subject, the more likely the dangers of countermeasures can be identified and nullified. Interestingly, the decision on whether to classify this research is not entirely unrelated to the physiological character of countermeasure techniques. If countermeasures have unique physiological signatures that cannot be masked or otherwise concealed, then classifying this research would be unnecessary. Lie detection would invariably identify countermeasures by these signatures whenever they were used, and potential examinees would learn to expect that countermeasures would be detected. Unfortunately, until the research is done, one cannot know whether countermeasures have such signatures. Ultimately, therefore, the decision whether to classify such research is a policy choice. Policy makers must weigh the danger of public knowledge of countermeasure techniques against the benefits of a robust research program that could be expected (though not guaranteed) to be more successful at identifying and nullifying countermeasure techniques.

References

Abrams, S.
    1999   A response to Honts on the issue of the discussion of questions between charts. *Polygraph* 28:223-228.

Aftergood, S.
    2000   Polygraph testing and the DOE national laboratories. *Science* 290:939-940.

Allen, J.J., and W.G. Iacono
    1997   A comparison of methods for the analysis of event-related potentials in deception detection. *Psychophysiology* 34:234-240.

American Psychological Association
    1999   *Standards for Educational and Psychological Testing.* Washington, DC: American Psychological Association.

Arvey, R.D., and J.E. Campion
    1982   The employment interview: A summary and review of recent research. *Personnel Psychology* 35:281-322.

Backster, C.
    1963   The Backster chart reliability rating method. *Law and Order* 1:63-64.
    1973   *Polygraph Examiner's Training Model.* New York: Backster School of Lie Detection.

Balding, D.J., and P. Donnelley
    1995   Inference in forensic identification. *Journal of the Royal Statistical Society, Series A* 158:21-53.

Bandettini, P.A., E.C. Wong, R.S. Hinks, R.S. Tikofsky, and J.S. Hyde
    1992   Time course EPI of human brain function during task activation. *Magnetic Resonance in Medicine* 25:390-397.

Bar-Hillel, M., and G. Ben-Shakhar
    1986   The a priori case against graphology. In *Scientific Aspects of Graphology*, B. Nevo, ed. Chicago: Charles C. Thomas.

Barland, G.H.
 1981   A Validation and Reliability Study of the Counterintelligence Screening Test. Fort
        George G. Meade, MD.
Barland, G.H., C.R. Honts, and S.D. Barger
 1989   Studies of the Accuracy of Security Screening Polygraph Examinations. Report
        No. DoDPI89-R-0001. Fort McClellan, AL: U.S. Department of Defense Poly-
        graph Institute.
Bartlett, M.S., J.C. Hager, P. Ekman, and T.J. Sejnowski
 1999   Measuring facial expressions by computer image analysis. *Psychophysiology* 36:
        253-263.
Begg, C.B., and R.A. Greenes
 1983   Assessment of diagnostic tests when verification is subject to selection bias. *Bio-
        metrics* 39:207-215.
Ben-Shakhar, G.
 1977   A further study of the dichotomization theory in detection of deception. *Psycho-
        physiology* 14(4):408-413.
 1989   Non-conventional methods in personnel selection. In *Assessment and Selection in
        Organizations*, P. Herriot, ed. Chichester, UK: Wiley.
Ben-Shakhar, G., and K. Dolev
 1996   Psychophysiological detection through the Guilty Knowledge technique: Effects
        of mental countermeasures. *Journal of Applied Psychology* 67(6):701-713.
Ben-Shakhar, G., and E. Elaad
 2002   The Guilty Knowledge Test (GKT) as an application of psychophysiology: Fu-
        ture prospects and obstacles. Pp. 87-102 in *Handbook of Polygraph Testing*, M.
        Kleiner, ed. San Diego: Academic Press.
 2003   The validity of psychophysiological detection of information with the guilty
        knowledge test: A meta-analytic review. *Journal of Applied Psychology.*
Ben-Shakhar, G., and J.J. Furedy
 1990   *Theories and Applications in the Detection of Deception: A Psychophysiological and
        International Perspective.* New York: Springer-Verlag.
Ben-Shakhar, G., M. Bar-Hillel, and M. Kremnitzer
 2002   Trial by polygraph: Reconsidering the use of the guilty knowledge technique in
        court. *Law and Human Behavior* 26:527-541.
Ben-Shakhar, G., M. Bar-Hillel, and I. Lieblich
 1986   Trial by polygraph: Scientific and juridical issues in lie detection. *Behavioral
        Science and the Law* 4:459-479.
Ben-Shakhar, G., I. Lieblich, and M. Bar-Hillel
 1982   An evaluation of polygraphers' judgments: A review from a decision theoretic
        perspective. *Journal of Applied Psychology* 67(6):701-713.
Ben-Shakhar, G., I. Lieblich, and S. Kugelmass
 1970   Guilty Knowledge Technique: Application of signal detection measures. *Journal
        of Applied Psychology* 54(5):409-413.
Ben-Shakhar, G., M. Bar-Hillel, Y. Bilu, E. Ben-Abba, and A. Flug
 1986   Can graphology predict occupational success? Two empirical studies and some
        methodological ruminations. *Journal of Applied Psychology* 71:645-653.
Berger, H.
 1929   Uber das elektrenkephalogramm des menschen. *Archiv fur Psychiatrie und
        Nervenkrankheiten* 87:527-580.
Berntson, G.G., J.T. Cacioppo, and K.S. Quigley
 1991   Autonomic determinism: The modes of autonomic control, the doctrine of auto-
        nomic space, and the laws of autonomic constraint. *Psychological Review* 98:459-
        487.

1993 Cardiac psychophysiology and autonomic space in humans: Empirical perspectives and conceptual implications. *Psychological Bulletin* 114:296-322.

Berntson, G.G., J.T. Cacioppo, P. F. Binkley, B.N. Uchino, K.S. Quigley, and A. Fieldstone
1994 Autonomic cardiac control. III. Psychological stress and cardiac response in autonomic space as revealed by pharmacological blockades. *Psychophysiology* 31:599-608.

Berntson, G.G., J.T. Bigger, D.L. Eckberg, P. Grossman, P.G. Kaufmann, M. Malik, H.N. Nagaraja, S.W. Porges, J.P. Saul, P.H. Stone, and M.W. van der Molen
1997 Heart rate variability: Origins, methods, and interpretive caveats. *Psychophysiology* 34:623-648.

Bishop, Y.M.M., S.E. Fienberg, and P.W. Holland
1975 *Discrete Multivariate Analysis: Theory and Practice.* Cambridge, MA: The MIT Press.

Blascovich, J.
2000 Psychophysiological methods. Pp. 117-137 in *Handbook of Research Methods in Social and Personality Psychology,* H.T. Reis and C.M. Judd, eds. Cambridge, UK: Cambridge University Press.

Blascovich, J., W.B. Mendes, S. Hunter, and B. Lickel
2000 Challenge, threat, and stigma. Pp. 307-333 in *The Social Psychology of Stigma,* T. Heatherton, R. Kleck, M.R. Hebl, and J.G. Hull, eds. New York: Guilford Press.

Blascovich, J., S.J. Spencer, D. Quinn, and C. Steele
2001a African Americans and high blood pressure: The role of stereotype threat. *Psychological Science* 12:225-229.

Blascovich, J., W.B. Mendes, S.B. Hunter, B. Lickel, and N. Kowai-Bell
2001b Perceiver threat in social interactions with stigmatized others. *Journal of Personality and Social Psychology* 80:253-267.

Bradley, M.T., and D. Ainsworth
1984 Alcohol and the psychophysiological detection of deception. *Psychophysiology* 21(1):63-71.

Bradley, M.T., and M.C. Cullen
1993 Polygraph lie detection on real events in a laboratory setting. *Perceptual and Motor Skills* 76(3/Pt. 1):1051-1058.

Bradley, M.T., and M.P. Janisse
1981 Accuracy demonstrations, threat, and the detection of deception: Cardiovascular, electrodermal, and pupillary measures. *Psychophysiology* 18(3):307-315.

Bradley, M.T., and K.K. Klohn
1987 Machiavellianism, the Control Question Test and the detection of deception. *Perceptual and Motor Skills* 64:747-757.

Bradley, M.T., and J. Rettinger
1992 Awareness of crime-relevant information and the Guilty Knowledge Test. *Journal of Applied Psychology* 77(1):55-59.

Brenner, M., H.H. Branscomb, and G. Schwartz
1979 Psychological stress evaluator—Two tests of a vocal measure. *Psychophysiology* 16(4):351-357.

Brownlie, C., G.J. Johnson, and B. Knill
1998 Validation Study of the Relevant/Irrelevant Screening Format. Unpublished manuscript. National Security Agency, Washington, DC.

Buckley, J.P., and L.C. Senese
1991 The influence of race and gender on blind polygraph chart analyses. *Polygraph* 20(4):247-258.

Buxton, R.B.
  2002   *Introduction to Functional Magnetic Resonance Imaging: Principles and Techniques.*
          New York: Cambridge University Press.
Cacioppo, J.T.
  1994   Social neuroscience: Autonomic, neuroendocrine, and immune responses to
          stress. *Psychophysiology* 31:113-128.
Cacioppo, J.T., and R.E. Petty
  1983   *Social Psychophysiology: A Sourcebook.* New York: Guilford Press.
  1986   Social processes. Pp. 646-679 in *Psychophysiology: Systems, Processes, and Applica-*
          tions, M.G.H. Coles, E. Donchin, and S. Porges, eds. New York: Guilford Press.
Cacioppo, J.T., and L.G. Tassinary
  1990a   Inferring psychological significance from physiological signals. *American Psy-*
          chologist 45:16-28.
  1990b   *Principles of Psychophysiology: Physical, Social, and Inferential Elements.* Cambridge,
          UK: Cambridge University Press.
Cacioppo, J.T., L.G. Tassinary, and G.G. Berntson, eds.
  2000a   *Handbook of Psychophysiology,* 2nd ed. New York: Cambridge University Press.
  2000b   Psychophysiological science. Pp. 3-26 in *Handbook of Psychophysiology,* 2nd ed.
          New York: Cambridge University Press.
Cacioppo, J.T., G.G. Berntson, J.T. Larsen, K.M. Poehlmann, and T.A. Ito
  2000   The psychophysiology of emotion. Pp. 173-191 in *The Handbook of Emotion,* 2nd
          ed. R. Lewis and J.M. Haviland-Jones, eds. New York: Guilford Press.
Cacioppo, J.T., G.G. Berntson, P.F. Binkley, K.S. Quigley, B.N. Uchino, and A. Fieldstone
  1994   Autonomic cardiac control. II. Noninvasive indices and baseline response as
          revealed by autonomic blockades. *Psychophysiology* 31:586-598.
Cacioppo, J.T., B.N. Uchino, S.L. Crites, Jr., M.A. Snydersmith, G. Smith, G.G. Berntson, and
P.J. Lang
  1992   Relationship between facial expressiveness and sympathetic activation in emo-
          tion: A critical review, with emphasis on modeling underlying mechanisms and
          individual differences. *Journal of Personality and Social Psychology* 62:110-128.
Cail-Sirota, J., and H.R. Lieberman
  1995   A Database of Research on Drugs Which Could Influence the Outcome of Psy-
          chophysiological Detection of Deception Examinations. Report No. DoDPI95-R-
          0005. Ft. McClellan, AL: U.S. Department of Defense Polygraph Institute.
Campion, M.A., D.K. Palmer, and J.E. Campion
  1997   A review of structure in the selection interview. *Personnel Psychology* 50:655-702.
Campion, M.A., E.D. Pursell, and B.K. Brown
  1988   Structured interviewing: Raising the psychometric properties of the employment
          interview. *Personnel Psychology* 41:25-42.
Cannon, W.B.
  1929   *Bodily Changes in Pain, Hunger, Fear, and Rage.* New York: Appleton-Century-
          Crofts.
Carson, R.E., M.E. Daube-Witherspoon, and P. Herscovitch
  1997   *Quantitative Functional Brain Imaging with Positron Emission Tomography.* San Di-
          ego: Academic Press.
Caton, R.
  1875   The electrical currents of the brain. *British Medical Journal* 1:278.
Cestaro, V.L.
  1996   A Comparison of Accuracy Rates Between Detection of Deception Examinations
          Using the Polygraph and the Computer Voice Stress Analyzer in a Mock Crime
          Scenario. Report No. DoDPI95-R-0004. Ft. McClellan, AL: U.S. Department of
          Defense Polygraph Institute.

Cestaro, V.L., and A.B. Dollins
  1994   An Analysis of Voice Responses for the Detection of Deception. Report No.
          DoDPI94-R-0001. Ft. McClellan, AL: U.S. Department of Defense Polygraph
          Institute.
Cohn, J.F., A.J. Zlochower, J. Lien, and T. Kanade
  1999   Automated face analysis by feature point tracking has high concurrent validity
          with manual FACS coding. *Psychophysiology* 36:35-43.
Cole, S.A.
  2001   *Suspect Identities: A History of Fingerprinting and Criminal Identification.* Cam-
          bridge, MA: Harvard University Press.
Coles, M.G.H., E. Donchin, and S.W. Porges, eds.
  1986   *Psychophysiology.* New York: Guilford Press.
Commission for Review of FBI Security Programs
  2002   A Review of FBI Security Programs. March 31. Submitted by William H. Webster,
          Chairman, to Attorney General John Ashcroft. Washington, DC: U.S. Depart-
          ment of Justice.
Commission on Science and Security
  2002   Science and Security in the 21st Century: A Report to the Secretary of Energy on
          the Department of Energy Laboratories. April 2002. Submitted by John J. Hamre,
          Chairman, to the Honorable Spencer Abraham, Secretary, U.S. Department of
          Energy.
Correa, E.I., and H.E. Adams
  1981   The validity of the preemployment polygraph examination and the effects of
          motivation. *Polygraph* 10(3):143-155.
Crider, A., and R. Lunn
  1971   Electrodermal lability as a personality dimension. *Journal of Research in Personal-
          ity* 5:145-150.
Critchley, H.D., R. Elliott, J. Mathias, and R.J. Dolan
  2000   Neural activity relating to generation and representation of galvanic skin conduc-
          tance responses: A functional magnetic resonance imaging study. *Journal of Neu-
          roscience* 20:3033-3040.
Crocker, J., B. Major, and C. Steele
  1998   Social stigma. Pp. 504-553 in *Handbook of Social Psychology, Volume 2*, S. Fiske, D.
          Gilbert, and G. Lindzey, eds. Boston, MA: McGraw-Hill Book Company.
Cronbach, L.J., and G.C. Gleser
  1965   *Psychological Tests and Personnel Decisions*, 2nd ed. Urbana: University of Illinois
          Press.
Cronbach, L.J., G.C. Gleser, H. Nanda, and N. Rajaratnam
  1972   *The Dependability of Behavioral Measurements: Theory of Generalizability for Scores
          and Profiles.* New York: Wiley.
Davidson, R.J.
  2002   Anxiety and affective style: Role of prefrontal cortex and amygdala. *Biological
          Psychiatry* 51:68-80.
Davidson, R.J., and W. Irwin
  1999   The functional neuroanatomy of emotion and affective style. *Trends in Cognitive
          Science* 3:11-21.
Davis, P.A.
  1939   Effects of acoustic stimuli on the waking human brain. *Journal of Neurophysiology*
          2:494-499.

Davis, R.C.
  1961   Physiological responses as a means of evaluating information. Pp. 142-168 in
          Manipulation of Human Behavior, A. Biderman and H. Zimmer, eds. New York:
          Wiley.
Dawson, M.E.
  1980   Physiological detection of deception: Measurement of responses to questions
          and answers during countermeasure maneuvers. *Psychophysiology* 17(1):8-17.
  2000   In *Handbook of Psychophysiology*, 2nd ed. J.T. Cacioppo, L.G. Tassinary, and G.G.
          Berntson, eds. New York: Cambridge University Press.
Dawson, M.E., A.M. Schell, and D.L. Filion
  1990   The electrodermal system. Pp. 295-324 in *Principles of Psychophysiology: Physical,
          Social, and Inferential Elements*, J.T. Cacioppo and L.G. Tassinary, eds. Cambridge,
          UK: Cambridge University Press.
Decicco, D.
  2000   Police officer candidate assessment and selection. *FBI Law Enforcement Bulletin*
          69(12):1-6.
DePaulo, B.M., J.I. Stone, and G.D. Lassiter
  1985   Deceiving and detecting deceit. Pp. 323-370 in *The Self and Social Life*, B.R.
          Schlenker, ed. New York: McGraw-Hill Book Company.
DePaulo, B.M., J.J. Lindsay, B.E. Malone, L. Muhlenbruck, K. Charlton, and H. Cooper
  in   Cues to deception. *Psychological Bulletin*.
  press
Dickson, W.
  1986   Pre-employment polygraph screening of police applicants. *FBI-Law-Enforcement-
          Bulletin* 55(4):7-9.
Dienstbier, R.A.
  1989   Arousal and physiological toughness: Implications for mental and physical
          health. *Psychological Review* 96(1):84-100.
Diven, K.
  1937   Certain determinants in the conditioning of anxiety reactions. *Journal of Psychol-
          ogy* 3:291-308.
Dollins, A.B.
  1997   Psychophysiological Detection of Deception Accuracy Rates Obtained Using the
          Test for Espionage and Sabotage: A Replication (Acronym: TESRep2). Report
          No. DoDPI97-P-0009. Ft. McClellan, AL: U.S. Department of Defense Polygraph
          Institute.
Dollins, A.B., D.J. Kraphol, and D.W. Dutton
  2000   A comparison of computer programs designed to evaluate psychophysiological
          detection of deception examinations: Bakeoff 1. *Polygraph* 29(3):237-257.
Donchin, E., and M.G.H. Coles
  1988   Is the P300 component a manifestation of context updating? *Behavioral and Brain
          Sciences* 11:343-356.
Dwyer,W., E. Prien, and J. Bernard
  1990   Psychological screening of law enforcement officers: A case for job relatedness.
          Journal of Police Science and Administration 17(3):176-182.
Ekman, P.
  2001   *Telling Lies: Clues to Deceit in the Marketplace, Politics, and Marriage*. 3rd ed. New
          York: W.W. Norton and Company.
Ekman, P., and M. O'Sullivan
  1991   Who can catch a liar? *American Psychologist* 46:913-920.

Ekman, P., M. O'Sullivan, and M.G. Frank
   1999   A few can catch a liar. *Psychological Science* 10(3):263-266.
Ekman, P., M. O'Sullivan, W.V. Friesen, and K.R. Scherer
   1991   Face, voice, and body in detecting deceit. *Journal of Nonverbal Behavior* 15:125-135.
Elaad, E., and G. Ben-Shakhar
   1991   Effects of mental countermeasures on psychophysiological detection in the guilty
           knowledge test. *International Journal of Psychophysiology* 11:99-108.
Elaad, E., A. Ginton, and G. Ben-Shakhar
   1994   The effects of prior expectations and outcome knowledge on polygraph examin-
           ers' decisions. *Journal of Behavioral Decision Making* 7:279-292.
   1998   The role of prior expectations in polygraph examiners decisions. *Psychology Crime
           and Law* 4(1):1-16.
Faigman, D.L., D.H. Kaye, M.J. Saks, and J. Sanders
   2002   *Modern Scientific Evidence: The Law and Science of Expert Testimony*, 2nd ed. Eagan,
           MN: West Publishing Company.
Farwell, L.A., and E. Donchin
   1991   The truth will out: Interrogative polygraphy ("lie detection") with event-related
           potentials. *Psychophysiology* 28:531-547.
Farwell, L.A., and S.S. Smith
   2001   Using brain MERMER testing to detect knowledge despite efforts to conceal. *Jour-
           nal of Forensic Science* 46:135-143.
Fiedler, K., J. Schmid, and T. Stahl
   in   What is the current truth about polygraph lie detection? *Basic and Applied Social
   press   Psychology* December, forthcoming.
Fienberg, S.E., and M. Finkelstein
   1996   Bayesian statistics and the law (with discussion). Pp. 129-146 in *Bayesian Statistics
           5*, J.M. Bernardo, J.O. Berger, A.P. Dawid, and A.F.M. Smith, eds. New York:
           Oxford University Press.
Fletcher, R.H., S.W. Fletcher, and E.H. Wagner
   1996   *Clinical Epidemiology: The Essentials, 3rd ed.* Baltimore: Williams and Wilkins.
           (pp. 53-57).
Fowles, D.C.
   1986   The eccrine system and electrodermal activity. Pp. 51-96 in *Psychophysiology:
           Systems, Processes, and Applications*, M.G.H. Coles, E. Donchin, and S.W. Porges,
           eds. New York: Guilford Press.
Fox, P.T., and M.E. Raichle
   1986   Focal physiological uncoupling of cerebral blood flow and oxidative metabolism
           during somatosensory stimulation in human subjects. *Proceedings of the National
           Academy of Sciences* 83:1140-1144.
Fox, P.T., M.E. Raichle, M.A. Mintun, and C. Dence
   1988   Nonoxidative glucose consumption during focal physiologic neural activity. *Sci-
           ence* 241:462-464.
Frahm, J., H. Bruhn, K.-D. Merboldt, and W. Hanicke
   1992   Dynamic MR imaging of human brain oxygenation during rest and photic stimu-
           lation. *Journal of Magnetic Resonance Imaging* 2:501-505.
Frank, M.G., and P. Ekman
   1997   The ability to detect deceit generalizes across different types of high-stake lies.
           Journal of Personality and Social Psychology 72:149-1439.
Frank, M.G., and T.H. Feeley
   in   To catch a liar: Challenges for research in lie detection training. *Journal of Applied
   press   Communication Research.*

Fredrikson, M., T. Furmark, M.T. Olsson, H. Fischer, J. Andersson, and B. Langstrom
  1998   Functional neuroanatomical correlates of electrodermal activity: A positrom emission tomographic study. *Psychophysiology* 35:179-185.
Furedy, J.J.
  1993   The "control" question "test" (CQT) polygrapher's dilemma: Logico-ethical considerations for psychophysiological practitioners and researchers. *International Journal of Psychophysiology* 15(3):263-267.
Fuss, T., B. McSheey, and L. Snowden
  1998   Under investigation: The importance of background investigations in North Carolina. *Police Chief* 65(4):169-172.
Gardner, W.L., S. Gabriel, and A.B. Diekman
  2000   Interpersonal processes. Pp. 643-664 in *Handbook of Physiology*, J.T. Cacioppo, L.G. Tassinary, and G.G. Berntson, eds. Cambridge, UK: Cambridge University Press.
Giesen, M., and M.A. Rollison
  1980   Guilty knowledge versus innocent associations: Effects of trait anxiety and stimulus context on skin conductance. *Journal of Research in Personality* 14:1-11.
Ginton, A., D. Netzer, E. Elaad, and G. Ben-Shakhar
  1982   A method for evaluating the use of the polygraph in a real-life situation. *Journal of Applied Psychology* 67(2):131-136.
Goffman, E.
  1963   *The Presentation of Self in Everyday Life*. New York: Anchor.
Goldberg, L.R., J.R. Grenier, R.M. Guion, L.B. Sechrest, and H. Wing
  1991   *Questionnaires Used in the Prediction of Trustworthiness in Preemployment Selection Decisions*. Washington, DC: American Psychological Association.
Green, D.M., and J.A. Swets
  1966   *Signal Detection Theory and Psychophysics*. New York: Wiley. [Reprinted by Peninsula Publishing, Los Altos, CA, 1988.]
Gudjonsson, G.H.
  1982   Some psychological determinants of electrodermal responses to deception. *Personality and Individual Differences* 3:381-391.
Guertin, W.H., and P.L. Wilhelm
  1954   A statistical analysis of the electrodermal response employed in lie detection. *The Journal of General Psychology* 51:153-160.
Gustafson, L.A., and M.T. Orne
  1963   Effects of heightened motivation on the detection of deception. *Journal of Applied Psychology* 47(6):408-411.
  1965   The effects of verbal responses on the laboratory detection of deception. *Psychophysiology* 2(1)10-13.
Hambleton, R., H. Swaminathan, and H. Rogers
  1991   *Fundamentals of Item Response Theory*. New York: Sage.
Hammond, D.L.
  1980   The Responding of Normals, Alcoholics and Psychopaths in a Laboratory Lie-Detection Experiment. A Ph.D. dissertation submitted to the California School of Professional Psychology, San Diego.
Hammond, K.R., L.O. Harvey, Jr., and R. Hastie
  1992   Making better use of scientific knowledge: Separating truth from justice. *Psychological Science* 3(2):80-87.
Harris, M.J., and R. Rosenthal.
  1985   Mediation of interpersonal expectancy effects: 31 meta-analyses. *Psychological Bulletin* 97:363-386.

Harvey, B., and L. Ward
  1996   Starting off on the right foot: The importance of proper background investiga-
         tions. *Police Chief* 63(4):51,53-54.
Hinton, J.W.
  1988   The psychophysiology of stress and personal coping styles. In *Social Psychophysi-
         ology and Emotion*, H.L. Wagner, ed. Chichester, England: John Wiley & Sons.
Honts, C.R.
  1986   Countermeasures and the Physiological Detection of Deception: A Psychophysi-
         ological Analysis. A Ph.D. dissertation submitted to the faculty of the Depart-
         ment of Psychology, The University of Utah.
  1994   Psychophysiological detection of deception. *American Psychological Society* 3(3):77-
         82.
Honts, C.R., and S. Amato
  1999   The Automated Polygraph Examination: Final Report to the Central Intelligence
         Agency. Applied Cognition Research Insititute. Boise, ID: Boise State Univer-
         sity.
  2002   Countermeasures. Pp. 251-264 in *Handbook of Polygraph Testing*, M. Kleiner, ed.
         San Diego: Academic Press.
Honts, C.R., and R.L. Hodes
  1983   The detection of physical countermeasures. *Polygraph* 12(1):7-17.
Honts, C.R., and M.V. Perry
  1992   Polygraph admissibility: Changes and challenges. *Law and Human Behavior*
         16(3):357-379.
Honts, C.R., S.L. Amato, and A.K. Gordon
  2001   Effects of spontaneous countermeasures used against the comparison question
         test. *Polygraph* 30(1):1-9.
Honts, C.R., R.L. Hodes, and D.C. Raskin
  1985   Effects of physical countermeasures on the physiological detection of deception.
         Journal of Applied Psychology 70(1):177-187.
Honts, C.R., D.C. Raskin, and J.C. Kircher
  1987   Effects of physical countermeasures and their electromyographic detection dur-
         ing polygraph tests for deception. *Journal of Psychophysiology* 1(3):241-247.
  1994   Mental and physical countermeasures reduce the accuracy of polygraph tests.
         Journal of Applied Psychology 79(2):252-259.
Honts, C.R., M.K. Devitt, M. Winbush, and J.C. Kircher
  1996   Mental and physical countermeasures reduce the accuracy of the concealed
         knowledge test. *Psychophysiology* 33:84-92.
Horowitz, S.W.
  1991   Empirical support for statement validity assessment. *Behavioral Assessment* 13:293-
         313.
Horvath, F.
  1978   An experimental comparison of the Psychological Stress Evaluator and the gal-
         vanic skin response in the detection of deception. *Journal of Applied Psychology*
         63:338-344.
  1979   The effects of differential motivation on detection of deception with the psycho-
         logical stress evaluator and the galvanic skin response. *Journal of Applied Psychol-
         ogy* 64:323-330.
Hugdahl, K.
  1995   *Psychophysiology*. Cambridge, MA: Harvard University Press.

Hunter, J.E., and R.F. Hunter
  1984   The validity and utility of alternative predictors of job performance. *Psychological Bulletin* 96:72-98.
Iacono, W.G.
  1991   Can we determine the accuracy of polygraph tests? Pp. 201-207 in *Advances in Psychophysiology: A Research Annual*, J.R. Jennings and P.K. Ackles, eds. London: Jessica Kingsley Publishers, Ltd.
  2000   The detection of deception. Pp. 772-793 in *Handbook of Psychophysiology*, J.T. Cacioppo, L.G. Tassinary, and G.G. Berntson, eds. New York: Cambridge University Press.
Iacono, W.G., G.A. Boisvenu, and J.A. Fleming
  1984   Effects of diazepam and methylphenidate on the electrodermal detection of guilty knowledge. *Journal of Applied Psychology* 69(2):289-299.
Iacono, W.G., A.M. Cerri, C.J. Patrick, and J.A.E. Fleming
  1992   Use of antianxiety drugs and countermeasures in the detection of guilty knowledge. *Journal of Applied Psychology* 77(1):60-64.
Ingram, E.M.
  1994   Effects of Electrodermal Lability and Anxiety on the Electrodermal Detection of Deception with a Control Question Technique. Report No. DoDPI94-R-0004. Fort McClellan, AL: U.S. Department of Defense Polygraph Institute.
Janniro, M.J., and V.L. Cestaro
  1996   Effectiveness of Detection of Deception Examinations Using the Computer Voice Stress Analyzer. Report No. DoDPI96-R-0005. Ft. McClellan, AL: U.S. Department of Defense Polygraph Institute.
Jansen, A.
  1973   Validation of Graphological Judgments: An Experimental Study. The Hague, Netherlands: Mouton Publishers.
Johnson, A.K., and E.A. Anderson
  1990   Stress and arousal. Pp. 216-252 in *Psychophysiology: Physical, Social and Inferential Elements*. New York: Cambridge University Press.
Johnson, M.M., and J.P. Rosenfeld
  1992   Oddball-evoked P300-based method of deception detection in the laboratory. II: Utilization of non-selective activation of relevant knowledge. *International Journal of Psychophysiology* 12:289-306.
Johnson, R., Jr., J. Barnhardt, and J. Zhu
  2002a   The Deceptive Brain: I. Contribution of Executive Processes. Unpublished manuscript. Queens College, City University of New York.
  2002b   The deceptive brain: II. Effect of Response Conflict and Strategic Monitoring on P300 and Episodic Retrieval-Related Brain Activity. Unpublished manuscript. Queens College, City University of New York.
  2002c   The deceptive brain: III. Effect of Practice on Behavioral and Event-Related Brain Potential Indices of Deception. Unpublished manuscript. Queens College, City University of New York.
Johnston, D.
  2002   Seven F.B.I. employees fail polygraph tests for security. *The New York Times* April 4.
Jones, E.E.
  1991   *Interpersonal Perception.* New York: W.H. Freeman.
Jones, E.E., and H. Sigall
  1971   The bogus pipeline: A new paradigm for measuring affect and attitudes. *Psychological Bulletin* 76:349-364.

Kahneman, D.
  1973   *Attention and Effort.* Englewood Cliffs, NJ: Prentice-Hall.
Kassin, S.M.
  1997   The psychology of confession evidence. *American Psychologist* 52(3):221-233.
  1998   More on the psychology of false confessions. *American Psychologist* 53:320-321.
Keller, J., B.D. Hicks, and G.A. Miller
  2000   Psychophysiology in the study of psychopathology. Pp. 719-750 in *Handbook of Psychophysiology,* L.G. Tassinary and J.T. Cacioppo, eds. New York: Cambridge University Press.
Kieren, N.M., and M.A. Gold
  2000   Pygmalion in work organizations: A meta-analysis. *Journal of Organizational Behavior* 2(8):913-928.
Kircher, J.C., and D.C. Raskin
  1988   Human versus computerized evaluations of polygraph data in a laboratory setting. *Journal of Applied Psychology* 73:291-302.
Kircher, J.C., S.W. Horowitz, and D.C. Raskin
  1988   Meta-analysis of mock crime studies of the control question polygraph technique. *Law and Human Behavior* 12(1):79-90.
Kircher, J.C., T. Packard, B.G. Bell, and P.C. Bernhardt
  2001   Effects of Prior Demonstrations of Polygraph Accuracy on Outcomes of Probable-Lie and Directed-Lie Polygraph Tests: Final Report. Unpublished manuscript, dated October 15.
Kircher, J.C., D.J. Woltz, B.G. Bell, and P.C. Bernhardt
  1998   Effects of Audiovisual Presentations of Test Questions During Relevant-Irrelevant Polygraph Examinations and New Measures: Final Report [to the Central Intelligence Agency]. University of Utah.
Kirksey, L., and B. Smith
  1998   Granting a stamp of approval. *Security Management* 42(5):62-69.
Kleiner, M.
  2002   *Handbook of Polygraph Testing,* M. Kleiner, ed. San Diego: Academic Press.
Kleinmuntz, B., and J.J. Szucko
  1984   Lie detection in ancient and modern times: A call for contemporary scientific study. *American Psychologist* 39(7)766-776.
Kosslyn, S.M., J.T. Cacioppo, R.J. Davidson, K. Hugdahl, W.R. Lovallo, D. Spiegel, and R. Rose
  2002   Bridging psychology and biology: The analysis of individuals in groups. *American Psychologist* 57:341-351.
Krapohl, D.J.
  1995   A Taxonomy of Polygraph Countermeasures. Unpublished paper. Available: *Polygraph,* Severna Park, MD.
Kubis, J.F.
  1962   *Studies in Lie Detection: Computer Feasibility Considerations.* RADC-TR 62-205, Contract AF 30(602)-2270. Air Force Systems Command, U.S. Air Force, Griffiss Air Force Base. New York: Rome Air Development Center.
Kugelmass, S., I. Lieblich, and Z. Bergman
  1967   The role of "lying" in psychophysiological detection. *Psychophysiology* 3(3):312-315.
Kwong, K.K., J.W. Belliveau, D. Chesler, I.E. Goldberg, R.M. Weiskoff, B.P. Poncelet, D.N. Kennedy, B.E. Hoppel, M.S. Cohen, R. Turner, et al.
  1992   Dynamic magnetic resonance imaging of human brain activity during primary sensory stimulation. *Proceedings of the National Academy of Sciences of the United States of America* 89:5675-5679.

Lacey, J.I.
1967 Somatic response patterning and stress: Some revisions of activation theory. In *Psychological Stress: Issues in Research*, M.H. Appley and R. Trumbell, eds. New York: Appleton-Century Crofts.

Lacey, J.L., J. Kagan, B.C. Lacey, and H.A. Moss
1963 The visceral level: Situational determinants and behavioral correlates of autonomic response patterns. In *Expression of the Emotions in Man*, P.H. Knapp, ed. New York: International University Press.

Lamb, M.E., K.J. Sternberg, P.W. Esplin, I. Hershkowitz, Y. Orbach, and M. Hovav
1997 Criterion-based content analysis: A field validation study. *Child Abuse & Neglect* 21(3):255-264.

Landis, C., and R. Gullette
1925 Studies of emotional reactions: III. Systolic blood pressure and inspiration-expiration ratios. *Journal of Comparative Psychology* 5:221-253.

Langleben, D.D., L. Schroeder, J.A. Maldjian, R.A. Gur, S. McDonald, J.D. Ragland, C.P. O'Brien, and A.R. Childress
2001 Brain activity during simulated deception: An event-related functional magnetic resonance study. *NeuroImage* (3):727-732.

Larson, J.A.
1922 The cardio-pneumo-psychogram and its use in the study of the emotions, with practical application. *Journal of Experimental Psychology* 5(5):323-328.

LeDoux, J.E.
1995 Emotion: Clues from the brain. *Annual Review of Psychology* 46:209-235.

Lee, T.M.C., H.L. Liu, L.H. Tan, C.C.H. Chan, S. Mahankali, C.M. Feng, J. Hou, P.T. Fox, and J.H. Gao
2002 Lie detection by functional magnetic resonance imaging. *Human Brain Mapping* 15:157-164.

Levey, A.B.
1988 Polygraphy: An Evaluative Review. Report prepared for the Management and Personnel Office of the Cabinet Office. Cambridge, UK: Medical Research Council.

Lijmer, J.G., B.W. Mol, S. Heisterkamp, G.J. Bonsel, M.H. Prins, J.H.P. van der Meulen, and P.M.M. Bossuyt
1999 Empirical evidence of design-related bias in studies of diagnostic tests. *Journal of the American Medical Association* 282(11):1061-1066.

Lindley, D.V.
1998 Bayes' theorem. Pp. 260-261 in *Encyclopedia of Biostatistics 1: A-Cox*, P. Armitage and T. Colton, eds. New York: Wiley.

Lombroso, C.
1882 *Genio e Follia: In Rapporto alla Medicina Legale, alla Critica ed alla Storia* (Fourth Edition). Rome: Bocca.
1895 *L'Homme Criminel*, 2nd ed. Paris: Felix Alcan.

Lykken, D.T.
1959 The GSR in the detection of guilt. *Journal of Applied Psychology* 43(6):385-388.
1981 *A Tremor in the Blood: Uses and Abuses of the Lie Detector*. New York: McGraw-Hill Book Company.
1998 *A Tremor in the Blood: Uses and Abuses of Lie Detection*. New York: Plenum Trade.
2000 Psychology and the criminal justice system: A reply to Haney and Zimbardo. *The General Psychologist* 35:11-15.

Lynch, B.F., and D.R. Henry
1979 A validity study of psychological stress evaluator. *Canadian Journal of Behavioural Science* 11:89-94.

Lynn, R.
1966   *Attention, Arousal, and the Orientation Reaction.* Oxford, UK: Pergamon Press.

MacLaren, V.V.
2001   A quantitative review of the guilty knowledge test. *Journal of Applied Psychology* 86:674-683.

Marston, W.M.
1917   Systolic blood pressure changes in deception. *Journal of Experimental Psychology* 2:117-163.

Maschke, G., and G. Scalabrini
no   The Lie Behind the Lie Detector. [Online] Available: www.antipolygraph.org.
date

Matte, J.A., and R.M. Reuss
1992   A study of the relative effectiveness of physiological data in field polygraph examinations. *Polygraph* 21(1):1-22.

McDonald, R.
1999   *Test Theory: A Unified Treatment.* New Jersey: Erlbaum.

McGuire, W.J.
1969   The nature of attitudes and attitude changes. In *The Handbook of Social Psychology,* 2nd ed,. Vol. 3. G. Lindzey and E. Aronson, eds. Reading, MA: Addison-Wesley.

McNatt, D.B.
2000   Ancient Pygmalion joins contemporary management: A meta-analysis of the result. *Journal of Applied Psychology* 85(2):314-322.

Mendes, W.B., M.D. Seery, and J. Blascovich
2000   Effects of Stigmatization on Cardiovascular Reactivity. Paper presented to the Society for Psychophysiological Research, San Diego, CA.

Metz, C.E.
1986   ROC methodology in radiologic imaging. *Investigative Radiology* 21:720-733.
1989   Some practical issues of experimental design and data analysis in radiological ROC studies. *Investigative Radiology* 24:234-245.
2002   ROC Analysis Programs. [Online] Available: http://xray.bsd.uchicago.edu/Krl/Toppagell.htm [October 21, 2002].

Meyer, R.G., and J.B. Youngjohn
1991   Effects of feedback and validity expectancy on responses in a lie detector interview. *Forensic Reports* 4:235-244.

Meyerhoff, J.L., G.A. Saviolakis, M.L. Koenig, and D.L. Yourick
2000   Physiological and Biochemical Measures of Stress Compared to Voice Stress Analysis Using the Computer Voice Stress Analyzer (CVSA). Report No. DoDPI98-P-0004. Ft. Jackson, SC: U.S. Department of Defense Polygraph Institute.

Miller, E.K., and J.D. Cohen
2001   An integrative theory of prefrontal cortex function. *Annual Review of Neuroscience* 24:167-202.

Motley, M.T.
1974   Acoustic correlates of lies. *Western Speech* 38:81.87.

Mueller, C.B., and L. Kirkpatrick
1995   *Modern Evidence: Doctrine and Practice.* New York: Little, Brown and Company.

Murphy, K.
1987   Detecting infrequent deception. *Journal of Applied Psychology* 72:611-614.
1993   *Honesty in the Workplace.* Monterey, CA: Brooks/Cole.

Nakayama, M.
2002   Practical use of the Concealed Information Test for criminal investigation in Japan. Pp. 49-86 in *Handbook of Polygraph Testing,* M. Kleiner, ed. San Diego: Academic Press.

National Research Council

1992   *DNA Technology in Forensic Science.* Committee on DNA Technology in Forensic Science. Commission on Life Sciences. Washington, DC: National Academy Press.

1994   *Under the Influence: Drugs and the American Workforce,* Committee on Drug Use in the Workplace, J. Normand, R. Lempert, and C. O'Brien, eds. Commission on Behavioral and Social Sciences and Education. Washington, DC: National Academy Press.

1996a   *The Evaluation of Forensic DNA Evidence.* Committee on DNA Forensic Science: An Update. Commission on Life Sciences. Washington, DC: National Academy Press.

1996b   *Understanding Risk: Informing Decisions in a Democratic Society,* Committee on Risk Characterization, P.C. Stern and H.V. Fineberg, eds. Washington, DC: National Academy Press.

Nelson, K.

1999   To select the best: A survey of selecting police officer applicants. *Law and Order* 47(10):42-45.

Neter, E., and G. Ben-Shakhar

1989   The Predictive Validity of Graphological Inferences: A Meta-Analytic Approach. *Personality and Individual Differences* 10(7):737-745.

Newman, M.L., J.W. Pennebaker, D.S. Berry, and J.M. Richards

2002   Lying words: Predicting deception from linguistic styles. *Journal of Personality and Social Psychology.*

Nierenberg, A.A., and A.R. Feinstein

1988   How to evaluate a diagnostic marker test. Lessons from the rise and fall of dexamethasone suppression test. *Journal of the American Medical Association* 259(11): 1699-1702.

Nunnally, J.C., and I.H. Bernstein

1994   *Psychometric Theory* (Third Edition). New York: McGraw-Hill Book Company.

O'Bannon, R.M., L.A. Goldinger, and J.D. Appleby

1989   *Honesty and Integrity Testing: A Practical Guide.* Atlanta, GA: Applied Information Resources.

Ogawa, S., T.M. Lee, A.R. Kay, and D.W. Tank

1990   Brain magnetic resonance imaging with contrast dependent on blood oxygenation. *Proceedings of the National Academy of Sciences* 87:9868-9872.

Ogawa, S., D.W. Tank, R. Menon, J.M. Ellermann, S.-G. Kim, H. Merkle, and K. Ugurbil

1992   Intrinsic signal changes accompanying sensory stimulation: Functional brain mapping with magnetic resonance. *Proceedings of the National Academy of Sciences* 89:5951-5955.

O'Hair, D., and M.J. Cody

1987   Gender and vocal stress differences during truthful and deceptive information sequences. *Human Relations* 40:1-13.

Olsen, D.E, J.C. Harris, M.H. Capps, and N. Ansley

1997   Computerized polygraph scoring system. *Journal of Forensic Sciences* 42(1):61-71.

Ones, D.S., C. Viswesvaran, and F.L. Schmidt

1993   Comprehensive meta-analysis of integrity test validities: Findings and implications for personnel selection and theories of job performance. *Journal of Applied Psychology* 78:679-703.

Orne, M.T., R.I. Thackray, and D.A. Paskewitz

1972   On the detection of deception: A model for the study of physiological effects of psychological stimuli. In *Handbook of Psychophysiology,* N.S. Greenfield and R.A. Sternbach, eds. New York: Holt, Rinehart, and Winston.

O'Toole, D., J.C. Yuille, C.J. Patrick, and W.G. Iacono
    1994   Alcohol and the physiological detection of deception: Arousal and memory in-
            fluences. *Psychophysiology* 31:253-263.
Palmatier, J.J.
    1996   The Validity and Comparative Accuracy of Voice Stress Analysis as Measured by
            the CVSA: A Field Study Conducted in a Psychophysiological Context. Ap-
            peared as incomplete Report No. DoDPI97-P-0003 (published in 1996), under the
            same title. Note: Also unfinished draft title assigned Report No. DoDPI97-P-
            0002. U.S. Department of Defense Polygraph Institute, Ft. Jackson, SC.
Patrick, C.J., and W.G. Iacono
    1989   Psychopathy, threat, and polygraph test accuracy. *Journal of Applied Psychology*
            74(2):347-355.
Pavlidis, I., N.L. Eberhardt, and J.A. Levine
    2002   Seeing through the face of deception. *Nature* 415:35.
Pavlov, I.P.
    1927   *Condition Reflex.* Oxford, UK: Clarendon Press.
Pennebaker, J.W., M.E. Francis, and R.J. Booth
    2001   *Linguistic Inquiry and Word Count: LIWC 2001.* Mahwah, NJ: Erlbaum.
Peterson, W.W, T.G. Birdsall, and W.C. Fox
    1954   The theory of signal detectability. *Transactions of the IRE Professional Group on
            Information Theory* 4:171-212. [Reprinted in *Readings in Mathematical Psychology*,
            R.D. Luce, R.R. Bush, and E. Galanter, eds., pp. 167-211. 1963. New York: Wiley.]
Podlesny, J.A., and D.C. Raskin
    1977   Physiological measures and the detection of deception. *Psychological Bulletin*
            84:782-799.
Pollina, D.A., and A. Ryan
    2002   The Relationship Between Facial Skin Surface Temperature Reactivity and Tradi-
            tional Polygraph Measures Used in the Psychophysiological Detection of Decep-
            tion: A Preliminary Investigation. U.S. Department of Defense Polygraph Insti-
            tute, Ft. Jackson, SC.
Porter, S., and J.C. Yuille
    1995   Credibility assessment of criminal suspects through statement analysis. *Psychol-
            ogy, Crime, and Law* 1:319-331.
    1996   The language of deceit: An investigation of the verbal clues to deception in the
            interrogation context. *Law and Human Behavior* 20:443-458.
Pringle, D.
    1994   "The prosecutor's fallacy": Who's the DNA fingerprinting pointing at? *New
            Scientist* 29:51-52.
Prokasy, W.F., and D.C. Raskin
    1973   *Electrodermal Activity in Psychological Research.* New York: Academic Press.
Quigley-Fernandez, B., and J.T. Tedeschi
    1978   The bogus pipeline as lie detector: Two validity studies. *Journal of Personality and
            Social Psychology* 36:247-256.
Rafaeli, A., and R.J. Klimoski
    1983   Predicting Sales Success Through Handwriting Analysis: An Evaluation of the
            Effects of Training and Handwriting Sample Content. *Journal of Applied Psychol-
            ogy* 68:212-217.
Raichle, M.E.
    1987   Circulatory and metabolic correlates of brain function in normal humans. Pp.
            643-674 in *Handbook of Physiology: The Nervous System V. Higher Functions of the
            Brain*, F. Plum, ed. Bethesda, MD: American Physiological Society.

Raine, A., G.P. Reynolds, and C. Sheard
1991   Neuroanatomical correlates of skin conductance orienting in normal humans: A magnetic resonance imaging study. *Psychophysiology* 28:548-558.

Ransohoff, D.F., and A.R. Feinstein
1978   Problems of spectrum and bias in evaluating the efficacy of diagnostic tests. *New England Journal of Medicine* 299(17):926-930.

Raskin, D.C., and R.D. Hare
1978   Psychopathy and detection of deception in a prison population. *Psychophysiology* 15(2):126-136.

Raskin, D.C., and C.R. Honts
2002   The Comparison Question Test. Pp. 1-48 in *Handbook of Polygraph Testing*, M. Kleiner, ed. San Diego: Academic Press.

Raskin, D.C., and J.C. Kircher
1990   *Development of a Computerized Polygraph System and Physiological Measures for Detection of Deception and Countermeasures: A Pilot Study* Preliminary Report. Contract No. 88-L655330-000. Salt Lake City: Scientific Assessment Technologies, Inc.

Raskin, D.A., S.W. Horowitz, and J.C. Kircher
1989   *Computerized Analysis of Polygraph Outcomes in Criminal Investigation.* Report of Research and Results of Phase II of Contract TSS 86-18 from the U.S. Secret Service. Salt Lake City, Utah.

Raskin, D.A., J.C. Kircher, C.R. Honts, and S.W. Horowitz
1988   *A Study of the Validity of Polygraph Examinations in Criminal Investigation.* Final Report to the National Institute of Justice (Grant No. 85-U-CX-0040). Salt Lake City: University of Utah.

Reed, S.D.
no   TES Expansion Study. Unpublished document. Fort McClellan, AL: U.S.
date   Department of Defense Polygraph Institute.
1993   Subcultural Report: Effects of Examiner's and Examinee's Race on Psychophysiological Detection of Deception Outcome Accuracy. Report No. DoDPI94-R-0012. Ft. McClellan, AL: U.S. Department of Defense Polygraph Institute.

Reid, M.C., M.S. Lachs, and A.R. Feinstein
1995   Use of methodological standards in diagnostic test research: Getting better but still not good. *Journal of the American Medical Association* 274(1):645-651.

Reilly, R.R., and G.T. Chao
1982   Validity and fairness of some alternate employee selection procedures. *Personnel Psychology* 35:1-67.

Rosenfeld, J.P., A. Angell, M. Johnson, and J.H. Qian
1991   An ERP-based, control-question lie detector analog: Algorithms for discriminating effects within individuals' average waveforms. *Psychophysiology* 28:319-335.

Rosenfeld, J.P., V.T. Nasman, R. Whalen, B. Cantwell, and L. Mazzeri
1987   Late vertex positivity in event-related potentials as a guilty knowledge indicator: A new method of lie detection. *International Journal of Neuroscience* 34:125-129.

Rosenthal, R.
1966   *Experimenter Effects in Behavioral Research.* New York: Appleton Century-Crofts.
1979   The "file drawer problem" and tolerance for null results. *Psychological Bulletin* 86(3):638-641.
1980   On telling tales when combining results of independent studies. *Psychological Bulletin* 88:496-497.
1994   Interpersonal expectancy effects: A 30-year perspective. *Current Directions in Psychological Science* 3:176-179.

Rosenthal, R., and Fode, K.L.
  1963   Psychology of the scientist: V. Three experiments in experimenter bias. *Psychological Reports* 12:491-511.
Rosenthal, R.R., and L. Jacobson
  1968   *Pygmalion in the Classroom.* New York: Holt, Rinehart and Winston.
Rosenthal, R., and D.B. Rubin
  1978   Interpersonal expectancy effects: The first 345 studies. *Behavioral and Brain Sciences* 3:377-386.
Sackett, P.R., L.R. Burris, and C. Callahan
  1989   Integrity testing for personnel selection: An update. *Personnel Psychology* 42:491-529.
Sapir, A.
  1987   *Scientific Content Analysis (SCAN).* Phoenix, AZ: Laboratory for Scientific Interrogation.
Sarter, M., G.G. Berntson, and J.T. Cacioppo
  1996   Brain imaging and cognitive neuroscience: Toward strong inference in attributing function to structure. *American Psychologist* 51:13-21.
Saxe, L., and G. Ben-Shakhar
  1999   Admissibility of polygraph tests: The application of scientific standards post-Daubert. *Psychology, Public Policy, and Law* 5(1):203-223.
Scheck, B., P. Neufeld, and J. Dwyer
  2000   *Actual Innocence: Five Days to Execution, and Other Dispatches from the Wrongly Convicted.* New York: Doubleday.
Schmidt, F.L., and J.E. Hunter
  1999   The validity and utility of selection methods in personnel psychology: Practical and theoretical implications of 85 years of research findings. *Psychological Bulletin* 124:262-274.
Schmidt, F.L., J.E. Hunter, R.C. McKenzie, and T.W. Muldrow
  1979   Impact of valid selection procedures on workforce productivity. *Journal of Applied Psychology* 64:609-626.
Shah, N.J., J.C. Marshall, O. Zafiris, A. Schwab, K. Zilles, H.J. Markowitsch, and G.R. Fink
  2001   The neural correlates of person familiarity: A functional magnetic resonance imaging study with clinical implications. *Brain* 124:804-815.
Shapiro, D., and A. Crider
  1969   Psychophysiological approaches to social psychology. Pp. 1-49 in *The Handbook of Social Psychology* (2nd ed, Volume 3), G. Lindzey and E. Aronson, eds. Reading, MA: Addison-Wesley.
Sinai, L.
  1988   Employee honest tests move to new frontiers. *Business Insurance* 22(38):3,14-16.
Smith, N.
  2001   Reading Between the Lines: An Evaluation of the Scientific Content Analysis Technique (SCAN). Police Research Series Paper 135. London: Home Office Policing and Reducing Crime Unit.
Snyder, M.
  1992   Motivational foundations of behavioral confirmation. Pp. 67-114 in *Advances in Experimental and Social Psychology*, Vol. 25, M.P. Zanna, ed. San Diego: Academic Press.
Snyder, M., and J.A. Haugen
  1994   Why does behavioral confirmation occur? A functional perspective on the role of the perceiver. *Journal of Economic and Social Policy* 30:218-246.

Snyder, M., E.D. Tanke, and E. Berscheid
   1977   Social perception and interpersonal behavior: On the self-fulfilling nature of social stereotypes. *Journal of Personality and Social Psychology* 35:656-666.
Society for Industrial and Organizational Psychology
   1987   *Principles for the Validation and Use of Personnel Selection Procedures* (Third Edition). College Park, MD: Society for Industrial and Organizational Psychology, Inc.
Sokolov, A.N.
   1963   *Perception and the Conditioned Reflex.* Oxford: Pergamon Press.
Spence, S.A., T.F.D. Farrow, A.E. Herford, I.D. Wilkinson, Y. Zheng, and P.W.R. Woodruff
   2001   Behavioural and functional anatomical correlates of deception in humans. *NeuroReport* 12:2849-2853.
Steller, M., and G. Koehnken
   1989   Criteria-based statement analysis. Pp. 217-246 in *Psychological Methods in Criminal Investigation and Evidence,* D.C. Raskin, ed. New York: Springer Verlag.
Strube, M.J.
   1990   Psychometric principles: From physiological data to psychological constructs. In *Principles of Psychophysiology,* J.T. Cacioppo and L.G. Tassinary, eds. New York: Cambridge University Press.
Swets, J.A.
   1986a Indices of discrimination or diagnostic accuracy: Their ROCs and implied models. *Psychological Bulletin* 99(1):100-117.
   1986b Form of empirical ROCs in discrimination and diagnostic tasks: Implications for theory and measurement of performance. *Psychological Bulletin* 99(2):181-198.
   1988   Measuring the accuracy of diagnostic systems. *Science* 240:285-1293.
   1992   The science of choosing the right decision threshold in high-stakes diagnostics. *American Psychologist* 47(4):522-532.
   1996   *Signal Detection Theory and ROC Analysis in Psychology and Diagnostics.* Mahwah, NJ: Erlbaum.
Swets, J.A., R.M. Dawes, and J. Monahan
   2000   Better decisions through science. *Scientific American* October:70-75.
Swinford, J.
   1999   Manually scoring polygraph charts utilizing the seven-position numerical analysis scale at the Department of Defense Polygraph Institute. *Polygraph* 28:10-28.
Szucko, J.J., and B. Kleinmuntz
   1981   Statistical versus clinical lie detection. *American Psychologist* 36(5):488-496.
Timm, H.W.
   1991   Effect of posthypnotic suggestions on the accuracy of preemployment polygraph testing. *Journal of Forensic Sciences* 36(5):1521-1535.
Tippett, R.G.
   1995   Comparative analysis study of the CVSA and the polygraph. *NITV Journal of Continuing Education* First Half 1995:9-26.
Tourangeau, R., T.W. Smith, and K.A. Rasinski
   1997   Motivation to report sensitive behaviors on surveys: Evidence from a bogus pipeline experiment. *Journal of Applied Social Psychology* 27:209-222.
Tranel, D., and H. Damasio
   1994   Neuroanatomical correlates of electrodermal skin conductance responses. *Psychophysiology* 31:427-438.
Tsivilis, D., L.J. Otten, and M.D. Rugg
   2001   Context effects on the neural correlates of recognition memory: An electrophysiological study. *Neuron* 16:497-505.

Tursky, B., M. Lodge, M.A. Foley, R. Reeder, and F. Foley
   1976   Evaluation of the cognitive component of political issues by the use of classical conditioning. *Journal of Personality and Social Psychology* 34:865-873.

Tziner, A., J. Chantale, and S. Cusson
   1993   *La sélection du personnel.* Laval, Québec: Éditions Agence D'Arc.

U.S. Department of Defense
   2000   *Annual Polygraph Report to Congress.* Fiscal Year 2000. Office of the Assistant Secretary of Defense (Command, Control, Communications, and Intelligence). Washington, DC: U.S. Department of Defense. [Online] Available: www.fas.org/sgp/othergov/polygraph/dod-2000.html [October 21, 2002].
   2001   *Annual Polygraph Report to Congress.* Fiscal Year 2001. Office of the Assistant Secretary of Defense (Command, Control, Communications, and Intelligence). Washington, DC: U.S. Department of Defense. [Online] Available: www.fas.org/sgp/othergov/polygraph/dod-2001.html [October 21, 2002].

U.S. Department of Defense Polygraph Institute
   1995a   A Comparison of Psychophysiological Detection of Deception Accuracy Rates Obtained Using the Counterintelligence Scope Polygraph and the Test for Espionage and Sabotage Question Formats. Report No. DoDPI94-R-0008. Fort McClellan, AL: U.S. Department of Defense Polygraph Institute.
   1995b   Psychophysiological Detection of Deception Accuracy Rates Obtained Using the Test for Espionage and Sabotage. Report No. DoDPI94-R-0009. Fort McClellan, AL: U.S. Department of Defense Polygraph Institute.
   2001   Project Report Listing Table of Contents. E-mail reference list. February 7.

U.S. General Accounting Office
   2001   Investigative Technique: Federal Agency Views on the Potential Application of "Brain Fingerprinting". Report to the Honorable Charles E. Grassley, U.S. Senate. October. Washington, DC: U.S. General Accounting Office.

U.S. Office of Technology Assessment
   1983   Scientific Validity of Polygraph Testing: A Research Review and Evaluation, A Technical Memorandum. OTA-TM-H-15, NTIS order #PB84-181411. Washington, DC: U.S. Government Printing Office.

Wagner, H.L.
   1988   The theory and application of social psychophysiology. In *Social Psychophysiology and Emotion*, H.L. Wagner, ed. Chichester, England: John Wiley & Sons.

Waid, W., ed.
   1983   *Sociophysiology.* Pp. 117-138. New York: Springer-Verlag.

Waid, W.M., and M.T. Orne
   1980   Individual differences in electrodermal lability and the detection of information and deception. *Journal of Applied Psychology* 65(1):1-8.

Waid, W.M., E.C. Orne, M.R. Cook, and M.T. Orne
   1981   Meprobamate reduces accuracy of physiological detection of deception. *Science* 212:71-72.

Wakamatsu, T.
   1987   Effects of motivating the suspect to deceive the polygraph test. *Polygraph* 16(2):129-144.

Waln, R.F., and R.G. Downey
   1987   Voice stress analysis: Use of telephone recordings. *Journal of Business and Psychology* 1:379-389.

Weinstein, M.C., and H.V. Fineberg
   1980   *Clinical Decision Analysis.* Philadelphia: W.B. Saunders.

Wiesner, W.H., and S.F. Cronshaw
1988   A meta-analytic investigation of the impact of interview format and degree of structure on the validity of the interview. *Journal of Occupational Psychology* 61:275–290.

Wilkinson, D.J., J.M. Thompson, G.W. Lambert, G.L. Jennings, R.G. Schwarz, D. Jefferys, A.G. Turner, and M.D. Esler
1998   Sympathetic activity in patients with panic disorder at rest, under laboratory mental stress, and during panic attacks. *Archives of General Psychiatry* 55(6): 511-520.

Williams, D.
1996   *How to Sting the Polygraph*. Chicksha, OK: Sting Publications.

Williams, L.M., M.J. Brammer, D. Skerrett, J. Lagopoulos, C. Rennie, K. Kozek, G. Olivieri, A. Peduto, and E. Gordon
2000   The neural correlates of orienting: An integration of fMRI and skin conductance orienting. *NeuroReport* 11:3011-3015.

Williams, L.M., M.L. Phillips, M.J. Brammer, D. Skerrett, J. Lagopoulos, C. Rennie, H. Bahramali, G. Olivieri, A.S. David, A. Peduto, and E. Gordon
2001   Arousal dissociates amygdala and hippocampal fear responses: Evidence from simultaneous fMRI and skin conductance recording. *NeuroImage* 14:1070-1079.

Wright, T.
1991   Pre-employment background investigations. *FBI Law Enforcement Bulletin* 60(11):16-21.

Zahn, T.P., J. Grafman, and D. Tranel
1999   Frontal lobe lesions and electrodermal activity: Effects of significance. *Neuropsychologia* 37:1227-1241.

Zuckerman, M., and R.E. Driver
1985   Telling lies: Verbal and nonverbal correlates of deception. Pp. 129-147 in *Multichannel Integrations of Nonverbal Behavior*, A.W. Siegman and S. Feldstein, eds. Hillsdale, NJ: Erlbaum.

Zuckerman, M., B.M. DePaulo, and R. Rosenthal
1981   Verbal and nonverbal communication of deception. In *Advances in Experimental Social Psychology, Volume 14*, L. Berkowitz, ed. New York: Academic Press.
1986   Humans as deceivers and lie detectors. Pp. 13-35 in *Nonverbal Communication in the Clinical Context*, P.D. Blanck, R. Buck, and R. Rosenthal, eds. University Park, PA: The Pennsylvania State University Press.

Appendix A

Polygraph Questioning Techniques

All polygraph questioning techniques that aim at some form of standardization or reproducibility involve comparisons of physiological responses to questions of central interest for the investigation or screening ("relevant questions") against physiological responses to other questions ("comparison questions"). Questioning techniques may differ in the nature of the comparison questions, the sequencing of questions, or the choice of which comparison questions in a sequence of questions will be compared with which relevant questions. They are also typically associated with particular approaches to conducting pretest interviews and interpreting polygraph charts. This appendix briefly describes some of the main polygraph questioning techniques and some of their variants.

All polygraph testing techniques normally begin with a pretest interview. The examinee and examiner discuss the test, test procedure, examinee's medical history, and details of the test issues. The examiner also observes the behavior of the examinee and, in test formats that allow for discretion in question design, may gather information to be used in choosing comparison questions for the test. Depending on the complexity of the case, examiner-examinee interactions, and testing technique, the pretest interview may last from 30 minutes to 2 hours or longer (Krapohl and Sturm, 2001).

RELEVANT-IRRELEVANT TEST

As its name implies, the relevant-irrelevant test format compares examinee responses to relevant and irrelevant questions. A *relevant question* is one that deals with the real issue of concern to the investigation. These questions include asking whether the examinee perpetrated the target act or knows who did it and perhaps questions about particular pieces of evidence that would incriminate the guilty person. An *irrelevant question* is one designed to provoke no emotion (e.g., "Is today Friday?). Irrelevant questions are typically placed in the first position of a question list because the physiological responses that follow the presentation of the first question are presumed to have no diagnostic value; they are also placed at other points in the question sequence. Guilty examinees are expected to show stronger reactions to relevant than to irrelevant questions; innocent examinees are expected to react similarly to both question types.

The relevant-irrelevant test format was the first widely used polygraph testing format and was long the dominant format. The format was originally used in criminal testing. Currently, it is also used in multiple-issue screening applications, for example, at the U.S. National Security Agency.

Relevant-irrelevant polygraph tests are not normally standardized for question selection or for interpretation. Examiners typically interpret the test results globally by inspecting the charts to see whether or not there is a pattern of stronger responses to relevant questions. The lack of standard procedures for administration and scoring makes the relevant-irrelevant test unsuitable for scientific evaluation. It is not possible to support general conclusions about its accuracy because the procedure can vary uncontrollably across examiners and examinations. Polygraph researchers generally consider the test outmoded. For example, Raskin and Honts (2002:5) conclude that the relevant-irrelevant test "does not satisfy the basic requirements of a psychophysiological test and should not be used."

COMPARISON QUESTION (CONTROL QUESTION) TEST

Comparison question tests (also called control question tests) compare examinees' responses to relevant questions to their responses to other questions that are believed to elicit physiological reactions from innocent examinees. Relevant questions are defined as in the relevant-irrelevant test. Comparison questions ask about general undesirable acts, sometimes of the type of an event under investigation. For example, in a burglary investigation, one comparison question might be "Have you ever stolen anything?" In *probable-lie* comparison question tests, the instructions are designed to induce innocent people to answer in the negative, even though most are lying. Innocent examinees are expected to experience concern about these answers that shows in their physiological responses. In *directed-lie* tests, examinees are instructed to respond negatively and untruthfully to comparison questions (e.g., "During the first 20 years of your life, did you ever tell even one lie?"). In both forms of test, the expectation is that innocent examinees will react more strongly to the comparison questions, and guilty examinees will react more strongly to relevant questions.

Comparison question tests are widely applicable and are used both in specific-incident investigation and in screening. Some of the varieties of comparison question tests are described very briefly below. They vary in question selection, test construction, test scoring and interpretation, and other characteristics not discussed here (see Raskin and Honts, 2002, for more detail).

Reid Comparison Question Test

The Reid comparison question test, also known as the modified general question test, was the earliest form of comparison question test. It includes probable-lie comparison questions and is interpreted by the examiner's global evaluation of the charts, combined with other observations made during the examination. Other characteristics of the test include a discussion of the examinee's moral values during the test procedure and the use of a "stimulation" test between the first and second presentations of the questions (see Reid and Inbau [1977] or Raskin and Honts [2002] for more detail).

Zone Comparison Test

The zone comparison test, which was developed by Backster (1963), is named for the three "zones" or blocks of time during the test: the relevant questions (called the red zone), the probable-lie comparison questions (the green zone), and other questions (the black zone). Black zone questions are included to uncover examinee concerns about an issue outside of the scope of the red and green zones, such as involvement in another crime. Each zone is presumed to be threatening to someone; however, depending on the examinee's mental set, it is anticipated that one particular zone is more threatening than are the other two (information from Donald Krapohl, U.S. Department of Defense Polygraph Institute, private communication, October 5, 2001). This was the first comparison question test to incorporate a numerical scoring system. It used a seven-point rating scale applied to each physiological measure for each relevant question on the test.

Utah Probable-Lie Test

The Utah probable-lie test, developed by Raskin and colleagues (Raskin and Honts, 2002) is constructed with question modules, typically consisting of irrelevant, probable-lie comparison, and relevant questions. Examiners are instructed to conduct the test, including the pretest interview, in the low-key manner of a psychological interview rather than in the confrontational manner of an interrogation that is common in some other questioning formats: "It is critical that the examiner's demeanor and behavior be professional and objective" (Raskin and Honts, 2002:18). Attention is paid to going over the questions with the examinee carefully during the pretest period. Charts are scored on a numerical scale that is a modification of the one developed for the zone comparison test. Computer interpretation programs have also been developed for this test.

Utah Directed-Lie Test

The Utah directed-lie test was developed to address some problems that were associated with the Utah probable-lie test, including the perceived need for highly skilled examiners, problems of standardizing the questions, and the possibility that examinees may misunderstand the purpose of the probable-lie questions and therefore fail to respond as the theory presumes. The test is administered and scored like the probable-lie version. The comparison questions are like those in the Utah probable-lie test, except that the examinee is told that anyone who gives a negative answer would be lying and is then asked to give a negative answer.

Test of Espionage and Sabotage

The Test of Espionage and Sabotage is a directed-lie test that was developed at the U.S. Department of Defense Polygraph Institute and is used by some U.S. government agencies, including the U.S. Department of Energy, for security screening. A repeated series of relevant and directed-lie comparison questions is used to address multiple issues (espionage, sabotage, unauthorized foreign contacts, and unauthorized release of information). This test is scored by the conventional seven-position scoring system used in the Utah tests, with the total score being the sum across the three examination parameters for each question on all charts. Numerical thresholds are predefined for judging whether or not a test indicates a significant response that might indicate deception or is inconclusive. A judgment of a significant response is normally followed by further questioning and possibly further testing with single-issue format polygraph tests.

Stimulation Test

The stimulation test, sometimes called the stim test or acquaintance test, is used by examiners in some test formats either during the pretest or between charts. Examinees are presented with a question set of very similar items and directed to lie about one. The examinee may be asked to pick one of several playing cards (card test) or to pick a number between three and seven (numbers test), and then to deny having picked each of the cards or numbers while connected to the polygraph machine. The main purpose of the procedure is to induce or strengthen in examinees the expectation that the polygraph can accurately determine the truthfulness of their answers.

CONCEALED INFORMATION TEST

Concealed information tests (more often called guilty knowledge or concealed knowledge tests) present examinees with sets of very similar items, much in the manner of stimulation tests, except that the similar items include one true and several (usually, four) false details of some aspect of an incident under investigation that has not been publicized, so that the true answer would be known only to the investigators and to those present at the incident. In a burglary, examinees might be asked about several possible points of entry into the house, one of which the burglar actually used. (For more detail about question construction and administration of concealed information tests, see Nakayama [2002].) When an examinee is asked whether he or she used each of these routes, the answer is expected to be negative regardless of the examinee's innocence or guilt. Guilty examinees are expected to reveal their concealed knowledge by responding more strongly to the true item than to the others.

Concealed information tests are applicable only under restricted conditions: when there is a specific incident, activity, or thing that can be the subject of questioning and when there are several relevant details that are known only to investigators and those present at the incident. Thus, these tests are not applicable in typical screening situations in which the only possible relevant questions concern generic events, such as unspecified acts of espionage that may or may not have occurred.

PEAK-OF-TENSION TEST

The peak-of-tension test is similar in format to concealed information tests, but is distinct because questions are asked in an easily recognized order (e.g., "Was the amount of stolen money $1,000? $2,000? $3,000?" etc.). A guilty examinee is expected to show a pattern of responsiveness that increases as the correct alternative approaches in the question sequence and decreases when it has passed. Stimulation tests often have this format. In a known-solution peak-of-tension test, the examiner knows which alternative is the one truly connected to the incident and evaluates the examinee's pattern of responses for evidence of involvement in the incident. It is also possible to use the peak-of-tension test in a searching mode when the examiner does not know which answer is connected to the event but wants to use the test for help in an investigation. It is assumed that the pattern of a guilty person's autonomic responses will reveal the correct answer.

REFERENCES

Backster, C.
  1963   The Backster chart reliability rating method. *Law and Order* 1:63-64.
Krapohl, D.J., and S.H. Sturm
  2001   *Terminology Reference for the Science of Psychophysiological Detection of Deception*, updated from 1997 book by the American Polygraph Association.
Nakayama, M.
  2002   Practical use of the concealed information test for criminal investigation in Japan. Pp. 49-86 in M. Kleiner, ed. *Handbook of Polygraph Testing*. San Diego, CA: Academic Press.
Raskin, D.C., and C.R. Honts
  2002   The comparison question test. Pp. 1-47 in *Handbook of Polygraph Testing*, M. Kleiner, ed. San Diego, CA: Academic Press.
Reid, J.E., and F.E. Inbau
  1977   Pp. 13-71 in *Truth and Deception: The Polygraph ("Lie-Detector") Technique*. 2nd ed. Baltimore, MD: The Williams & Wilkins Company.

Appendix B

Use of Polygraph Screening in the U.S. Department of Energy and Other Federal Agencies

T his report responds to questions stimulated by the polygraph security screening program at the U.S. Department of Energy (DOE). The first part of this appendix provides an overview of the DOE's polygraph screening program. The second part characterizes in less detail the polygraph screening programs at other federal agencies: It shows the considerable variety across agencies in who is given polygraph examinations, the purposes of the examinations, the test formats, and so forth. The third part reproduces the DOE regulations on polygraph examinations.

U.S. DEPARTMENT OF ENERGY[1]

The U.S. Department of Energy conducts counterintelligence polygraph examinations on individuals who are either applicants for or incumbents in DOE "high-risk" positions that are designated in law and regulation.[2] A DOE counterintelligence polygraph examination covers six issues: espionage, sabotage, terrorism, unauthorized disclosure of classified information, unauthorized contacts with foreign nationals, and deliberate damage to or malicious misuse of a United States government or defense system. The majority of covered positions involve individuals who have already been hired (including contractor employees), have their clearances, and are being tested to determine whether they should be granted access to particular information. However, all applicants for employment in such "high-risk" positions must also undergo polygraph examinations, as an announced requirement of specific jobs involving access to designated programs. The relevant polygraph examination regulations (below) cover how the agency uses polygraph examination results and the specific actions that can be taken regarding an individual's job assignment as a result of the decisions made based on the polygraph examination.

An individual has the right to decline to take a polygraph examination, and an individual being examined may terminate the examination at any time. The DoE regulations provide details about the consequences, which include refusal to employ, assign, or detail the individual to the identified position.

According to Sec. 709.4 of the regulations (see below), people in a wide variety of positions are required to take a polygraph examination. Whether an employee or an applicant, the individual must be notified in advance and in writing. Positions in the Offices of Counterintelligence, Security, and Independent Oversight and Performance Assurance; Special Access Programs (SAPs); the Personnel Security Assurance Program (PSAP); the Personnel Assurance Program (PAP); programs that involve need-to-know or access to information specifically designated by the secretary of energy regarding the design and operation of nuclear weapons and associated use/control features; and individuals with access to "sensitive compartmented information" are subject to additional five-year periodic as well as aperiodic (i.e., irregular) reinvestigation polygraph testing.

A polygraph examination at DOE is considered to include three phases: (1) the pretest interview, (2) the in-test phase, and (3) the post-test phase. If the examination does not reveal any issues that must be resolved, it can be completed in an average time of about two-and-a-half hours. However, if it does reveal such issues, the examination process may extend into additional testing.

The methods and procedures used by polygraph examiners are standardized and follow established guidelines. The Test for Espionage and Sabotage (TES) is normally the initial format for all DOE counterintelligence scope polygraph examinations. However, the DOE polygraph examiners have the authority to determine and use the best technique(s) for the examination, based on the circumstances encountered during the pretest interview.

All DOE examiners are trained at the U.S. Department of Defense Polygraph Institute (DoDPI), and each has had his or her basic, advanced, and specialized training at or sanctioned by DoDPI. During training, examiners practice both giving examinations and scoring them under the supervision of experienced instructors. Each federal examiner is required to serve a minimum of a 6-month internship under a certified examiner.

Pretest Interview

The pretest interview begins with obtaining the examinee's consent to be tested, followed by an in-depth and detailed explanation of the process and rationale behind the polygraph examination. The functioning of the polygraph instrument is then explained. Next, the questions to be asked are introduced and explained in substantial depth and detail to the examinee. These questions are then reviewed with the examinee to ensure his or her understanding. Finally, the examinee provides his or her answers to the questions prior to beginning the test.

In order to focus the examinee's attention on specific aspects of the legally defined counterintelligence subject matter, individualized pretest interviews are intermingled with the actual in-test phase of the polygraph examination. The length of the pretest interview depends on the specific counterintelligence subject matter covered by the examination and the examiner's interactions with the individual being pretested. This length depends on how long it takes to satisfy the examiner that the person being tested understands and is fully prepared to begin the testing process. The pretest phase also involves the recording of a number of "control" questions as a baseline for evaluating physiological data collected during the in-test phase.

The U.S. Department of Energy currently uses the Lafayette Computerized Polygraph System. Each examination is recorded on videotape, in color, and with sound. Also, polygraph tests are monitored remotely by supervisory examiners as they are being conducted. This process is explained to the examinee prior to the beginning of the examination.

In preparation for the in-test phase, sensors designed to detect and transmit data on respiration, electrodermal activity, and cardiovascular activity to the computerized instrument are attached to the examinee. One convoluted pneumatic tube is placed around the upper chest and another is placed around the abdomen to record the individual's respiration during the test. Two finger plates are generally placed on the first and third fingers of one of the examinee's hands to record electrodermal activity. A standard medical blood pressure cuff is placed over the brachial artery on one of the person's upper arms to record cardiovascular activity. When the sensors are in place and the examiner is able to monitor and record satisfactory physiological recordings, the test begins.

In-Test Phase

Questions asked and their sequence vary according to the test being used and the matter of concern. In a screening polygraph using the TES, typical relevant questions that might be used include: "Have you committed sabotage against the United States?" "Have you been involved in espionage against the United States?" "Have you disclosed classified information to any unauthorized person?" "Have you had any unauthorized foreign contact?"

The examinee is instructed to answers the questions with a simple and unemotional "yes" or "no" response, as appropriate. The respiration, electrodermal activity, and cardiovascular activities are recorded on the computer. A test may take from 4 to 7 minutes from start to finish. There may be numerous tests within an examination. Cuff pressure is deflated during breaks between tests so that an examinee will be able to rest until the next test is taken.

During the testing process, the physiological data are transmitted in real time from the computerized polygraph instrument and recorded, as indicated above, on digital videotape. The supervisory examiner monitors the recorded data on a computer screen as the examination proceeds. The result is a videotape that displays the physiological recordings on one half of the screen and a full frontal view of the examinee on the other.

Post-Test Phase

During the post-test, the examiner evaluates the collected physiological data and formulates an opinion of the test results. That opinion could be "no significant response," "significant response," or "no opinion." A *no significant response* opinion would indicate that the examiner did not identify significant physiological responses to the relevant questions. A *significant response* opinion would indicate that the examiner did identify significant physiological responses and would result in additional testing, inquiry, interview, or investigation. *No opinion* would indicate that the data were insufficient for the examiner to formulate an opinion.

The data are evaluated by the administering examiner, a peer examiner, a supervisory examiner, and a quality control examiner. This process is completed on the day of testing or as circumstances allow. If the test is determined to be nondeceptive by the examiners available to evaluate the test results during the session, the examinee is advised that the test results will be subjected to final quality control and the session is ended. If a test is determined to be clearly deceptive either during the examination or by the supervisory and quality control process completed soon thereafter, steps are initiated to determine and implement the next procedure, which could include additional testing, inquiry, interviewing, investigation, referral to other agencies, or several of these steps.

OTHER FEDERAL AGENCIES

A number of federal agencies in addition to DOE give polygraph screening examinations. These include the Air Force, the Central Intelligence Agency, the Defense Intelligence Agency, the Drug Enforcement Administration, the Federal Bureau of Investigation, the National Reconnaissance Office, the National Security Agency, the Naval Criminal Investigative Service, and the Secret Service. Each has its own practices regarding the groups of people given polygraph examinations and the purposes of those examinations (e.g., preemployment screening, employee screening). In addition, test formats and polygraph equipment vary, as do the ways the agencies use the polygraph examination and its results. The following brief descriptions of the use of polygraphs by these agencies suggests this variation.

The Air Force trains polygraph examiners through its Office of Special Investigations (see http://www.af.mil/news/factsheets/Air_ Force_ Office_ Special_I.html), as part of a professional investigative service to commanders of all Air Force activities, primarily in criminal and fraud and counterintelligence investigations, and also in counterespionage and intelligence operations (see Dohm and Iacono, 1993).

At the Central Intelligence Agency (see wysiwyg://71/http://www. cia.gov/cia /employment/before.htm), each applicant for a position must undergo a thorough background investigation examining his or her life's history, character, trustworthiness, reliability, and soundness of judgment, among other personal characteristics. The polygraph is used to check the veracity of this information. The agency also has a security reinvestigation program that includes the use of the polygraph (personal communication, William E. Fairweather, chief, Polygraph Division).

Defense Intelligence Agency (DIA) employees may be subject to initial and periodic Counterintelligence Scope Polygraph testing (see http://www.dia.mil/Careers/Instructions/conditions.html). DIA polygraph examiners use polygraph techniques to aid in determining attempts at deception by individuals involved in personnel security, criminal, fraud, and counterintelligence investigations and operations (personal communication, Jerry Craig, chief, Security Investigations and Polygraph).

Drug Enforcement Administration special agent applicants and intelligence research specialist applicants must complete a polygraph examination and an exhaustive background investigation. A diversion investigator applicant may be subject to a polygraph examination and an exhaustive background investigation. Not all postings require a polygraph examination (personal communication, Jeffrey Behrmann, polygraph program manager).

At the Federal Bureau of Investigation (see http://www.fbi.gov/employment/policies.htm), each applicant who successfully completes the initial application process, including testing and interviews, is required to successfully complete a polygraph examination before being declared eligible for employment.

The National Reconnaissance Office (see http://www.nro.gov/contact.html) employs personnel from within the Department of Defense and the Central Intelligence Agency, whose polygraph testing requirements follow the guidelines of the agency that appointed them.

At the National Security Agency, a security clearance must be granted prior to employment (see http://www.nsa.gov/programs/employ/apply.html). An applicant is required to undergo extensive preemployment processing, including aptitude testing, an interview with a psychologist, a security interview conducted with the aid of a polygraph, and a personnel interview (personal communication, Charles White, deputy chief, polygraph program).

The Naval Criminal Investigative Service (see http://www.ncis.navy.mil/aboutNCIS.html) requires an applicant for special agent to submit to a urinalysis and a polygraph examination (see http://www. ncis.navy.mil/careers/HowToApply.html).

In the Secret Service, to be hired as a special agent (see http://www.ustreas.gov/usss /opportunities_agent.htm) and in some other positions, a complete background investigation, which includes in-depth interviews, drug screening, a medical examination, and a polygraph examination, is necessary.

U.S. DEPARTMENT OF ENERGY POLYGRAPH EXAMINATION REGULATIONS[3]

Title 10 - Energy
Chapter III – U.S. Department of Energy, Part 709 - Polygraph Examination Regulations
Subpart A—General Provisions

Sec. 709.1 What is the purpose of this part?

This part:

(a) Describes the categories of individuals who are eligible for counterintelligence-scope polygraph testing; and

(b) Provides guidelines for the use of counterintelligence-scope polygraph examinations and for the use of exculpatory polygraph examinations, upon the request of an individual, in order to resolve counterintelligence investigations and personnel security issues; and

(c) Provides guidelines for protecting the rights of individual DOE, and DOE contractor, and employees subject to this rule.

Sec. 709.2 What is the scope of this part?

This part includes:

(a) A description of the conditions under which DOE may administer and use polygraph examinations;

(b) A description of the positions which DOE may subject to polygraph examination;

(c) Controls on the use of polygraph examinations; and

(d) Safeguards to prevent unwarranted intrusion into the privacy of individuals.

Sec. 709.3 What are the definitions of the terms used in this part?

For purposes of this part:

Accelerated Access Authorization Program or AAAP means the program for granting interim access to classified matter and special nuclear material based on a drug test, a National Agency Check, a psychological assessment, and a counterintelligence-scope polygraph examination consistent with this part.

Access means the admission of DOE and contractor employees and applicants for employment, and other individuals assigned or detailed to Federal positions at DOE to the eight categories of positions identified in Sec. 709.4(a)(1)-(8).

Access authorization means an administrative determination that an individual is eligible for access to classified matter or is eligible for access to, or control over, special nuclear material.

Adverse personnel action means (1) With regard to a DOE employee, the removal, suspension for more than 14 days, reduction in grade or pay, or a furlough of 30 days or less as described in 5 U.S.C. Chapter 75; or (2) With regard to a contractor employee, the discharge, discipline, or denial of employment or promotion, or any other discrimination in regard to hire or tenure of employment or any term or condition of employment.

Contractor means a DOE contractor or a subcontractor at any tier.

Control questions means questions used during a polygraph examination that are designed to produce a physiological response, which may be compared to the physiological responses to the relevant questions.

Counterintelligence means information gathered and activities conducted to protect against espionage, other intelligence activities, sabotage, or assassinations conducted by or on behalf of foreign governments or elements thereof, foreign organizations, or foreign persons, or international terrorist activities.

Deception indicated means an opinion that indicates that an analysis of the polygraph charts reveal physiological responses to the relevant questions that were indicative of evasion.

DOE means the U.S. Department of Energy.

Eligibility evaluation means the process employed by the Office of Counterintelligence to determine whether DOE and contractor employees and applicants for employment, and other individuals assigned or detailed to Federal positions at DOE will be recommended for access or continued access to the eight categories of positions identified in Sec. 709.4(a)(1)-(8).

Intelligence means information relating to the capabilities, intentions, or activities of foreign governments or elements thereof, foreign organizations or foreign persons.

Local commuting area means the geographic area that usually constitutes one area for employment purposes. It includes any population center (or two or more neighboring ones) and the surrounding localities in which people live and can reasonably be expected to travel back and forth daily to their usual employment.

No deception indicated means an opinion that indicates that an analysis of the polygraph charts revealed the physiological responses to the relevant questions were not indicative of evasion.

No opinion refers to an evaluation of a polygraph test in which the polygraph examiner cannot render an opinion based upon the physiological data on the polygraph charts.

Personnel Assurance Program or PAP means the human reliability program set forth under 10 CFR part 711 designed to ensure that individuals assigned to nuclear explosive duties do not have emotional, mental or physical incapacities that could result in a threat to nuclear explosive safety.

Personnel Security Assurance Program or PSAP means the program in subpart B of 10 CFR part 710.

Personnel security clearance means an administrative determination that an individual is eligible for access to classified matter or is eligible for access to, or control over, special nuclear material.

Polygraph means an instrument that (1) Records continuously, visually, permanently, and simultaneously changes in cardiovascular, respiratory, and electrodermal patterns as minimum instrumentation standards; and (2) Is used, or the results of which are used, for the purpose of rendering a diagnostic opinion regarding the honesty or dishonesty of an individual.

Polygraph examination means a process that encompasses all activities that take place between a polygraph examiner and individual during a specific series of interactions, including the pretest interview, the use of the polygraph instrument to collect physiological data from the individual while the polygraph examiner is presenting a series of tests, the test data analysis phase, and the post-test phase.

Polygraph examination records means all records of the polygraph examination, including the polygraph report, audio-video recording, and the polygraph consent form.

Polygraph report refers to a polygraph document that may contain identifying data of the individual, a synopsis of the basis for which the examination was conducted, the relevant questions utilized and the polygraph examiner's conclusions.

Polygraph test means that portion of the polygraph examination during which the polygraph instrument collects physiological data based upon the individual's responses to test questions from the examiner.

Relevant questions are those questions used during the polygraph examination that pertain directly to the issues for which the examination is being conducted.

Special Access Program or SAP means a program established under Executive Order 12958 for a specific class of classified information that imposes safeguarding and access requirements that exceed those normally required for information at the same classification level.

Unresolved issues refers to an opinion which indicates that the analysis of the polygraph charts revealed consistent, significant, timely physiological responses to the relevant questions in personnel screening.

Sec. 709.4 To whom does the polygraph examination requirement under this part apply?

(a) Except as provided in paragraph (b) of this section, this part applies to DOE and contractor employees and applicants for employment, and other individuals assigned or detailed to federal positions at DOE, who are in:

(1) Positions that DOE has determined include counterintelligence activities or access to counterintelligence sources and methods;

(2) Positions that DOE has determined include intelligence activities or access to intelligence sources and methods;

(3) Positions requiring access to information that is protected within a non-intelligence special access program (SAP) designated by the Secretary of Energy;

(4) Positions that are subject to the Personnel Security Assurance Program (PSAP);

(5) Positions that are subject to the Personnel Assurance Program (PAP);

(6) Positions that DOE has determined have a need-to-know or access to information specifically designated by the Secretary regarding the design and operation of nuclear weapons and associated use control features;

(7) Positions within the Office of Independent Oversight and Performance Assurance, or any successor thereto, involved in inspection and assessment of safeguards and security functions, including cyber security, of the Department;

(8) Positions within the Office of Security and Emergency Operations, or any successor thereto;

(9) The Accelerated Access Authorization Program (AAAP); and

(10) Positions where the applicant or incumbent has requested a polygraph examination in order to respond to questions that have arisen in the context of counterintelligence investigations or personnel security issues. These examinations are referred to in this part as exculpatory polygraph examinations.

(b) This part does not apply to:

(1) Any individual for whom the Director of the Office of Counterintelligence (D/OCI), gives a waiver, based upon certification from another federal agency that the individual has successfully completed a full scope or counterintelligence-scope polygraph examination administered within the last five years;

(2) Any individual who is being treated for a medical or psychological condition or is taking medication that, based upon consultation with the individual, the DOE Test Center determines would preclude the individual from being tested; or

(3) Any individual for whom the Secretary of Energy gives a written waiver in the interest of national security.

(c) The Program Manager responsible for each program with positions identified in paragraphs (a)(1)-(8) of this section identifies in the first instance, in order of priority, those specific positions that will be polygraphed.

(d) The Program Manager submits positions identified under paragraph (c) of this section to the D/OCI for review and concurrence. The D/OCI forwards the positions, with suggested additions or deletions, to the Secretary for approval.

Sec. 709.5 How will an individual know if his or her position will be eligible for a polygraph examination?

(a) All positions in the programs described in Sec. 709.4(a)(1)-(8) are eligible for polygraph examination. When a polygraph examination is scheduled, DOE must notify the individual, in accordance with Sec. 709.21.

(b) Any job announcement or posting with respect to any position in those programs must indicate that the selection of an individual for the position may be conditioned upon his or her successful completion of a counterintelligence-scope polygraph examination.

Sec. 709.6 How often will an individual be subject to polygraph examination?

Positions identified in Sec. 709.4(a)(1)-(8) are subject to a five year periodic, as well as an aperiodic, reinvestigation polygraph.

Subpart B—Polygraph Examination Protocols and Protection of National Security

Sec. 709.11 What types of topics are within the scope of a polygraph examination?

(a) DOE may ask questions that are appropriate to a counterintelligence-scope examination or that are relevant to the matter at issue in an exculpatory examination.

(b) A counterintelligence-scope polygraph examination is limited to topics concerning the individual's involvement in espionage, sabotage, terrorism, unauthorized disclosure of classified information, unauthorized foreign contacts, and deliberate damage to or malicious misuse of a U.S. government information or defense system.

(c) DOE may not ask questions that:

(1) Probe a person's thoughts or beliefs;

(2) Concern conduct that has no counterintelligence implication; or

(3) Concern conduct that has no direct relevance to an investigation.

Sec. 709.12 How does DOE determine the wording of questions?

The examiner determines the exact wording of the polygraph questions based on the examiner's pretest interview of the individual, the individual's understanding of the questions, and other input from the individual.

Sec. 709.13 May an individual refuse to take a polygraph examination?

(a) Yes. An individual may refuse to take a counterintelligence-scope or exculpatory polygraph examination, and an individual being examined may terminate the examination at any time.

(b) If an individual terminates a counterintelligence-scope or exculpatory polygraph examination prior to the completion of the examination, DOE may treat that termination as a refusal to take a polygraph examination under Sec. 709.14.

Sec. 709.14 What are the consequences of a refusal to take a polygraph examination?

(a) If an individual is an applicant for employment, assignment, or detail to one of the positions described in Sec. 709.4(a)(1)-(8), and the individual refuses to take a counterintelligence polygraph examination required by statute as an initial condition of access, DOE and its contractors must refuse to employ, assign, or detail the individual to the identified position.

(b) If the individual is an applicant for employment, assignment, or detail to one of the positions described in Sec. 709.4(a)(1)-(8) and the individual refuses to take a counterintelligence polygraph examination otherwise required by this part, DOE and its contractors may refuse to employ, assign, or detail the individual to the identified position.

(c) If an individual is an incumbent in a position described in Sec. 709.4(a)(1)-(8) and the individual refuses to take a counterintelligence polygraph examination required by statute as a condition of continued access, DOE and its contractors must deny the individual access to the information or involvement in the activities that justified conducting the examination, consistent with Sec. 709.15. If the individual is a DOE employee, DOE may reassign or realign the individual's duties, within the local commuting area, or take other action, consistent with that denial of access.

(d) If the individual is an incumbent in a position described in Sec. 709.4(a)(1)-(8), and the individual refuses to take a counterintelligence polygraph examination as required by this part, DOE and its contractors may deny that individual access to the information or involvement in the activities that justified conducting the examination, consistent with Sec. 709.15. If the individual is a DOE employee, DOE may reassign or realign the individual's duties, within the local commuting area, or take other action, consistent with that denial of access.

(e) If the individual is a DOE employee whose current position does not require a counterintelligence polygraph examination and is an applicant for employment, assignment, or detail to one of the positions described in Sec. 709.4(a)(1)-(8), the individual's refusal to take a polygraph examination will not affect the individual's current employment status.

(f) If an individual refuses to take a polygraph examination as part of the Accelerated Access Authorization Program, DOE must terminate the accelerated authorization process and the individual may continue to be processed for access authorization under the standard DOE personnel security process.

(g) Since an exculpatory polygraph examination is administered at the request of an individual, DOE and its contractors may not take any adverse personnel action against an individual for refusing to request or take an exculpatory polygraph examination. DOE and its contractors may not record an individual's refusal to take an exculpatory polygraph examination in the individual's personnel security file, or any investigative file. DOE also may not record the fact of that refusal in a DOE employee's personnel file.

(h) If a DOE employee refuses to take a counterintelligence polygraph examination, DOE may not record the fact of that refusal in the employee's personnel file.

Sec. 709.15 How does DOE use polygraph examination results?

(a) If, following the completion of the polygraph test, there are any unresolved issues, the polygraph examiner must conduct an in-depth interview of the individual to address those unresolved issues.

(b) If, after the polygraph examination, there are remaining unresolved issues that raise significant questions relevant to the individual's access to the information or involvement in the activities that justified the polygraph examination, DOE must so advise the individual and provide an opportunity for the individual to undergo an additional polygraph examination. If the additional polygraph examination is not sufficient to resolve the matter, DOE must undertake a comprehensive investigation of the individual, using the polygraph examination as an investigative lead.

(c) The Office of Counterintelligence (OCI) will conduct an eligibility evaluation that considers examination results, the individual's personnel security file, and other pertinent information. If unresolved issues remain at the time of the eligibility evaluation, DOE will interview the individual if it is determined that a personal interview will assist in resolving the issue. No denial or revocation of access will occur until the eligibility evaluation is completed.

(d) Following the eligibility evaluation, D/OCI must recommend, in writing, to the Program Manager responsible for the access that the individual's access be approved or retained, or denied or revoked.

(1) If the Program Manager agrees with the recommendation, the Program Manager will notify the individual, in writing, that the individual's access has been approved or retained, or denied or revoked.

(2) If the Program Manager disagrees with the D/OCI's recommendation the matter will be referred to the Secretary for a final decision.

(3) If the Program Manager denies or revokes the individual's access, and the individual is a DOE employee, DOE may reassign the individual or realign the individual's duties within the local commuting area or take other actions consistent with the denial of access.

(4) If the Program Manager denies the individual's access and the individual is an applicant for employment, assignment, or detail to one of the positions described in 709.4(a)(1)-(8), DOE and its contractors may refuse to employ, assign or detail the individual to the identified position.

(5) If the Program Manager revokes the access of an individual assigned or detailed to DOE, DOE may remove the individual from access to the information that justified the polygraph examination and return the individual to the agency of origin.

(6) If the Program Manager denies or revokes the access for an individual applying for a DOE access authorization or already holding a DOE access authorization, DOE may initiate an administrative review of the individual's clearance eligibility under the DOE regulations governing eligibility for a security clearance at 10 CFR part 710.

(7) For cases involving a question of loyalty to the United States, DOE may refer the matter to the FBI as required by section 145d of the AEA.

(e) DOE and contractor employees, applicants for employment, and other individuals assigned or detailed to federal positions within DOE whose access to the categories described in Sec. 709.4(a)(1)-(8) is denied or revoked may request reconsideration by the relevant head of the departmental element, as identified in the notice of denial or revocation. Individuals who decline to take the counterintelligence scope polygraph examination will not be afforded these reconsideration rights.

(f) Utilizing the DOE security criteria used to grant or deny access to classified information, OCI will make a determination whether an individual completing a counterintelligence polygraph examination has made disclosures that warrant referral, as appropriate, to the Office of Security and Emergency Operations or the Manager of the applicable Operations Office. OCI will not report minor security infractions that do not create a serious question as to the individual's eligibility for a personnel security clearance.

Subpart C—Safeguarding Privacy and Employee Rights

Sec. 709.21 When is an individual notified that a polygraph examination is scheduled?

When a polygraph examination is scheduled, DOE must notify the individual, in writing, of the date, time, and place of the polygraph examination, and the individual's right to obtain and consult with legal counsel or to secure another representative prior to the examination. DOE must provide a copy of this part to the individual. The individual must receive the notification at least ten days, excluding weekend days and holidays, before the time of the examination except when good cause is shown or when the individual waives the advance notice provision.

Sec. 709.22 What rights to counsel or other representation does an individual have?

(a) At the individual's own expense, an individual has the right to obtain and consult with legal counsel or another representative prior to the polygraph examination. The counsel or representative may not be present during the polygraph examination. No one other than the individual and the examiner may be present in the examination room during the polygraph examination.

(b) At the individual's own expense, an individual has the right to obtain and consult with legal counsel or another representative at any time during an interview conducted in accordance with Sec. 709.15(c).

Sec. 709.23 How does DOE obtain an individual's consent to a polygraph examination?

DOE may not administer a polygraph examination unless DOE has:

(a) Notified the individual of the polygraph examination in writing in accordance with Sec. 709.21; and

(b) Obtained written consent from the individual.

Sec. 709.24 What other information is provided to the individual prior to a polygraph examination?

Before administering the polygraph examination, the examiner must:

(a) Inform the individual of the use of audio and video recording devices and other observation devices, such as two-way mirrors and observation rooms;

(b) Explain to the individual the characteristics and nature of the polygraph instrument and examination;

(c) Explain the physical operation of the instrument and the procedures to be followed during the examination;

(d) Review with the individual the control questions and relevant questions to be asked during the examination;

(e) Advise the individual of the individual's privilege against self-incrimination; and

(f) Provide the individual with a pre-addressed envelope addressed to the D/OCI in Washington, D.C., which may be used to submit comments or complaints concerning the examination.

Sec. 709.25 Are there limits on use of polygraph examination results that reflect "deception indicated" or "no opinion"?

(a) DOE or its contractors may not:

(1) Take an adverse personnel action against an individual solely on the basis of a polygraph examination result of "deception indicated" or "no opinion"; or

(2) Use a polygraph examination that reflects "deception indicated" or "no opinion" as a substitute for any other required investigation.

(b) The Secretary or the D/OCI may suspend an individual's access based upon a written determination that the individual's admission of involvement in one or more of the activities covered by the counterintelligence polygraph, when considered in the context of the individual's access to one or more of the high risk programs identified in Sec. 709.4(a)(1)-(8), poses an unacceptable risk to national security or defense. In such cases, DOE will investigate the matter immediately and make a determination of whether to revoke the individual's access.

Sec. 709.26 How does DOE protect the confidentiality of polygraph examination records?

(a) DOE owns all polygraph examination records and reports.

(b) Except as provided in paragraph (c) of this section, the Office of Counterintelligence maintains all polygraph examination records and reports in a system of records established under the Privacy Act of 1974, 5 U.S.C. 552a.

(c) The Office of Intelligence also may maintain polygraph examination reports generated with respect to individuals identified in Sec. 709.4(a)(2) in a system of records established under the Privacy Act.

(d) Polygraph examination records and reports used to make AAAP determinations or generated as a result of an exculpatory personnel security polygraph examination are maintained in a system of records established under the Privacy Act of 1974.

(e) DOE must afford the full privacy protection provided by law to information regarding an employee's refusal to take a polygraph examination.

(f) With the exception of the polygraph report, all other polygraph examination records are destroyed ninety days after the eligibility evaluation is completed, provided that a favorable recommendation has been made to grant or continue the access to the position. If a recommendation is made to deny or revoke access to the information or involvement in the activities that justified conducting the polygraph examination, then all the records are retained at least until the final resolution of any request for reconsideration by the individual or the completion of any ongoing investigation.

Subpart D—Polygraph Examination and Examiner Standards

Sec. 709.31 What are the DOE standards for polygraph examinations and polygraph examiners?

(a) DOE adheres to the procedures and standards established by the U.S. Department of Defense Polygraph Institute (DODPI). DOE administers only DODPI approved testing formats.

(b) A polygraph examiner may administer no more than five polygraph examinations in any twenty-four hour period. This does not include those instances in which an individual voluntarily terminates an examination prior to the actual testing phase.

(c) The polygraph examiner must be certified to conduct polygraph examinations under this part by the DOE Psychophysiological Detection of Deception/Polygraph Program Quality Control Official.

(d) To be certified under paragraph (c) of this section, an examiner must have the following minimum qualifications:

(1) The examiner must be an experienced counterintelligence or criminal investigator with extensive additional training in using computerized instrumentation in Psychophysiological Detection of Deception and in psychology, physiology, interviewing, and interrogation.

(2) The examiner must have a favorably adjudicated single-scope background investigation, complete a counterintelligence-scope polygraph examination, and must hold a "Q" access authorization, which is necessary for access to Secret Restricted Data and Top Secret National Security Information. In addition, he or she must have been granted SCI access approval.

(3) The examiner must receive basic Forensic Psychophysiological Detection of Deception training from the DODPI.

(4) The examiner must be certified by DOE to conduct the following tests:

(i) Test for Espionage, Sabotage, and Terrorism;

(ii) Counterintelligence-Scope Polygraph Tests;

(iii) Zone Comparison Tests;

(iv) Modified General Question Tests;

(v) Peak of Tension Tests; and,

(vi) Relevant and Irrelevant and Directed Lie Control Tests.

Sec. 709.32 What are the training requirements for polygraph examiners?

(a) Examiners must complete an initial training course of thirteen weeks, or longer, in conformance with the procedures and standards established by DODPI.

(b) Examiners must undergo annual continuing education for a minimum of forty hours training within the discipline of Forensic Psychophysiological Detection of Deception.

(c) The following organizations provide acceptable curricula to meet the training requirement of paragraph (b) of this section:

(1) American Polygraph Association,

(2) American Association of Police Polygraphists, and

(3) U.S. Department of Defense Polygraph Institute.

NOTES

1. Information on polygraph examination procedures at the U.S. Department of Energy was provided by DOE staff members Douglas Hinckley, Anne P. Reed, and David M. Renzelman. We thank these individuals for this information and their consistently helpful assistance in our efforts throughout the study.
2. The text that follows describes the DOE employee polygraph screening program as it operated in 2001; it was suspended by the 107th Congress on December 13, 2001 (National Defense Authorization Act for Fiscal Year 2002, S1438, Sec. 3152, U.S. Department of Energy Counterintelligence Polygraph Program). This study was requested in order to inform decisions about the future of this program.
3. This section is taken from Code of Federal Regulations, Title 10, Volume 4, Parts 500 to end; Revised as of January 1, 2000. It was provided to the committee by Douglas Hinckley, U.S. Department of Energy.

REFERENCE

Dohm, T.E., and W.G. Iacono
   1993   *Design and Pilot of a Polygraph Field Validation Study: Appendices.* DoDPI93-R-0006. Fort McClellan, AL: U.S. Department of Defense Polygraph Institute.

Appendix C

The Wen Ho Lee Case
and the Polygraph

The Los Alamos National Laboratory investigation of Wen Ho Lee in connection with espionage and security violations has taken on mythical proportions, and claims about whether or not he "passed" his polygraph examinations have been central to many of the newspaper and other media accounts. Different members of the committee were given varying accounts about a polygraph examination conducted by the U.S. Department of Energy (DOE), but this information was not provided to the committee on the record.

This appendix summarizes information extracted from a number of sources, including the publicly released parts of the final report of a U.S. Department of Justice review of the handling of the entire case (Attorney General's Review Team, 2000; hereafter referred to as the FBI report).[1] We include this information because it illuminates the background of this study. It was the Wen Ho Lee case that led Congress to require polygraph screening in the DOE and that, indirectly, triggered this study. In addition, the case illustrates the fine line that sometimes divides polygraph screening from event-specific investigation: Wen Ho Lee's polygraph tests included a number of generic screening-type questions, even though the investigators were sometimes interested in specific contacts between Lee and foreign scientists during which specific information may have been passed to the foreigners. The FBI report covers investigations of security lapses at Los Alamos National Laboratory linked to Wen Ho Lee, beginning in 1982 and running through 1999. It describes the results of three different polygraph tests administered to Wen Ho Lee, in 1984 by the FBI, in 1998 by DOE, and in 1999 by the FBI again. The details available for the first and third remain largely classified although their "results" are described in the released version of the FBI report, as well as in two recently published books (Lee, 2001; Stober and Hoffman, 2001).

THE 1984 FBI POLYGRAPH

Following reports that Wen Ho Lee had unauthorized contacts with representatives of the Peoples' Republic of China (PRC), the FBI began an extensive investigation of Lee that included physical surveillance, examination of telephone and other records, and a series of interviews with Lee. On January 24, 1984, Lee took a polygraph examination conducted by an FBI examiner "to resolve any questions which may have arisen concerning the information he had furnished" in an FBI interview on January 3, 1984. The questions asked during this examination, the format of the test, and the polygraph examiner's evaluation of his initial responses are not described in the FBI report, but Lee (2001:26) claims that one of the questions he was asked was: "Did you pass any classified information to an unauthorized person?"—to which he answered "No."

The FBI report suggests that he was subjected to follow-up questioning because of concerns regarding deceptive responses (p. 39):

> Lee insisted that he had not furnished classified information to any unauthorized person nor had he ever agreed to work for any non-U.S. intelligence agency. Further testing was conducted to verify Lee's truthfulness.

> The FBI examiner determined that Lee had been non-deceptive in his answers to follow-up questions regarding [deleted].

A follow-up FBI memo documents the results as follows (p. 39):

> The subject of this matter has been interviewed and has substantially admitted all allegations and has explained why he made certain contacts. . . . In view in the fact that the subject has been interviewed, has explained his actions and has passed a polygraph examination, this matter is being placed in a closed status.

There is some dispute over how this information was shared with DOE, and issues regarding Lee's activities arose again in 1988 in connection with a background check done by the Office of Personnel Management in connection with Lee's Q clearance. In June 1993, Lee's Q clearance was officially continued, although in the interim he had traveled twice to the PRC, once in 1986 and again in 1988, and during those trips met with a number of PRC scientists. Later, he arranged for the visit to Los Alamos of a Chinese graduate student, and the details surrounding this visit and his interactions with this student also became a matter of investigation.

THE 1998 DOE POLYGRAPH

The FBI investigations into Wen Ho Lee's foreign contacts and activities began again in earnest in 1995 and culminated in a polygraph administered on December 23, 1998, by Wackenhut Security, contractors for DOE in Albuquerque, following an extensive interview of Lee by the FBI and DOE investigators. In the pretest interview, Lee made a "significant disclose" (p. 631), the details of which have been withheld in the released report. Both Lee (2001) and Stober and Hoffman (2001) report that Lee revealed a previously unreported 1988 meeting he had in his Bejing hotel room with Hu Side and Zheng Shaoteng, two Chinese nuclear weapons scientists. Zheng had asked Lee about the detonation system for the "primary" of the W88 warhead, and Lee claimed that he told Zheng that he did not know the answer.

The main polygraph examination asked Lee four relevant questions, ones that appear to be variations of the TES (Test of Espionage and Security) espionage question and focused toward specific activities (pp. 631-632):

A. Have you ever committed espionage against the United States?

B. Have you ever provided any classified weapons data to any unauthorized person?

C. Have you had any contact with anyone to commit espionage against the United States?

D. Have you ever had personal contact with anyone you know who has committed espionage against the United States?

According to the FBI report, Lee answered all of the questions "no" and the polygraph examiner concluded that Lee "was not deceptive when answering the questions above" (p. 632). The report raises concerns about the questions and the meaning of the term "espionage" and suggests that the post-test interview should have been more extensive, given that Lee had admitted in the pretest to being solicited in a 1988 hotel room encounter to provide classified information to an unauthorized individual.

But the real issue the report raises concerns the review of the charts and tape of the polygraph interview by DOE supervisors in January 1999. In that review, they determined that "the initial NDI [no deception indicated] opinion could not be duplicated or substantiated" and that they were "unable to render an opinion pertaining to the truthfulness of the examinee's answers to the relevant questions of this test" (p. 645). In a

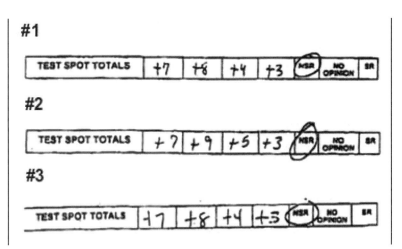

FIGURE C-1   "Independent" scoring by three different polygraphers of Wen Ho
Lee's responses to questions in a polygraph examination.
SOURCE: CBS News (2000: Available: http://www.cbsnews.com/stories/2000/
02/05/national/main157338.shtml).   Copyright CBS Worldwide, Inc.   Used by
permission.

discussion with the principal DOE supervisor who rescored the examination, he confirmed to the committee his concern with the original scoring
of the charts and his concern with the FBI statement that he recommended
calling Lee back for a follow-up interview.   In the meantime, the FBI
received copies of the tape and the charts, and its polygraph unit concluded that Lee "did not pass the exam," and that he "seemed to be
inconclusive if not deceptive" in his answers to the polygraph (pp. 645-
646).

CBS News (2000), as part of its February 5, 2000, broadcast, reproduced Figure C-1, which purports to be the "independent" scoring by
three different polygraphers of Lee's responses to the four questions
(there is no information on which chart—i.e., for which time the questions were asked).   The first line (#1) in the figure was by the original
Wackenhut polygrapher, the second (#2) by a supervisor, and the third
(#3) by a quality control reviewer.   All three have circled "NSR" meaning "no significant response."   In the particular numerical scoring method
being used, scores of less than –3 lead to conclusions of deception, scores
between –3 and +3 are inconclusive, and those of more than +3 are considered nondeceptive.   Without the actual polygraph readings, one cannot interpret the different accounts of the DOE test results.

THE 1999 FBI POLYGRAPH

On February 10, 1999, the FBI administered a third polygraph to Lee; the contents and format are not disclosed in the FBI report. The report notes, however, that Lee was found inconclusive on two of the relevant questions posed and deceptive on the other two. Stober and Hoffman (2001:187) report that at some point the relevant questions included:

> "Have you ever given [two sensitive nuclear-weapon] codes to any un-authorized person?"

as well as a follow-up question on W88 information. The format used appears to have been a relevant/irrelevant one, and Lee claims that some of the irrelevant questions included:

> "Are you married?"
> "Do you work at Los Alamos?"
> "Do you drink wine often?"
> "Do you smoke?"
> "Do you gamble illegally?"
> "Do you dislike black people?"
> "Do you ever cheat on your publications?"

A DOE polygraph supervisor reported to the committee that these were not the precise wordings of the questions used.

Lee (2001:58) contrasts the set-up and environment of this polygraph test with the one administered by DOE, which he describes as "comfortable." After the first chart, Lee was told that he had failed the test badly.

There appear to have been admissions made by Lee in the post-test interview that led to a confrontational FBI interview of Lee and ultimately to fairly exhaustive searches of Lee's office and computer files.

AN OFFER OF A FOURTH POLYGRAPH

After the second FBI polygraph, the investigation turned from whether Lee was responsible for the transmittal of information on the W88 to the Chinese to issues of security violations associated with the movement of computer files from secure systems to nonsecure ones at Los Alamos and the preparation of tapes of these files. Stober and Hoffman (2001:248) report that in December 1999 Lee's lawyers contacted the U.S. Attorney's Office offering that Lee would take "a polygraph test, administered by a mutually agreed upon operator, on the narrow questions of whether he had destroyed the tapes he had made and whether he had ever given their contents to an unauthorized person." The committee does not know the outcome of this offer.

NOTE

1. The full report numbers some 779 pages, and was submitted in May 2000, as a "top secret" classified document. Following a Freedom of Information Act request, an edited version of the report was declassified and publicly released.

REFERENCES

Attorney General's Review Team
    2000   *Final Report.* Attorney General's Review Team of the Handling of the Los Alamos National Laboratory Investigation. Washington, DC: U.S. Department of Justice.
CBS News
    2000   Lee polygraph scores. February 5. [Online] Available: http://www.cbsnews.com/stories/2000/02/05/national/main157338.shtml [Accessed: August 19, 2002].
Lee, W.H., and H. Zia (contributor)
    2001   *My Country Versus Me.* New York: Hyperion.
Stober, D., and I. Hoffman
    2001   *Convenient Spy: Wen Ho Lee and the Politics of Nuclear Espionage.* New York: Simon and Schuster.

Appendix D

Physiological Processes
Measured by the Polygraph

This appendix summarizes scientific knowledge about the three main physiological processes that are measured by the polygraph: cardiovascular, electrodermal, and respiratory.

CARDIOVASCULAR ACTIVITY

Cardiovascular activity is governed by the sympathetic and parasympathetic nervous systems, with the former acting through the postganglionic neurotransmitter norepinephrine to speed the heart and increase blood pressure and the latter acting through the postganglionic acetylcholine to slow the heart and lower blood pressure. The baroreceptor-heart rate reflex serves to maintain blood pressure: baroreceptors (pressure-sensitive receptors) mostly within the carotid sinus increase firing in afferents to the nucleus of the tractus solitarius in response to an increase in blood pressure, which in turn inhibits sympathetic motor neurons in the intermediolateral cell column of the cord and excites the parasympathetic source nuclei in the nucleus ambiguus and dorsal motor nucleus of the vagus. The resulting decrease in sympathetic activation further slows heart rate and reduces ventricular contractility and reciprocal increase in parasympathetic activation slows the beat of the heart and reduces cardiac output. Together with reductions in adrenergic vasoconstrictor tone, the baroreceptor actions compensate for the disturbance and restore blood pressure. The opposite pattern of autonomic control (i.e., sympathetic activation and reciprocal parasympathetic withdrawal) is triggered by a sudden lowering of blood pressure (e.g., during assumption of an upright posture) (Berntson, Cacioppo, and Quigley, 1991).

The baroreflex displays the essential characteristics of a feedback-regulated, homeostatic servomechanism that responds to perturbations and acts to restore basal blood pressure. But blood pressure regulation is far more complex. Indeed, blood pressure changes can be seen in antici-pation of a perturbation, before any change in baroreceptor afference. Examples include the increased blood pressure just prior to assumption of an upright posture or in anticipation of threat or danger. To some extent, these likely reflect simple Pavlovian conditioning, in which stimuli (environmental or cognitive) that predict an impending perturbation can serve as conditioned stimuli for an anticipatory, compensatory adjust-ment (Dworkin, 2000).

Not only can sympathetic and parasympathetic activation within the autonomic nervous system be reciprocal—as implied by arousal theo-ries—but it can also be uncoupled, coactivated or coinhibited (e.g., Berntson, Cacioppo, and Quigley, 1991, 1993). Reciprocal activation fos-ters a rapid and dramatic change in effector status (e.g., heart rate); un-coupled activation affords more fine tuning (e.g., vagal withdrawal in response to mild exercise); and coactivation or coinhibition can regulate or mute the functional consequences of underlying neural adjustments.

Importantly for the interpretation of polygraph data, individual dif-ferences in the mode of autonomic activation to acute psychological stres-sors have been identified, with some individuals showing primarily sym-pathetic increases, others primarily vagal withdrawal, and others showing reciprocal sympathetic activation (Berntson et al., 1994; Cacioppo et al., 1994). In addition, Obrist, Light, and colleagues demonstrated that active coping tasks (those with which one copes by doing something, e.g., men-tal arithmetic) tend to elicit beta-adrenergic (e.g., cardiac) activation and increased blood pressure, whereas passive coping tasks (those with which one copes by enduring; e.g., cold pressor) tend to elicit alpha-adrenergic (e.g., vasomotor) activation (e.g., Light, Girdler, and Hinderliter, in press) and increased blood pressure. Individual differences have been found in these cardiovascular patterns as well, with some individuals showing greater cardiac reactivity and others greater vasomotor reactivity (Light et al., 1993; Kasprowicz et al., 1990; Sherwood, Dolan, and Light, 1990).

In sum, cardiovascular responses to stimuli that may be considered arousing are multiply determined, and there are individual differences in terms of the direction and extent of cardiovascular reactivity that is ob-served. These findings call into question assumptions about cardiovascu-lar signals of arousal that are consistent across individuals.

ELECTRODERMAL ACTIVITY

The most sensitive measure in laboratory studies of the detection of deception has been electrodermal activity (e.g., Orne, Thackray, and Paskewitz, 1972). Electrodermal activity varies as a function of the eccrine glands, which are innervated by the sympathetic branch of the autonomic nervous system, but the postganglionic neurotransmitter is acetylcholine rather than norepinephrine (the postganglionic sympathetic neurotransmitter for most visceral effectors). This means that circulating catecholamines (epinephrine, norepinephrine), which can have an excitatory effect on autonomic effectors, have no effect on eccrine gland or electrodermal activity.

Electrodermal activity is measured by passing a small current through the skin to measure skin resistance or its reciprocal, skin conductance. Deviations from basal levels (e.g., responses to relevant and control questions) are called electrodermal responses (EDRs). Whether the electrodermal activity is measured and depicted in terms of skin resistance or skin conductance is not arbitrary. For instance, whether the EDR is interpreted as larger to a relevant question or a control question can vary depending on type of measurement and basal electrodermal activity levels (Dawson, 2000).

Eccrine glands can be thought of as tiny tubes with openings at the surface of the skin (Stern, Ray, and Quigley, 2001). The more activation of a given eccrine gland, the greater the secretion into the gland or onto the surface of the skin and, consequently, the lower the resistance to current flow across this area of the skin. Because eccrine glands are concentrated in the palms of the hands and soles of the feet, the set of eccrine glands between two electrodes on the fingers or palms can be conceived as variable resistors wired in parallel. The total electrodermal activity (or output of eccrine glands) at any given moment, therefore, can be measured by summing the values of all the active resistors wired in parallel. Because the sum of resistors in parallel equals the sum of the conductances, changes in skin conductance need not be corrected for basal levels to measure the effect of a given stimulus.

In polygraphy, this means that the deflections associated with relevant or control questions can be used to gauge an individual's response to the question only if the readout is in terms of skin conductance. Even when measuring skin conductance, however, stimuli that elicit the responses are so numerous as to make it difficult to isolate its specific psychological antecedent (e.g., Landis, 1930).

RESPIRATORY ACTIVITY

Respiration can be modified by the central and the autonomic nervous systems. The respiratory centers in the medulla and pons contain neurons that fire spontaneously to initiate inspiration. In addition, respiration is modified by autonomic reflexes arising from the lungs, heart, blood vessels, and upper airways. For instance, central chemoreceptors (e.g., in the brainstem) are responsive to carbon dioxide concentrations, peripheral chemoreceptors near the large vessels of the heart are sensitive to oxygen concentrations in the blood, and stretch receptors in the lungs are sensitive to the extent of lung inflation.

Respiration is easily brought under voluntary control, and variations in respiration can produce changes in heart rate and electrodermal activity. Therefore, respiration needs to be monitored to determine whether responses to relevant and control questions are artifacts. For instance, a sharp sniff can reliably produce an electrodermal response. If an examinee were to sniff sharply following control but not relevant questions, it might appear that the individual's responses to the relevant questions were relatively small and, therefore, reflected general stress, arousal, or anxiety rather than deception. In polygraph testing, the rate and depth of respiration are measured by strain gauges positioned around the chest and abdomen because breathing can produce fluctuations in the girth of either or both. The strain gauge provides a measure of relative amplitude; if the strain gauge moves during the session, amplitudes recorded prior to this movement could not be compared to those recorded following the movement.

REFERENCES

Berntson, G.G., J.T. Cacioppo, and K.S. Quigley
    1991   Autonomic determinism: The modes of autonomic control, the doctrine of autonomic space, and the laws of autonomic constraint. *Psychological Review* 98:459-487.
    1993   Cardiac psychophysiology and autonomic space in humans: Empirical perspectives and conceptual implications. *Psychological Bulletin* 114:296-322.
Berntson, G.G., J.T. Cacioppo, P.F. Binkley, B.N. Uchino, K.S. Quigley, and A. Fieldstone
    1994   Autonomic cardiac control. III. Psychological stress and cardiac response in autonomic space as revealed by pharmacological blockades. *Psychophysiology* 31:599-608.
Cacioppo, J.T., G.G. Berntson, P.F. Binkley, K.S. Quigley, B.N. Uchino, and A. Fieldstone
    1994   Autonomic cardiac control. II. Noninvasive indices and baseline response as revealed by autonomic blockades. *Psychophysiology* 31:586-598.
Dawson, M.E.
    2000   In *Handbook of Psychophysiology*, 2nd ed., J.T. Cacioppo, L.G. Tassinary, and G.G. Berntson, eds. New York: Cambridge University Press.

Dworkin, B.R.
  2000   In *Handbook of Psychophysiology*, 2nd ed., J.T. Cacioppo, L.G. Tassinary, and G.G. Bernstson, eds. New York: Cambridge University Press.
Kasprowicz, A.L., S.B. Manuck, S.B. Malkoff, and D.S. Krantz
  1990   Individual differences in behaviorally evoked cardiovascular response. *Psychophysiology* 27:605-619.
Landis, C.
  1930   Psychology and the psychogalvanic reflex. *Psychological Review* 37:381-398.
Light, K.C., S.S. Girdler, and A.L. Hinderliter
  in   Case study: Genetic and behavioral factors in combination influence risk of
  press   hypertensive heart disease. In *Expanding the Boundaries of Health: Bio-Behavioral-Social Perspectives*, N. Anderson, F. Kessel, and P. Rosenfeld, eds. New York: Oxford University Press.
Light, K.C., R.J. Turner, A.L. Hinderliter, and A. Sherwood
  1993   Race and gender comparisons: I. Hemodynamic responses to a series of stressors. *Health Psychology* 12:354-365.
Orne, M.T., R.I. Thackray, and D.A. Paskewitz
  1972   On the detection of deception. A model for the study of physiological effects of psychological stimuli. Pp. 743-786 in *Handbook of Psychophysiology*, N.S. Greenfield and R.A. Sternbach, eds. New York: Holt, Rinehart, and Winston.
Sherwood, A., C.A. Dolan, and K.C. Light
  1990   Hemodynamics of blood pressure responses during active and passive coping. *Psychophysiology* 27:656-668.
Stern, R., W.J. Ray, and K.S. Quigley
  2001   *Psychological Recording*, 2nd ed. New York: Oxford University Press.

Appendix E

Historical Notes on the Modern Polygraph

I n the course of the committee's work, we reviewed some material on the origin and history of polygraph testing. Some of this material is presented here because it provides interesting context and shows that several themes in the polygraph debate have very long histories: criticism by scientists of the scientific basis of polygraph testing, the development in the popular culture of a mystique of infallibility for polygraph lie detection, the use of the polygraph for security screening despite scientific criticism, policy debates leading to decisions to end polygraph security screening programs, and debates over openness in polygraph research. In addition, this material provides context for the legal history of polygraph admissibility in courts and shows the link between early polygraph research and the work of the National Research Council. We include it as part of a complete record.

The polygraph literature variously attributes the origins of the modern polygraph machine to Benussi (1914) or to Larson, who constructed the prototype of the multi-channeled polygraph in 1921 (see McCormick, 1927; Larson, 1932) and to Keeler (1933). But in many ways we can trace the idea of using psychophysiological recordings—in particular, systolic blood pressure—to measure deception in laboratory and legal settings to William Moulton Marston, largely while he was a graduate student at Harvard University from 1915 to 1921. (Precursors for recording from other channels to detect deception go back even earlier.) Marston's work has a curious history that is linked to work of the National Research Council.

WILLIAM MOULTON MARSTON,
THE NATIONAL RESEARCH COUNCIL, AND WONDER WOMAN

William Moulton Marston was over the course of his career a psychologist, a feminist theorist, an inventor, and comic-strip writer. He obtained an A.B. from Harvard in 1915 and then a law degree in 1918 and a Ph.D. in psychology in 1921. He began working on his blood pressure approach to deception in 1915 as a graduate student under the direction of Hugo Munsterberg in the Harvard Psychological Laboratory. According to Marston's son, it was his mother Elizabeth, Marston's wife, who suggested to him that "When she got mad or excited, her blood pressure seemed to climb" (Lamb, 2001). Although Elizabeth is not listed as Marston's collaborator in his early work, Lamb, Matte (1996), and others refer directly and indirectly to Elizabeth's work on her husband's deception research. She also appears in a picture taken in his polygraph laboratory in the 1920s (reproduced in Marston, 1938).

After the United States entered World War I, Marston attempted to interest the Committee on Psychology at the National Research Council (which at the time was acting as the Department of Science and Research of the Council of National Defense) in his work and its potential to detect espionage. The committee was chaired at the time by Robert M. Yerkes, who had written on the uses of psychological methods for the detection of crime. Most accounts of Marston's work at the time claim that he actually worked at the National Research Council (NRC), but a review of material in the archives of the council make clear that, despite extended correspondence between Marston and Yerkes, and review by the committee of Marston's work, the NRC never officially hired Marston nor sponsored his work (see Marston, 1938; Matte, 1996).

Accompanying a letter to Yerkes dated October 9, 1917, Marston submitted a proposal for the next phase of his research on the topic of deception detection. On October 13, the committee voted to set up a subcommittee, under the chairmanship of John F. Shepard, to consider "the value of methods of testing for deception" and to evaluate Marston's proposal. Two weeks later, following the set-up of apparatus in the Harvard Laboratory, Marston wired Yerkes with the message: "Remarkable results thirty deception tests under iron clad precautions letter following." This was followed by a letter detailing the work that Marston had carried out with Harold E. Burt and Leonard T. Troland, and the subsequent testing of another 20 cases in Boston Municipal Court. Shepard reported back to the committee on December 14 on Marston's work, and the committee decided to pursue the use of Marston's approach further. Shepard's written report, however, was not quite so positive. He expressed strong skepticism about the use of blood pressure tests, based on flaws in similar work from the past, and suggested that "galvano-psychic and vaso-motor reactions [would] be more delicate indicators than blood pressure; but the same results would be caused by so many different circumstances, anything demanding equal activity (intellectual or emotional), that it would be practically impossible to divide any individual case." His report went on to suggest alterations in the experimental protocol to protect against suspected biases. Many of the problems cited are familiar to modern critics of the polygraph test.

At this point, Marston was also completing his law degree at Harvard, and his correspondence with Yerkes focused on seeking employment with the government, first the War Department and then the Department of Justice, in lieu of actual service in the armed forces. Marston appears to have been successful and secured a commission to carry out further work in the Sanitary Corps, where he completed research described initially in an unpublished report dated December 18, 1918, and subsequently published (Marston, 1921). According to Marston (1938), he and his colleagues tested a total of 100 criminal cases in Boston criminal court, and his systolic blood pressure test led to correct determinations in 97 of them (see Lykken, 1991). There are no further references to Marston's work in the NRC files except for an inquiry in 1935 from J. Edgar Hoover, director of the Federal Bureau of Investigation. The NRC response referred Hoover to Marston's publications (1917, 1920, 1921, 1925, and 1929). Both Marston (1938) and Bunn (1997) refer to his having used his test on spies during this period, but no details are available.

After World War I, Marston pursued an academic career, and he appeared as an expert witness in the now famous 1923 Frye case, in which the defense unsuccessfully attempted to introduce his expert testimony as to the innocence of the defendant on the basis of his systolic blood pressure test. According to Marston (1938), Frye was accused of murder in the District of Columbia and, after first denying all knowledge of the event, confessed and provided police with correct details of the killing. A few days later, Frye recanted the confession, claiming that he admitted to the crime because he had been promised a share of the reward for his own conviction. Marston then gave Frye his deception test in a D.C. jail and found his claim of innocence to be entirely truthful. When Marston was introduced as an expert witness at trial, the presiding judge excluded the evidence on the grounds that the test had been administered in jail 10 days before Frye testified in court and that it was irrelevant to the veracity of his testimony. Frye was convicted of murder (*Frye v. United States*, 293 F.1013 [D.C. Cir. 1923]). The case was appealed on the ground that the trial judge erroneously excluded Marston's testimony. On appeal, the circuit court argued that the judge was correct in excluding the evidence:

Just when a scientific principle or discovery crosses the line between the experimental and the demonstrable stages is difficult to define. Somewhere in this twilight zone the evidential force of the principle must be recognized, and while courts will go a long way in admitting expert testimony deduced from a well-organized scientific principle or discovery, the thing from which the deduction is made must be sufficiently established to have gained general acceptance in the particular field in which it belongs.

We think the systolic blood pressure deception test has not yet gained such standing and scientific recognition among physiological and psychological authorities as would justify the courts in admitting expert testimony deduced from the discovery, development, and experiments thus far made.

While Marston's (1938) account of his proffered testimony in the *Frye* case suggests that the circumstances of the case and the original ruling were somewhat different than what this opinion suggests, the *Frye* test standard stood as the dominant rule regarding the admissibility of scientific expert testimony for the next 70 years. While most courts refused to admit testimony about polygraph evidence over the years, often with reference to *Frye*, some state and local courts did allow it, and Marston (1938) describes one such case in which he testified in an Indianapolis City Court, the year following *Frye*. In 1993, the Supreme Court's *Daubert* ruling altered the approach to admissibility in the federal courts in significant ways, and the admissibility of polygraph evidence is once again in dispute (*Daubert v. Merrell Dow Pharmaceuticals, Inc.*, 509 U.S. 579 [1993]); see Chapter 5.

After the war, Marston moved for 10 years from one academic post to another, including stints at American University, Columbia University, New York University, and Tufts University. It was during this period that Marston developed his theory of emotions, borrowing from related literature, and developed his own personality test to measure four important personality factors. The factors he chose were called dominance, influence, steadiness, and compliance, from which the DISC theory takes its name. In 1926, Marston published his findings in a book entitled *The Emotions of Normal People*, which included a brief description of the personality test he had developed. Then, in 1929, he left academia and traveled to Universal Studios in California, where he spent a year as director of public services.

In the 1930s, Marston continued to popularize his approach to testing deception in such outlets as *Esquire, Family Circle,* and *Look* magazines. His favorite test subjects were sorority members: He would attend their clandestine initiation parties, at which the young women would tie one another up and sometimes wrestle. Using his deception test, Marston monitored their systolic blood pressure while they watched the hazing rites. Sorority girls were also the subject of a few of Larson's early case studies of deception (Matte, 1996).

Marston also was featured in a razor blade advertisement that appeared in several popular magazines including the *Saturday Evening Post* and *Life*. The ad shows Marston analyzing a polygraph tracing while a man is shaving and includes the following text (*Saturday Evening Post*, October 8, 1938):

> Strapped to Lie Detectors, the same scientific instruments used by G-men and police officers throughout the country, hundreds of men take part in an astounding series of tests that blast false claims and reveal the naked truth about razor blades. These men, shaving under the piercing eye of Dr. William Moulton Marston, eminent psychologist and originator of the famous Lie Detector test, come from all walks of life, represent all types of beards and every kind of shaving problem. Knowing that the Lie Detector tells all . . . these men shave one side of the face with a Gillette Blade, the other side with substitute brands.

In 1940, when he was serving as an educational consultant for Detective Comics, Inc. (now known as DC Comics), Marston asked why there was not a female hero. Max Gaines, then head of DC Comics, was intrigued by the concept and told Marston that he could create a female comic book hero—a "Wonder Woman"—which he did, using a pen name that combined his middle name with Gaines's: Charles Moulton.

Wonder Woman first appeared in a nine-page center spread in the December-January 1941 issue of *All Star Comics*. Then, in January 1942, she debuted in *Sensation Comics* number one, with a full version of her origin and her first adventure, armed with her bulletproof bracelets, magic lasso, and her Amazonian training. For our purposes, Wonder Woman's magic lasso is her most notable possession and a link to the original and modern myth of the invincibility of the polygraph:

> The magic lasso was supposedly forged from the Magic Girdle of Aphrodite, which Wonder Woman's mother was bequeathed by the Goddess. Hephastateus borrowed the belt, removed links from it, and that is where the magic lasso came from. It was unbreakable, infinitely stretchable, and could make all who are encircled in it tell the truth (http://www.hastur.com/WonderWoman/marston.html).

In a 1943 issue of *The American Scholar*, Marston said:

> Not even girls want to be girls so long as our feminine archetype lacks force, strength, and power. Not wanting to be girls, they don't want to be tender, submissive, peace-loving as good women are. Women's strong qualities have become despised because of their weakness. The

obvious remedy is to create a feminine character with all the strength of Superman plus all the allure of a good and beautiful woman.

William Moulton Marston died in 1947, but Wonder Woman and the legend of his work at the National Research Council creating the polygraph live on.

SOME OTHER HISTORICAL NOTES ON THE POLYGRAPH

Some writers have attributed the origins of the modern polygraph to John August Larson or Leonarde Keeler, rather than to Marston, because of their development of actual prototypes of multichannel polygraph machines. Alder (1998) provides an informative history of their competing claims and interactions. According to his account, Larson chose an "open science" strategy for pursuing his polygraph research and publishing in scientific journals. Throughout his career, he publicly expressed doubts about the suitability of polygraph tests as evidence in the courts. Keeler, by contrast, patented the hardware for his polygraph machine, controlled who could buy the machines, and marketed his approach to business and government; he did not systematically subject it to peer review. He actively sought to have polygraph evidence, using his machine and with himself as the expert examiner-witness, admitted into testimony in criminal proceedings. Larson worked hard to develop standardized approaches to the polygraph interview, and Keeler stressed the role of the polygraph as an interrogation device and advocated enhancing the discretion of the examiner.

Keeler, like Marston, pursued the use of the polygraph for security purposes, cultivating the market for security screening during the 1940s. In particular, Alder (1998:515-516) describes Keeler's initiation of polygraph testing at the Oak Ridge nuclear facility beginning in 1946:

> There he interrogated all 690 employees of the Atomic Energy Commission subcontractor, Carbide and Carbon Chemical Co. These executives, scientists, engineers, skilled and unskilled laborers were asked to submit voluntarily to testing upon hiring, on a routine basis during employment, and upon termination. Only a tiny percentage dared refuse. The tests resulted in the firing of many employees, and the Oak Ridge program came to an end in 1953 amid accusations of coercion.

REFERENCES

Alder, K.
  1998   To tell the truth: The polygraph exam and the marketing of American expertise. *Historical Reflections* 24:487-525.
Benussi, V.D.
  1914   Die atmungssymptome der lüge. *Archiv Fuer Die Gesamte Psychologie* 31:244-273. English translation printed in 1975 *Polygraph* 4(1):52-76.
Bunn, G.C.
  1997   The lie detector, Wonder Woman and liberty: The life and works of William Moulton Marston. *History of the Human Sciences* 10:91-119.
Keeler, L.
  1933   Scientific methods for criminal detection with the polygraph. *Kansas Bar Association* 2:22-31.
Lamb, M.
  2001   Who was Wonder Woman 1? *Bostonia.* [Online] Available: http://www.bu.edu/alumni/bostonia/fall2001/ww/index.html/ [Accessed: April 24, 2002].
Larson, J.A.
  1932   *Lying and Its Detection.* Chicago: University of Chicago Press.
Lykken, D.T.
  1991   What's wrong with psychology anyway? Pp. 3-39 in *Thinking Clearly About Psychology.* Volume 1: Matters of Public Interest, D. Chiccetti and W. Grove, eds. Minneapolis: University of Minnesota Press.
Marston, W.M.
  1917   Systolic blood pressure symptoms of deception. *Journal of Experimental Psychology* 2:117-163.
  1920   Reaction times of deception. *Journal of Experimental Psychology* 5:72-87.
  1921   Psychological possibilities in the deception tests. *Journal of Criminal Law and Criminology* 11(4):551-570.
  1925   Negative-type reaction times of deception. *Psychological Review* 32:241-247.
  1926   *The Emotions of Normal People.* New York: Harcourt, Brace.
  1929   Bodily symptoms of elementary emotions. *Psyche* 38:70-86.
  1938   *The Lie Detector Test.* New York: Richard R. Smith.
  1943   Why 100,000,000 Americans Read Comics. *The American Scholar* (13)1:42.
Matte, J.A.
  1996   *Forensic Psychophysiology Using the Polygraph.* Williamsville, NY: J.A.M. Publications.
McCormick, C.T.
  1927   Deception-tests and the law of evidence. *California Law Review* 15(484):491-492.

Appendix F

Computerized Scoring of Polygraph Data

INTRODUCTION

A critical part of polygraph examination is the analysis and interpretation of the physiological data recorded on polygraph charts. Currently, polygraph examiners rely on their subjective global evaluation of the charts, various partly objective numerical scoring methods, computerized algorithms for chart scoring, or some combination of the three. Computerized systems have the potential to reduce bias in the reading of charts and eliminate problems of imperfect inter-rater variability that exist with human scoring. The extent to which they can improve accuracy depends on how one views the appropriateness of using other knowledge available to examiners, such as demographic information, historical background of the subject, and behavioral observations.[1]

Computerized systems have the potential to perform such tasks as polygraph scoring better and more consistently than human scorers. This appendix summarizes the committee's review of existing approaches to such scoring systems. Specifically, it focuses on two systems: the Computerized Polygraph System (CPS) developed by Scientific Assessment Technologies based on research conducted at the psychology laboratory at the University of Utah, and the PolyScore® algorithms developed at Johns Hopkins University Applied Physics Laboratory. We also comment on the Axciton™ and Lafayette™ polygraph instruments that use the PolyScore algorithms.

The statistical methods used in classification models are well developed. Based on a set of data with predictor variables (features in the polygraph test) of known deceptive and nondeceptive subjects, one attempts to find a function of the predictor variables with high values for deceptive and low values for nondeceptive subjects. The conversion of continuous polygraph readings into a set of numeric predictor variables requires many steps and detailed decisions, which we outline below. In particular, we discuss aspects of choosing a small number of these predictors that together do the best job of predicting deception, and we consider the dangers of attempting to use too many variables when the test data set is relatively small.

We examined the two scoring systems with sufficient documentation to allow evaluation. The CPS system has been designed with the goal of automating what careful human scorers currently do and has focused from the outset on a relatively small set of data features; PolyScore has been developed from a much larger set of features, and it is more difficult to evaluate because details of development are lacking. Updates to these systems exist, but their details are proprietary and were not shared with us. The description here focuses on the PolyScore and CPS scoring algorithms since no information is publicly available on statistical methods utilized by these more recently developed algorithms, although the penultimate section includes a summary of the performance of five algorithms, based on Dollins, Kraphol, and Dutton (2000).[2]

Since the 1970s, papers in the polygraph literature have proffered evidence claiming to show that automated classification algorithms could accomplish the objective of minimizing both false positive and false negative error rates. Our own analyses based on a set of several hundred actual polygraphs from criminal cases provided by the U.S. Department of Defense Polygraph Institute (DoDPI), suggest that it is easy to develop algorithms that appear to achieve perfect separation of deceptive and nondeceptive individuals by using a large number of features or classifying variables selected by discriminant analysis, logistic regression, or a more complex data-mining technique. Statisticians have long recognized that such a process often leads to "overfitting" of the data, however, and to classifiers whose performance deteriorates badly under proper cross-validation assessment (see Hastie, Tibshirani, and Friedman [2001] for a general discussion of feature selection). Such overestimation still occurs whenever the same data are used both for fitting and for estimating accuracy even when the appropriate set of features is predetermined (see Copas and Corbett, 2002). Thus, on a new set of data, these complex algorithms often perform less effectively than alternatives based on a small set of simple features.

In a recent comparison, various computer scoring systems performed similarly and with only modest accuracy on a common data set used for validation (see Dollins, Krapohl, and Dutton, 2000). The committee believes that substantial improvements to current numerical scoring may be possible, but the ultimate potential of computerized scoring systems depends on the quality of the data available for system development and application and the uniformity of the examination formats with which the systems are designed to deal.

STATISTICAL MODELS FOR
CLASSIFICATION AND PREDICTION

Before turning to the computer algorithms themselves, we provide some background on the statistical models that one might naturally use in settings such as automated polygraph scoring. The statistical methods for classification and prediction most often involve structures of the form:

$$\text{response variable} = g(\text{predictor variables, parameters, random noise}). \tag{1}$$

For prediction, the response variable can be continuous or discrete; for classification, it is customary to represent it as an indicator variable, y, such that, in the polygraph setting, $y = 1$ if a subject is deceptive, and $y = 0$ is the subject is not. Some modern statistical approaches, such as discriminant analysis, can be viewed as predicting the classification variable y directly, while others, such as logistic regression, focus on estimating its functions, such as $\Pr(y = 1)$. Typically, such estimation occurs conditional on the predictor variables, $\mathbf{x}$, and the functional form, g.

Thus, for linear logistic regression models, with k predictor variables, $\mathbf{x} = (x_1, x_2, x_3, x_4, \ldots, x_k)$, the function g is estimated in equation (1) using a linear combination of the k predictors:

$$score(\mathbf{x}) = \beta_0 + \beta_1 x_1 + \beta_2 x_2 + \beta_3 x_3 + \beta_4 x_4 + \ldots + \beta_k x_k, \tag{2}$$

and the "response" of interest is

$$P(deception \mid \mathbf{x}) = P(y \mid \mathbf{x}) = \frac{e^{score(\mathbf{x})}}{1 + e^{score(\mathbf{x})}}. \tag{3}$$

(This is technically similar to choosing $g = score(\mathbf{x})$, except that the random noise in equation (1) is now associated with the probability distribution for y in equation (3), which is usually taken to be Bernoulli.) The observations on the predictor variables here lie in a k-dimensional space and, in essence, we are using an estimate of the score equation (2) as a hyperplane to separate the observations into two groups, deceptives and nondeceptives. The basic idea of separating the observations remains the same for nonlinear approaches as well. Model estimates do well (e.g., have low errors of misclassification) if there is real separation between the two groups.

Model development and estimation for such prediction/classification models involve a number of steps:

1. Specifying the list of possible predictor variables and features of the data to be used to assist in the classification model (1). Individual variables can often be used to construct multiple prediction terms or features.

2. Choosing the functional form g in model (1) and the link function to the classification variable, y, as in equation (3).

3. Selecting the actual features from the feature space to be used for classification.

4. Fitting the model to data to estimate empirically the prediction equation to be used in practice.

5. Validating the fitted model through classification of observations in a separate dataset or through some form of cross-validation.

Hastie, Tibshirani, and Friedman (2001) is a good source of classification/prediction models, cross-validation, related statistical methodologies and discussions that could be applied to the polygraph problem. Recently, another algorithmic approach to prediction and classification problems has emerged from computer science, which is also called data mining. It focuses less on the specification of formal models and treats the function g in equation (1) more as a black box that produces predictions. Among the tools used to specify the black box are regression and classification trees, neural networks, and support vector machines. These still involve finding separators for the observations, and for any method one chooses to use, step 1 and algorithmically oriented analogues of steps 2-5 listed above still require considerable care.

Different methods of fitting and specification emphasize different features of the data. The standard linear discriminant analysis is developed under the assumption that the distributions of the predictors for both the deceptive group and the nondeceptive group are multivariate normal, with equal covariance matrices (an assumption that can be relaxed), which gives substantial weight to observations far from the region of concern for separating the observations into two groups. Logistic regression models, in contrast, make no assumptions about the distribution of the predictors, and the maximum likelihood methods typically used for their estimation put heavy emphasis on observations close to the boundary between the two sets of observations. Common experience with all prediction models of the form (1) is that with a large number of predictor variables, one can fit a model to the data (using steps 1 through 4) that completely separates the two groups of observations. However, implementation of step 5 often shows that the achieved separation is illusory. Thus, many empirical approaches build cross-validation directly into the fitting process and set aside a separate part of the data for final testing.

The methods used to develop the two computer-based scoring algorithms, CPS and PolyScore, both fit within this general statistical framework. The CPS developers have relied on discriminant function models, and the PolyScore developers have largely used logistic regression models. But the biggest differences that we can discern between them are the data they use as input, their approaches to feature development and selection, and the efforts that they have made at model validation and assessment. The remainder of this appendix describes the methodologies associated with these algorithms and their theoretical and empirical basis.

DEVELOPMENT OF THE ALGORITHMS

A common goal for the development of computer-based algorithms for evaluating polygraph exams is accuracy in classification, but the devil is in the details. A proper evaluation requires an understanding of the statistical basis of classification methods used, the physiological data collected for assessment, and the data on which the methods have been developed and tested.

CPS builds heuristically on the Utah numerical manual scoring, which is similar in spirit to the Seven-Position Numerical Analysis Scale, a manual scoring system currently taught by DoDPI. PolyScore, in contrast, does not attempt to recreate the manual scoring process that the examiners use. Neither appears to rely on more fundamental research on information in the psychophysiological processes underlying the signals being recorded, except in a heuristic fashion.

CPS was developed by Scientific Assessment Technologies based on research conducted at the psychology laboratory at the University of Utah by John Kircher and David Raskin (1988) and their Computer Assisted Polygraph System developed in the 1980s. While the latter system was developed on data gathered in the laboratory using mock crime scenarios, the newer CPS versions have been developed using polygraph data from criminal cases provided by U.S. Secret Service Criminal Investigations (Kircher and Raskin, 2002). The CPS scoring algorithm is based on standard multivariate linear discriminant function analysis followed by a calculation that produces an estimate of the probability of truthfulness or equivalently, deception (Kircher and Raskin, 1988, 2002). The most recent version utilizes three features in calculating a discriminant score: skin conductance amplitude, the amplitude of increase in the baseline of the cardiograph, and combined upper and lower respiration line-length (excursion) measurement (Kircher and Raskin, 2002).

PolyScore was developed by Johns Hopkins University Applied Physics Laboratory (JHU-APL), and version 5.1 is currently in use with the Axciton and Lafayette polygraph instruments. The algorithm has been developed on polygraph tests for actual criminal cases provided by the DoDPI. The input to PolyScore is the digitized polygraph signal, and the output is a probability of deception based either on a logistic regression or a neural network model. The PolyScore algorithm transforms these signals on galvanic skin response, blood pressure (cardio), and upper respiration into what its developers call "more fundamental" signals that they claim isolate portions of the signals that contain information relevant to deception. It is from these signals that the PolyScore developers extracted features for use, based on empirical performance rather than a priori psychophysiological assumptions.

The next sections describe how the two algorithms treat data used, signal processing, feature extraction, statistical analysis, and algorithm evaluation. These descriptions provide the basis for a discussion of possible future efforts at algorithm development and assessment. Since virtually all of the development and testing of algorithms has been done on specific-incident data, with highly varying formats and structures, some of the observations and comments on the algorithms may not always have as much relevance to highly structured screening polygraph tests, like the Test for Espionage and Sabotage (TES), but other problems, such as low base rates, do have salience for the TES. The final sections of this appendix on algorithm evaluation and summary describe some of these issues.

Data Used

Current polygraph machines typically record four signals during a polygraph examination: thoracic and abdominal respirations, a cardiovascular signal, and an electrodermal signal. Differences between specific analog and digital machines exist in the recording of the physiological measurements. Sampling rates may vary between different systems. Analog to digital conversion, filtering, and pen adjustments may also vary. One crucial difference lies in the recording of the electrodermal channel, which is believed by many polygraph researchers to be the most diagnostic (Kircher and Raskin, 2002). Stoelting (and CPS) records skin conductance; Lafayette appears to record skin resistance, a signal that requires further filtering in order to stabilize the baseline of the response; Axciton actually uses a hybrid of skin resistance and skin conductance

(Dollins, Kraphol, and Dutton, 2000) (see the discussion of the advantages and disadvantages of these two measures in Appendix D). Kircher and Raskin (2002) provide more details on the physiological recordings and conversion of analog to digital signal, although they focus mainly on the procedures used by CPS. These matters are, in effect, precursors to the development of automated scoring algorithms, which presume that the analyzed signals "accurately" reflect the psychophysiological phenomena that are capable of distinguishing deception and nondeception.

PolyScore® 3.0 was developed by analyzing polygraph data from 301 presumed nondeceptive and 323 presumed deceptive criminal incident polygraph examinations, with six Axciton instruments. The apparatus specifications for these cases are not available. "Truth" for these cases was obtained in three ways:

1. confession or guilty plea,
2. consensus on truthful subjects by two or more different examiners, or
3. confirmed truthful.

Version 5.1 of PolyScore used Zone Comparison Test (ZCT) and Modified General Question Test (MGQT) data from 1,411 real cases (J. Harris, personal communication, Johns Hopkins University Applied Physics Laboratory, 2001).

Chapters 2 and 4 of this report describe many of the biases that can result from the use of field cases selected from a larger population on the basis of truth and point out that consensus among multiple examiners is not acceptable as a criterion of deceptive/nondeceptive status. In effect, the use of such data can be expected to produce exaggerated estimates of polygraph accuracy. Nonetheless, most of the discussion that follows sets these concerns aside. Using field data, especially from criminal settings, to develop algorithms poses other difficulties. Actual criminal case polygraphs exhibit enormous variability, in the subject of investigation, format, structure, and administration, etc. These data are hard to standardize for an individual and across individuals in order to develop generalizable statistical procedures.

We analyzed polygraph data from 149 criminal cases using the ZCT and MGQT test formats, data that overlapped with those used in the development of PolyScore. Besides differences in the nature of the crime under investigation, our analyses revealed diverse test structures, even for the same test format, such as ZCT. The questions varied greatly from test to test and were clearly semantically different from person to person, even within the same crime. The order of questions varied across charts for the same person. In our analyses, we found at least 15 different sequences for relevant and control questions, ignoring the positioning of the irrelevant questions. The number of relevant questions asked varied. Typically, there were three relevant questions. Accounting for irrelevant/control questions substantially increases the number of possible sequences. These types of differences across cases pose major problems for both within- and between-subject analyses, unless all the responses are averaged. Finally, in the cases we examined there was little or no information available to control for differences among examiners, examiner-examinee interactions, delays in the timing of questions, etc. Some of these problems can be overcome by careful systematic collection of polygraph field data, especially in a screening setting, and others cannot. Controlling for all possible dimensions of variation in a computer-scoring algorithm, however, is a daunting task unless one has a large database of cases.

The laboratory or mock crime studies so commonly found in the polygraph literature typically remedy many of these problems, but they have low stakes, lack realism, and do not replicate the intensity of the stimulus of the real situations. Laboratory test formats are more structured. The same sequence of questions is asked of all the subjects, making these exams more suitable for statistical analysis. For laboratory data, the experimental set-up predetermines a person's deceptive and nondeceptive status, thus removing the problem of contaminated truth. Laboratory studies can have more control over the actual recording of the measurements and running of the examinations, as well as information on examiners, examinees, and their interactions. A major shortcoming of laboratory polygraph data for developing computer-based algorithms, however, is that they do not represent the formats that will be ultimately used in actual investigations or screening settings. Similarly, laboratory subject populations differ in important ways from those to whom the algorithms will be applied.

Signal Processing

With modern digital polygraphs and computerized systems, the analog signals are digitized, and the raw digitized electrodermal (skin conductance), cardiovascular and respiratory (abdominal and thoracic) signals are used in the algorithm development. The analog-to-digital conversion process may vary across different polygraph instruments. We were unable to determine Axciton instrument specifications. Kircher and Raskin (1988) provide some procedures used by Stoelting's polygraph instruments for CPS. Once the signals have been converted, the primary objective of signal processing is to reduce the noise-to-information ratio.

This traditionally involves editing of the data, e.g., to detect artifacts and outliers, some signal transformation, and standardization.

Artifact Detection and Removal

Artifacts indicate distortions in the signal that can be due to the movement of the examinee or some other unpredicted reactions that can modify the signal. Outliers account for both extreme relevant and control responses. The PolyScore algorithms include components for detecting artifacts and deciding if a signal is good or not. Kircher and Raskin (2002) report that they developed algorithms for artifact removal and detection in the 1980s, but they were not satisfied with their performance and did not use them as a part of CPS. Thus, examiners using CPS need to manually edit artifacts before the data are processed any further.

PolyScore tests each component of each question for artifacts and outliers. If any are detected, the algorithms remove those portions of the record from scoring, but examiners can review the charts and change the labeled artifacts, if they find it appropriate. Olsen et al. (1997) report that PolyScore labels a portion of a record as an extreme reaction (outlier) if it accounts for more than 89 percent of the variability among all the responses on the entire polygraph exam for a person; although the precise meaning of this is not totally clear, a portion of the individual's data would probably need to be totally off the scale to account for so much of the variation.

The committee was told that the PolyScore algorithms are proprietary and not available for evaluation. Thus, we were unable to examine the appropriateness of the procedures used in connection with artifact adjustment and the accuracy of any of the related claims.

Signal Transformation

A second step in data editing is signal transformation. Both CPS and PolyScore algorithms transform the raw digitized signals in different ways, but with a common goal of further signal enhancement.

PolyScore detrends the galvanic skin response and cardio signals by removing the "local mean," based on 30-second intervals both before and after the point, from each point in the signal, thus removing long-term or gradual changes unrelated to a particular question. This removes pen adjustments caused by the examiner. After detrending, PolyScore separates the cardio signal through a digital filter into the high-frequency portion representing pulse and the low-frequency component corresponding to overall blood volume. The derivative of the detrended blood volume then measures the rate of change and uncovers the remnants of the pulse in the blood volume signal, which are further eliminated by a second filter. The respiration signal, like the cardio signal, has two frequency components: a high frequency corresponding to each breath and a low frequency representing the residual lung volume. Baselining, achieved by matching each low point of exhalation between breaths to a common level, separates these frequencies and makes it easier to compare the relative heights of breaths (Harris et al., 1994).

CPS creates response curves (waveforms) for the digitized signals of skin conductance, thoracic respiration, and abdominal respiration by the sequence of stored poststimulus samples for a 20-second period following the onset of each question (Kircher and Raskin, 1988). To produce the blood pressure response waveform, CPS averages the systolic and diastolic levels for each second. Finger pulse amplitude is a second-by-second waveform like the blood pressure. However, this waveform is the difference of diastolic and systolic levels, not the average. Diastolic levels at 2 seconds prestimulus and 20 seconds poststimulus are subtracted from the corresponding systolic levels. Twenty poststimulus ratios are calculated by dividing each poststimulus amplitude by the average of the two pre-stimulus values. Each proportion is then subtracted from unity, reflecting the finger pulse amplitude waveform that rises with decrease in amplitude of finger pulse. Features are extracted from the times and levels of inflection points.

Signal Standardization

PolyScore performs signal standardization to standardize the extracted features; CPS does not. Harris et al. (1994) stress the importance of this step in the development of PolyScore. The goal of this step is to allow amplitude measurements across different charts or individuals to be scored by a common algorithm. Typically, standardization is performed by subtracting the mean of the signal from each data point and dividing this difference by the standard deviation. JHU-APL points out that since the data contain outliers, this method is inaccurate and thus PolyScore standardizes by subtracting the median from each data point and dividing it by the interquartile range (1st and 3rd quartiles are used, corresponding to the 25th and the 75th percentile).

Feature Extraction

The discussion of general statistical methodology for prediction and classification at the beginning of this appendix noted the importance of feature development and selection. The goal is to obtain a set of features from the raw data that can have some relevance in modeling and classification of internal psychological states, such as deception. For polygraph data, a feature can be anything measured or computed that represents an emotional signal. The mapping between psychological and physiological states remains a substantial area of investigation in psychophysiology. Some commonly used features in the manual scoring are changes in amplitude in respiration, galvanic skin response and cardiovascular response, changes in baseline of respiration, duration of a galvanic skin response, and change in rate of cardiovascular activity. Computerized analysis of digitized signals offers a much larger pool of features, some of them not easily observable by visual inspection.

The general psychophysiological literature suggests describing the skin conductance response using such features as level, changes in the level, frequency of nonspecific responses, event-related response amplitude, latency, rise time, half recovery time, number of trials before habituation, and rate of change of event-related amplitude. Dawson, Schell, and Filion (2000) note that the rise time and half recovery time might be redundant measures and not as well understood as amplitude in association with psychophysiological responses. Similarly, cardiovascular activity is typically analyzed using heart rate and its derivatives, such as the heart rate variability or the difference of the maximum and minimum amplitudes. Brownley, Hurwitz, and Schneiderman (2000), however, state that reliability of heart rate variability as a measure is controversial, and they suggest the use of respiratory sinus arrhythmia, which represents the covariance between the respiratory and heart rate activity. This approach implies a need for frequency-domain analysis in addition to time-domain analysis of the biological signals. Harver and Lorig (2000) suggest looking at respiratory rate and breathing amplitude as possible features that describe respiratory responses. They also point out that recording changes only of upper or only of lower respiration is not adequate to estimate relative breathing amplitude. In general, area measures (integrated activity over time) are less susceptible to high-frequency noise than peak measures, but amplitude measurements are more reliable than latency (Gratton, 2000).

Early research focusing specifically on the detection of deception suggested that the area under the curve and amplitudes of both skin conductance and cardiovascular response can discriminate between deceptive and truthful subjects. Other features investigated included duration of rise to peak amplitude, recovery of the baseline, and the overall duration of the response. Kircher and Raskin (1988) report that line length, the sum of absolute differences between adjacent sample points, which captures some combination of rate and amplitude, is a good measure of respiration suppression.

Harris (1996, personal communication) reports that the initial feature space for PolyScore 3.0 had 4,488 features and that about 10,000 features were considered for the 5.1 version. PolyScore's main focus for feature development and selection appears to have been on reaction time (i.e., where the reaction starts, peaks, ends) and the reaction's magnitude (i.e., amplitude), described by four numerical characterristics: percentile, derivative, line length, and latency period. JHU-APL evaluated the features using different window sizes (response intervals) for different signals.

PolyScore 3.2 uses a logistic regression model incorporating ten features: three each that describe galvanic skin response and blood volume and two each that describe pulse and respiration (Olsen et al., 1997). PolyScore 5.1 uses a neural network incorporating 22 features. JHU-APL declined to provide the committee with the specific features used by either program or detailed information on their selection.

Kircher and Raskin (1988, 2002) report that CPS initially considered 12 features describing the response waveforms for its discriminant analysis:

- skin conductance amplitude,
- blood pressure amplitude,
- finger pulse amplitude,
- skin conductance rise time,
- skin conductance full recovery time,
- blood pressure duration of half recovery time,
- finger pulse amplitude duration of half recovery time,
- skin conductance rise rate,
- blood pressure half recovery rate,
- skin conductance full recovery rate,
- electrodermal burst frequency, and
- respiration line length.

The most recent version of the CPS algorithm, however, uses only three features: skin conductance amplitude, the amplitude of increases in the baseline of the cardiograph and a line length composite measure of thoracic and abdominal respiration excursion (Kircher and Raskin, 2002). These features differ from those selected for use in PolyScore and appear to resemble more closely those that polygraph examiners attempt to identify in practice than do the vast majority of features incorporated into Polyscore feature selection spaces. In numerical scoring of polygraph charts, examiners typically combine upper and lower respiration scores into one score as well. Respiration line length is a more sophisticated measurement, however, which an examiner cannot easily calculate from the paper chart.

Feature Standardization

To score a polygraph exam, one needs to be able to compare the examinee's responses on relevant questions to those on the control questions. These comparisons need to be done for one person, but the statistical models also need to be able to account for between subject-variability. Both algorithms attempt to standardize the extracted features for relevant and control questions, thereby calibrating all subjects to the same scale (Olsen et al., 1997), but they do not do it quite the same way.

PolyScore standardizes relevant responses from subject i' to the control responses from subject i' as follows:

$$R^*_{i_i} = \frac{R_i - \mu_C}{\sigma_{CR}}, \tag{4}$$

$$\sigma^2_{CR} = \frac{\sum (R_i - \mu_R)^2 + \sum (C_i - \mu_C)^2}{\# \, of \, questions - 2}, \tag{5}$$

where R_i is the ith relevant question feature, C_i is the ith control question feature, μ_C is the mean of the control features, μ_R is the mean of the relevant features, and σ_{CR} is the pooled standard deviation, all determined within subject i'.

Unlike traditional manual scoring where each relevant question is compared to its "closest" control question, PolyScore computes the 80th percentile of each relevant standardized feature thus reducing the information from an entire examination to a single value for each feature.

CPS calculates a standardized response, a z-score, for each relevant and comparison question by subtracting the common within-subject mean from the calculated response and dividing by the common within-subject standard deviation. Podlesny and Kircher (1999) claim that the difference between the PolyScore and CPS methods of computing standard errors is small and not significant. If there are three relevant and three control questions per chart, then the common mean and standard deviation are calculated using all repeated measurements (typically 18 if there are three charts). CPS uses the z-score for multiple comparisons. Each standardized relevant question is compared with the averaged standardized control questions across all charts for a particular measure. These values are used to assess the strength of the different responses on the different relevant questions. However, CPS uses the difference of the averaged standardized control and averaged standardized relevant responses for its discriminant analysis.

Both algorithms combine the data from all three charts. In field uses of automated algorithms, standardization and comparison across charts for an individual and across individuals is problematic since the questions can be semantically different. For example, for the same person, the first relevant question on the first chart may not be the same as the first relevant question on the third chart since the question sequence may vary across charts. Laboratory experiments typically eliminate this problem: they ask the same number of questions and same type of questions in the same sequence, repeated three times for all the subjects. This is not the case in actual specific incident polygraphs using the MGQT or ZCT type test formats. The Test of Espionage and Sabotage (TES) is more standardized in this respect and hence more suitable for the statistical analysis accounting for within- and between-subject variability. Our preliminary analyses of a set of polygraph tests from widely varying criminal cases suggest that the similar features work for each chart, and that the first chart alone is a relatively good but far from perfect discriminator, and that the information from the following charts improves the classification of nondeceptive people.

Statistical Analysis

Statistical analysis involves feature evaluation and selection in the context of specific forms of scoring and methods of translating scores into an actual classification rule. The latter problem is the focus of much discussion elsewhere in this report. This section reviews aspects of feature selection and other aspects of statistical modeling involving the development of scoring rules.

While the availability of the digitized signal and computerized analyses create a large number of possible features, this does not solve the problem of discovering all the variables actually *relevant* to distinguishing between deception and nondeception, nor does it answer the question of how they are related to one another. The statistical classification modeling problem involves extracting a subset of relevant features that can be used to minimize some function of the two types of classification error, false positives and false negatives, when applied to inputs more general than the training dataset from which the features are selected.

Feature Selection

If the feature space is initially small, some analysts believe that the surest method of finding the best subset of features is an *exhaustive* search of all possible subsets. Ideally, for each subset, one designs a classifier, tests the resulting model on independent data, and estimates its associated error rates. One can then choose the model with the smallest combination of error rates. While this strategy may be feasible when the number of features is small, even the preliminary list of 12 features used in the development of the CPS algorithm poses problems. According to Kircher and Raskin (2002), they performed all-possible-subset regression analysis, but they do not provide details on possible transformations considered or how they did cross-validation.

When the number of features is larger, the exhaustive approach is clearly not feasible. If one has a small training set of test data (and repeatedly uses the same test data) one can obtain features that are well suited for that particular training or test data but that do not constitute the best feature set in general. One also needs to be careful about the number of selected features. The larger the number of features or variables, the more likely they will overfit the particular training data and will perform poorly on new data. The statistical and data-mining literatures are rife with descriptions of stepwise and other feature selection procedures (e.g., forward selection, backward elimination, etc.), but the multiplicity of models to be considered grows as one considers transformations of features (every transformation is like another feature) and interactions among features. All of these aspects are intertwined: the methodological literature fails to provide a simple and unique way to achieve the empirical objectives of identifying a subset of features in the context of a specific scoring model that has good behavior when used on a new data set. What most statisticians argue is that fewer *relevant* variables do better on cross-validation, but even this claim comes under challenge by those who argue for model-free, black-box approaches to prediction models (e.g., see Breiman, 2001). For the polygraph, the number of cases used to develop and test models for the algorithms under review was sufficiently small that the apparent advantages of these data-mining approaches are difficult to realize.

For the development of PolyScore, JHU-APL's primary method of feature selection was a linear logistic regression model where "statistical significance" of the features was a primary aspect in the selection process. Harris (personal communication) claims that he and his colleagues primarily chose those features with higher occurrence rate across different iterations of model fitting (e.g., galvanic skin response). We were unable to determine the detailed algorithmic differences between the 3.0 and 5.1 logistic regression versions of PolyScore. For version 5.1, JHU-APL extracted a set of features from its feature space of 10,000 based on statistical significance and then checked their ability to classify by applying the estimated model to a random holdout test set involving 25 percent of the 1,488 cases in its database. This procedure yielded several good models with varying numbers of features, some subsets of others, some overfitting, and some underfitting the data. Ultimately, JHU-APL claims to have chosen a model based on overall performance and not on the individual features themselves. There are natural concerns about claims for model selection and specification from 10,000 features using a database of only 1,488 cases, concerns that are only partially addressed by the random holdout validation strategy used by JHU-APL.

None of the JHU-APL claims or statements has been directly verifiable because JHU-APL refused to make any details or documentation available to the committee, including the variables it ultimately chose for its algorithm. The only way one could evaluate the performance of the algorithm is to apply it to a fresh set of data not used in any way in the model development and validation process and for which truth regarding deception is available from independent information.

Further Details on Statistical Modeling

In polygraph testing, the ultimate goal of classification is to assign individuals (cases) to classes in a way that minimizes the classification error (i.e., some combination of false positives and false negatives). As we noted above, CPS uses discriminant function analysis and PolyScore has algorithms based on logistic regression and neural networks.

PolyScore's logistic regression procedure can be thought of as having two parts (although the two are actually intertwined). First, the score is calculated as a linear combination of weighted features using maximum likelihood estimation, for example:

$$\text{score} = \text{intercept} + \hat{\beta}_1 x_1 + \hat{\beta}_2 x_2 + \hat{\beta}_3 x_3 + \hat{\beta}_4 x_4 + \hat{\beta}_5 x_5. \tag{6}$$

Table F-1 reports the values of the estimated logistic regression coefficients, or weights, for the five features presented by Harris et al. (1994). A positive sign for a weight indicates an increase in the probability of deception, while a negative sign denotes a decrease. The absolute value of a weight suggests something about the strength of the linear association with deception. These results agree with the general results of CPS, which also claims that the stronger measure is the skin conductance measure, and they assign the most weight to it, while the respiration measure has a negative correlation with deception.

Second, one can estimate the probability of deception from the logistic regression:

$$\hat{P}(deception \mid x) = \hat{P}(y \mid x) = \frac{e^{score(x)}}{1 + e^{score(x)}}, \tag{7}$$

TABLE F-1 Features Implemented in Version 3.0 of PolyScore with Their Estimated Coefficients

Features	Weights $(\hat{\beta})$
x_1 GSR Range	+5.5095
x_2 Blood Volume Derivative 75th Percentile	+3.0643
x_3 Upper Respiration 80th percentile	−2.5954
x_4 Pulse Line Length	−2.0866
x_5 Pulse 55th Percentile	+2.1633

and then choose the cutoffs for the estimated probabilities (7) with values above the upper cutoff being labeled as deceptive and those below the lower cutoff as nondeceptive. The currently used cutoffs are 0.95 and 0.05, respectively. Different methods can be used to produce the scoring equation (6), and there is a lack of clarity as to precisely what method was used for the final PolyScore algorithm.

The CPS algorithm relies on the result of a multivariate discriminant analysis, which is known as a less robust method than the logistic regression with respect to departures from assumptions and which gives more weight to extreme cases in building a classifier. Kircher and Raskin (1988) report that they used all-possible-subsets regression analysis on the 12 feature differences of scores to choose the best model and retained the five features listed in Table F-2. However, Kircher and Raskin's (2002) most recent model relies on only three features: skin conductance amplitude, the amplitude of increases in the baseline of the cerograph, and the respiration length.

Kircher and Raskin's discriminant analysis provided "optimal" maximum likelihood weights for these variables to be used in a classification equation of the form (6) to produce a score for each subject in the two

TABLE F-2 Features Implemented in CPS (reported by Kircher and Raskin, 1988) and Their Estimated Coefficients

Features	Weights $(\hat{\beta})$
x_1 SC Amplitude	+0.77
x_2 SC full recovery time	+0.27
x_3 EBF	+0.28
x_4 BP Amplitude	+0.22
x_5 Respiration Length	−0.40

groups. Note that these coefficients are essentially on a different scale than those of the PolyScore logistic regression model. They need to be converted into estimates for the probabilities of observing the scores given deception and nondeception by means of the normal probability density function. Kircher and Raskin allow these probability functions to have different variances:

$$\hat{P}(Score \mid ND) = \frac{1}{\sqrt{2\pi}} \frac{1}{\hat{\sigma}_{ND}} e^{-1/2[(Score-\hat{\mu}_{ND})/\hat{\sigma}_{ND}]^2} , \tag{8}$$

$$\hat{P}(Score \mid D) = \frac{1}{\sqrt{2\pi}} \frac{1}{\hat{\sigma}_{D}} e^{-1/2[(Score-\hat{\mu}_{D})/\hat{\sigma}_{D}]^2} , \tag{9}$$

where $\hat{\mu}_{ND}$ and $\hat{\sigma}_{ND}$ are the estimates of the mean and standard deviation, respectively, of the discriminant scores from the nondeceptive subjects, and $\hat{\mu}_{D}$ and $\hat{\sigma}_{D}$ are the estimates of the mean and standard deviation, respectively of the discriminant scores from the deceptive subjects.[3] Finally, one can convert these estimated values into estimated probabilities of deception through Bayes' theorem:

$$\hat{P}(D \mid Score) = \frac{P(D)\hat{P}(Score \mid D)}{P(D)\hat{P}(Score \mid D) + P(ND)\hat{P}(Score \mid ND)} , \tag{10}$$

where $P(ND)$ and $P(D)$ are the prior probabilities of being nondeceptive (ND) and deceptive (D), respectively. Kircher and Raskin take these prior probabilities to be equal to 0.5. Despite the use of Bayes' theorem in this final step, this is not a proper Bayesian approach to producing a classification rule.

Kircher and Raskin (1988) report that if $\hat{P}(ND \mid Score)$ based on three charts is greater than 0.70 they classify that person as nondeceptive, and if $\hat{P}(ND \mid Score)$ is less than 0.30, the person is classified as deceptive. For those whose estimated probability is between these two cutoff points, they calculate a new discriminant score based on five charts and then recalculate $\hat{P}(ND \mid Score)$ and use the same cutoff points. At that point, they label the test for subjects whose scores fall between 0.30 and 0.70 as inconclusive.

Both PolyScore and CPS seem to rely on the presumption of equal base rates for deceptive and nondeceptive cases, and they have been "evaluated" on databases with roughly equal sized groups. The performance of the algorithm in new instances or with differently structured "populations" of examinees is conjectural, and appropriate prior probabilities and operational cutoff points for algorithms for use in security screening are unclear.

Algorithm Evaluation

We lack detailed information from the developers on independent evaluations of the PolyScore and CPS algorithms. We do have limited information on a type of cross-validation and a jackknife procedure to evaluate PolyScore® 3.0, neither of which provides a truly independent assessment of algorithm performance in light of the repeated reanalyses of the same limited sets of cases.

Kircher and Raskin (2002) report the results of 8 selected studies of the CPS algorithm, none involving more than 100 cases, and most of which are deeply flawed according to the criteria articulated in Chapter 4. Moreover, only one of the two field studies described includes comparative data for deceptive and nondeceptive individuals. They report false negative rates ranging from 0 to 14 percent, based on exclusion of inconclusives. If inconclusives are included as errors, the false negative rates range from 10 to 36 percent. Similarly, they reported false positive rates ranging from 0 to 19 percent, based on exclusion of inconclusives. If inconclusives are included in the calculation of error rates, as for example in the calculation of ROC (receiver operating characteristics) curves, then the false positive rates ranges from 8 to 37 percent. It would be a mistake to treat these values as illustrative of the validity of the CPS computer scoring algorithm. Kircher and Raskin also list a ninth study (Dollins, Krapohl, and Dutton, 2000) that, as best we have been able to determine, is the only one that attempts independent algorithm evaluation. The values for false positive and false negative error rates that it reports appear to be highly exaggerated, however, because of the selection bias associated with the cases used.

Dollins and colleagues (Dollins, Krapohl, and Dutton, 2000) compared the performance of five different computer-based classification algorithms in late 1997: CPS, PolyScore, AXCON, Chart Analysis, and Identifi. Each developer was sent a set of 97 charts collected with Axciton instruments for "confirmed" criminal cases and used the versions of their software available at the time. Test formats included both ZCT and MGQT. None of the developers at the time of scoring knew the truth, confirmed by a confession or from indisputable corroborating evidence. An examination was labeled as nondeceptive if someone else confessed to the crime. The data contained 56 deceptive and 41 nondeceptive cases and came from a mix of federal and nonfederal agencies. All of the computer programs were able to read the Axciton proprietary format except the CPS program, and Axciton Systems, Inc., provided the CPS developers with a text-formatted version of the data (see below).

Dollins and associates (Dollins, Krapohl, and Dutton, 2000) report that there were no statistically significant differences in the classification powers of the algorithms. All programs agreed in correctly classifying 36 deceptive and 16 nondeceptive cases. And all incorrectly classified the same three nondeceptive cases, but there was not a single case that *all* algorithms scored as inconclusive. CPS had the greatest number of inconclusive cases and the least difference between the false positive and false negative rates. Four other algorithms all showed tendencies toward misclassifying a greater number of innocent subjects. The results, summarized in Table F-3, show false negative rates ranging from 10 to 27 percent and false positive rates of 31 to 46 percent (if inconclusives are included as incorrect decisions).

As Dollins and colleagues (Dollins, Krapohl, and Dutton, 2000) point out, there are a number of problems with their study. The most obvious is a sampling or selection bias associated with the cases chosen for evaluation. The data were submitted by various federal and nonfederal agencies to the DoDPI and *most* of these were correctly classified by the original examiner and are supported by confessions. This database is therefore not representative of any standard populations of interest. If the analyzed cases correspond, as one might hypothesize given that they were "correctly" classified by the original examiner, to the easy classifiable tests, then one should expect all algorithms to do better on the test cases than in uncontrolled settings. Because all algorithms produce relatively high rates of inconclusive tests even in such favorable circumstances, performance with more difficult cases is likely to degrade. There was no control over the procedures that the algorithm developers used to classify these cases, and they might have used additional editing and manual

TABLE F-3 Number of Correct, Incorrect, and Inconclusive Decisions by Subject's Truth

Algorithm	Deceptive ($n = 56$)			Nondeceptive ($n = 41$)		
	Correct	Incorrect	Inconclusives	Correct	Incorrect	Inconclusive
CPS	41	4	11	28	3	10
PolyScore	49	1	6	26	7	8
AXCON	50	1	5	24	9	8
Chart Analysis	49	2	5	22	8	11
Identifi	49	1	6	22	8	11

SOURCE: Dollins, Krapohl, and Dutton (2000:239).

examination of the data, as well as modifications to the software for classification cutoffs. The instrumentation used was also a possible problem in this study, particularly for the CPS algorithm. Data were collected with the Axciton instrument that records a hybrid of skin conductance and skin resistance. The CPS algorithm relies on true skin conductance and the data recorded with the Stoelting instrument. The CPS algorithm was unable to process the Axciton proprietary data and was provided with the text format, in which there was also a possibility of error in rounding the onsets of the questions with further negative effect on the CPS performance. The other algorithms performed very similarly, which is not surprising because they were developed on data collected with Axciton instruments and in most cases with very similar databases.

IMPLICATIONS FOR TES

JHU-APL is currently working on a beta-test version of PolyScore 5.2 that has prototype algorithms for scoring screening test formats such as TES and relevant/irrelevant formats. The current version of the TES-format algorithm uses the same features as the ZCT/MGQT–format algorithm, but this may change. Polygraph examiners review each chart in a TES separately; PolyScore analyzes them together. We are not aware of other scoring algorithms for the TES format.

Table F-4 reports very preliminary results of the TES algorithm provided to us by JHU-APL. The current difficulty in developing this algorithm is the overall small number of deceptive cases. As a result, they are giving up the power to detect (that is, keeping the sensitivity of the test at lower levels) in order to keep the false positive rates lower, in effect changing the base rate assumptions. These data indicate that sensitivity of 70 percent may be attained in conjunction with 99 percent specificity (1 percent false positive rate). JHU-APL believes these numbers can be im-

TABLE F-4 Preliminary TES Results

Type of Analysis	Total Number	Inc	Corr	TN	FP	FN	TP
Binary[a]	716	0	707	692	4	5	15
Ternary	524	192	520	510	3	1	10

NOTES: Inc, inconclusive; Corr, correct; TN, true negative; FP, false positive; FN, false negative; TP, true positive.

[a]Inconclusives forced to deceptive, nondeceptive.

proved. Of about 2,100 cases, one-third have been used strictly for training, one-third for training and testing, and one-third have been withheld for independent validation, a step that has not yet occurred. A major problem with this database is independent determination of truth.

SUMMARY

The PolyScore and CPS computerized scoring algorithms take the digitized polygraph signals as inputs and produce estimated probabilities of deception as outputs. They both assume, a priori, equal probabilities of being truthful and deceptive. PolyScore was developed on real criminal cases, and the Computer Assisted Polygraph System (CAPS) (the precursor to CPS) was developed on mock crimes. CAPS truth came solely from independent blind evaluations, while PolyScore relied on a mix of blind evaluations and confessions. The more recent CPS versions seem to rely on actual criminal cases as well although we have no details.

Both algorithms do some initial data transformation of the raw signals. CPS keeps these to a minimum and tries to retain as much of the raw signal as possible. PolyScore uses more initial data editing tools such as detrending, filtering, and baselining. PolyScore and CPS standardize signals, using different procedures and on different levels. They extract different features, and they seem to use different criteria to find where the maximal amounts of discriminatory information lie. Both, however, give the most weight to the electrodermal channel.

PolyScore combines all three charts into one single examination record and considers reactivities across all possible pairs of control and relevant questions. CAPS compares adjacent control and relevant questions as is done in manual scoring, but it also uses difference of averaged standardized responses on the control and relevant questions to discriminate between guilty and nonguilty people. CPS does not have an automatic procedure for the detection of artifacts, but it allows examiners to edit the charts themselves before the algorithm calculates the probability of truthfulness. PolyScore has algorithms for artifacts and outliers detection and removal, but JHU-APL treats the specific details as proprietary and will not reveal them. While PolyScore uses logistic regression or neural networks to estimate the probability of deception from an examination, CPS uses standard discriminant analysis and a naïve Bayesian probability calculation to estimate the probability of deception.[4]

Overall, PolyScore claims to do as well as experienced examiners on detecting deceptives and better on detecting truthful subjects. CPS claims to perform as well as experienced evaluators and equally well on detection of both deceptive and nondeceptive people. Computerized systems clearly have the potential to reduce the variability that comes from bias and inexperience of examiners and chart interpreters, but the evidence that they have achieved this potential is meager. Porges and colleagues (1996) evaluated PolyScore and critiqued the methodology it used as unscientific and flawed. Notwithstanding the adversarial tone taken by Porges and colleagues, many of the flaws they identified apply equally to CPS, such as the lack of adequate evaluation.[5]

Dollins and associates (Dollins, Krapohl, and Dutton, 2000) compared the performance of these two algorithms with three other algorithms on an independent set of 97 selected confirmed criminal cases. CPS performed equally well on detection of both innocent and guilty subjects, while the other algorithms were better at detecting deceptive examinees than clearing nondeceptive ones. Unfortunately, the method of selecting these cases makes it difficult to interpret the reported rates of misclassification.

One could argue that computerized algorithms should be able to analyze the data better than human scorers because they incorporate potentially useful analytic steps that are difficult even for trained human scorers to perform (e.g., filtering and other transformations, calculation of signal derivatives), look at more information, and do not restrict comparisons to adjacent questions. Moreover, computer systems never get careless or tired. The success of both numerical and computerized systems, however, still depends heavily on the pretest phase of the examination. How well examiners formulate the questions inevitably affects the quality of information recorded.

PolyScore is currently working on algorithms for scoring the screening data coming from TES and relevant/irrelevant tests. An a priori base rate might be introduced in these algorithms to increase accuracy and to account for the low number of deceptive cases.

There has yet to be a proper independent evaluation of computer scoring algorithms on a suitably selected set of cases, for either specific incidents or security screening, which would allow one to accurately assess the validity and accuracy of these algorithms.

NOTES

1. Some computerized systems store biographical information such as examinee's name, social security number, age, sex, education, ethnicity, marital status, subject's health, use of drugs, alcohol, and prior polygraph history (e.g., see www.stoelting.com), but it is unclear how this type of information would be appropriately used to improve the diagnostic accuracy of a computer scoring system.
2. Matte (1996) and Kircher and Raskin (2002) provide more details on the actual polygraph instruments and hardware issues and some of the history of the development of computerized algorithms.
3. Under the assumption of unequal variance for the two groups, which Kircher and

Raskin say they are using, a more statistically accepted procedure is to calculate a score using a quadratic discriminant function.

4. A proper Bayesian calculation would be far more elaborate and might produce markedly different results.

5. The distinctions made regarding the logistic regression and discriminant analysis methods used by the two systems are not especially cogent for present purposes.

REFERENCES

Breiman, L.
  2001 Statistical modeling: The two cultures (with discussion). *Statistical Science* 16:199-231.
Brownley, K.A., B.E. Hurwitz, and N. Schneiderman
  2000 Cardiovascular psychophysiology. Chapter 9, pp. 224-264, in *Handbook of Psychophysiology*, 2nd ed., J.T. Cacioppo, L.G. Tassinary, and G.G. Bernston, eds. New York: Cambridge University Press.
Copas, J.B., and P. Corbett
  2002 Overestimation of the receiver operating characteristic curve for logistic regression. *Biometrika* 89:315-331.
Dawson, M., A.M. Schell, and D.L. Filion
  2000 The electrodermal system. Chapter 8, pp. 200-223, in *Handbook of Psychophysiology*, 2nd ed., J.T. Cacioppo, L.G. Tassinary, and G.G. Bernston, eds. New York: Cambridge University Press.
Dollins, A.B., D.J. Krapohl, and D.W. Dutton
  2000 A comparison of computer programs designed to evaluate psychophysiological detection of deception examinations: Bakeoff 1. *Polygraph* 29(3):237-257.
Gratton, G.
  2000 Biosignal Processing. Chapter 33, pp. 900-923, in *Handbook of Psychophysiology*, 2nd ed., J.T. Cacioppo, L.G. Tassinary, and G.G. Bernston, eds. New York: Cambridge University Press.
Harris, J.
  1996 Real Crime Validation of the PolyScore® 3.0 Zone Comparison Scoring Algorithm. Unpublished paper. The Johns Hopkins University Applied Physics Laboratory.
Harris, J., et al.
  1994 *Polygraph Automated Scoring System.* U.S. Patent Document. Patent Number: 5,327,899.
Harver, A., and T.S. Lorig
  2000 Respiration. Chapter 10, pp. 265-293, in *Handbook of Psychophysiology*, 2nd ed., J.T. Cacioppo, L.G. Tassinary, and G.G. Bernston, eds. New York: Cambridge University Press.
Hastie, T., R. Tibshirani, and J. Friedman
  2001 *The Elements of Statistical Learning: Data Mining, Inference and Prediction.* New York: Springer-Verlag.
Kircher, J.C., and D.C. Raskin
  1988 Human versus computerized evaluations of polygraph data in a laboratory setting. *Journal of Applied Psychology* 73:291-302.
  2002 Computer methods for the psychophysiological detection of deception. Chapter 11, pp. 287-326, in *Handbook of Polygraph Testing*, M. Kleiner, ed. London: Academic Press.

Matte, J.A.
  1996   *Forensic Psychophysiology Using Polygraph–Scientific Truth Verification Lie Detection.*
          Williamsville, NY: J.A.M. Publications.
Olsen, D.E, J.C. Harris, M.H.Capps, and N. Ansley
  1997   Computerized Polygraph Scoring System. *Journal of Forensic Sciences* 42(1):61-71.
Podlesny, J.A., and J.C. Kircher
  1999   The Finapres (volume clamp) recording method in psychophysiological detection
          of deception examinations: Experimental comparison with the cardiograph
          method. *Forensic Science Communication* 1(3):1-17.
Porges, S.W., R.A. Johnson, J.C. Kircher, and R.A. Stern
  1996   Unpublished Report of Peer Review of Johns Hopkins University/Applied Phys-
          ics Laboratory to the Central Intelligence Agency.

Appendix G

Process for Systematic Review of Polygraph Validation Studies

"Systematic review" describes a relatively formal approach to evaluating a body of research literature that has over the past two decades gradually been supplanting the classical "expert summary" review article. The latter, while often an intellectual *tour de force*, is nevertheless prone to idiosyncratic literature selection and overemphasis on the reviewer's experience and predispositions. Systematic reviews incorporate a common set of steps, conducted and documented so that, as with primary scientific studies, it is possible for other researchers to replicate the systematic review process to confirm its results. The five common steps, each of which may be elaborated in a variety of ways, are question formulation, literature search and compilation, critical characterization and data extraction, integration of results, and contextual evaluation. Our systematic review was less formal than many, due largely to the breadth of the task and the scope of available resources, but we are confident in the approach and the resulting primary scientific conclusions.

QUESTION FORMULATION

The questions addressed by this review were largely dictated by the committee's charge. These are:

• How strong is the correspondence between polygraph test results and actual deception in empirical studies that allow such assessment?

• Does the strength of correspondence vary substantially across different test settings, questioning methods, study populations, or other variables of potential practical importance?

• To what degree are the quality and generalizability of the polygraph research literature sufficient to support policy decisions regarding use of the polygraph, with particular emphasis on national security screening applications?

LITERATURE SEARCH AND COMPILATION

Many thousands of works have been written on the polygraph. An extensive bibliography compiled two decades ago (Ansley, Horvath, and Barland, 1983) listed some 3,400 references, and there have certainly been thousands of works on the subject since then. Our interest for this review was in the small proportion of this literature that includes polygraph validation studies, that is, studies that (a) report measurements of one or more of the physiological responses measured by the polygraph and (b) link these physiological responses to the respondent's truth or deception. Only such studies offer empirical evidence that can be used to assess the criterion validity of the polygraph.

We used several approaches in an effort to obtain as much as possible of the entire corpus of polygraph validation studies. One was a normal literature search using computerized bibliographic databases such as PsycInfo, Social Science Citation Index, Medline, and so forth, using relevant keywords. In addition, we sent requests by regular or electronic mail to a variety of individuals and organizations that we believed might have, or be able to lead us to, research reports useful for this study. These requests went to all U.S. government agencies that do security screening by polygraph, to polygraph websites known to us, and to leading researchers of all persuasions in the polygraph controversy. All contacted were additionally asked to forward our request to others who might also have information potentially useful to us. Finally, we periodically checked our growing bibliography against major published and unpublished bibliographies and reviews of the polygraph literature (e.g., Ansley, Horvath, and Barland, 1983; U.S. Office of Technology Assessment, 1983; Kircher, Horowitz, and Raskin, 1988; Urban, 1999; Ben-Shakhar, personal communication; Defense Information Systems Agency, 2001; U.S. Department of Defense Polygraph Institute, personal communication; Ben-Shakhar and Elaad, 2002). We sought out validation studies regardless of whether or not they had undergone peer review. Through this procedure, we attempted to be as inclusive as possible in collecting material to review, in order to limit publication bias and make our own judgments of research quality.

CRITICAL CHARACTERIZATION AND DATA EXTRACTION

The many documents we collected included 217 reports of 194 unique polygraph validation studies. These varied greatly in quality of research design, choice and standardization of measurement techniques, thoroughness of control for confounding variables, statistical analyses, and various other factors that affect their scientific value.

We used a four-stage process to select studies from the polygraph validation literature for qualitative evaluation and to extract data from those studies for quantitative summarization. The process involved: (1) initial staff screening of collected research reports by a set of basic criteria for acceptability and for special interest; (2) detailed reading of reports by committee members, with characterization by a larger set of criteria; (3) resolution of unresolved issues from initial staff screen and elimination of remaining redundant reports and those without appropriate data for baseline receiver operating characteristic (ROC) curve assessment; and (4) extraction of datasets for ROC assessment from remaining study reports. Stages (3) and (4) were performed by a subgroup of committee statisticians and staff.

Initial Staff Screen

Polygraph validation reports were reviewed by staff for conformity to six basic criteria of scientific acceptability and potential usefulness for baseline ROC assessment. The criteria were initially discussed by all involved staff and a committee research methodologist. Multiple reviewers evaluated a substantial selection of the reports and discussed and collectively resolved discrepancies, in the process clarifying policies for classification. The rest of the reports were evaluated by two staff coders, who discussed any discrepancies and agreed on classifications. We used six screening criteria:

1. **Documentation of examination procedures sufficient to allow a basic replication. To meet this criterion, a study had to pass all the following tests:**

• *Question selection.* Studies passed if they specified the questions used for each polygraph test, provided a superset of questions from which the questions used were selected and a reproducible selection process, or otherwise provided enough detail about the method of question selection or construction, as for instance in field application of a comparison question technique, to allow for essential replication of the process.

• *Physiological measures used.* Studies passed if they specified the measures recorded (even if these were of questionable value).

• *Instrumentation.* Studies passed if they specified the equipment used to collect physiological measures.

• *Scoring method.* Studies passed if they specified how the physiological measures were converted to the dependent-variable measures that were compared to truth.

2. **Independently determined truth.** Studies passed if (a) guilt or innocence was predetermined by the conditions of an experiment or (b) in a nonexperimental study, if truth was defined by a confession, adjudication by a legal process, or review of the case facts by a panel who were uninformed about the results of the polygraph examination. An experimental study was defined as one in which guilt or innocence is manipulated by the researcher. Such studies may be carried out either in laboratories or in more realistic settings. In nonexperimental studies, examinees are tested with regard to crimes or transgressions committed in the world outside the laboratory, of which they are innocent or guilty.

3. **Inclusion of both guilty and innocent individuals, as determined by criterion 2 (truth).** Studies also passed this screen if they used a within-subjects design in which the same individual provided truthful and deceptive responses to highly similar questions.

4. **Sufficient information for an accuracy analysis.** Studies passed if: (a) scores were classified as deceptive, nondeceptive, and inconclusive (or the equivalent) for both innocent and guilty respondents; (b) inconclusive cases were absent because of an explicit decision rule that forced a definite choice on all cases; or (c) data were recorded on an ordinal, interval, or ratio scale, allowing for accuracy analysis with multiple cutoff points. Studies failed if charts that were scored inconclusive were rejected from the data analysis and not reported.

5. **Scoring conducted with masking to truth.** Experimental studies passed the screen if they stated or showed that both the polygraph examiners and scorers were kept unaware of the examinee's guilt or innocence, even if the procedures to achieve this masking might have been flawed. Nonexperimental studies passed if scorers were kept uninformed about all case information relevant to determining truth, even if the original polygraph examiners were not uninformed. Studies using scoring methods that left no room for individual judgment (e.g., automated scoring methods) also passed.

6. **Appropriate assignment to experimental groups germane to validity assessment (mainly, guilt and innocence).** This criterion was ap-

plied only to experimental studies, and they passed if (a) they stated that or explained how subjects were randomly assigned to groups; (b) they compared truthful and deceptive responses of the same individual in a within-subjects design (e.g., concealed information technique studies); or (c) they put subjects in a situation that tempted them to guilty action and allowed them to choose whether or not to commit the acts or to deceive.

In applying the above criteria, staff were instructed to err in the direction of inclusiveness, by forwarding to the committee for full examination and resolution reports with ambiguities about whether the criteria were all met. In addition, reports that appeared to have uniquely interesting design features, that seemed particularly relevant to screening, or that considered other issues of particular importance to the committee's charge (e.g., countermeasures, effects of examinee differences) were also forwarded to the committee even if they failed the above screening criteria.

Of the 217 reports reviewed in this initial screen, 23 were later found to be duplicate reports of the same research, leaving 194 unique studies.[1] Staff forwarded 102 unique reports to the entire committee, which conducted a detailed review of them. Of the total, there were 61 studies that clearly satisfied the six criteria above. Reports of 41 other studies also received detailed review because they either (a) appeared to fail only one screen, with the possibility that the failure was due only to omission of a detail in the written report or, for observational field studies, an inherent logistical limitation; (b) considered factors of particular relevance on which literature was sparse (e.g., countermeasures); or (c) exhibited special features of research design that staff judged potentially important enough to justify further examination, despite failing the screen. These studies were provided to all committee members along with information on how they had been classified according to the screening criteria. Additional studies from the full list of 189 were made available to members as requested.

Committee Review

All committee members read many studies, with choices dictated by their particular interests and areas of expertise, testimony to the committee, and background readings. Committee meetings included comprehensive discussions of the body of literature and specific subsets of it. Designated subgroups reviewed and commented upon all reports in special categories of studies (e.g., of countermeasures).

Two members were assigned to review each of the 115 reports forwarded from the initial screen. The assigned committee members classified each study with regard to 16 study characteristics.

1. *Setting.* Studies were categorized as laboratory or field studies. "Laboratory" refers to studies in a controlled environment using polygraph examinations conducted specifically for research purposes. "Field" refers to studies of polygraph performance using examinations conducted to detect deception primarily for practical purposes other than research, e.g., in criminal investigations, civil litigation, or employee screening.

2. *Test format.* Studies were classified as using comparison question, concealed information, relevant-irrelevant, or other techniques. Comparison question techniques include both probable-lie and directed-lie variants.

3. *Question range.* Studies were classified as to whether relevant questions referred to knowledge of specific facts or participation in specific events or, instead, addressed only categories of events, as is commonly the case with screening polygraphs.

4. *Skin measurement.* Studies that measured electrodermal response were classified as to whether skin conductance or skin resistance was recorded.

5. *Primary outcome scale.* Studies were classified in terms of whether polygraph results were reported in two categories (e.g., deception indicated or no deception indicated), in three categories (including an inconclusive category), in multiple categories indicating degrees of evidence pointing to deception or truthfulness, or as summary scores on numerical scales.

6. *Masking to base rate.* Studies were classified as to whether polygraph examiners or scorers knew the base rate of deceptive individuals in the examinee population.

7. *Scoring reliability.* Studies were placed in one of three categories based on the stringency of control for observer variability: human scoring without data on inter-rater reliability; multiple human scorers with inter-rater reliability data; or automated (computerized) scoring.

8. *Consequences of test.* Studies were classified according to the seriousness (trivial, moderate, or severe) of the reward for appearing nondeceptive and, separately, of the punishment for appearing deceptive.

9. *Case selection.* Scorers noted whether or not the examinees came from a defined population potentially allowing replication (e.g., military recruits, people tested in criminal investigations in a particular jurisdiction).

10. *Truth.* Field studies were classified by how truth was determined:

by confession, retraction, judicial procedures (including jury trials and jury-like panels), or other methods.

11. *Documentation of research protocol.* Scorers rated the research report as providing detailed and clear, adequate, or minimal documentation of the study procedures covered in screening criterion 1. "Detailed and clear" required use of generally sound methods.

12. *Quality of data analysis.* Scorers rated the quality of procedures used for analyzing the polygraph data as high, adequate, or low.

13. *Internal validity.* Scorers rated each study comprehensively on a 1-5 scale, with 1 representing the highest scientific standards for research methodology and 5 representing the minimum standards consistent with the initial screening criteria. Scorers considered the above factors, additional potential sources of bias and confounding, sample size, and discussion of their ramifications for conclusions.

14. *Overall salience to the field.* Each study was similarly rated 1-5, incorporating internal validity as well as broader issues. For experimental studies, considerable weight was given to external validity, including how well an experiment mimicked actual polygraph testing situations with regard to choices of engaging in or refraining from the target activity and to be deceptive or forthcoming and the consequences of being found deceptive on the test. Scorers also considered the importance of the measures and variables examined to the major practical questions concerning polygraph validity.

15. *Funding.* Studies were classified on the basis of information in the research reports as follows: intramural research funded by an agency with a polygraph program; extramural research funded by such an agency; extramural research funded by another source; research locally funded by an academic or research organization; and other or unable to determine.

16. *Comparative analyses.* Reviewers noted whether each study included internal comparisons on variables of special interest: examinees' age, gender, or race; type of crime or transgression; levels of motivation or "stakes"; examinees' psychopathology; use of countermeasures; or other internal comparisons.

Disagreements between qualitative categorizations were resolved by a third committee member acting as a judge or, in some cases, through discussion by the raters. Ordinal numerical scores within one unit on a five-point scale were averaged. Disparities of more than one unit were resolved by discussion among the reviewers, by averaging if such discussion did not produce a consensus or, in a few cases where this discussion was difficult to arrange, by adjudication by a third committee member.

Reviewers also extracted the basic data on polygraph accuracy provided by the study. Typically, these data could be conveyed in simple tabular form to show test outcomes for deceptive and nondeceptive examinees. If studies included multiple conditions or internal comparisons, either a primary summary table was extracted, or tables were reported for each of several conditions or subgroups. This process yielded from one to over a dozen datasets from the individual studies, depending on the number of conditions and subpopulations considered. Often, multiple datasets reflected the same subjects tested under different conditions or different scoring methods applied to the same polygraph examination results.

Resolution of Unresolved Issues and Extraction of Datasets for ROC Analysis

To gain a baseline impression of empirical polygraph validity, we used data primarily from the studies that passed the six first-stage screening criteria. After committee review of the reports passed on by staff with unresolved status in this regard, 74 were determined to satisfy the initial criteria. Those criteria were relaxed to allow 6 others that failed no more than one criterion, either on grounds of documentation or impracticality in a field context, and that came either from a source of particular relevance (U.S. Department of Defense Polygraph Institute, DoDPI) or exhibited features of special interest (e.g., field relevance). During this process, we identified redundant reports of the same study, and used the report with the most comprehensive data reporting or that reported data in a form most suitable for our purpose.

Some studies that had passed our screen and initially appeared suitable for ROC analysis were not ultimately used for this purpose. Specifically, studies that exclusively reported polygraph decisions made on the basis of averaging raw chart scores of multiple examiners were excluded. While this approach shares with computer scoring the laudable intent of reducing errors due to examiner variability, to our knowledge such a scoring method is never used in practice, and it will often exaggerate the validity of a single polygraph examination.

We also excluded, for this particular purpose, data from an otherwise interesting research category: studies of concealed information tests using subjects as their own controls that did not also include subjects who had no concealed information about the questions asked. These studies compared responses of research subjects to stimuli about which they had information to responses to other stimuli, in various multiple-choice contexts. In them, each examinee was deceptive to some questions and nondeceptive to others. Some of these studies were quite strong in the sense of controlling internal biases and quite convincing in demonstrating a statistical association between polygraph responses and deception in uncontaminated laboratory settings. However, various design features of these studies seriously limited the relevance of their measurements of polygraph accuracy. Some of them designated deception or truthfulness based on relative rankings within a group of examinees rather than for an individual or used extremely artificial stimulus sets (e.g., playing cards or family names). Most importantly, these studies lacked uncontaminated nondeceptive control subjects, so that their assessments of accuracy are based on a priori assumptions about how such subjects would have responded, and do not account for the possibility that nondeceptive examinees may respond differentially to stimuli that commonly have emotional connotations even for nondeceptive individuals.

Since our purpose was to use multiple studies to get a general sense of polygraph accuracy, we excluded from this analysis studies in which examinees came only from population subgroups distinguished by psychological aberration. Finally, we excluded from the quantitative analysis any study with fewer than five individuals in either the deceptive or nondeceptive groups, on the grounds that results from such studies were inherently too statistically unstable to provide much useful information.

This winnowing process left 57 unique studies (listed below) judged useful for gaining a general sense of polygraph validity through ROC analysis. Most of these studies reported multiple datasets. To avoid implicitly weighting studies by the multiplicity of conditions and subgroups considered, in all but two instances (noted in 3 below) we extracted only one set of validation data for further examination from each study from which reviewers had reported multiple datasets. These datasets were determined by one or more committee members and the consultant, working under the following rules:

1. Multiple polygraph channels. In studies that evaluated polygraph tracings from separate channels independently and reported the results separately, we used the results based on the composite of all tracings if these were reported, and the results based on skin conductance/resistance if no composite results were provided. Studies comparing the contributions of skin resistance, cardiovascular, and respiratory responses have generally found skin resistance to have the most discriminating power of the polygraph channels and most have found the additional contributions of cardiovascular and respiratory responses to be modest.

2. Demographically distinct subgroups. Results from demographic subgroups tested under the same conditions were pooled, after excluding subgroups selected for extreme deviancy, such as psychopaths. While deviant subgroups were potentially of interest in their own regard, they were considered inappropriate for a core evaluation of polygraph validity.

3. Subgroups tested under different conditions. Results from subgroups tested under different conditions (e.g., variants of the same questioning method, different sets of instructions or methods of psychological preparation, modestly different mock crime scenarios) were pooled. Statistically important differences in results of such variants were rare. For studies contrasting major variants against testing under a standard paradigm, such as a probable lie comparison question test, we used data from the control group tested using the standard paradigm. Two reports included data from administration of comparison question and concealed information polygraph tests to different groups of subjects. We extracted one dataset for each type of testing procedure from each of these two studies. In studies of countermeasures in which certain groups were instructed to use countermeasures, we used data only from examinees who were not instructed to use countermeasures. In studies of "spontaneous" countermeasure use by examinees who were not instructed to use countermeasures, we pooled all examinees.

4. Different scoring methods or scorers. Data from human scorers masked to information about truth were selected in preference to those from human scorers not so masked, such as the original examiner. Results from masked scorers separate the information in the polygraph charts from other information present during the examination (e.g., demeanor) or in the examinee's history (e.g., past offenses) that might influence expectations of the scorer and hence scoring results.

Despite the fact that computer scoring shares these advantages with masked human scoring, we chose the results of a human scorer over those of computer scoring when both were available, even when the human scorer was not masked. Computers are not commonly used for primary scoring in current polygraph practice. In the studies we reviewed, computer scoring was not noticeably superior to human scoring except on data used to train the computer, where computer success rates are known to be spuriously elevated. (See Appendix F for more detailed discussion of issues involving studies of computer scoring.)

Some studies reported separate results of multiple human scorers in the same generic category, e.g., three masked scorers. In such cases, the proportions of examinees allocated to each decision category were averaged across examiners to form a single dataset. Some studies reported results of different methods of scoring, for instance, variations in the cutoffs applied to summary scores from charts to distinguish those that suggested deception from nondeceptive or inconclusive charts. Often these scoring methods were applied to the same set of charts. In such instances, we chose data reflecting the "control," that is, the most widely accepted scoring paradigm.

5. Indistinguishable datasets. In a very few (< 5) instances, multiple (usually two) datasets remained with none taking precedence on the above grounds. In these instances, the dataset most favorable to polygraph testing was used.

This stage of review was accomplished by a small subgroup of committee members, staff, and the consultant, under oversight of a committee member specializing in research methodology.

INTEGRATION OF RESULTS AND CONTEXTUAL EVALUATION

We have conducted a systematic review but not a meta-analysis. A meta-analysis is a systematic review that integrates the compiled results of either the totality of selected studies or homogeneous subgroups of them into one or a few simple numerical summaries, each of which usually addresses both statistical significance (e.g., p-value) and the magnitude of an observed relationship (effect size). The best meta-analyses also include a search for systematic explanations of heterogeneity in the results of the studies compiled. Initially proposed to overcome the sample size limitations of individual studies and misinterpretations of negative statistical hypothesis tests, meta-analysis has seen widespread application as a general tool for research synthesis in the social and health sciences. Others have made efforts to do meta-analyses for all or part of the literature on the use of the polygraph for the detection of deception or the presence of concealed information (e.g., see Kircher et al., 1988; Urban, 1999; and Ben-Shakhar and Elaad, 2002). We have not attempted such numerical reduction here. In view of the widespread expectation that critical literature reviews lead to such comprehensive summaries, we offer some explanation for this decision.

There are both technical and substantive reasons for not using meta-analytic methods in this report. We do not use these methods in part because the literature does not allow us to deal adequately with the heterogeneity of the available studies. The laboratory studies employ instruments measuring different physiological parameters, multiple scales of measurement and systems of scoring, varying methods of interviewing, examiners of different levels of experience, and multiple study populations. The field studies present all these kinds of heterogeneity and more: they include variation within studies in the deceptions of concern, in examiners' expectancies, and in multiple unrecorded aspects of the social interaction during the polygraph examination. Appropriate meta-analytic summaries would handle this diversity either by hypothesizing that these variations do not affect the relationship between polygraph measurement and deception and empirically testing this hypothesis, or by modeling heterogeneity across the studies as a random effect around some central measure of the relationship's strength, perhaps also correcting estimates of the observed variability in effect sizes for sampling error, which is likely to be a serious concern in a research literature where small samples are the norm. However, the literature contains too few studies of adequate quality to allow meaningful statistical analysis of such hypotheses or models. Without such analysis, it is not clear that there is any scientific or statistical basis for aggregating the studies into a single population estimate. Were such an estimate obtained, it would be far from clear what combination of population and polygraph test conditions it would represent.

Our main substantive concern is with the relevance of the available literature to our task of reviewing the scientific evidence on polygraph testing with particular attention to national security screening applications. There is only a single study that provides directly relevant data addressing the performance of the polygraph in this context (Brownlie et al., 1998), and because it uses global impressionistic scoring of the polygraph tests, its data do not meet our basic criteria for inclusion in the quantitative analysis. The great majority of the studies address the accuracy of specific-issue polygraph tests for revealing deception about specific criminal acts, real or simulated. Even in the few studies that simulate security screening polygraph examinations, the stakes are low for both the examiners and the examinees, the base rate for deception is quite high (that is, the examiners know that there is a high probability that the examinee is lying), and there is little or no ambiguity about ground truth (both examiners and examinees know what the specific target transgression is, and both are quite clear about the definitions of lying and truthfulness). Given the dubious relevance to security screening of even the closest analog studies, as well as the heterogeneity of the literature, we do not believe there is anything to be gained by using precise distributional models to summarize their findings.

Rather than developing and testing meta-analytic models, we have taken the simpler and less potentially misleading approach of presenting descriptive summaries and graphs. The studies vary greatly in quality and include several with extreme outcomes due to sampling variability, bias, or non-generalizable features of the study design. Thus, we do not give much weight to the studies with outcomes at the extremes of the group, and summarize the sample of studies with values of the accuracy index (A) that are most representative of the distribution of study outcomes—the median and the interquartile range. As Chapter 5 and Appendix I show, such a tabulation reveals sufficiently for our purposes the main things the empirical research shows about the accuracy of polygraph testing, particularly inasmuch as the literature does not adequately represent the performance of polygraph tests in screening contexts.

NOTE

1. The duplications usually involved master's theses, Ph.D. dissertations, or agency reports that were subsequently published.

STUDIES INCLUDED IN QUANTITATIVE ANALYSIS

Barland, G.H., and D.C. Raskin
  1975   An evaluation of field techniques in detection of deception. *Psychophysiology* 12(3):321-330.
Barland, G.H., C.R. Honts, and S.D. Barger
  1989   Studies of the Accuracy of Security Screening Polygraph Examinations. Report No. DoDPI89-R-0001. Fort McClellan, AL: U.S. Department of Defense Polygraph Institute.
Ben-Shakhar, G., and K. Dolev
  1996   Psychophysiological detection through the Guilty Knowledge technique: Effects of mental countermeasures. *Journal of Applied Psychology* 67(6):701-713.
Blackwell, N.J.
  1996   PolyScore: A Comparison of Accuracy. Fort McClellan, AL: U.S. Department of Defense Polygraph Institute.
  1998   PolyScore 3.3 and Psychophysiological Detection of Deception Examiner Rates of Accuracy When Scoring Examinations from Actual Criminal Investigations. Report DoDPI97-R-0006. Fort McClellan, AL: U.S. Department of Defense Polygraph Institute.
Bradley, M.T.
  1988   Choice and the detection of deception. *Perceptual and Motor Skills* 66(1):43-48.
Bradley, M.T., and M.C. Cullen
  1993   Polygraph lie detection on real events in a laboratory setting. *Perceptual and Motor Skills* 76(3/Pt. 1):1051-1058.
Bradley, M.T., and M.P. Janisse
  1981   Accuracy demonstrations, threat, and the detection of deception: Cardiovascular, electrodermal, and papillary measures. *Psychophysiology* 18(3):307-315.
Bradley, M.T., and K.K. Klohn
  1987   Machiavellianism, the Control Question Test and the detection of deception. *Perceptual and Motor Skills* 64:747-757.
Bradley, M.T., and J. Rettinger
  1992   Awareness of crime-relevant information and the Guilty Knowledge Test. *Journal of Applied Psychology* 77(1):55-59.
Bradley, M.T., V.V. MacLaren, and S.B. Carle
  1996   Deception and nondeception in Guilty Knowledge and Guilty Actions polygraph Tests. *Journal of Applied Psychology* 81(2):153-160.
Craig, R.A.
  1997   The Use of Physiological Measures to Detect Deception in Juveniles: Possible Cognitive Developmental Influences. A Ph.D. dissertation submitted to the faculty of the Department of Psychology, The University of Utah.

Davidson, P.O.
   1968   Validity of the guilty-knowledge technique: The effects of motivation. *Journal of Applied Psychology* 52(1):62-65.
Dawson, M.E.
   1980   Physiological detection of deception: Measurement of responses to questions and answers during countermeasure maneuvers. *Psychophysiology* 17(1):8-17.
Driscoll, L.N., C.R. Honts, and D. Jones
   1987   The validity of the positive control physiological detection of deception technique. *Journal of Police Science and Administration* 15(1):46-50.
Elaad, E., and M. Kleiner
   1990   Effects of polygraph chart interpreter experience on psychophysiological detection of deception. *Journal of Police Science and Administration* 17:115-123.
Giesen, M., and M.A. Rollison
   1980   Guilty knowledge versus innocent associations: Effects of trait anxiety and stimulus context on skin conductance. *Journal of Research in Personality* 14:1-11.
Hammond, D.L.
   1980   The Responding of Normals, Alcoholics and Psychopaths in a Laboratory Lie-Detection Experiment. A Ph.D. dissertation submitted to the California School of Professional Psychology, San Diego.
Honts, C.R.
   1986   Countermeasures and the Physiological Detection of Deception: A Psychophysiological Analysis. A Ph.D. dissertation submitted to the faculty of the Department of Psychology, The University of Utah.
Honts, C.R., and S. Amato
   1999   The Automated Polygraph Examination: Final Report to the Central Intelligence Agency. Applied Cognition Research Insititute. Boise, ID: Boise State University.
Honts, C.R., and B. Carlton
   1990   The Effects of Incentives on the Detection of Deception. Report No. DoDPI90-R-0003. Fort McClellan, AL: U.S. Department of Defense Polygraph Institute.
Honts, C.R., and M.K. Devitt
   1992   Bootstrap Decision Making for Polygraph Examinations. Report No. DoDPI92-R-0002. Fort McClellan, AL: U.S. Department of Defense Polygraph Institute.
Honts, C.R., and D.C. Raskin
   1988   A field study of the validity of the directed lie control question. *Journal of Police Science and Administration* 16(1):56-61.
Honts, C.R., S. Amato, and A. Gordon
   2000   Validity of Outside-Issue Questions in the Control Question Test. Final Report on Grant No. N00014-8-1-0725. Boise, ID: The Applied Cognition Research Institute.
Honts, C.R., R.L. Hodes, and D.C. Raskin
   1985   Effects of physical countermeasures on the physiological detection of deception. *Journal of Applied Psychology* 70(1):177-187.
Honts, C.R., D.C. Raskin, and J.C. Kircher
   1987   Effects of physical countermeasures and their electromyographic detection during polygraph tests for deception. *Journal of Psychophysiology* 1(3):241-247.
Honts, C.R., M.K. Devitt, M. Winbush, and J.C. Kircher
   1996   Mental and physical countermeasures reduce the accuracy of the concealed knowledge test. *Psychophysiology* 33:84-92.

Horowitz, S.W.
    1989   The Role of Control Questions in Physiological Detection of Deception. A Ph.D. dissertation submitted to the faculty of the Department of Psychology, The University of Utah.
Iacono, W.G., G.A. Boisvenu, and J.A. Fleming
    1984   Effects of diazepam and methylphenidate on the electrodermal detection of guilty knowledge. *Journal of Applied Psychology* 69(2):289-299.
Iacono, W.G., A.M. Cerri, C.J. Patrick, and J.A.E. Fleming
    1992   Use of antianxiety drugs and countermeasures in the detection of guilty knowledge. *Journal of Applied Psychology* 77(1):60-64.
Ingram, E.M.
    1994   Effects of Electrodermal Lability and Anxiety on the Electrodermal Detection of Deception with a Control Question Technique. Report No. DoDPI94-R-0004. Fort McClellan, AL: U.S. Department of Defense Polygraph Institute.
    1996   Test of a Mock Threat Scenario for Use in the Psychophysiological Detection of Deception: I. Report No. DoDPI96-R-0003. Fort McClellan, AL: U.S. Department of Defense Polygraph Institute.
    1996   Test of a Mock Threat Scenario for Use in the Psychophysiological Detection of Deception: III. Report No. DoDPI97-R-0003. Fort McClellan, AL: U.S. Department of Defense Polygraph Institute.
    1998   Test of a Mock Theft Scenario for Use in the Psychophysiological Detection of Deception: VI. Report No. DoDPI98-R-0002. Fort McClellan, AL: U.S. Department of Defense Polygraph Institute.
    1998   Test of a Mock Theft Scenario for Use in the Psychophysiological Detection of Deception: VII. Report No. DoDPI98-R-0003. Fort McClellan, AL: U.S. Department of Defense Polygraph Institute.
Jayne, B.C.
    1990   Contributions of physiological recordings in the polygraph technique. *Polygraph* 19(2):105-117.
Kircher, J.C., and D.C. Raskin
    1988   Human versus computerized evaluations of polygraph data in a laboratory setting. *Journal of Applied Psychology* 73(2):291-302.
Lykken, D.T.
    1959   The GSR in the detection of guilt. *Journal of Applied Psychology* 43(6):385-388.
Matte, J.A., and R.M. Reuss
    1989   A field validation study of the quadri-zone comparison technique. *Polygraph* 18(4):187-202.
O'Toole, D., J.C. Yuille, C.J. Patrick, and W.G. Iacono
    1994   Alcohol and the physiological detection of deception: Arousal and memory influences. *Psychophysiology* 31:253-263.
Patrick, C.J., and W.G. Iacono
    1989   Psychopathy, threat, and polygraph test accuracy. *Journal of Applied Psychology* 74(2):347-355.
    1991   Validity of the control question polygraph test: The problem of sampling bias. *Journal of Applied Psychology* 76(2):229-238.
Podlesny, J.A., and J.C. Kircher
    1999   The Fianpres (volume clamp) recording method in psychophysiological detection of deception examinations. *Forensic Science Communications* 1(3).

Podlesny, J.A., and D.C. Raskin
 1978   Effectiveness of techniques and physiological measures in the detection of decep-
         tion. *Psychophysiology* 15(4):344-359.
Podlesny, J.A., and C.M. Truslow
 1993   Validity of an expanded-issue (Modified General Question) polygraph technique
         in a simulated distributed-crime-roles context. *Journal of Applied Psychology*
         78(5):788-797.
Raskin, D.C., and R.D. Hare
 1978   Psychopathy and detection of deception in a prison population. *Psychophysiology*
         15(2):126-136.
Raskin, D.C., and J.C. Kircher
 1990   *Development of a Computerized Polygraph System and Physiological Measures for De-
         tection of Deception and Countermeasures: A Pilot Study (Preliminary Report).* Con-
         tract No. 88-L655330-000. Salt Lake City, UT: Scientific Assessment Technolo-
         gies, Inc.
Reed, S.
 no   TES Expansion Study. Unpublished paper. U.S. Department of Defense
 date   Polygraph Institute, Fort McClellan, AL.
Rovner, L.I.
 1979   The Effects of Information and Practice on the Accuracy of Physiological Detec-
         tion of Deception. A Ph.D. dissertation submitted to the faculty of the Depart-
         ment of Psychology, The University of Utah.
Stern, R.M., J.P. Breen, T. Watanabe, and B.S. Perry
 1981   Effect of feedback of physiological information on responses to innocent associa-
         tions and guilty knowledge. *Journal of Applied Psychology* 66:677-681.
Suzuki, A., K. Ohnishi, K. Matsuno, and M. Arasuma
 1979   Amplitude rank score analysis of GSR in the detection of deception: Detection
         rates under various examination conditions. *Polygraph* 8:242-252.
U.S. Department of Defense Polygraph Institute
 1998a   *Test of a Mock Theft Scenario for Use in the Psychophysiological Detection of Deception:
         IV.* Report No. DoDPI97-R-0007. Ft. McClellan, AL: U.S. Department of Defense
         Polygraph Institute.
 1998   Test of a Mock Theft Scenario for Use in the Psychophysiological Detection of
         Deception: V. Report No. DoDPI98-R-0001. Fort McClellan, AL: U.S. Depart-
         ment of Defense Polygraph Institute.
Waid, W.M., S.K. Wilson, and M.T. Orne
 1981   Cross-modal physiological effects of electrodermal lability in the detection of de-
         ception. *Journal of Personality and Social Psychology* 40(6):1118-1125.
Waid, W.M., E.C. Orne, M.R. Cook, and M.T. Orne
 1981   Meprobamate reduces accuracy of physiological detection of deception. *Science*
         212:71-72.
Yankee, W.J.
 1993   *An Exploratory Study of the Effectiveness of Event-Related Stimuli as a Control Proce-
         dure in the Psychophysiological Detection of Deception.* Report No. DoDPI93-R-0003.
         Fort McClellan, AL: U.S. Department of Defense Polygraph Institute.
Yankee, W.J., and D. Grimsley
 2000   Test and retest accuracy of a psychophysiological detection of deception test.
         Polygraph 29(4):289-298.

REFERENCES

Ansley, N., F. Horvath, and G.H. Barland
   1983   *Truth and Science: A Bibliography* (Second Edition). Lithicum Heights, MD: American Polygraph Association.

Ben-Shakhar, G., and E. Elaad
   2002   The Validity of Psychophysiological Detection of Information with the Guilty Knowledge Test: A Meta-analytic Review. Unpublished manuscript. Hebrew University, Israel.

Brownlie, C., G.J. Johnson, and B. Knill
   1998   Validation Study of the Relevant/Irrelevant Screening Format. Unpublished paper. National Security Agency, Baltimore, MD.

Defense Information Systems Agency
   2001   Technical Report Bibliography: Polygraph. Search Control No. (T95332 01/06/12 – BIB). Unclassified. U.S. Department of Defense.

Kircher, J.C., S.W. Horowitz, and D.C. Raskin
   1988   Meta-analysis of mock crime studies of the control question polygraph technique. *Law and Human Behavior* 12(1):79-90.

Urban, G.D.
   1999   A Meta-Analysis of the Validity of the Polygraph for the Detection of Deception. Unpublished manuscript. Northern Michigan University.

U.S. Office of Technology Assessment
   1983   Scientific Validity of Polygraph Testing: A Research Review and Evaluation, A Technical Memorandum. OTA-TM-H-15, NTIS order #PB84-181411. Washington, DC: U.S. Government Printing Office.

Appendix H

Quantitative Assessment of Polygraph Test Accuracy

This appendix provides additional details regarding the data on polygraph test accuracy extracted during our systematic literature review, as well as technical background on methods we used for estimating a receiving operator characteristic (ROC) curve and associated area from each set of data.

Characteristics of Studies As described in Chapter 5 and Appendix G, we extracted 59 datasets from 57 studies (52 laboratory, 7 field) including 3,681 polygraph examinations (3,099 laboratory, 582 field). Of the 57 studies, 41 (34 laboratory, 7 field) reported data allowing ROC curve estimation from two points, while 17 laboratory studies provided only one estimated ROC point and a single laboratory study provided ten estimated points on its single ROC. The median sample size in a dataset, including both genuine or programmed deceptive and nondeceptive examinees, was 49, with mean 62.4 (median and mean 48 and 59.6, respectively, for laboratory datasets, and 100 and 83.1, respectively, for field datasets). Only one (laboratory) dataset had fewer than 20 examinees, while only nine datasets (five laboratory, four field studies) had as many as 100 examinees. As best as could be determined, 21 studies were funded by agencies with operational polygraph programs, of which 16 were internal reports of such agencies. Of studies not funded by polygraph agencies, 20 were locally funded studies at academic or other research institutions, two were internally funded at other organizations without operational polygraph programs, and 14 were externally funded studies at academic or other research institutions without operational polygraph programs.

Of the laboratory datasets, 37 described comparison question tests, 13 described concealed information tests, 1 described the relevant-irrelevant test, and 1 described another procedure; among field studies, 6 described comparison question tests and 1 a peak-of-tension concealed information procedure. Questioning referred to specific incidents in all cases but one. The electrodermal measure was skin conductance for 23 datasets (22 laboratory, 1 field), skin resistance for 22 (18 laboratory, 4 field), and could not be determined for 14 datasets (12 laboratory, 2 field). For 36 datasets (33 laboratory, 3 field), both committee reviewers agreed that the studies were silent as to whether examiners or scorers (or both) were masked to the base rate of deception in the examinee pool, and reviewers of 3 others (2 laboratory, 1 field) agreed that the base rate was known by examiners and scorers. For only 3 of the remaining datasets did the reviewers agree as to nature of masking. Twenty-two datasets (21 laboratory, 1 field) reported on computer scoring, 5 alone (all laboratory) and 16 (15 laboratory, 1 field) in conjunction with human scoring. Of the 54 datasets (47 laboratory, 7 field) that reported on human scoring, 28 (23 laboratory, 5 field) presented results of multiple scorers with information on inter-rater variability, while 26 (24 laboratory, 2 field) either reported only on single scorers or used multiple human scorers but did not report on inter-rater variability.

Our documentation categories of detailed and clear, adequate, and minimal were assigned respective scores of 0, 1, and 2. Study scores averaged 1.2 of 2, with 26, 21, and 10 studies respectively scoring above, at, and below 1.0. The average analytic quality rating scores similarly averaged 1.0, with 14, 29, and 14 studies above, equal to, and below 1.0, respectively. On a five-point scale (best score 1.0), internal validity scores averaged 3.04 (median = 3.0), with 10 studies at 2.0 or better, 25 studies 2.0+ to 3.0 inclusive, 20 studies 3.0+ to 4.0 inclusive, and 2 studies scored 4.5. On the same scale, salience scores averaged 3.3 (median = 3.5), with 5 studies at 2.0 or better, 19 studies at 2.0+ to 3.0 inclusive, 26 studies 3.0+ to 4.0 inclusive, and 7 studies 4.0+ to 5.0 inclusive. Scores for laboratory and field studies were generally similar, with laboratory studies faring about half a point better on internal validity, and field studies having a modestly smaller advantage on salience. Field studies also were rated slightly better than laboratory studies on documentation and data analysis. The quality scores for protocol documentation, data analysis, internal validity, and salience were correlated as might be anticipated. With signs adjusted so that positive correlations represent agreement in quality, correlations of salience score with protocol documentation score, data analysis score, and internal validity score were respectively 0.33, 0.42, and 0.49.

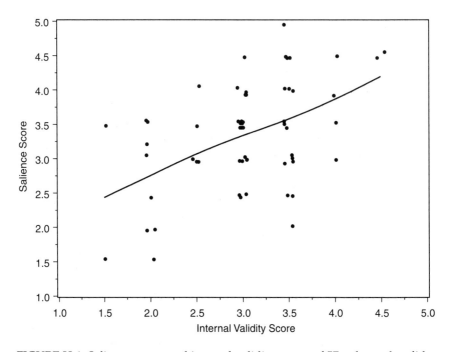

FIGURE H-1 Salience scores and internal validity scores of 57 polygraph validation studies.
NOTE: Scores represent means of two (occasionally three) committee reviewers.

Correlations of internal validity score with protocol documentation and
data analysis scores were 0.37 and 0.66, respectively, with a correlation of
0.30 between documentation and data analysis scores. Figure H-1 plots
salience against internal validity scores, with points jittered slightly left
and right to avoid overlap. A smoothing spline portrays the association.

Method of Estimating Accuracy We used the area under an ROC
curve extrapolated from each dataset to summarize polygraph accuracy
as manifested in that dataset. Since only one dataset gave more than two
points for ROC extrapolation, an underlying model was helpful to join
the small number of dots. (Here we follow the maxim, attributed to the
statistician G.E.P. Box, that "all models are wrong, but some models are
useful.") The dominant model in the signal detection theory research
assumes that the criterion on which decisions are based (here, the polygraph chart score) has different normal (Gaussian) distributions among
groups with signal absent and present (here, nondeceptive and deceptive
examinees). These distributions are presumed to have different means

and may also have different standard deviations (a measure of spread). To extrapolate an ROC curve from only one point using this Gaussian model requires that we additionally assume these standard deviations are equal. Figure H-2 shows six theoretical ROCs from this "equivariance" binomial model, with respective A values of 0.5, 0.6, 0.7, 0.8, 0.9, 0.95, along with the reverse diagonal line corresponding to sensitivity = (1– false positive rate), which can alternately be interpreted as false positive rate = false negative rate. On this line, the probability that the test is correct is the same whether the examinee is deceptive or nondeceptive. The intersection of each ROC with this line highlights the difference be-

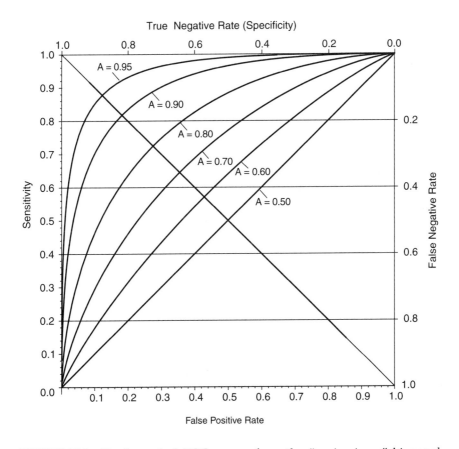

FIGURE H-2 Six theoretical ROC curves from the "equivariance" binomial model.
NOTE: Curves are binomial equivalence ROCs with accuracy index (A) values of 0.5, 0.6, 0.7, 0.8, 0.9, and 0.95.

tween A and the probability that the test is correct. Note that, for these curves, when the test is correct with the same probability for deceptive as for nondeceptive examinees, this shared probability is between 5 percent and 10 percent lower than the value of A for each ROC. Elsewhere on the ROC, percent correct depends heavily on the base rate and, in some circumstances, may not be lower than the value of A.

Under this model, the method of maximum likelihood estimation is commonly used to estimate the ROC, and hence A. However, this method fails without at least one observation in each of the categories used to determine the ROC points. When some categories are only sparsely filled, it also can produce unstable and inadmissible results: that is, ROC curves that idiosyncratically dip below the 45-degree diagonal instead of increasing steadily from the lower left to the upper right-hand corners of the graph. In either of these instances, we estimated A directly from the empirical ROC data, by connecting points from the same study to each other, the leftmost point to the lower left-hand corner, and the rightmost point to the upper right-hand corner, and determining A as the area within the polygon generated by those lines and the lower and right-hand plotting axes. In the signal detection theory literature, this is known as the "trapezoidal estimate." For our data, where one-point ROCs with equivariance binomial maximum likelihood estimates exist, the resulting estimates of A tended to be higher than the trapezoidal estimates by about 0.1; for two-point ROCs, the discrepancy between the trapezoidal and binomial (possibly with unequal variances) estimates of A was much smaller, generally 0.01-0.03. Had sample sizes been large enough to allow the use of a binomial estimate in all cases, we conjecture that the median values of A reported in Chapter 5 and below would have increased by 0.02-0.03 for laboratory studies and perhaps 0.01 for field studies.

Accuracy in Laboratory Studies Figure H-3 plots values of A from the extrapolated ROCs from our 52 laboratory datasets, in descending order of A from left to right. Below each point is suspended a line of length equal to the estimated standard error of the associated A, to give an indication of the inherent variability in these numbers given the sizes of the various studies. From the lengths of most of these lines, it is clear that few of these studies estimate A precisely. Furthermore, the apparent precision of the high estimates at the upper left may well be due to the fact that values of A that are near the maximum due to chance necessarily produce unduly low estimates of variability. We note, in any event, that the large majority of A values are between 0.70 and 0.95, and that half the studies fall between the lower and upper quartiles of A = 0.813 and 0.910, represented by the horizontal lines.

One might suspect that the highest and lowest values of A would

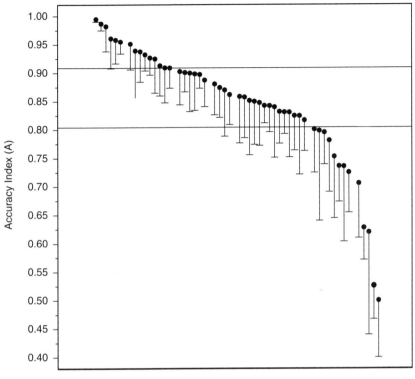

FIGURE H-3 Accuracy index (A) values calculated from 52 datasets from laboratory studies.
NOTE: Vertical lines are the length of one standard error; they extend downward from the accuracy index value for convenience of presentation.

have arisen by chance from studies with particularly small sample sizes, but in fact these groups of studies have sample sizes comparable to the larger collection. It is also interesting to note that values of A have not been increasing over time, as they might be expected to do if, as some members of the polygraph community have suggested to the committee, older studies underestimate the accuracy of current polygraph testing due to recent improvements in technique. The 6 datasets with the lowest A values were all reported in the 1990s, while the 7 datasets with highest A values were reported between 1968 and 1989, and none of the 9 datasets with A exceeding 0.95 were among the 22 datasets reported after 1992. Looked at another way, the median A for 8 datasets (7 laboratory, 1 field) reported prior to 1980 was 0.94, for 21 datasets (19 laboratory, 2 field)

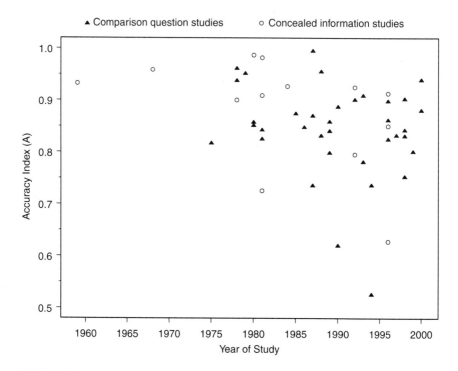

FIGURE H-4 Accuracy index (A) values for laboratory studies over time.

reported in the 1980s was 0.86, and for the 30 most recent datasets (26 laboratory, 4 field) was 0.85. Figure H-4 shows the relationship of A to time, distinguishing between data on comparison question tests and concealed information or guilty knowledge tests. Although there are many more comparison question than concealed information datasets, the trend appears downward for both.

In view of the low methodological quality ratings that we assigned to many of these studies, we readdressed the above points in the subset of 14 laboratory studies with internal validity scores better than 3 on a 1-5 scale (with 1 as best). These studies included 721 polygraph tests. Figures H-5, H-6, and H-7 are the counterparts within this subgroup of studies of Figures 5-1, H-3, and H-4 for the laboratory studies with the best internal validity. The situation portrayed is much the same as for the full group of laboratory studies. Outliers excluded, the negative time trend in A values from comparison question test datasets appears similar in the high internal validity subgroup, and the decline is not visible in the concealed information test datasets of which, however, only three are included. In Figure H-7, each dataset is symbolized on the plot by the salience score

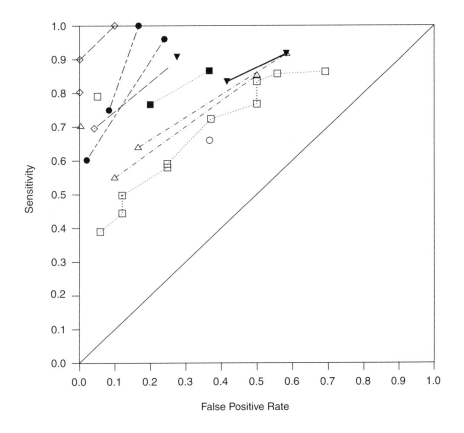

FIGURE H-5 Sensitivity values and false positive rates for 14 laboratory datasets with high internal validity.
NOTE: Points connected by lines come from the same dataset.

that committee reviewers assigned to the study from which it was derived. Datasets from studies with higher salience (i.e., lower salience scores) tend to fall in the middle of the range of A values on the plot.

In view of the issue of possible research bias associated with the sponsorship of research, we attempted to classify studies by source of funding: internal studies by agencies with and without polygraph programs, studies by other groups externally funded by agencies with and without polygraph programs, and locally funded studies by academics. It was not always possible to do this without ambiguity, because funding sources were not always fully clear from the publications and because of the close connections of most researchers in the field to the polygraph

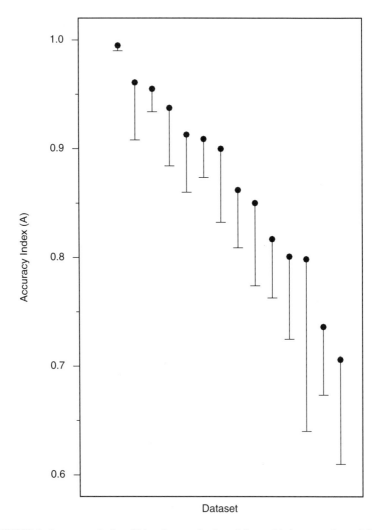

FIGURE H-6 Accuracy index (A) values calculated from 14 datasets from laboratory studies with high internal validity.
NOTE: Vertical lines are the length of one standard error; they extend downward from the accuracy index value for convenience of presentation.

profession or one or more government polygraph agencies. The attempt
was made, nevertheless. Figure H-8 shows boxplots of values of A from
the datasets we selected from studies in each of these five funding groups.
For each group, the central box contains the middle half of the values of
A, with the median value marked by a dot and horizontal line. The

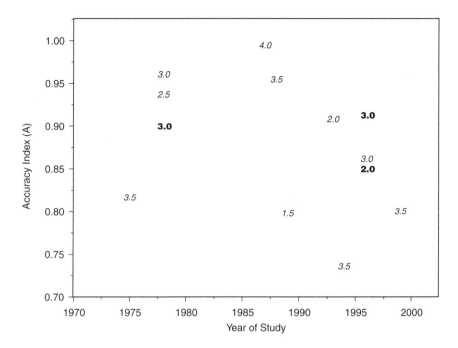

FIGURE H-7 Accuracy index (A) values for comparison question and concealed information laboratory polygraph studies with high internal validity, by year and salience score.
NOTES: Each dataset is symbolized on the plot by the salience score that committee reviewers assigned to the study from which it was derived. Boldface type indicates concealed information studies; italic type indicates comparison question studies.

"whiskers" extend to the largest and smallest values within 1.5 times the interquartile range of the edge. Any values farther out are marked by detached dots and horizontal lines. The data in Figure H-8 suggest that studies internal to or funded by polygraph agencies do not report higher measures of polygraph validity than studies funded by other sources.

Figure H-9 shows parallel boxplots for the entire group of 52 datasets, the subgroup of 14 datasets with internal validity score better than 3, and the subgroup of four datasets with both internal validity and salience scores better than 3. Restricting to high validity and salience does not change the overall impression conveyed by these data, that characteristic values of A from laboratory studies fall in the broad range between 0.70 and 0.95, with the most characteristic values falling in or slightly above the 0.81-0.91 range, which contains half (26 of 52) of our selected datasets.

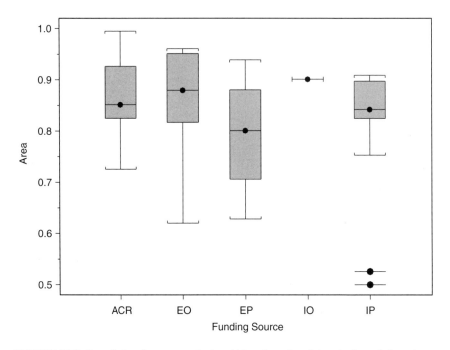

FIGURE H-8 Boxplots of accuracy index (A) values for datasets from laboratory studies, by funding source.

NOTE: ACR, academic research organization (n = 19); EO, externally funded by agency without polygraph program (n = 14); EP, externally funded by agency with polygraph program (n = 5); IO, internally funded by agency without polygraph program (n = 1); IP, internally funded by agency with polygraph program (n = 13).

Accuracy in Field Studies Figure H-10 displays A values for the 7 field datasets (i.e., specific-incident polygraphs) discussed in Chapter 5, in the same manner as Figure H-3 for the 52 laboratory datasets. As noted above, the median value of 0.89 is roughly the same as the median of 0.86 for the laboratory datasets, with the difference about what might be expected from the more frequent use of trapezoidal estimates of area for the laboratory studies. The standard errors are a bit smaller for the field studies (which have larger sample sizes) than for the laboratory studies, with that for the first study shown in Figure H-10 artificially small due to the proximity of the estimate to the maximum. The two studies with lowest values of A were done 20 years apart, one in the late 1970s and the other in the late 1990s. The five other studies were done in 1988-1991.

The types of funding used to support of these studies illustrate why the categories we used, which are reasonable and quite distinct at face

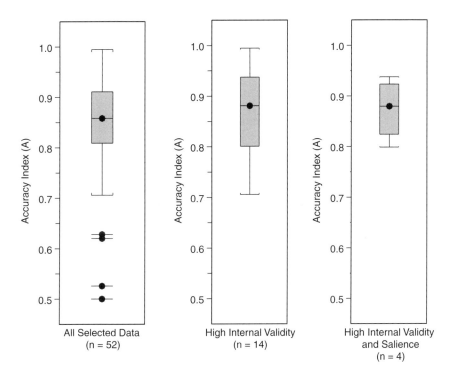

FIGURE H-9 Boxplots of accuracy index (A) values for all 52 laboratory datasets, the subgroup of 14 datasets with internal validity scores better than 3, and the subgroup of 4 datasets with both internal validity and salience scores better than 3.

value, often blur in the context of polygraph research. Only three of these seven studies were funded by agencies with polygraph programs. However, one study classified as locally funded academic research was conducted in the university laboratory of a polygraph examiner and former employee of the U.S. Department of Defense Polygraph Institute. Another, with A essentially equal to 1.0 in the above figures, was the doctoral dissertation of the president of a polygraph company, based on data from polygraph tests that used a specific variant of the control question test, with an associated scoring mechanism, that the author had developed some years earlier. Of 122 polygraph tests from criminal investigations that were examined in this particular study, there were seven inconclusive tests but no false positive or false negative errors.

Due to the small number of field studies available, we use a slightly more lenient criterion in restricting to higher quality studies and consider

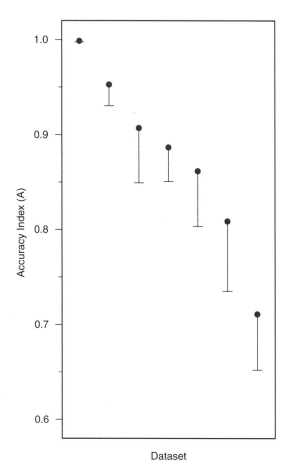

FIGURE H-10 Accuracy index (A) values for seven field datasets.
NOTE: Vertical lines are the length of one standard error; they extend downward from the accuracy index value for convenience of presentation.

the smaller set of studies with internal validity rating of less than or equal
to 3 (contrasting with the criterion of less than 3 used for laboratory
studies). Only two of the seven field studies met this criterion and also
had salience ratings of better (i.e., lower) than 3. Their associated A
values were 0.91 and 0.89, close to the median A of 0.89 for the seven
datasets. Thus, the results of the field studies, if taken literally, suggest
that the average accuracy of polygraph testing in field specific-incident
investigations is similar to and may be slightly higher than that found in
polygraph accuracy studies using laboratory models. However, inas-

much as none of these studies isolates the determination of truth from performance on the polygraph examination, they share a bias that must inflate apparent accuracy, perhaps to a significant degree. This result, in conjunction with the tendency for diagnostic test performance to degrade in field application relative to under laboratory conditions, leads us to believe that actual polygraph test performance in the field, if it could be measured against actual truth, would show a lower level of accuracy than indicated by the field or laboratory datasets we examined.

Appendix I

False Positive Index Values for Polygraph Testing

Table I-1 illustrates the effects of accuracy and thresholds on the false positive index, with four illustrative base rates (the false positive index is the number of false positive test results for each true positive test result). It shows that increasing test accuracy makes for more attractive tradeoffs in using the test. For example, it shows that that for any base rate, if the threshold is set so as to correctly detect 50 percent of truly positive cases, or major security risks (shown in Table I-1B), a diagnostic with $A = 0.80$ has a false-positive index of about three times that of a diagnostic with $A = 0.90$; a diagnostic with $A = 0.70$ has an index of about six times that of a test with $A = 0.90$; and a diagnostic with $A = 0.60$ has an index of about eight times that of a test with $A = 0.90$. These ratios vary somewhat with the threshold selected, but they illustrate how much difference it would make if a high value of A could be achieved for field polygraph testing. If the diagnosis of deception could reach a level of $A = 0.90$, testing would produce much more attractive tradeoffs between false positives and false negatives than it has at lower levels of A. Nevertheless, if the proportion of major security risks in the population being screened is equal to or less than 1 in 1,000, it is reasonable to expect even with optimistic assessments of polygraph test accuracy that each spy or terrorist that might be correctly identified as deceptive would be accompanied by at least hundreds of nondeceptive examinees mislabeled as deceptive, from whom the spy or terrorist would be indistinguishable by polygraph test result. The possibility that deceptive examinees may use countermeasures makes this tradeoff even less attractive.

Figures I-1 through I-4 enable readers to derive values of the false

TABLE I-1A Values of the False Positive Index with Decision
Thresholds Set for 80 Percent Sensitivity

Base rate	A = 0.90	A = 0.80	A = 0.70	A = 0.60
0.001	208	452	634	741
0.01	21	45	63	73
0.10	1.9	4.1	5.7	6.7
0.50	0.21	0.45	0.63	0.74

TABLE I-1B Values of the False Positive Index with Decision
Thresholds Set for 50 Percent Sensitivity

Base rate	A = 0.90	A = 0.80	A = 0.70	A = 0.60
0.001	70	232	411	545
0.01	7.0	23	41	54
0.10	0.63	2.1	3.7	4.9
0.50	0.07	0.23	0.41	0.55

TABLE I-1C Values of the False Positive Index with Decision
Thresholds Set for 20 Percent Sensitivity

Base rate	A = 0.90	A = 0.80	A = 0.70	A = 0.60
0.001	20	104	240	370
0.01	2.0	10	24	37
0.10	0.18	0.94	2.2	3.3
0.50	0.02	0.10	0.24	0.37

positive index (FPI) from assumptions about the base rate of deceptive
examinees in a population to be given polygraph tests, the level of accuracy achieved by the polygraph, and the decision threshold, defined in
terms of the sensitivity, or proportion of deceptive individuals to be identified correctly. The figures show values for accuracy rates (A) of 0.90,
0.80, 0.70, and 0.60 and sensitivities of 80, 50, and 20 percent. The figures
are based on the binormal, equivariance model and are presented on
logarithmic scales to make it easier to get accurate readings for very low
base rates than is possible with standard scales such as presented in Figures 7-1 and 7-2.

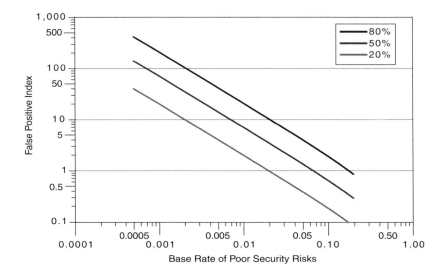

FIGURE I-1 False positive index values as a function of base rate of deception for a diagnostic procedure with an accuracy index (A) of 0.90 and threshold values achieving sensitivities of 80 percent, 50 percent, and 20 percent.

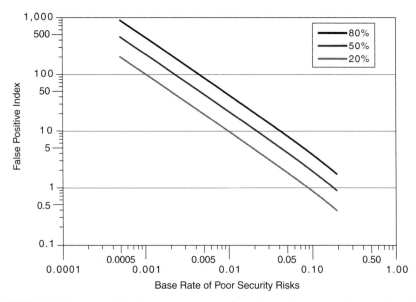

FIGURE I-2 False positive index values as a function of base rate of deception for a diagnostic procedure with an accuracy index (A) 0.80 and threshold values achieving sensitivities of 80 percent, 50 percent, and 20 percent.

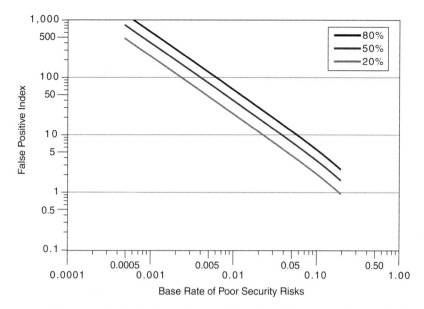

FIGURE I-3 False positive index values as a function of base rate of deception for a diagnostic procedure with an accuracy index (A) of 0.70 and threshold values achieving sensitivities of 80 percent, 50 percent, and 20 percent.

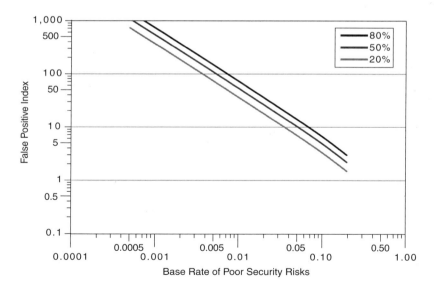

FIGURE I-4 False positive index values as a function of base rate of deception for a diagnostic procedure with an accuracy index (A) of 0.60 and threshold values achieving sensitivities 80 percent, 50 percent, and 20 percent.

Appendix J

Decision Analysis of Polygraph Security Screening

In recent decades, decision scientists and policy advisers have worked to develop systematic methods for resolving hard decision problems that arise in business, medicine and public policy (Raiffa, 1968; Quade, 1989; Gold et al., 1996; Hammond, Keeney, and Raiffa, 1999). These methods are used explicitly in many scientific articles, and they are used implicitly in practical advice, where the goal is to get decision makers to think systematically before acting.

It is useful to consider what such an analysis of counterespionage personnel policy, or of polygraph testing in that context, would entail. Six steps of such an analysis are typically recommended (Hammond, Keeney, and Raiffa, 1999): (1) understanding the problem and context of decision; (2) defining the goals and objectives of policy; (3) generating the alternative choices; (4) predicting their consequences; (5) evaluating those consequences and trading off results in different domains; and (6) using the analysis to help make the decision.

The different uses of polygraph examinations—for periodic screening of employees, preemployment screening, and event-specific investigation—present different decision problems. Consequently, the problems must be specified in each situation, even though some objectives, such as minimizing costs, are relevant to all situations.

Consider the example of periodic screening for espionage (the logic is the same for sabotage or terrorism, though the analysis would need to consider each of these separately). The main goal of periodic screening is to limit the damage to national interests by employees who are spies by detecting them and by deterring others who might otherwise be induced to become spies. A secondary goal is to reduce the damage from information leaks following security violations. Personnel programs might be evaluated against a variety of criteria, including the number of undetected spies working in the agency and the potential damage each could do, the financial costs of the program itself, and the costs to individuals and society of careers interrupted or changed because of false positive test results. We note that, currently, postemployment polygraph screening often involves periodic testing at known intervals, a policy that is likely to be less effective than aperiodic testing at unanticipated intervals.

Policy analysis must consider some set of alternatives for dealing with the problem. One might consider three alternative programs: periodic screening that includes a polygraph test like the Test for Espionage and Sabotage (TES); no security screening or a lower cost interrogation without the polygraph; and an intense screening with replacements or supplements for the polygraph, such as more pencil-and-paper testing or more extensive background investigation of finances and activities. Any final assessment would have to define the programs precisely, including major differences that distinguish different programs.

Formal policy analysis would then predict the consequences of each alternative policy, perhaps by mathematical modeling, using parameters that represent the key factors affecting results. Different parts of the analysis might use different kinds of models. Game theory might be useful for modeling deterrent effects and the use of countermeasures, while standard statistical models might be used for estimating the number of spies caught in the next year. The analysis would set a time horizon within which effects will be counted and specify how long the programs are assumed to be in place. The effects of detecting spies would be immediate, but deterrece might have longer range effects. We first discuss three key parameters and then explain how the modeling might be performed. For simplicity, we consider only the goal of limiting the damage from espionage. (The analysis for other security violations is quite similar.)

The first parameter is $p(a)$, the probability of a spy operating under screening policy a. If a is a tough screening policy that makes spying less attractive, $p(a)$ would be lower than the probability given no rescreening. A second parameter is $C(a)$, the annual costs of screening program a, which would normally be modeled as the sum of fixed costs, $F(a)$, and a per-screen variable cost, $V(a)$: $C(a) = F(a) + N(a)V(a)$, with $N(a)$ representing the number of employees screened under policy a per year. (Other, more subjective, costs are considered later as part of the evaluation of consequences.)

With tests that perfectly discriminate spies from others, the mathematics of prediction is simple and implies that one should only use the cheapest of the perfect tests, and use it if the annual costs of the test itself and of spying between tests were less than the annual costs of spies with no screening. Unfortunately, all currently known screening tests are imperfect. A third parameter, $P(a)$, represents the performance (accuracy) of screening program a for detecting spies and avoiding false accusations. Because polygraph screening programs involve more than just the polygraph test (for example, the effect of the interrogation depends on examinees' perceptions of polygraph accuracy), $P(a)$ depends on more than just the polygraph test alone, and may be different from the accuracy index (A) of the polygraph test procedure. Bayes' theorem can be used to calculate the number of false positives and true positives as a function of policy and to select the appropriate threshold for labeling an employee as deceptive (or, more specifically, as a security risk or a spy), given the calculations of net costs.

To estimate the parameters for the model, one would need to use judgment (preferably informed by statistical evidence) to calculate the base rate of espionage and a plausible range of values. For example, the estimate of the probability that an employee is a spy might be based on the 139 known spies from 1940-1994 (Taylor and Snow, 1997) added to an estimate of the spies that were caught but not reported for security reasons, and the estimated number of spies who were not caught in this period, divided by the number of people working in that period with access to critical information. This probability would vary from agency to agency and over time.

The variable costs of a screening program are primarily labor and could be estimated from the number of cases done each year, multiplied by the average salaries paid to examiners and examinees for the time they spend in the screening process. Fixed costs might be estimated by some standard overhead amount or by a detailed costing. Alternatively, the total monetary costs might be estimated by taking the annual polygraph program budget and estimating the portion used in screening activities.

Chapter 5 is primarily concerned with assessing the accuracy of polygraph testing in various situations. Accuracy may depend on the testing procedure, the situation, and characteristics of examiners and examinees, as well as the base rate of espionage and the decision threshold selected for each decision point in a screening program. Historical data on performance is needed for estimating the likely numbers of false positives and false negatives, as well as a subjective assessment of the relationship of the historical data to the current context.

To evaluate the predicted consequences for each policy, it is necessary to frame the analysis by choosing a common perspective for all programs, which in this case would be a societal viewpoint, rather than that of a particular agency. The simplest way to combine outcomes in differ-

TABLE J-1 Outcomes Under Alternative Screening Policies

Policies Under Consideration	Number Screened	Costs of Screen	Number of Spies Remaining	Number of False Accusations	Number of Security Violations
No screening					
Low-cost interrogation without polygraph					
Some TES screening					
Much TES screening					
High-cost screening, no polygraph					

ent domains is by a cost-consequence table, as shown in Table J-1 (Gold et al., 1996). Usually, the entries are incremental relative to a single reference program, such as interrogation without polygraph. If no one policy is dominant (best on all dimensions), this table might be used in a subjective assessment of the tradeoffs to get to the best choice. People might disagree on those tradeoffs, but the table entries, if correct, give the information needed for a reasoned choice.

There are many difficulties in estimating the costs for the analysis. It is easier to compute the total costs of polygraph examinations than their incremental costs and their effects in comparison with interrogation without polygraphs. The total costs are the incremental costs if polygraph examinations are added to whatever else is done and any confessions are due solely to the polygraph, but this assumption probably overstates both the incremental costs and benefits.

In principle, an alternative table might replace or supplement the columns for the number of spies remaining and number of false accusations by estimates of their costs. All cost estimates should include costs to the examinee and spillover costs, in addition to the direct costs of running the screening program.

The costs per false positive are much lower for preemployment screening than for periodic employee screening. In preemployment screening, there is a cost to the government of hiring less qualified people and a cost to an applicant of not getting a desired job. Unless the skills sought are very specialized, the government costs will be small. The costs to an applicant include bad feelings from failing the polygraph and the need to search for a different job. Costs are much higher in employee screening because national security jobs by their nature rely on specific human capital that must be learned on the job. For an employee who has not committed any serious security violations and who has settled into a social setting and learned many skills specific to his or her job, the costs to the government of putting that employee in some state of limbo involve training a replacement and perhaps damage to national security caused by the replacement of a valuable contributor with an inexperienced one. The costs to the employee include bad feelings, a waste of job-specific skills and knowledge, and perhaps a search for a new, probably inferior job. The costs to the government will be higher if there are negative side effects on morale or productivity of coworkers or on the ability to attract potentially productive employees.

The hardest estimate to make is the expected costs per undetected spy or terrorist. These will vary greatly by the potential of that person to do damage: from virtually none for ineffective spies to enormous amounts for successful ones who may compromise agents or give away invaluable technical information. A report on information collected on the 139 Americans who were officially charged with spying between 1940 and 1994 showed many to be low-level personnel who needed money and naively tried to sell some secrets (Taylor and Snow, 1997). Since 1978, 38 percent of spies caught were caught on their first attempt. In recent years, ideology has become much less important as a motive. Taylor and Snow (1997) credit the 1978 Foreign Intelligence Surveillance Act for both detecting and successfully prosecuting more spies than before. Despite the end of the cold war, foreign governments are still interested in U.S. secrets, with economic and nonmilitary technical information becoming relatively more important than they used to be.

The expected costs of an isolated security violation, such as taking classified information home, are the product of the value of that information to an adversary and the probability that the adversary gets it. Because many people with access to classified information slip up from time to time, it is fortunate that the probability of those mistakes leading to an important disclosure is quite small. This probability is hard to estimate, but the expected costs per violation might be approximated by dividing the costs of all leaks through inadvertent security violations (as opposed to espionage or hacking) by the number of such violations. An area with a very lax security system might attract attention from adversaries and increase the chance that any particular infraction there turns out badly.

For some purposes, it is useful to combine all the outcomes into one or two measures. In a cost-benefit analysis, all outcomes are replaced by an estimate of their dollar value, and if all outcomes but one are replaced by their dollar value, the one nonfinancial outcome is called the effect in a cost-effectiveness analysis. Typically in the health field, the effect is some measure of incremental health, such as years of life added. In employee screening, the effect would be undetected spies, so that the programs could be rated on their cost in relation to the number of undetected spies (because of deterrence, this is slightly different from the cost per detected spy). To get to a cost-benefit analysis, one would need to put a dollar value on the cost of each undetected spy. Indirect effects of the program are also included in a thorough analysis. These would include the effects of detected spies on deterrence, the effects of false positives on morale and on the quality of scientific personnel that work in an agency, and the effects on other parts of the security system (for example, placing too much reliance on polygraph screening may result in loosening of ordinary security precautions, thus increasing the chances that a spy who is cleared by a polygraph examination will succeed in stealing secrets).

Most of the uncertainty in calculation and evaluation relates to modeling assumptions and subjective judgments rather than statistical noise. Also, policy makers typically are looking for choices that remain good even if conditions or goals change. For these reasons, analysts typically use sensitivity analysis to examine how choices and conclusions are affected by varying the subjective assumptions and parameter estimates over a reasonable range, rather than attempting to compute confidence intervals or make probabilistic statements about the best choice.

From this brief discussion it should be evident that there would be considerable difficulties involved in any quantitative policy analysis of the use of polygraph in periodic or aperiodic screening. An argument for conducting such an analysis despite the difficulties is that it may lead to better decision making than alternative strategies for making choices. For instance, leaving the choice to specialists may lead to inertia in maintaining policies that are no longer appropriate to changed conditions. Also, professionals have been noted to emphasize service to their clients rather than to society as a whole and may come to have undue faith in what they do (Fischhoff et al., 1981).

REFERENCES

Fischhoff, B., S. Lichtenstein, P. Slovic, S. Derby, and R. Keeney
  1981   *Acceptable Risk.* New York: Cambridge University Press.
Gold, M.R., J.E. Siegel, L.B. Russell, and M.C. Weinstein
  1996   *Cost Effectiveness in Health and Medicine.* New York: Oxford University Press.
Hammond, J.S., R.L. Keeney, and H. Raiffa
  1999   *Smart Choices, A Practical Guide to Making Better Decisions.* Boston: Harvard Business School Press.
Quade, E.S. (revised by G.M. Carter)
  1989   *Analysis for Public Decisions, 3rd ed.* New York: North Holland.
Raiffa, H.
  1968   *Decision Analysis, Introductory Lectures on Choices Under Uncertainty.* Reading, MA: Addison Wesley.
Taylor, S.A., and D. Snow
  1997   Cold war spies: Why they spied and how they got caught. *Intelligence and National Security* 12(2):101-125.

Appendix K

Combining Information Sources in Medical Diagnosis and Security Screening

In medical diagnosis, a physician uses a patient's medical history, the clinical interview, reported symptoms, and physician-observed clinical signs to decide what tests to undertake. Subsequently, the physician combines test results with the other information sources in arriving at a diagnosis. In terms of the use of information, the problem is similar enough to that of security screening that much of the extensive literature on medical diagnosis may be consulted for insights relevant to security screening.

In making judgments about whether an examinee is a security risk or has committed security violations, government security officials might take into account polygraph charts and at least five other types of information:

1. Biographical data on the examinee, such as might be gathered by a background check, including any specific incriminating information when a particular crime (e.g., act of espionage) is in question.

2. Contextual information that might affect the dynamics between the examinee and examiner or otherwise affect the interpretation of the charts. This information might include the examinee's race, sex, educational level, and native language and the social status of both examiner and examinee.

3. The examiner's observations during the examination on the subject's demeanor: affect, body language, voice patterns, facial expressions, etc.

4. Follow-up information, including additional polygraph examinations to elucidate problem areas in the initial examination.

5. Other objective measures that might supplement or replace the polygraph: examples include voice stress measurements, infrared measures of skin temperature, and various direct measures of brain activity (see Chapter 6).

This appendix provides an overview of approaches used for combining information with statistical or other formal objective numerical algorithms, largely with reference to the medical diagnosis literature. These approaches, increasingly though inconsistently applied in clinical medical practice, contrast greatly with what we have seen in government security screening programs, in which polygraph and other information are combined essentially by clinical judgment, which can be considered as an informal, practitioner-specific algorithm incorporating hunches and rules of thumb. There are two major classes of formal methods for combining information, statistical classification approaches and expert systems (computer-aided diagnosis); we discuss each in turn.

STATISTICAL CLASSIFICATION

Statistical classification systems assume, at least implicitly, an underlying probability model relating the diagnostic groups (class labels) and the classifying information. These methods start with a training set or design sample, consisting of cases with known diagnoses and a dataset containing values for a vector, $\mathbf{x}$, of q potential classifier variables or features. For example, if one summarized the information in a polygraph test by overall scores for each of the four channels, there would be only four (q) classifiers. One expects the distributions of these variables to be different for deceptive and nondeceptive individuals. If $f(\mathbf{x} \mid i)$ is the joint probability function of the classifying variables for diagnostic group i, one can mentally visualize these q classifying variables as "inhabiting" a geometric space of q dimensions. The goal of statistical classification methods is to divide this space into regions, one for each diagnostic group, so that the rule which classifies all individuals whose vectors fall into region k as belonging to group k has good properties.

One widely used criterion is minimization of overall risk. This is defined as the expected total cost of all classification errors. Technically, this is the sum of costs c_{ij} associated with misclassifying a person of class i into class j, summed over j, then weighted by the class i prevalences (probability of occurrence), denoted by p_i and summed over i. Thus,

$$Risk = \sum_i p_i r_i = \sum_i p_i \left(\sum_j c_{ij} \int_{Rj} f(x \,|\, i) \, dx \right).$$

Forming the regions, R_j, to minimize the overall risk is the Bayes classification rule.

When misclassification costs, prevalences, and group-specific distributions are known, one can find this rule in a straightforward fashion. For two diagnostic groups, we chose the region R_1 to consist of all those points

$$f(x \,|\, 1)/f(x \,|\, 2) > p_2 c_{12}/p_1 c_{21,}$$

with R_2 making up the rest of the space. In Bayesian statistical terminology, region j consists of points with a relatively large posterior probability of membership in group j. This basic idea holds for any number of groups (for details, see Hand, 1998).

Unfortunately, the misclassification costs, prevalences, and group-specific probability distributions are rarely known. The distributions can be estimated from a training sample, consisting of representative (ideally, random and large) samples from each of the diagnostic groups with each individual measured on (ideally) all variables thought to be potentially useful classifiers. The group prevalences and misclassification costs are typically estimated from other sources of information.

It is tempting to simply plug these estimates into the Bayes classification formula, but this approach is fraught with pitfalls. First, it can at best be an approximation to a proper Bayesian solution, and the only way to assess its quality is to perform a full statistical assessment of the unknown, estimated components of the formula. For this reason, the Kircher and Raskin approach to computerized scoring (see Appendix F) is not really a Bayesian approach.

Second, estimating the components is not easy. Estimating the costs often requires an in-depth policy analysis. Estimating the joint distributions can be unreliable, especially when the number of classifiers is large.

One can get a sense of at least one of the pitfalls by addressing the specification of joint probability function $f(x \,|\, i)$. Suppose each of the p variables can take any one of L possible values. Then each joint probability function $f(x \,|\, i)$ will assign a probability to each of L^p cells. This requires a sample size much larger than L^p. This exponential growth in the problem size as the number of variables increases is often dramatically termed the "curse of dimensionality." Thus, one really needs to use some type of statistical model to estimate the probability distribution. Methods differ in how they deal with this exponential growth problem, typically by imposing restrictions on the numbers of variables, on the probability distributions assumed, or on the shapes and configurations of the regions. There are six main approaches: (1) linear or quadratic discrimination; (2) logistic regression; (3) nearest neighbor and kernel methods; (4) recursive partitioning (e.g., classification and regression trees, CART); (5) Bayes independence models; (6) artificial neural networks. The first two approaches are discussed in Appendix F. Hastie, Tibshirani, and Friedman (2001) and Hand (1992, 1998) give useful overviews. All these methods have proponents and critics and are supported by examples of excellent performance in which they equaled or surpassed that of experienced clinicians in a reasonably narrowly defined domain of disease or treatment. These methods have been applied in many areas, not just to problems of medical classification.

Two simple special cases of the logistic regression method reduce to simple calculations and do not require the technical details of logistic regression to describe. We describe these here because they exemplify some common aspects of methods for combining information and are often considered to provide useful guidance in medical diagnostic analyses. They also have relevance for polygraph screening.

Independent Parallel Testing

Independent parallel testing assumes that a fixed collection of diagnostically informative dichotomous variables is obtained for each subject. The disease or other feature that is the target of detection is inferred to be present if any of the individual tests is positive. Consequently, the parallel combination test is negative only when all of its component tests are negative. In personnel security screening, one might consider the polygraph test, the background investigation for clearance, and various psychological tests administered periodically as the components of a parallel test: security risk is judged to be absent only if all the screens are negative for indications of security risk.

Under the assumed independence among tests, the specificity (1 − false positive rate) of the parallel combination test is the product of the specificities of the individual component tests. Since the component specificities are below 1, the combined or joint specificity must be lower than that of any components. Similarly, the false negative rate of the parallel combination test is the product of the false negative rates of the individual component tests, hence, also lower than that of any component. Consequently, the sensitivity of the parallel combination test is higher than the sensitivity of any component test, and the parallel combination yields a test of higher sensitivity but lower specificity than any component.

As shown in Chapter 2, a similar tradeoff of specificity for sensitivity can be obtained with a single test based on a continuous measurement by changing the cutoff or threshold used for classification on the basis of the test result and thus moving to the right on the receiver operating characteristic (ROC) curve for that test. The virtue of the parallel combination is that it brings more information to bear on the problem. Hence, if one begins with component tests of fixed cutoff points and generates the parallel combination test from them, the result will have a greater sensitivity and lower specificity than any of the component tests using the same cutoff point. In general, sensitivity is the test characteristic that most strongly drives negative predictive value, which in turn governs the ability to rule out a diagnosis. Hence, negative parallel tests are often used in medical care for the explicit purpose of excluding a disease diagnosis.

If the component tests each have some discriminating power, the parallel test will often also have a greater sensitivity than any component test calibrated to the specificity achieved by the combination. The gain in accuracy, however, is limited by the degree to which each new test in the parallel combination is correlated with the feature one is trying to detect. Any dependence between tests would reduce the amount of new information available, and consequently, diminish the potential gain. With many tests, it is unlikely that the best discriminating function will be obtained by requiring that a person is classified negative only if all tests are negative—better decision rules will come from the various classification methods listed above.

The independent parallel testing argument suggests that polygraph testing might be useful in the security screening context even if it were not sufficiently valid by itself to be useful. A negative polygraph examination combined with other negative data might increase the certainty of a decision to grant or continue access to sensitive information. The degree to which the polygraph improved the decision-making process in such a context, however, would depend on whether polygraph test results can appropriately be treated as statistically independent of other screening modalities, as well as on the discriminating power of the polygraph. The false positive rate of the parallel combination will exceed that of any component, so the polygraph cutoff in a parallel investigation might have to be set accommodate this (that is, to increase the range of scores considered as indicating truthfulness) with a corresponding sacrifice in sensitivity.

Independent Serial Testing

In independent serial testing a sequence of tests is specified, with each test used only if its predecessors in the sequence have all been positive. Serial tests are the general rule in medical practice, especially if one considers nonlaboratory components of medical diagnosis as informal tests within an information collection sequence. By comparison with parallel tests, serial tests are cost-effective because the most powerful and expensive tests are not performed on many examinees. A serial test usually begins with relatively inexpensive and noninvasive measures and proceeds to more expensive and more invasive procedures as the accumulation of information makes the presence of the feature of interest increasingly likely. One can imagine a polygraph test as the first step in a personal security screening sequence, with more expensive background checks, detailed interrogations, and possibly levels of surveillance as later stages in the process. Indeed, at least one agency uses serial polygraph testing, where positive results of one type of test lead to a second test of somewhat different nature, and so on.

The accuracy of serial combination testing is much like that for parallel combination testing but with the roles of sensitivity and specificity—and, hence, of false positive and false negative rates—reversed. The feature of interest is not diagnosed unless all tests are positive, so the sensitivity of the serial combination is the product of the sensitivities of the component tests, and the false positive rate of the serial combination is the product of the false positive rates of the individual component tests. Thus, serial testing yields a combination with lower sensitivity but higher specificity than its components. In general, specificity drives the false positive index, and so positive serial tests are often used in medical care to arrive at a firm basis for taking action. As with parallel testing, the potential gain in accuracy of serial testing is limited by the accuracy and extent of dependence of each additional test added to the sequence. In contrast with parallel testing, however, each rearrangement of the ordering of a given set of tests yields a new serial test with different properties from other orderings of the component tests.

For personnel security screening, the relative inexpensiveness of polygraph makes it attractive as an early step in a serial screening process. But this requires other suitable tests with known degrees of accuracy for follow-up. Moreover, if one wanted to avoid large numbers of false positives and the associated costs of following them up, polygraph testing would have to be used at a high specificity, incurring the risk of early termination of the screening sequence for some serious security risks.

EXPERT SYSTEMS

In contrast to the above approaches, nonstatistical expert systems typically codify and represent existing knowledge using collections of rules, for instance, of the form "if-then-else," with deterministic or subjective probabilistic outcomes and heuristic "inference engines" for operating on these rules (see Buchanan and Shortliffe [1984] for an early example, and the overview in Laskey and Levitt [2001]). Examples can be found in psychiatric diagnosis from coded interview schedules, e.g., DMS III/DIS (Maurer et al., 1989) and PSE/CATEGO (Wing et al., 1974). There is evidence that combining rule-based systems and statistical classification in particular neural networks may help the dimensionality problem (Vlachonikolis et al., 2000). A general feature of rule-based systems, however, is that they require a substantial body of theory or empirical knowledge involving clearly identified features with reasonably straightforward logical or empirical relationships to the definition or determination of the outcome of interest. For screening uses of the polygraph, it seems clear that no such body of knowledge exists. This may severely limit the practical application of expert systems in this context.

Both statistical and expert system methods could in principle be implemented in the polygraph context. Indeed, some of these ideas are being explored in the context of computerized scoring of polygraph charts (Olsen et al., 1997). However, it is not clear that this can be fruitful. If the polygraph examination is low in accuracy, combining it with other information will not be helpful.

There are additional important caveats involving the manner of incorporating contextual variables and the adequacy of training samples in terms of size and representativeness. Regarding context, only recently are medical research and practice recognizing the importance of the social interaction between patient and physician in treatment. The contextual variables described above have thus far played little role in medical classification and computer-aided diagnosis. For any individual medical problem, it may be unclear how best to incorporate them into models. They may act as additional predictors or confounders as effect modifiers that change the relationships of selected other predictors to the target classification, or even as stratification variables that define separate groups in which potentially quite different prediction models may be necessary. Neither are such choices clear in the polygraph context. It is possible that having two distributions of variables, one for deceptive individuals and one for nondeceptive ones, is overly simple. A plausible example is the possibility that the distribution of blood pressure readings obtained during the polygraph examination may differ dramatically for African American and white examinees (evidence making this hypothesis plausible is reported by Blascovich et al., 2001).

We have noted above that the statistical pattern recognition approaches require the training sample to be representative of the target population. In many respects, one needs to question whether training samples based on samples of a community, college students, or basic trainees in the military are at all representative for target populations to be screened for espionage, terrorism, or sabotage at government weapons laboratories and other high-security installations. Ideally, a representative sample would include subpopulations of spies, terrorists, and saboteurs that might be screened, as well as truthful scientists, engineers, and technicians. And in the latter group, one would also want individuals who have committed minor security violations and are deceptive in their responses in that regard. Furthermore, as a consequence of the "curse of dimensionality," these techniques tend to require large samples. Medical classification studies typically involve at least several hundred in each diagnostic group. In contrast, in the standard polygraph field study the problem of objectively ascertaining truth means that it is difficult and unusual to obtain that many verified deception cases. In this circumstance, it is likely that uses of pattern recognition methods will have to be restricted to small numbers of variables.

Finally, realistic assessments of the performance of classification rules must be available. If the data used to develop the rule are also used to assess its performance, the result will typically suggest better—perhaps much better—performance than is likely to be found when the rule is applied to future data. This problem will exist whether misclassification rate, sensitivity and specificity, any other summary numbers or, when applicable, the entire ROC curve, are used. The expected discrepancy is inversely related to the number of individuals in the development dataset relative to the number of candidate variables and is negligible only when the sample size is at least an order of magnitude higher than the number of candidate variables. Thus, pattern recognition approaches that analyze dozens or hundreds of variables will significantly overestimate their true validity unless they are developed on training samples with hundreds or thousands.

Many methods for using the original data to give a more realistic assessment of future performance have been proposed. The most important are variants of cross-validation or what is sometimes referred to as the "leave-one-out" or "round-robin" approach. In the statistics literature, these methods go back to the 1940s and are now commonly linked to the jackknife and bootstrap techniques (Davison and Hinkley, 1997). In the simplest of the cross-validation approaches, each individual is omitted sequentially, classified using the rule developed on the basis of all the other individuals' data, and then applying the classification rule to the omitted case. But individuals can also be omitted in groups, with the other groups used for cross-validation. For cross-validation to give an honest estimate of the predictive value of the classification rule, one needs to incorporate the entire rule-building process, including any variable selection procedures, but this caveat is unfortunately too often ignored in practice.

Of course, the gold standard is assessment of performance on a genuinely new and independent data set. A recent editorial in the journal *Medical Decision Making* (Griffith, 2000:244) makes this point:

> The general problem is how to make probability-based clinical decision aids not only accurate on a specific dataset but also effective in general practice. Automated computational algorithms for estimation and decision making need to be held to the same standards that would be expected from a clinical research study. Thus, these prediction models must demonstrate high accuracy on independent datasets large enough to capture the inherent variability between patients at risk for a given medical outcome.

Appendix G addresses more explicitly the importance of this warning in the context of statistical approaches to computerized polygraph scoring.

REFERENCES

Blascovich, J., S.J. Spencer, D. Quinn, et al.
   2001   African Americans and high blood pressure: The role of stereotype threat. *Psychological Science* 12(3):225-229.
Buchanan, B., and E. Shortliffe
   1984   *Rule-based Expert Programs: The MYCIN Experiments of the Stanford Heuristic Programming Project*. Reading, MA: Addison Wesley.
Davison, A.C., and D.V. Hinkley
   1997   *Bootstrup Methods and Their Applications*. Cambridge, UK: Cambridge University Press.
Griffith, J.
   2000   Artificial neural networks: Are they ready for use as clinical decision aids? Editorial. *Medical Decision Making* 20(2):243-244.
Hand, D.J.
   1992   Statistical methods in diagnosis. *Statistics in Medical Research* 1:49-67.
   1998   Discriminant Analysis. Pp. 1168-1179 in *Encyclopedia of Biostatistics*, Volume 2, P. Armitage and P. Colton, eds. New York: John Wiley and Sons.
Hastie, T., R. Tibshirani, and J. Friedman
   2001   *The Elements of Statistical Learning: Data Mining, Inference and Prediction*. New York: Springer-Verlag.
Laskey, K.B., and T.S. Levitt
   2001   Artificial intelligence: Uncertainty. Pp. 799-805 in *International Encyclopedia of the Social and Behavioral Sciences*, Vol. 2, P. Baltes and N. Smelser, eds. Oxford: Elsevier.
Maurer, K., H. Biel, et al.
   1989   On the way to expert systems. *European Archives of Psychiatry and Neurological Sciences* 239:127-132.
Olsen, D.E., J. Harris, et al.
   1997   Computerized polygraph scoring system. *Journal of Forensic Sciences* 41(1):61-71.

Vlachonikolis, I.G., D.A. Karras, et al.
  2000 Improved statistical classification methods in computerized psychiatric diagnosis. *Medical Decision Making* 20(1):95-103.
Wing, J.K., J.E. Cooper, and N. Sartorius
  1974 *Measurement and Classification of Psychiatric Symptoms.* Cambridge, UK: Cambridge University Press.

Appendix L

Biographical Sketches of
Committee Members and Staff

STEPHEN E. FIENBERG (*chair*) is Maurice Falk university professor of statistics and social science, in the Department of Statistics and the Center for Automated Learning and Discovery at Carnegie Mellon University. He is a member of the National Academy of Sciences and currently serves on the advisory committee of the National Research Council's Division of Behavioral and Social Sciences and Education. He is a past chair of the Committee on National Statistics and has served on several of its panels. He has published extensively on statistical methods for the analysis of categorical data and methods for disclosure limitation. His research interests include the use of statistics in public policy and the law, surveys and experiments, and the role of statistical methods in censustaking.

JAMES J. BLASCOVICH is professor and chair of psychology and codirector of the Research Center for Virtual Environments and Behavior at the University of California, Santa Barbara. He is president-elect of the Society for Personality and Social Psychology (Division 8 of the American Psychological Association). His research interests include the psychophysiology and social psychophysiology of motivation and emotion, stigma and prejudice, and social influence processes in immersive virtual environments.

* JOHN T. CACIOPPO is the Tiffany and Margaret Blake distinguished service professor at the University of Chicago. He has pioneered the field

---

* Served on the committee until May 28, 2002.

of social neuroscience and cofounded the Institute for Mind and Biology to support multilevel integrative analyses of social behavior. His current research focuses on the mechanisms underlying affect and emotion and the cognitive and neural substrates of racial prejudice.

RICHARD J. DAVIDSON is the William James and Vilas Research professor of psychology and psychiatry at the University of Wisconsin-Madison, where he directs the W.M. Keck Laboratory for Functional Brain Imaging and Behavior. His research is focused on the neural substrates of emotion and disorders of emotion, and he is an expert on the use of psychophysiological and brain imaging measures to study emotion.

PAUL EKMAN is professor of psychology at the University of California, San Francisco. His areas of expertise are deception and demeanor and emotional expression. He is the author or editor of 13 books and has been the recipient of a Senior Scientist Award (Career Award) from the National Institute for Mental Health. He received the American Psychological Association's highest award for basic research, the Distinguished Scientific Contribution Award, a Doctor of Humane Letters from the University of Chicago, and was named William James Fellow by the American Psychological Society.

DAVID L. FAIGMAN is a professor of law at the University of California, Hastings College of the Law. He received both his M.A. (psychology) and J.D. degrees from the University of Virginia. He writes extensively on the law's use of science and constitutional law. His books include *Legal Alchemy: The Use and Misuse of Science in the Law,* and he is a coauthor of the four-volume treatise, *Modern Scientific Evidence: The Law and Science of Expert Testimony.* The treatise has been cited widely by courts, including several times by the U.S. Supreme Court. He lectures regularly to state and federal judges on issues concerning science and the law.

PATRICIA L. GRAMBSCH is associate professor of biostatistics in the School of Public Health, University of Minnesota. Her research expertise includes stochastic processes and mathematical modeling, with emphasis on time-to-event data. Her clinical collaborations involve clinical trials for chronic disease treatments and preventions. She is a fellow of the American Statistical Association.

PETER B. IMREY is a staff member of the Department of Biostatistics and Epidemiology, Cleveland Clinic Foundation, having previously been a professor in the Departments of Statistics and Medical Information Sciences, University of Illinois at Urbana-Champaign. His research includes statistical methods for categorical data analysis and epidemiologic studies, and he is active in extensive collaboration in design and analysis of biomedical and public health investigations. He is chair of the Statistics Section, American Public Health Association (APHA). He has previously served on the governing councils of APHA and the International Biometric Society and chaired the American Statistical Association's Biometrics Section and Section on Teaching Statistics in the Health Sciences.

EMMETT B. KEELER is a senior mathematician at RAND in Santa Monica, California. He teaches policy analysis methods as a professor in the RAND Graduate School and an adjunct professor in the Public Health School, University of California, Los Angeles. His research has dealt with the theoretical and empirical effects of financing arrangements on health care utilization, quality, and outcomes. His current research deals with evaluating attempts to improve the quality of care and developing a business case for providing higher quality care.

KATHRYN B. LASKEY is an associate professor of systems engineering at George Mason University. She was previously a principal scientist at Decision Science Consortium, Inc. Her primary research interest is the study of decision, theoretically based knowledge representation, and inference strategies for automated reasoning under uncertainty. She has worked on methods for knowledge-based construction of problem-specific Bayesian belief networks, specifying Bayesian belief networks from a combination of expert knowledge and observations, and for recognizing when a system's current problem model is inadequate. She has worked with domain experts to develop Bayesian belief network models for a variety of decision and inference support problem areas. She received a joint Ph.D. in statistics and public affairs from Carnegie Mellon University, an M.S. in mathematics from the University of Michigan, and a B.S. in mathematics from the University of Pittsburgh.

SUSAN R. McCUTCHEN has been on staff at The National Academies for over 20 years and worked in several Academy divisions and with many different boards, committees, and panels in those units. The studies in which she has participated have covered a broad range of subjects, including international affairs, technology transfer, aeronautics, natural disasters, education, needle exchange, and human factors. She has assisted in the production of a large number of Academy publications. A French major, with minors in English, Italian, and Spanish, her B.A. degree is from Ohio's Miami University, and her M.A. degree from Kent State University.

KEVIN R. MURPHY is a professor of psychology at Pennsylvania State University. His research areas include performance evaluation, psychological measurement, research methods, and honesty in the workplace. He serves as editor of the *Journal of Applied Psychology*, and he has consulted extensively with the Armed Forces and with private industry on the design and evaluation of personnel selection and appraisal systems.

MARCUS E. RAICHLE is professor and codirector of the Division of Radiological Sciences, Mallinckrodt Institute of Radiology, Washington University School of Medicine, St. Louis. He is a member of the National Academy of Sciences, the Institute of Medicine, and the American Academy of Arts and Sciences, and a fellow of the American Association for the Advancement of Science. Focusing on research on the functioning of the human brain, his work has been widely published in leading scientific journals. Dr. Raichle is also a member of the Society for Neuroscience, the American Neurological Association, the American Academy of Neurology, and the International Society on Cerebral Blood Flow and Metabolism.

RICHARD M. SHIFFRIN is Luther Dana Waterman research professor, distinguished professor, and director of the Cognitive Science Program, Indiana University. A recent winner of the Rumelhart Prize and member of the National Academy of Sciences (in which capacity he has been involved in many NRC and NAS activities), he constructs and tests models of cognition, especially memory, perception, attention, and decision making. Much of his research involves the extraction of signal from noise, in both perception and memory.

ALEKSANDRA SLAVKOVIC *(consultant)* is a Ph.D. student in the Department of Statistics at Carnegie Mellon University. She holds a B.A. (honors) in psychology from Duquesne University and an M.S. in human-computer interaction from the School of Computer Science, Carnegie Mellon University. Past and current research interests include usability evaluation methods, human performance in virtual environments, statistical data mining, and statistical approaches to confidentiality and data disclosure.

PAUL C. STERN *(study director)* also serves as study director of the Committee on the Human Dimensions of Global Change. His research interests include the determinants of environmentally significant behavior, particularly at the individual level, and participatory processes for informing environmental decision making. His recent books include *Environmental Problems and Human Behavior, 2nd ed.* (with G.T. Gardner,

Pearson, 2002), *Evaluating Social Science Research, 2nd ed.* (with L. Kalof, Oxford University Press, 1996); *Understanding Risk: Informing Decisions in a Democratic Society* (edited with H.V. Fineberg, National Academy Press, 1996), *International Conflict Resolution after the Cold War* (edited with D. Druckman, National Academy Press, 2000), and *The Drama of the Commons* (edited with E. Ostrom, T. Dietz, N. Dolsak, S. Stonich, and E.U. Weber, National Academy Press, 2002). He received his B.A. degree from Amherst College and his M.A. and Ph.D. degrees from Clark University.

JOHN A. SWETS is chief scientist emeritus at BBN Technologies in Cambridge, Massachusetts, lecturer on health care policy at Harvard Medical School, and senior research associate at the Brigham and Women's Hospital in Boston. He is a member of the National Academy of Sciences (immediate past chair of the psychology section) and of the American Academy of Arts and Sciences. He was a member and chair of the Commission of Behavioral and Social Sciences and Education of the NRC, and he is now a member of the NRC's Board on Behavioral, Cognitive, and Sensory Sciences. Other NRC activities include chairs of committees to design an international fire-alarm signal and to evaluate techniques for the enhancement of human performance, and recently served on two committees of the Institute of Medicine. His research emphasis has been on the development of signal detection theory for sensory and cognitive functions and on the theory's application to the diagnostic process in several practical fields.

Index

A

Accuracy measurement, 61
association measures, 62-63 n.7
Chi-square coefficient, 63 n.7
Cohen's kappa, 63 n.7
comparison group, 35
consistent approach to, 37-51
countermeasures and, 31, 36, 66, 78
and decision threshold, 40, 42-49,
61, 62 n.7, 63 n.8, 95, 104-105
n.16, 130, 148, 354-357
diagnostic models, 37-38, 40, 41, 43,
47, 48, 49, 61, 62 n.7, 63 n.11, 66,
84, 95, 127, 149
equivariance binormal model, 342-
344
false negative probability, 39
false positive index, 35, 36, 38, 39,
61, 62 n.6, 67, 68, 69, 122-123,
180-181, 182, 334, 354-357
false positive probability, 39, 89
funding source for research and,
119-120
limitations of data, 66, 68-69, 109, 115
log-odds ratio, 62-63 n.7

negative predictive value, 39
overestimation, 214
Pearson's r, 152 n.1
percentage correct index, 31, 43, 46,
49-50, 63 n.8, 129-130, 148
phi coefficient, 63 n.7
positive predictive value, 38, 39, 58-
60, 184
purpose of polygraph test and, 22-
23, 24, 31, 33-37, 40, 46-47, 48,
60, 101
Receiver operating characteristic
(ROC) curve estimation, 342-
344, 368
sensitivity and specificity, 38, 39,
43, 45, 48, 78, 85, 91, 94, 122-123,
211 nn.4&5, 318-319, 367-368,
369
theoretical basis, 38, 40, 42, 46, 61,
62-63 n.7, 102, 109, 127-128, 213,
343-344
trapezoidal estimate, 344, 350
used in this study, 43-44, 50-51,
342-344
and validity, 30-33, 66
Yule's Q, 62-63 n.7